COPYRIGHT HANDBOOK

COPYRIGHT HANDBOOK

Donald F. Johnston

R.R. BOWKER COMPANY
New York & London, 1978

Published by R.R. Bowker Company
1180 Avenue of the Americas, New York, N.Y. 10036
Copyright © 1978 by Xerox Corporation
All rights reserved
Printed and bound in the United States of America

Copyright is not claimed in the U.S. government
materials which are set forth in Appendixes 1–5,
8 and 9.

Library of Congress Cataloging in Publication Data

Johnston, Donald F.
  Copyright handbook.

  Includes bibliographical references and indexes.
    1. Copyright—United States. I. Title.
KF2994.J63   346'.73'0482   77-27449
ISBN 0-8352-0951-2

CONTENTS

PREFACE

Copyright law was conceived in order to encourage the development and distribution of works of authorship. It accomplishes this by giving authors certain exclusive rights to their works, including the right to authorize others to exercise those rights. If such protection were absent, neither authorship nor distribution would cease, but unauthorized reproduction and distribution would be so easily accomplished that the quantity and diversity of creative activity would be inhibited.

The United States Constitution recognized this problem of rights in the context of both inventions and works of authorship. Article I, Section 8 gives Congress the power "To promote the Progress of Science and useful Arts, by securing for limited Times to Authors and Inventors the exclusive Right to their respective Writings and Discoveries." Congress first exercised the Article I, Section 8 power in 1790. There have been major copyright law revisions from time to time, but there have been only two in the twentieth century: the Copyright Acts of 1909 and 1976. The latter, our new copyright law, became effective on January 1, 1978. It does not consist solely of the granting of exclusive rights to authors. Congress concluded that such a simplistic approach, that of solely granting authors exclusive rights, was not necessary to provide adequate incentives for authorship nor would it properly serve society as a whole. Consequently, in the new law Congress addressed not merely authors' rights, but users' rights as well. Of course, authors are users themselves.

The new copyright law represents many compromises among conflicting interest groups and among conflicting policy goals. The need to reach a legislative solution to the issue of copyright has resulted in many, but by no means all, provisions that are complex or incomplete, general or ambiguous. The purpose of this book is to explain the new copyright law and its complexities. It has been designed in an effort to offer a general understanding of the law and to provide an accessible format in which specific information can be expeditiously located. The book was conceived from the point of view that it would not necessarily be read from cover to cover. Some details will be of little practical interest to the general reader, while other details will be of great interest. Where the new law is not explicitly clear and when the potential consequences of an incorrect interpretation may be substantial, legal advice should be sought.

The volume is intended primarily for use by publishers, librarians, educators, and authors, who regularly, or from time to time, have need for direct access to information about the new law. It is also intended as a convenient source for attorneys when their particular information needs do not require exhaustive or more focused works, such as treatises, law review articles, or court decisions.

The first chapter is an introduction to the subject of copyright and to the main features of the new law. It also provides basic questions and answers about copyright as well as a context for the details of the law. The chapters that follow examine the components of the new copyright law and include such areas as copyrightable subject matter, copyright notices, registration, exclusive rights, fair use, and library reproduction rights.

The book relates only to the new copyright law. Foreign copyright laws and U.S. and foreign laws in other fields (e.g., antitrust, patents, trade secrets, contracts) are not within its scope, although they are referred to when especially relevant. In addition, there is not extensive coverage of the law in relation to either cable television or computers. Both of these areas are highly complex. The judgment has been made that detailed consideration of them would not be needed by most readers and that, because they are specialized areas, those who require extensive information about them would have access to pertinent publications or to legal counsel.

I presently serve as counsel to R.R. Bowker Company, the publisher of this book and a company in the publishing division of the Xerox Corporation. I was assisted in preparing this work by the following people whose contributions were generously given and gratefully received: Judy Garodnick, Morton David Goldberg, Chandler Grannis, Marge Lucia, Gerry McColgan, Corinne Naden, Nancy Riley, Dick Rudick, Bob Shafter, Catherine Shepherd, and Nancy Volkman. They are not responsible for any shortcomings in the text but deserve much credit for many that were avoided. On a less personal note, I would like to acknowledge those government officials and private citizens who contributed to the development of the new copyright law, many of whom worked beyond the requirements of their duties. The law that emerged from their efforts has flaws but may well be the best result that was possible.

In 1787 the Constitutional Convention convened and drew up the United States Constitution, and it was in this context that Benjamin Franklin addressed the president of the Convention and its representatives. Perhaps the thoughts he expressed about the Constitution in the year 1787 can be applied as well to the new copyright law, passed by Congress in 1976: ". . . when you assemble a number of men to have the advantage of their joint wisdom, you inevitably assemble with those men all their prejudices, their passions, their errors of opinion, their local interests, and their selfish views. From such an assembly can a perfect product be expected? It therefore astonishes me, Sir, to find this system approaching so near to perfection as it does. . . . Thus I consent, Sir, to this Constitution because I expect no better, and because I am not sure that it is not the best."

Donald F. Johnston

GUIDE TO USE

The detailed table of contents provides a reference to each particular area of the new copyright law. An alternate reference source is the index at the back of the book. It is suggested that readers seeking a background and context for the new law read the introductory chapter. Throughout *Copyright Handbook* the Copyright Act of 1976 is referred to as the new law or the new copyright law. The predecessor statute, the Copyright Act of 1909, is called the old law, the old copyright law, or the 1909 Act.

In the text itself, sentences are frequently followed by numbers, letters, and/or words in brackets. For example:

> The basic standards of copyrightability are that there must be an original work of authorship and it must be set down in a suitably tangible form [101 "fixed"; 102(a)].

The numbers in brackets, e.g. [101, 102], refer to the relevant section of the new law. The letters in parentheses, e.g. (a), refer to the relevant subsection of the new law. The words in quotes, e.g. ("fixed"), refer to specific terms defined in section 101 of the new law, a section which is a very long compilation of statutory definitions. These words are cited in brackets so the reader can find the definitions more easily within section 101. Sections or subsections may be found in Appendix 1, which contains the entire text of the new law. At times, the number in brackets is preceded by the phrase "Transitional and Supplementary Provisions." This phrase refers to provisions, set forth at the end of the new law, that were written into the new law in order to account for the problem of transition from the old law to the new law, as well as to amend other federal laws that referred to the old copyright law. Since these provisions sometimes bear the same numbers as sections in the main body of the new law, they are distinguished within the brackets not only by the phrase "Transitional and Supplementary Provisions," but also by the abbreviation "Sec." (Section). For example:

[Transitional and Supplementary Provisions, Sec. 102]

The Transitional and Supplementary Provisions of the new law are found on pages 186–190 of this volume.

The use of bracketed citations is intended to provide the reader with an immediate primary reference to the new copyright law and to reduce the need for innumerable notes and references. Chapter notes and references are used, but only when citing material other than that in the new copyright law; they are found in the section preceding the appendixes.

The appendixes contain the texts of the new and old copyright laws; copying guidelines for educators and librarians; material on U.S. international copyright relations; supplementary tables cross-referencing the old and new copyright laws; and Copyright Office forms and selected regulations.

1

INTRODUCTION

Congress passed a new copyright law in the fall of 1976. A very few provisions took effect immediately; all the rest were given an effective date of January 1, 1978 [Transitional and Supplementary Provisions, Sec. 102].

OLD AND NEW LAW: SIMILARITIES AND DIFFERENCES

Not since 1909 had Congress made a general restatement of U.S. copyright policies. (There had been piecemeal amendments to the 1909 Act from time to time.)[1] Many technological developments affecting copyright emerged or became significant in the 1909–1976 period (e.g., radio, motion pictures, tape recorders, television, computers, photocopiers, cable television, satellite communications). Nonetheless, the new law retains much of the general structure of the 1909 Act[2]:

Copyright continues to protect creators of original works of authorship through a statutory grant, to the author, of specified exclusive rights to use, and to authorize others to use, the created work [106, 201].

Users of copyrighted materials continue to have rights to make certain uses of copyrighted works without the need to obtain permission, e.g., to make "fair use" of copyrighted works [e.g., 107].

When works are published, an inclusion of a notice of copyright ordinarily is called for, as was the case under the old law [401–404].

The public distribution of copies generally has the effect of creating an obligation to deposit copies with the Copyright Office [407]. This was true under the old law as well.

A registration system for copyright claims has been retained [408].

In each of these areas—author's rights, user's rights, notice and deposit requirements, and registration procedures—there have been important changes as to specifics but the basic concepts have been retained. We will go over the changes later in this chapter and, in more detail, in subsequent chapters devoted to each topic.

Notwithstanding the general similarities between the old law and the new, the new law makes some major departures, of which the following are examples[3]:

> The old law generally left it up to the states to provide protection for unpublished works; the new law provides for federal protection for a work from the time it is set down in a sufficiently tangible form [302–304]. This single change does much to reduce the importance of"publication"as a major legal criterion, although it still retains significance for such matters as copyright notice rules.

> The old law provided for an initial term of copyright protection of 28 years and made a 28-year renewal term available if applied for. The new law retains a modification of this dual-term system for works published or federally registered before 1978 [304]. But for new works (and for unpublished pre-1978 works not federally copyrighted before 1978) a single term of copyright is established, generally one lasting for the author's lifetime plus 50 years [302–303].

> The new law makes it clear that *ownership* of a portion of the total rights in a copyright may be transferred [201(d)(2)]. Under the old law, a concept of indivisibility was extant and, to avoid the harsh results to which it sometimes could lead, strained interpretations of the law or the facts were sometimes made.

> The new law contains more detailed provisions than the old concerning the scope of one's rights to use copyrighted works without permission [107–118]. Among the new special provisions are those relating to reproduction rights of libraries and to cable carriage of broadcast signals [108, 111].

These and other departures from the old law are considered in summary later in this chapter and in more detail in subsequent chapters. Although the changes are many, anyone familiar with the old law can readily become reasonably comfortable with the new. This does not mean that the new law is a model of clarity that always points to unequivocal conclusions. Some problems were overlooked. Others were looked over and avoided. Still others met with only general solutions turning on words such as "fair." In cases of doubt, the more complex the issues or the more significant the potential consequences, the more likely it is that legal advice should be sought.

The new copyright law covers about 60 pages of fine print and is at least three times longer than the old. However, much of the new law's text concerns special situations. For example, one of the 60 pages covers rules that apply when there are copyright notice errors or omissions; three other pages concern jukebox performances of musical works [116, 405–406]. Thus, most persons who need to know quite a bit about copyright law will not have to be able to recall the entire statute in detail. It will suffice to have a general knowledge of the law as a whole together with more detailed knowledge of the legal areas of particular interest.

Following is a useful introduction to the material, posing and answering some questions of general interest about the new law. Unless otherwise indicated, the questions assume that no facts are involved that predate 1978, the effective date of the new law.

BASIC QUESTIONS AND ANSWERS

Q. How do I obtain a U.S. copyright?

A. By developing an original work of authorship and setting it down in a sufficiently tangible form. A typewritten page is sufficiently tangible, as is a videotape. A live performance on a television screen (and not recorded on tape) is not; the image is too transitory in duration [101 "fixed"; 102].

Q. What protection is there for original works of authorship *before* they are set down in a sufficiently tangible form?

A. The new copyright law, a federal statute, does not provide protection, but it does allow the states to do so [301(b)(1)].

Q. Do I have to publish my work to have federal copyright protection?

A. No [102–104; 302(a)].

Q. Is registration a prerequisite for copyright protection?

A. No [408(a)]. There are a few special circumstances when you must seek to register your claim of copyright, e.g., before you actually commence a suit for infringement of the copyright [411; see also 405(a)(2)]. But there is no general requirement to register all copyright claims. One important occasion to register is when a work was under federal copyright prior to 1978. Such works are subject to an initial copyright term and a renewal term. The latter is available only through a timely renewal registration process [304(a)].

Q. When is registration permissible?

A. When you have created an original work of authorship and set it down in a sufficiently tangible form. Publication is not a requirement for registration [408].

Q. If registration is not ordinarily required, why register except when it is required?

A. It gives you some extra rights. Put another way, you might lose some rights if you don't register. To illustrate, suppose your work is published in 1980 and someone infringes upon it in 1982. If you registered your claim of copyright before the infringement commenced, you have a chance to recover reasonable attorney's fees in your infringement lawsuit. If you did not so register, all of your attorney's bills will come out of your own pocket [412].

Q. What rights does my copyright give me?

A. The exclusive right to reproduce your copyrighted work, to prepare derivative works, and publicly to distribute, display, and perform it [106]. There are some limitations on these rights but they nonetheless are extensive [106–118, 202].

Q. If others have my permission to copy an excerpt from my work, is that enough for them to avoid infringement?

A. Theoretically, yes. Practically, also yes, if it is really *your* work they are copying. Complications arise when the excerpt to be copied is really someone else's copyrighted material, which *you* had permission to copy but not permission to allow others to copy. In such cases, you may inform the person requesting permission that *you* have no objection but that he or she nonetheless may have to get permission from the copyright owner of the excerpt.

Q. Does the copyright law require that any formalities be followed when I grant permission?

A. If your permission is so extensive that it amounts to a transfer of *ownership* of a copyright, the transfer is supposed to be by a signed writing [204]. Examples would be the assignment of all copyrights or the grant of an exclusive right. Other permissions, i.e., nonexclusive licenses, need not follow any particular formalities insofar as copyright law is concerned, although written understandings are desirable for other reasons. It is sometimes advantageous, for copyright law purposes, to have exclusive and nonexclusive copyright licenses recorded in the Copyright Office [205(c)].

In the remainder of this chapter, we will examine copyright law on a more systematic basis.

OVERVIEW OF GENERAL COPYRIGHT STANDARDS

We will first consider nine categories of copyright rules:

1. copyrightable subject matter;
2. copyright formalities;
3. copyright ownership and transfers;
4. the five exclusive rights of copyright;
5. the consequences of copyright infringement;
6. the duration of copyright protection;
7. international considerations;
8. relation of the new copyright law to the old;
9. relation of the copyright law to other laws.

Then we will discuss five additional categories—those authorizing certain uses of copyrighted works without the necessity of obtaining the copyright owner's consent.

Copyrightable Subject Matter

The basic standards of copyrightability are that there must be an original work of authorship and it must be set down in a suitably tangible form [101 "fixed"; 102(a)]. With such broad criteria, copyright is by no means confined to written words. For example, music, paintings, sculptures, jewelry, and fabric designs can be covered.

The first of the two standards—original work of authorship—is broader and narrower in scope than is often supposed. It is broader in that very little originality or creativity is required to qualify for copyright protection.[4] It is narrower in that your rights in your original work of authorship do not give you protection as to everything about it, e.g., it does not protect your "idea" [102(b)].

Copyrightable subject matter is detailed in Chapter 2.

Copyright Formalities

Copyright Notices.   When a work is published by authority of the copyright owner, it should bear a notice of copyright. A typical notice would be the symbol © 1979 Author's Name [401]. For sound recording copyrights, a Ⓟ is used instead of a © [402].

Notice requirements are important. Errors or omissions can result in loss of copyright. However, provisions of the new law sometimes allow such a fatal consequence to be avoided [405, 406].

Copyright notices are discussed in Chapter 3.

Deposit of Copies.   Generally, when a work is published in the United States with notice of copyright, two copies should be deposited with the Copyright Office for the benefit of the Library of Congress [407]. There are some exceptions provided by Copyright Office regulations. When deposit is required, there are provisions for fines in the event of noncompliance after demand [407(d)].

Deposit requirements are discussed in Chapter 4.

Registrations.   The law provides for registration of copyright claims [408]. Although registration is rarely absolutely essential, failure to register early sometimes will mean that the full array of copyright protection will not be available against an infringer. Registration calls for the completion of an application, the payment of a $10 fee, and, usually, the deposit of two copies of the work [408(a)].

Registration is discussed in Chapter 5.

Recording Documents.   The law allows documents relating to copyright to be recorded in the Copyright Office, e.g., a transfer of ownership of one of the rights of copyright. The recording system allows a person with an interest in a copyright to notify the world—or at least those who choose to look—of that interest [203(a)(4)(A); 205(a); 302(c), (d); 304(c)(4)(A)].

Registration documents are considered in Chapter 5. Other documents that may be recorded are discussed in other chapters where relevant.

Ownership, Transfers, and Licenses

The law generally provides that initial ownership of copyright belongs to the author [201]. The author may transfer ownership rights in a work—i.e., one or more exclusive rights of copyright—to others or may license others, on a nonexclusive basis, to use the work [106; 201(d)].

Ownership, transfers, and licenses are discussed in Chapter 6.

Exclusive Rights of Copyright

The exclusive rights of copyright are the rights of reproduction, preparation of derivative works, public distribution, public performance, and public display [106]. As we shall see later, these exclusive rights have some qualifiers [107–118, 202]. Nonetheless, the exclusivity is broad.

The exclusive rights of copyright are considered in Chapter 7. The qualifiers are considered in Chapters 11 through 14.

Consequences of Copyright Infringement

An infringer is someone who exercises one or more of the exclusive rights of copyright without authorization from the copyright owner and without any exception, such as fair use, being applicable [501].

A court generally has the power to enjoin infringements from continuing, to order the infringer to compensate the copyright owner for the damages caused, to order the infringer to pay over to the copyright owner the profits made from the infringement, and to order the infringer to pay the copyright owner's reasonable attorney's fees [502–505]. Those are the principal remedies—injunction, damages, profits, and attorney's fees. Where an infringement was commenced before the copyright owner registered the claim of copyright with the Copyright Office, the copyright owner sometimes is ineligible to recover attorney's fees and certain types of damages [412].

Infringement remedies are discussed in Chapter 8.

Duration of Copyright Protection

The general rule is that copyright lasts for the life of the author plus 50 years (and to the end of that last calendar year) [302, 303, 305].

Special rules apply for anonymous and pseudonymous works and for works where the "author" is the employer rather than the individual who actually prepared the work. The rule in those situations generally is that copyright lasts for 75 years from publication or 100 years from the time the work was created, whichever term expires first [302(c); 305].

Another special rule applies for all works published with notice of copyright or otherwise federally copyrighted before 1978. Copyright duration for these works is initially 28 years from the date copyright was secured. A renewal term of 47 years more is available only if the copyright is renewed prior to the end of the initial term. Works already in their renewal term on October 19, 1976 (or renewed prior to 1978) get the benefit of the 47-year renewal term even though a shorter renewal term was provided by the old law [304].

Copyright duration rules are detailed in Chapter 9.

International Considerations

U.S. Protection for Noncitizens. The law makes U.S. copyright protection available for U.S. citizens. Foreign citizens are covered for both unpublished works and for works first published in the United States. Protection is also available for foreign-published works by citizens of foreign countries when those countries have international copyright relations with the United States [104]. There are a great many such countries and they are listed in Appendix 5.

Foreign Copyright Laws. All of the statements in this book concern only U.S. copyright law except where there is an express statement otherwise.

The copyright laws of other countries often contain many similarities to our own and, by virtue of international arrangements, many countries grant to U.S. citizens the same rights under their copyright law as they grant to their own citizens. You maximize the possibility of qualifying for such rights by using the © symbol as part of your copyright notice. It is a copyright symbol recognized by the Universal Copyright Convention.

Manufacturing Clause. There are U.S. import restrictions on certain works if they are not manufactured in the United States or Canada. Only nondramatic literary materials by an American author or a resident alien author are potentially affected and there are detailed provisions that narrow the scope of the so-called manufacturing clause still further [601]. Under the new law, the manufacturing clause will expire by its own terms on July 1, 1982 [601(a)].

Censorship. Congress recognized the possibility that a foreign government might acquire citizen's rights by a compulsory transfer and then keep the work out of the United States by withholding copyright permissions. A section of the new law is designed to block any such practice [201(e)].

International considerations are discussed further in Chapter 10.

Relation of New Law to Old Law

The new law never resurrects a copyright that passed into the public domain under the old [Transitional and Supplementary Provisions, Sec. 103].

The new law sometimes enlarges the rights that the old law provided. For example, a work published in 1970 then had a potential copyright life of 56 years. Under the new law, the potential copyright life of that work is 75 years [304].

The new law explicitly provides that the old law continues to govern infringement lawsuits insofar as they relate to pre-1978 infringements [Transitional and Supplementary Provisions, Sec. 112].

Many standards of the old copyright law have been brought forward into the new. Consequently, judicial decisions made under the 1909 Act will continue to have life as precedents in interpreting the new law, albeit precedents to be used with a cautionary eye for possible distinctions arising from the new law's changes.

In the remaining chapters, we will not consider the old law–new law relationship as a separate topic but will discuss it in the context of particular issues for which it is especially relevant.[5] For general reference purposes, a copy of the 1909 Act is included as Appendix 2. Appendix 7 cross-references sections of the new law with the old and vice versa.

Copyright and Other U.S. Laws

The copyright law coexists with other federal laws such as the federal patent, trademark, and antitrust statutes, and the Federal Communications Act.

State or local laws stand in a different posture. Those that purport to govern matters exclusively within the scope of the copyright law are preempted by the new law [301(a)–(c)]. The problem sometimes will be to determine if a particular state or local law does indeed come within the domain of the new copyright law.

The relation of U.S. copyright law to other federal, state, and local laws is discussed in Chapter 7.

USER RIGHTS

Thus far our attention has largely been on the issues relating to the creation, management, and breadth of copyrights. What about users of copyrighted materials? Do they have rights too? With permission, of course. But otherwise?

Definitely. For example, since copyright does not protect an "idea," users have the right, insofar as copyright law is concerned, to use an author's ideas without permission. That right arises from what a copyright is not, i.e., what falls outside the scope of "copyrightable subject matter." Thus it makes sense for users of copyrighted material to have an understanding of what it is that copyright basically does and does not cover. In addition, there are copyright rules that expressly authorize certain uses of copyrighted materials even though the uses might ordinarily infringe on copyright. In this chapter, we will consider the principal rules within these five general categories:

1. fair use (section 107);
2. library reproduction rights (section 108);
3. public performances;
4. public displays;
5. compulsory licenses.

In each category there are user rights that operate as limitations on one or more of the five exclusive rights of copyright—reproduction, preparation of derivative works, public distribution, public performances, and public display.

Fair Use: Section 107

Notwithstanding a copyright owner's five exclusive rights, the fair use of a copyrighted work is not an infringement of copyright [107].

"Fair use" is an equitable rule of reason. Its application turns on the particular facts involved in each situation and its lack of specificity is sometimes frustrating. With time, this vagueness in the law may be further clarified, but a degree of flexibility is inherent in it. In addition, fair use may eventually become inapplicable to certain areas and more precise, though somewhat arbitrary, standards may be substituted.

Some guidelines have been developed to clarify fair use within the context of specific teaching activities.

Fair use is discussed in depth in Chapter 11.

Library Reproductions: Section 108

Have fair-use guidelines also been developed for librarians to cover situations they frequently confront?

No. However, Congress did provide a special standard, section 108 of the new law. It allows eligible libraries, under defined circumstances, to reproduce and distribute a copy of a copyrighted work without concern over whether the activity would be covered by section 107's fair use. Section 108 is filled with ups and downs, curves and bumps. As an introductory sampling, consider the following: You can make a copy. Do not make two copies at the same time. You can make a second copy later. However, it must be on a truly separate occasion; then it may be allowed by the section. But not if you are engaging in "systematic" copying or distribution. However, you will not be doing so if you are merely obtaining an interlibrary copy without the purpose or effect of substituting for a subscription or purchase.

We will try to make more sense of that later. The point now is that section 108 is complex. It will not solve all your library copying problems, whether you are a librarian, publisher, or author. It was a first step toward greater clarity as to some of the things that a library may properly do. It may have been a wise step, but it was not one of graceful simplicity. The conflicting policy considerations were strong. The issues were not simple. There was not a broad enough consensus as to what was "right."

Library reproduction rights are discussed further in Chapter 12.

Public Performance Exceptions

Under the old law, there were a number of categories of copyrighted works (e.g., most musical works) for which the copyright owner had no public performance right generally, but only a right with respect to public performances "for profit." The for-profit distinction was sometimes murky. Congress concluded that it was too unsophisticated a line of demarcation.[6] The new law gives the copyright owner certain rights as to public performances, regardless of whether they are for profit, if the work is in one of the following categories: literary, musical, dramatic, choreographic, audiovisual, and pantomimic.

A "literary" work, in the sense the term is used in the statute, is a very broad category and does not imply esthetic criteria [101 "literary works"].[7] Consequently, the principal works excluded from the above list are sound recordings and pictorial, graphic, and sculptural works. The last three are covered by a "public display" right.

Although Congress broadened copyright owners' public performance rights, it was not as simple as all that. Exceptions were engrafted to take particular situations into account. These relate, under specific conditions, to: teaching activities (including instructional broadcasts); performances for religious or charitable purposes; performances for the handicapped; and even to incidental performances at record shops and at agricultural or horticultural fairs [110].

Keep in mind that we have been considering limitations on the copyright owner's "public" performance rights. The copyright owner does not have a "private" performance right under copyright law [106].

Rules concerning public performance and public display exceptions are addressed in Chapter 13.

Public Display Exceptions

Under the new law, a copyright owner has an exclusive right to display the following types of works publicly: literary, musical, dramatic, choreographic, pantomimic, pictorial, graphic, sculptural, and individual images of audiovisual works. Except for the addition of pictorial, graphic, and sculptural works, these are the same categories as for the public performance right.

Users' rights with respect to public displays generally are the same as those applicable to public performances [e.g., 110]. An important addition is that the statute gives the owner of a lawful copy of a copyrighted work the right to display that particular object (to viewers present at the place where the copy is located) without the need to obtain the copyright owner's consent [109(b)].

In addition to the specific limitations on the copyright owner's public performance and display rights, the general fair-use limitation will be available in particular circumstances.

Compulsory Licenses

Within the four categories just considered—fair use, library reproductions, public performances, and public displays—the users' rights, when applicable, allow the copyrighted work to be used for free and without permission. Thus, in a sense, the copyright owner has no right of copyright in specific situations. There is another category of users' rights where the user does not need permission, but does incur statutory payment obligations and obligations to follow certain prescribed procedures. These are called "compulsory-license" situations.

Under the old law, we had only one form of compulsory license. It related to the making of recordings of musical compositions.[8] Under the new, we retain that one and add three others, each of which we shall consider below. We also have a new government body—the Copyright Royalty Tribunal—one of whose tasks is to set royalty rates, from time to time, in the four compulsory license areas [801–804]. The Tribunal will also preside over the allocation of funds among copyright owners in those cases where royalty payments are to be made to the Copyright Office rather than directly to particular copyright owners [801]. The four compulsory licenses relate to recording of nondramatic musical compositions, jukebox performances, noncommercial broadcasting, and cable television.

Musical Compositions: Recording Rights [115].   Under defined circumstances, a party has a right to make a sound recording of a musical composition once a recording has been publicly distributed in the United States by authority of the copyright owner. This *does not* authorize the making of duplicates of the initial recording, but only the making of new recordings of the composition.

Jukebox Performances [116].   A jukebox exemption existed under the old law—no part of the coin that went into the machine saw its way to the copyright owner.[9] Under the new law, the coins still don't flow back directly to the copyright owner. However, the jukebox operator pays an annual $8 license fee to the Copyright Office. Copyright owners can make claims to the Copyright Royalty Tribunal for their fair shares of those fees.

Noncommercial Broadcasting [118].   The new law establishes a compulsory-license system for noncommercial broadcasters. The license relates to published nondramatic musical works and to published pictorial, graphic, and sculptural works. The royalty rates are to be established through negotiations or, if and when necessary, by the Copyright Royalty Tribunal.

Cable Television [111]. Whether a cable television system may, as of right, carry a particular broadcast signal is a matter within the province of the Federal Communications Act.[10] When a system is authorized by the FCC (Federal Communications Commission) to carry such a broadcast signal, the new copyright law governs whether any copyright payment need be made. Generally, the cable system will, semiannually, pay a percentage of its revenue to the Copyright Office as a general license fee. As was the case with the jukebox license, the royalty payments are made to the Copyright Office and copyright owners make claims to their fair share.

The four compulsory licenses are discussed further in Chapter 14.

UNRESOLVED COPYRIGHT ISSUES

It is appropriate at this point to note that U.S. copyright law may change more frequently in the future than it has in the past. Indeed, when Congress passed the new law, it deliberately left some loose ends for study and possible legislative action over the next several years. Among the significant pending matters are those concerned with (1) performance rights in sound recordings, (2) computers and photocopiers, (3) noncommercial broadcast rights, (4) governmental works, (5) ornamental designs of useful articles, and (6) library reproduction rights. Since copyright law revision efforts understandably do not have the highest congressional priority and often involve substantial controversy, legislative changes in some or all of these areas may proceed rather slowly.

Performance Rights

When a musical recording is played on radio or television, the copyright law recognizes that the composer should be entitled to a payment. However, there is no comparable "performance" recognition for the performers or record producers who made the recording. At the request of Congress, the Register of Copyrights has submitted a report about this "performance rights" issue to Congress.

New Technologies

At the end of 1974, Congress established CONTU (the National Commission on New Technological Uses of Copyrighted Works) to study and make recommendations concerning copyright policies as they relate to modern data processing and reproduction technology.[11] Legislation calls for CONTU's final report by the end of July 1978.

Noncommercial Broadcasting

The compulsory license for noncommercial broadcasters did not cover nondramatic literary works. Would such coverage be a good idea? Should the noncommercial broadcasters be able to use such material royalty free? Congress has requested the Register of Copyrights to submit a report [118(e)(2)].

U.S. Government Works

Under the new law, there is no U.S. copyright protection for a work prepared by an officer or employee of the United States government as part of that person's official duties [101 "work of the United States Government"; 105]. NTIS (the National Technical Information Service), a part of the Department of Commerce, convinced the House of Representatives that there should be a limited exception to that rule for the benefit of NTIS. The exception was deleted in the House–Senate Conference Committee. The September 1976 Conference Report recommended the NTIS request be considered "early in the next session" of Congress.[12]

Ornamental Designs of Useful Articles

In 1976 the Senate, as part of the copyright law revision process, passed a bill providing protection for ornamental designs of useful articles.[13] Comparable provisions were not passed by the House and thus were not enacted into law. The House Judiciary Committee's September 1976 report on the copyright bill stated: "It will be necessary to reconsider the question of design protection in new legislation during the 95th Congress."[14]

Library Reproductions: Section 108

Section 108—the special provision concerning library reproductions—is something of an experiment. The Register of Copyrights is to report on it to Congress by January of 1983 [108(i)].

2

COPYRIGHTABLE SUBJECT MATTER

AUTHORSHIP; TANGIBLE FORM

The new copyright law has two basic criteria covering what is copyrightable. First, there must be an original work of authorship [102(a)]. Second, it must be set down in a tangible form sufficiently permanent to permit it to be communicated for a period of more than transitory duration, e.g., sheet music instead of a hum [101 "fixed"; 102(a)].

If a work fails to meet the first test, original work of authorship, it has no potential for copyright protection under the new law. If a work fails to meet only the second test, tangibility, it is not yet a work under U.S. copyright, but it may become one.

Original Work

The term "original work of authorship" appears to have about the same breadth of copyright coverage as under the old law. Of course, we have a new statute, with new word combinations and their implicit invitation to new arguments. Thus it is possible that original work of authorship may bring some significant changes to the old rules. However, such does not seem to be the case at the moment. Instead, there appears to be continuity of concept.[1]

The requirement that the work be "original" is somewhat misleading. It requires only that it be original to the author; i.e., he or she did not copy it. It need not be original—or "novel"—to the world.[2] Of course, the more that the work is like something else, the more one will question if it, indeed, was original to the author. This may sometimes be unfair. At least if the two works are fairly simple, their similar expressions may well have indeed come from two "originators," each perhaps having made his own product from the same threads of ideas.

To be an original work of authorship, there must be some element of creativity, however minimal. A most banal effort may yield enough to qualify, but not always. One case, involving a tinkered-up version of a standard sales form, failed to make the grade.[3]

As you can see, copyright can protect far more than top quality work—and indeed, far less. That is not a foolish arrangement. It makes it possible for the courts to avoid becoming critics, a probable benefit to all. Besides, the author does not obtain exclusive rights to the ideas that he or she expresses, only to the right to stop others from copying expression. Actually, the author may not obtain even that right, as in the case where there are only a few practical ways to express something, e.g., some simple contest rules.[4]

Tangible Form

To be eligible for copyright protection under the new law, the work must be fixed in a tangible medium of expression from which it can be communicated for a period of more than transitory duration.[5] Consider these examples:

1. performance of a song on stage;
2. performance of a song on radio;
3. performance of a song on television;
4. songwriter's score.

The first three would not, by themselves, establish enough to bring a federal copyright into being. The fourth example would. The original work of authorship must be "fixed" [102]. A work is fixed when its embodiment (by or under authority of the copyright owner) in a material object is sufficiently stable to permit it to be perceived, reproduced, or otherwise communicated for a period of more than transitory duration [101 "fixed"].

Prior to the work's being fixed, state law rather than federal law applies for protection [301(b)(1)].

WORKS OF AUTHORSHIP CATEGORIES

The new law lists seven categories of works of authorship, not purporting to be exhaustive:

1. literary works;
2. musical works, including any accompanying words;
3. dramatic works, including any accompanying music;
4. pantomimes and choreographic works;
5. pictorial, graphic, and sculptural works;
6. motion pictures and other audiovisual works;
7. sound recordings [102].

This listing is not of paramount importance in that we do not have a seven-part copyright law, one for each category. Nonetheless, an understanding of the categories is helpful. We will consider each of them plus two others (derivative works and compilations) that, so to speak, cross party lines. Actually, the seven also are not totally separate from one another.

Literary Works

This first category in the statute is really the catchall. It includes works, other than audiovisual, expressed in verbal or numerical symbols or indicia [101 "literary works"]. A novel would fall into this category as would a copyrightable catalog or a copyrightable compilation of data in computer-tape form.[6]

Musical and Dramatic Works

These categories are specifically mentioned in the statute not only because they are important areas of copyright, but also because there are a number of special provisions in the statute concerning variant terms, such as nondramatic musical and nondramatic literary works [e.g., 110(2); 115; 116; 118].

Pantomimes, Choreographic Works

The element of "fixation" often will be missing for these types of works but films and tapes, and sometimes notations, can supply it.

The legislative history states that social dance steps and simple routines are not included in choreographic works.[7]

Pictorial, Graphic, Sculptural Works

Works are included in this category insofar as their forms, but not their utilitarian aspects, are concerned [101 "pictorial," etc.].

The design of a useful article falls within this category only to the extent that it incorporates pictorial, graphic, or sculptural features that can be identified separately from, and are capable of existing independently of, the utilitarian aspects of the article [101 "pictorial," etc.; see also 113].

The House Judiciary Committee's legislative report on these provisions states that the committee does not regard the "design of typeface" to be within the new law's definition of pictorial, graphic, or sculptural work. As for architectural works, the committee concluded that drawings would be eligible for copyright protection. As for a structure itself, copyright protection would not be available where the only elements of shape in the design are conceptually inseparable from the utilitarian aspects of the structure.[8]

Motion Pictures, Other Audiovisuals

Audiovisual works are those that consist of related images that are intrinsically intended to be shown by the use of equipment such as projectors. "Motion pictures" are types of audiovisual works where the images, when shown in succession, impart an impression of motion [101 "audiovisual works," "motion pictures"].

Sound Recordings

The old copyright law at one time left room for argument as to whether someone could, without permission, copy a particular musical recording and sell it so long as he or she had permission to make a recording of the underlying musical composition. The resulting uncertainty was a factor in the development of a booming "record piracy" business. In 1971 Congress amended the old law to provide a separate copyright in sound recordings as such. That law became effective for those sound recordings that were recorded, for the first time, after February 14, 1972. The new law continues that protection and allows the states to provide similar protection for sound recordings first fixed before that date [102; 114; 301(c)].[9]

The copyrightable elements in a sound recording often will involve authorship on the part of both the performers and the record producers.[10] A sound recording is usually the type of copyrightable work that is based on a prior copyrighted work, e.g., a recorded song derived from sheet music. Both types of copyright must be kept in mind.

Derivative Works

A copyright in a derivative work, e.g., a translation, is distinct from the copyright in the underlying work [103(b)]. That rule is illustrative of a broader principle—*your* copyright covers only *your* original work of authorship. If you used material from someone else, do not claim you own *that*.

An interesting feature about a derivative work (or a compilation) is that a portion that *unlawfully* uses a preexisting copyrighted work is not entitled to copyright protection as a derivative work [103(a)].

Compilations

A compilation is a work formed by the collection and assembling of preexisting materials that are selected, coordinated, or arranged in such a way that the resulting work, as a whole, constitutes an original work of authorship [101 "compilation"]. It is possible to create a new work of authorship solely by combining preexisting material.[11]

COPYRIGHTABILITY LIMITS

Ideas and Others

In no case does copyright protection for an original work of authorship extend to any of the following: idea, concept, principal, discovery, procedure, process, system, or method of operation [102(b)]. The form of expression may be protected (when there is original work of authorship in that), but not the underlying idea, concept, or other.

The above list of exclusions makes some sense, particularly since copyright protection lasts for so long a period, and it would be unwise for that protection to cover anything as fundamental as an underlying idea or concept. But the exclusions of ideas and others are not founded solely on such practical considerations as copyright duration. Tradition and precedent combine to confine copyright protection to what an author does qua author.[12] Whatever that is, and however much it has been expanded to include some "uncreative" works, Congress still thinks of "authorship" when it thinks of copyright.[13] Concepts, principles, systems, processes—and ideas in that context—are more closely associated not with authorship or copyright, but with legal areas such as patents and trade secrets (see Chapter 7).

Although the exclusions do make sense, they also make for some confusion on occasion. A fine copyright scholar, Judge Learned Hand, put it this way, for ideas, in an infringement suit where a movie, *The Cohens and the Kellys*, was charged to have infringed on a play, *Abie's Irish Rose:*

> Upon any work, and especially upon a play, a great number of patterns of increasing generality will fit equally well, as more and more of the incident is left out. The last may perhaps be no more than the most general statement of what the play is about, and at times may consist only of its title; but there is a point in the series of abstractions where they are no longer protected, since otherwise the playwright could prevent the use of his "ideas," to which, apart from their expression, his property is never extended. . . . Nobody has ever been able to fix that boundary, and nobody ever can. . . .
>
> [The playwright's] copyright did not cover everything that might be drawn from the play; its content went to some extent into the public domain. We have to decide how much, and while we are as aware as anyone that the line, wherever it is drawn, will seem arbitrary, that is no excuse for not drawing it. . . .[14]

Facts, News

The eight exclusions listed in the preceding section are expressly mentioned in the statute. There are two other exclusions—a "fact" and "news"—that are not expressly mentioned, but that nonetheless are not considered to be within the meaning of an original work of authorship. However, a *compilation* of facts may be a work of authorship as may be the manner of expression of news.[15]

In the case of a fact compilation, authorship can derive from the arrangement of the facts and from the selection process—what to include and what to exclude. It will sometimes be difficult to judge how much of a fact compilation may be used, and in what manner, without running afoul of copyright.[16] Often, and almost always for significant undertakings, it is advisable to consult an attorney.

In the case of news, authorship can derive from the selection activities already mentioned, and from the arrangement of the news facts and the way in which they are expressed. But statements such as "In a copyrighted news story release today, the *Bromley Bugle* . . ." do not mean that only *that* publication is entitled to make use of the *information* the publication reported. The *Bugle's* use of a separate copyright notice, in its own name, on a story would probably be intended to convey the thoughts that the paper: (1) considered that it has a major story, (2) did not want to have substantial copying without its consent, and (3) thought that those journalists who pass on the news should give credit to the *Bugle* when so doing.

Short Phrases, Titles, Trademarks

Short phrases, titles, and trademarks often represent creative expression. Nonetheless, they have not been included under the copyright law.[17]

U.S. Government Works

A work prepared by an officer or employee of the U.S. government, as part of that person's official duties, is not eligible for U.S. copyright protection [101, 105]. This exclusion is a narrow one. It does not rule out copyright for *all* works by federal employees, but only for those works prepared as part of the employee's official duties. And, even as to those works, the exclusion applies only to U.S. copyright protection. Secton 105 does not prohibit the United States from seeking copyright protection under the laws of other countries.

The exclusion does not prohibit the United States from *owning* copyrights. For example, the government may accept bequests of copyrights and may obtain copyrights in works prepared by nonemployees under federal funding if the funding contract so provides.[18]

Computer Uses

Under the new law, the form of a copyrightable work is not a barrier to federal copyright protection so long as the form is sufficiently tangible [101 "fixed"; 102]. A copyrightable compilation of data on computer readable tape is subject to copyright protection, as is a copyrightable computer program.[19] However, Congress does not wish to resolve copyright–computer issues in full until CONTU (the National Commission on New Technological Uses of Copyrighted Works) reports on the issues. As a stopgap measure, Congress provided, in section 117, that the new law does not give a copyright owner any greater or lesser rights, with respect to the use of a work in conjunction with computers, than those available under the federal copyright law and other state and federal laws in effect on December 31, 1977 [117].

In its report to Congress, CONTU is expected to address such issues as: (1) whether the notice and deposit requirements should be different for works in computer form than for works in more traditional formats[20]; (2) the application of fair use in the context of the use of data bases[21]; (3) whether a computer program should be copyrightable and, if so, the limits of the scope of copyright protection in light of the traditional concept that copyright does not protect systems, plans, or methods of operation[22]; and (4) the extent to which copyright law should preempt state "trade secret" law insofar as computer programs are concerned.[23]

Even after CONTU's recommendations, Congress may take considerable time before revising the law. Meanwhile, those with a proprietary interest in computer programs and data bases would do well to consult counsel as to whether, in light of the new law's provisions, prior practices should be retained or changed.

3

COPYRIGHT NOTICES

USE OF COPYRIGHT NOTICE

A notice of copyright should be used when a work protected under U.S. copyright is published by authority of the copyright owner. The new law calls for the use of notice even when the work is published outside of the United States [401(a); 402(a)].

COPIES AND PHONORECORDS

The development of the U.S. copyright law has been somewhat different for sound recordings than for older forms of authorship, and copyrights in sound recordings use a different form of notice from that used for other types of works. A copyright in a sound recording is indicated by the symbol Ⓟ, e.g., Ⓟ 1979 Your Name, whereas a notice for other types of works uses Ⓒ or "Copyright" or "Copr.," e.g., Ⓒ 1979 Your Name.

A sound recording is a work that results from the fixation of a series of sounds (but not including the sounds accompanying a motion picture or other audiovisual work). The material objects in which the sounds are fixed are termed "phonorecords" (even if they happen to be audio-tapes). Material objects in which works *other than* sound recordings are fixed are "copies" [101]. The traditional type of copyright notice goes on copies. The Ⓟ type of notice goes on phonorecords.

Generally, in this book we use the word "copy" and its variants for convenience to embrace both copies and phonorecords and make the distinction between the two where it is relevant. The subject of copyright notices is one such area and we will focus on the difference between copies and phonorecords where appropriate.

Not every physical embodiment of a work is a copy or a phonorecord. These terms do not include material objects from which the work is capable of being perceived for only a transitory duration [101 "fixed"]. Thus, when a television screen carries a performance, the screen image is not a copy of the work.[1] A videotape, however, would be a copy. The terms "copy" and "phonorecord" include the original as well as the duplicates [101 "copies," "phonorecords"].

PUBLICATION

When a work protected under U.S. copyright is published by authority of the copyright owner, a notice of copyright should be placed on all publicly distributed phonorecords and on all publicly distributed copies from which the work may be visually perceived either directly or with the aid of a machine or device [401(a); 402(a)].

A work is "published" when copies are distributed to the public by sale, or by other transfer of ownership, or by rental, leasing, or lending [101 "publication"]. The legislative history says that "to the public" means, generally, to persons under no explicit or implicit restrictions with respect to disclosure of the work's contents.[2]

A work is also published when an offer to distribute copies is made to a group of persons for purposes of further distribution (such as books to wholesalers) or public performance (such as records to broadcast stations) or public display [101 "publication"].

The public performance or public display of a work does not, by itself, constitute publication [101 "publication"]. Thus, a play is not published if nothing more than its performance occurs. The public display of a painting does not, by itself, result in the painting's being published.

ELEMENTS OF COPYRIGHT NOTICE

A required copyright notice consists of three elements. The first element serves to notify the reader that copyright is claimed. Typically, the internationally recognized © is used for copies; ℗ is used for phonorecords. The second element is the year of first publication of the work. The third element is the name of the copyright owner [401(b); 402(b)].

As we shall see later, the year date may be omitted in certain cases, e.g., on illustrated greeting cards [401(b)(2)].

On rare occasions, a copyrightable work will consist preponderantly of one or more works of the U.S. government. (As discussed in the previous chapter, a work prepared by an officer or employee of the U.S. government, as part of that person's official duties, is not eligible for U.S. copyright protection [101, 105].) In these cases, an additional notice is required. It notifies the reader that the work consists of much that is not protected by U.S. copyright [101 "work of the United States Government"; 105; 403].

When a work consists of a number of separate and independent works assembled into a collective whole (e.g., a magazine, an anthology, or an encyclopedia), the separate contributions need not contain their own copyright notice. A single notice for the collective work as a whole suffices to meet the law's notice requirements. One exception is advertisement in the collective work by persons other than the copyright owner. These ads should bear a separate notice if copyright is claimed [101 "collective work"; 404].

Even when a separate notice on a contribution is not required, it will sometimes be desirable, particularly in the case of periodical articles. Such separate notice means that photocopies of the articles are likely to bear the relevant copyright information. Also, if the author of the contribution retains copyright ownership, that status will be expressly stated, whereas the copyright notice for the collective work will ordinarily show a different name. Finally, where an author writes many articles during a year, the consistent use of separate notices enables the author to obtain a single copyright registration that will cover each article [408(c)(2)].

The fact that a separate copyright notice is not required by copyright law for a contribution to a collective work does not prevent the author from arranging contractually that it be carried, if the publisher will agree.

Claim of Copyright

In the case of sound recordings, the symbol ℗ is used in the copyright notice to indicate a claim of copyright [101 "sound recordings"; 402(b)]. The symbol is recognized in international copyright treaties and stands for "phonogram."[3]

For works other than sound recordings, the symbol © or the word "Copyright," or the abbreviation "Copr." is used. The use of the symbol © is recommended, either alone or with Copyright or Copr. Its use may afford some rights abroad under the Universal Copyright Convention; i.e., foreign signatory countries will excuse you from some of the formal requirements they might otherwise impose as a condition of copyright protection in their countries.[4]

In addition to the ©, you may wish to use "All Rights Reserved." This may be of benefit in some Latin American countries that are not parties to the Universal Copyright Convention.[5] Usually, this phrase is used after the copyright owner's name, e.g., © 1979 Your Name. All Rights Reserved.

Year Date of First Publication

Date of First Publication. The year date to be used is the year of first publication of the work or sound recording [401(b)(2); 402(b)(2)]. If a second printing is made the next year, the original year date would still be used in the copyright notice because it remains the year of first publication.

Derivative Works, Compilations. When the work is a derivative work or compilation, the date of first publication of the derivative work or compilation suffices on copies. The date of first publication of the pre-existing published material is not required by copyright law, at least in the case of copies [401(b)(2)].[6] For instance, a translation would not have to include the date of first publication of the work translated.

Of course, we are assuming here that the derivative work or compilation itself has enough original authorship to qualify as a separately copyrightable work. If changes in the original work are so insubstantial that this is not true, the date of first publication of the original work would be used.

Greeting Cards and Others. In one class of works—which we will call the greeting card category—the year date may be omitted in the notice. To fall within this class, there must be a pictorial, graphic, or sculptural work reproduced in or on greeting cards, postcards, stationery, jewelry, dolls, toys, or in or on any useful articles. The right to omit the year date applies even if there is accompanying textual matter [401(b)(2)].

Unpublished Works. Under the new law it is acceptable to put a copyright notice on a copyrightable work that is not yet published; however, it is not required. If you do use a notice, it will not be in exactly the general form we have been considering. There would not be a year date of first publication to include. You might simply state:

> This is an unpublished manuscript
> in which copyright subsists
>
> Your Name
> June 5, 1979

Some form of notice—no particular words required—is worth considering when you are distributing the manuscript to several people, but not in such a manner as to constitute publication.

In addition to the use of an informal notice, it is sometimes appropriate to add a cautionary statement such as "This copy is not for distribution to the public." While not legally required, such a statement may stop an inappropriate distribution. Failing that, it at least notifies the receiver that the copy was probably not distributed with the copyright owner's authority. If a copy originally made for use in unpublished form is later publicly distributed, a notice appropriate for a published work should of course be added.

Name of Copyright Owner

The copyright notice on a published work should include the name of the owner of copyright in the work. An abbreviation by which the name can be recognized is also acceptable as is a generally known alternative designation of the owner [401(b)(3); 402(b)(3)].

Even if there is an error in the name of the owner of copyright, the copyright itself is not in jeopardy [406(a)]. However, as discussed later in this chapter, a third party sometimes can rely on a grant of rights from the person named in the notice even though that person did not have a valid authority to make the grant. Instances of such improper grants will be rare. However, if you want maximum protection against that possibility you should, when the correct owner is not named, have the work registered in the Copyright Office promptly and have any transfer of rights under it also recorded promptly [205(c)-(f); 406(a)].

A single notice applicable to a collective work as a whole suffices to meet the notice requirements with respect to the separate contributions (with the advertising exception mentioned earlier). However, the owner of copyright named in the collective work will not necessarily be the owner of copyright in any particular contribution. In that event, and absent a separate notice for the contribution, the statute states that the contribution is treated as if its notice of copyright had a name error [404]. The effect of a name error is considered later in this chapter.

U.S. Government Works

A work prepared by an officer or employee of the U.S. government, as part of that person's official duties, is not eligible for U.S. copyright protection. If another work, which *is* subject to U.S. copyright protection, happens to consist *preponderantly* of one or more works of the U.S. government, then the copyright notice calls for a new element of information in addition to the usual three. It should include a statement identifying those portions of the work protected by U.S. copyright. The statement may be by way of inclusion or exclusion [403].

COPYRIGHT NOTICE PLACEMENT

In the case of copyrightable sound recordings, the required copyright notice should be placed on the surface of the phonorecord or on the phonorecord label or container, in "such manner and location as to give reasonable notice of the claim of copyright" [402(c)]. Since phonorecords are not copies of the underlying musical compositions, the new law does not require separate ©-type notices on the phonorecords to protect the underlying musical compositions.[7] However, a ©-type notice might be used for words or artwork accompanying the phonorecord.

In the case of works other than phonorecords, there is just the general requirement for placement that the notice be affixed to the copies in "such manner and location as to give reasonable notice of the claim of copyright" [401(c)]. For a book, the title page and the obverse side of the title page would be reasonable locations. Regulations of the Register of Copyrights give examples of reasonable copyright notice positions for various types of works and also of reasonable methods for affixing the notices. The Register's examples are not to be construed as the only possible reasonable positions and methods of affixation [401(c)]. It would seem that an unreasonable notice placement (or method of affixation) would be equated to a notice that has been omitted.

PRE-1978 WORKS

The notice provisions thus far discussed apply to copies and phonorecords distributed on or after January 1, 1978. In the case of a work published before 1978, copies or phonorecords publicly distributed in 1978 or later are deemed to have an adequate notice if the notice complies with the requirements of either the old law or the new law [Transitional and Supplementary Provisions, Sec. 108].

EFFECT OF NOTICE ERRORS AND OMISSIONS

In this section we will examine the *new* law's standards about errors in, and omissions of, copyright notices. You should note, however, that the *old* law's copyright notice standards were more rigid, and errors and omissions could readily result in loss of copyright.[8] If notice error occurred prior to 1978 that had the effect of putting the work into the public domain, the new law does not revive the copyright [Transitional and Supplementary Provisions, Sec. 103].

In considering notice errors and omissions, keep in mind that the new law requires a copyright notice only when a work is published and only as to publicly distributed copies. Should you become concerned about a particular error or omission, do not ignore the possibility that the work was not published in the legal sense or that the copies were not publicly distributed.

Also keep in mind that the error and omission rules we are considering apply to copies distributed by authority of the copyright owner. They do not apply to copies distributed unlawfully. They also do not apply to copies distributed lawfully but by authority of the statute alone (e.g., by the fair-use provisions of section 107) rather than by authority of the copyright owner [405(a); 406(a)].[9]

Omission of Notice

Avoidance of Copyright Invalidation. The omission of a required copyright notice, from 1978 on, does not invalidate the copyright in a work if the notice has been omitted from no more than a relatively small number of copies distributed to the public [405(a)(1)].

Invalidation is also avoided if the notice is omitted in violation of an express written requirement that the copies bear the prescribed notice. The requirement must be made as a condition of the copyright owner's authorization of the public distribution of copies [405(a)(3)].

Invalidation may also be avoided by meeting two conditions. First, a reasonable effort must be made to add the required notice to all copies that are distributed to the public in the United States after the omission has been discovered. Second, registration of the work must have been made before the publication without notice *or* must be made within five years after the publication without notice [405(a)(2)].

Effect of Omission on Innocent Infringer. Suppose someone innocently infringes a copyright by relying on the absence of a notice in a copy that was, in fact, authorized by the copyright owner. If that person is able to prove that he or she was misled by the omission of the notice, damages need not be paid for any infringing acts committed before receiving actual notice that registration of a claim of copyright in the work has been made. However, the innocent infringer is still potentially exposed to other sanctions, e.g., an injunction against future infringement or an obligation to pay over, to the copyright owner, profits arising from the past infringement. But the court has discretionary power to give the infringer some relief even as to these two items [405(b)].

Note that the misled innocent infringer is given the statutory defense only with respect to an omission on a copy "publicly distributed by authority of the copyright owner."

Notice Error Equivalent to Notice Omission. If a copy bears no ©, ℗, or other appropriate signal that copyright is being claimed, the notice may well be sufficiently defective to equate with a notice omission. (The new law does not expressly say.) However, there would possibly be tolerance for mistakes where notice of copyright claim is nonetheless fairly given, e.g., the use of "(c)" instead of a ©.[10]

If a copy contains no name or no date that could reasonably be considered a part of the notice, the copy is considered to have been published without any notice [406(c)]. (In the case of a sound recording, if its producer is named on the phonorecord labels or containers, the producer's name shall be considered a part of the notice if no other name appears in conjunction with the notice [402(b)(3)].)[11]

If the year date in a copyright notice is more than one year later than the year in which publication first occurred, the work is considered to have been published without any notice [406(b)].

When a work consists preponderantly of one or more works of the U.S. government, the failure to include the special notice required is equated to an omission of copyright notice [403; 405(a)].[12]

The notice-omission rules apply to omissions on copies "publicly distributed by authority of the copyright owner" [405, 406]. The same is true concerning the notice-error rules that follow.

Notice Error Not Equated to Omission

Year Date Earlier. If the year date in the notice is *earlier* than the year in which publication first occurred, the notice is not equated to an omission. However, the date actually used can become the controlling date where copyright duration depends on the date of first publication [406(b)].

Year Date Only One Year Later. If the year date in the notice is not more than one year later than the year in which publication first occurred, there are no adverse copyright consequences insofar as copies publicly distributed after 1978 are concerned [406(b)]. This provision derives from the fact that such notice errors are not major in a copyright context and are quite common for works published near the end of a year.[13]

Name of Copyright Owner. When the person named in a copyright notice is not the owner of copyright, the validity and ownership of the copyright are not affected. However, if a party is misled by the notice error and begins an infringement in good faith, based on a purported transfer or license from the person named in the notice, that party may have a complete defense against the infringement claim [406(a)]. The defense is not available if registration for the work was made in the name of the owner of copyright before the infringing undertaking was begun. It is also not available if, before that undertaking, a document executed by the person named in this notice, and showing the true ownership of the copyright, has been recorded in the Copyright Office [406(a)(1), (2)].

The accompanying table summarizes the notice-error rules in the new law.

TABLE OF NEW LAW'S NOTICE-ERROR RULES

Type of Post-1977 Notice Error	Error Equated to Omission of Notice?	References*
No copyright owner named	Yes	406(c)
Wrong copyright owner named	No	406(a)
No year date of first publication (when required)	Yes	406(c)
Year date too early	No	406(b)
Year date one year later	No	406(b)
Year date more than one year later	Yes	406(b)
Omission of special notice when work consists preponderantly of U.S. government work(s)	Yes	403, 405(a)

*Denotes sections of the new copyright law.

INFORMATION DERIVABLE FROM COPYRIGHT NOTICES

When you see a copyright notice on a work that was first published in the United States, what information can you derive from it, assuming that the notice is accurate? The answer is surprisingly little for certain, but quite a bit in terms of probabilities.

Let us consider this notice on a book:

© 1979 Name of Author

From the copyright notice itself, you know that copyright is claimed by the named author in *something* related to the book. However, the notice does not tell you in *what*. That is because a simple notice, such as in this example, is all that is required even though the book may contain much material in the public domain or much material for which the copyright is owned by others (the author, for example, having used the material with permission). Here are some illustrations:

Example: Anthology. The author of the book may be claiming only a copyright in the compilation of the stories included in it. He or she may have authored none of the stories. Others may own those copyrights.

Example: Translation. The author may be claiming only copyright in the translation. Copyright in the work that was translated may belong to someone else. If you want permission to adapt the translation, you would ordinarily need authorization that covers both the translation and the work translated.

Example: Reprint of a classic. The author's claim of copyright may relate only to his or her introduction. However, it is also possible that the author edited the classic. If the changes were more than minimal, the author may be claiming copyright in the revision. You might need permission to copy the revision even though you would be free to copy the original version.

Thus, as a theoretical matter, the mere fact of a copyright notice does not tell you much. As a practical matter, you can become familiar with possibilities such as given in these examples and, from the nature of the copyright work, you can make reasonably good judgments as to what the copyright is likely to cover. In many cases, the book lists "credits" that provide further facts. Additional information may be obtainable from the author, the publisher, or from Copyright Office records that may exist relating to the work. Copyright information that can be derived from the date of publication in a notice will be reviewed in Chapter 9.

4

DEPOSIT COPIES FOR LIBRARY OF CONGRESS

When a copyrighted work is published in the United States with notice of copyright, as a general rule two copies must be deposited with the Copyright Office [407(a)]. This deposit requirement of section 407 is for the benefit of the Library of Congress. It is an obligation independent of the obligation to deposit copies when you register a claim of copyright [408]. However, under prescribed conditions, a deposit for Library of Congress purposes will also suffice to meet the section 408 deposit obligation [408(b)].

APPLICABILITY

When a work is published with notice of copyright in the United States, the deposit requirements of section 407 apply. Any required deposit is supposed to be made within three months after the date of that publication [407(a)].

A work is "published" when copies are distributed to the public by sale or other transfer of ownership, or by rental, lease, or lending. A work also is published by an offering to distribute copies to a group of persons for purposes of further distribution, public performance, or public display [101 "publication"]. There is no copy, and thus no deposit obligation, if the material object containing the copyrighted work holds it for only a brief duration [101 "copies"]. Thus, the television broadcast you see on your screen is not a copy and does not, by itself, invoke a copyright owner's obligation under section 407. However, if videotapes of the program are publicly distributed, there should be a notice of copyright and the section 407 deposit requirement would apply.

A public performance or public display of a work would not, by itself, constitute publication [101 "publication"].

DEPOSITED MATERIAL

The general rule calls for the deposit of two complete copies of the best edition. In the case of a sound recording, two complete phonorecords of the best edition would be deposited together with two copies of the material published with the phonorecord, e.g., the album jacket [407(a)].

The "best edition" of a work is the edition, published in the United States at any time before the date of deposit, that the Library of Congress determines to be most suitable for its purposes [101 "best edition"]. The Library of Congress has adopted a policy statement entitled "Best Edition of Published Copyrighted Works for the Collections of the Library of Congress." The policy statement establishes criteria for selecting the "best edition" when two or more editions of the same version of the same work have been published before the deposit requirement is met. A copy of the policy statement is included at the end of the Deposit Requirements section in Appendix 9.

EXCEPTIONS TO GENERAL DEPOSIT REQUIREMENT

By regulation, the Register of Copyrights may exempt categories of materials from the deposit requirement, or may require the deposit of only one copy or phonorecord, or may require the deposit of a substitute for copies or phonorecords [407(c)]. An example for each of the three types of exceptions follow:

Three-dimensional sculptural work	No section 407 deposit
Three-dimensional relief map	One copy
A lithograph of which less than five copies have been published and as to which an individual author is the owner of copyright	Photographs of the work are acceptable

The regulations include other examples and also a general provision whereby special relief from the normal regulatory deposit requirements may be granted by the Register of Copyrights when appropriate (see Appendix 9).

There are occasions where the section-407 exceptions are not repeated or are not always the same as for section-408 deposit rules. This is because the section-407 deposit is designed to serve the Library of Congress' needs whereas the section 408 deposit also serves another need—registration information. For example, the Library of Congress does not want to receive each type of published stationery for which copyright is claimed; therefore, no section 407 deposit is required. However, the Copyright Office would like to see the stationery, when registration is sought, in order to make a judgment of whether the stationery qualifies as a copyrightable work. Thus, a deposit is required if registration is sought.

DEPOSIT RESPONSIBILITIES; FEES

The deposit obligation of section 407 applies to the owner of copyright or the owner of the exclusive right of publication in the work published [407(a)].

When the owner of copyright and the owner of the exclusive right of publication are different persons, each has a potential deposit obligation but only one or the other need fulfill it. It will often make sense for them to agree as to which one thought the agreement would not relieve either party of its *statutory* responsibility.

Under section 407, no fee is required to deposit a work. If a receipt for the deposit is desired, it must be requested and the receipt charge is $2 [407(b); 708(a)(3)].

SANCTIONS FOR FAILURE TO DEPOSIT

Copyright is not lost if you fail to meet the deposit requirements of section 407 [407(a)].

A fine can be imposed if the required deposit is not made after demand by the Register of Copyrights. The demand may be made at any time after publication of the work and may be made upon the owner of copyright or the owner of the exclusive right of publication in the work. If deposit is not made after the demand, there can be a fine of up to $250. In addition, an amount comparable to the acquisition price of the materials may be demanded. The fine may be raised an additional $2,500 if there is willful and repeated failure to comply [407(d)].

Since the sanctions apply only when there is a failure to deposit after demand, the new law may not provide a strong enough penalty to encourage deposits. However, as we shall consider in Chapter 5, the law provides some benefits for registering claims of copyright. Since registration generally also calls for the deposit of copies, there is more than just a potential fine to motivate deposits.

DISPOSITION OF MATERIALS DEPOSITED

The materials deposited pursuant to section 407 are the property of the United States [704(a)]. They are available to the Library of Congress for its collections or for exchange or transfer to another library [704(b)]. If the Library of Congress doesn't select particular published materials, the Copyright Office retains them for a period it and the Library of Congress consider practicable. Thereafter, the materials may be destroyed or otherwise disposed of unless they were deposited under section 408 as well as section 407 and a request for retention was made (see Chapter 5).

UNPUBLISHED TRANSMISSION PROGRAMS

It is possible for copyrighted material to be transmitted to the public without the work's having been published so as to create a deposit obligation under section 407(a). Special provisions have been included in section 407 that make it possible for the Library of Congress to obtain copies of these transmission programs. These provisions authorize the establishment of regulations that would permit the Library of Congress to make a copy of the program [101 "transmission program"; 407 (e) (1)]. The provisions also authorize regulations whereby the Register of Copyrights, under defined circumstances, may demand a copy from the owner of the right of transmission in the United States [407(e)(2),(3)].

5

COPYRIGHT REGISTRATION

There are three types of copyright registrations. The first type is what we will call a basic registration. The second type is called a supplementary registration. It is used only if a basic registration has been made for the work. It serves to correct an error in a basic registration or to amplify the information given in a basic registration [408(d)]. The third type of registration is a renewal registration. It is used only for works that were published with copyright notice prior to 1978 or otherwise federally copyrighted by then. Although the renewal registration is technically also a "basic" registration, it has enough special characteristics that, for discussion purposes here, it is considered as a separate category later on in this chapter.

BASIC REGISTRATIONS: GENERAL

To receive a certificate of registration for your initial claim of copyright in your work, you must deliver to the Copyright Office: (1) a completed application for registration, (2) a deposit of two copies of the work or an acceptable substitute deposit, and (3) an application fee [408(a)]. The Copyright Office examines the application and the submitted material and either issues a certificate of registration or notifies you of the reasons for refusal [410].

BASIC REGISTRATIONS: WHO REGISTERS

Ordinarily, a particular work will have only one basic registration. It may be applied for by the author or by the owner of copyright or of an exclusive right in the work. Where only one basic registration is permitted, Copyright Office standards in effect provide that the first registration precludes basic registrations by others. However, the Copyright Office also takes the position that the statutory benefits of registration, to be considered later, are not personal to the one who registered and are not confined to the exclusive rights of that registrant.

When the first basic registration relates to a work in unpublished form, a second basic registration may be sought for the work in published form [408(e)]. A second basic registration will also be allowed where its applicant asserts that an earlier basic registration was unauthorized and legally invalid. It also is allowed by an author of the work who is not named as copyright claimant in the first registration.

Keep in mind that the general rule of one basic registration applies to a particular work. There can be a "family" of related copyrightable works, each of which is separately registrable by a basic registration, e.g., a revised edition and an original edition where the revision has sufficient new or different copyrightable material.

When there is a basic registration outstanding and a second basic registration is not authorized, those who would have liked to have made the basic registration often may get their particular facts on record, if they like, by obtaining a supplementary registration or by recording a transfer of ownership, whichever is applicable.

Because of the general rule of one basic registration, when two or more persons are entitled to apply, they may choose to agree among themselves as to which one will apply for it and to give that person priority if he or she does apply within a specified time. While the agreement would not be binding on the Copyright Office, it would accomplish the desired objective if the private parties abided by it.

The Register of Copyrights may, by regulation, permit a single basic registration to cover a group of related works [408(c)(1)]. Such regulations are required in the case of an individual author's periodical contributions, published within a twelve-month period, when such contributions each bore a separate notice of copyright containing the same copyright owner name [408(c)(2)].

BASIC REGISTRATIONS: PROCEDURES

Application Forms

There are four different application forms for basic registrations. The one to use depends upon the type of work to be registered. Form TX is for nondramatic literary works. Form PA is for performing arts materials, e.g., dramatic and musical works and motion pictures. Form VA is for pictorial, graphic, and sculptural works. Form SR is for sound recordings. It is also to be used when the same copyright claimant seeks to register not only the sound recording but also the musical, dramatic, or literary work embodied in the sound recording.

The following table lists the forms used for a basic registration under both the old law and the new law. The new forms are to be used whether or not the work was created or published before 1978.

Form Used Under the Old Law	New Form to Be Used
A, A-B Foreign, A-B ad interim, B, BB, C	TX
D, E, E-Foreign, L-M	PA
F, G, H, I, J, K, KK	VA
N	SR

Each of the four basic registration forms includes a "continuation sheet" for use when the basic form does not provide sufficient answering space; for example, form TX/CON is the continuation sheet for form TX. There is also a form for renewal registrations (form RE), a form for supplementary registrations (CA), and a form to be used when an individual's contributions to periodicals are to be registered by means of a single registration (GR/CP).

A copy of each of the forms is included in Appendix 8 in reduced format. Copies of the official forms, which are larger in size and easier to work with, may be obtained from the Copyright Office, Library of Congress, Washington, D.C. 20559.

In general, each of the four basic registration forms calls for the same information, but details in the forms and related instructions vary to take into account different characteristics among the types of work in each grouping. In the discussion that follows we will consider the principal information called for by form TX. Further explanation is provided by the form itself and the instructions that accompany it.

Title of Work. The title of the work to be registered will be given as well as previous or alternative titles. For periodicals, the volume, number, and issue date will also be provided. When it is a contribution to a collective work that is the work being registered, the applicant will use the title of the contribution and will also provide information about the collective work itself.

Author Information. The full name of the author or the work to be registered ordinarily will be given together with: (1) the year of the author's birth (optional) and, if the author is dead, the year of death; (2) the author's citizenship and domicile; and (3) a brief description of the contribution of the author to the work being registered; e.g., "Entire work," or "Chapters 15–17." The first page of the form provides space for three author listings. A "Continuation Sheet," designated TX/CON, provides room for additional names.

When the contribution to be reported upon, with respect to a particular author, falls into the category of an anonymous or pseudonymous contribution—terms that are defined in section 101—that fact is noted and it is not necessary to name that author. However, citizenship and domicile information must be given and the author's contribution should be described if possible.

When the contribution to be reported upon for a particular author falls into the category of a work made for hire—a term discussed in Chapter 6—that fact is noted and the employer or the party who specially ordered or commissioned the work is named as the author.

Year Work Created. The form calls for reporting the year the "creation" of work to be registered was completed. A work is considered to have been "created" when it is set down in a copy or phonorecord for the first time [101 "created"]. You may be creating a work each time you sit down at your typewriter and type out a single page of your thoughts. However, the year of creation of the work to be registered will be the year that work was completed.

Date and Nation of First Publication. In the case of a published work, the date of first publication of the work to be registered and the nation where first publication took place will be given. The same application form is used for both published and unpublished works, publication data obviously being omitted in the latter case.

Name and Address of Copyright Claimant. The copyright claimant is either the author of the work to be registered or one who has obtained ownership of copyright initially belonging to the author (see Chapter 6). The copyright claimant may be more than one person. Under present regulations, a transferee who obtained ownership of less than all rights of U.S. copyright would not be considered the copyright claimant for purposes of the application form's "claimant" section.

When a copyright claimant is not the author, the application should contain a brief statement of how the claimant obtained ownership of copyright.

Previous Registration. The form calls for reporting whether the work (or an earlier version) to be registered has been previously registered. If it has been, the registration number and year of registration is requested and the applicant is asked for a reason why the registration is being sought, e.g., that it is the first published edition of a work previously registered in unpublished form.

Compilations; Derivative Works. If the work to be registered is a compilation or a derivative work, the applicant will (a) identify any preexisting work or works that the work is based on or incorporates and (b) provide a brief, general statement of the material added to the work to be registered in which copyright is claimed.

Manufacturing Data. If the work to be registered has been published and consists preponderantly of nondramatic literary material, the new law's manufacturing clause—considered in Chapter 10—may apply. If it does, the applicant should provide (a) the name of those who, with respect to the material, performed the processes indicated below, and (b) the places where the processes were performed [601(c)]:

1. the typesetting or the platemaking—if the copies were printed directly from type that was set, or directly from plates made from such type;
2. the platemaking—if the making of plates by a lithographic or photoengraving process was a final or intermediate step preceding the printing;
3. the printing or other final process of producing copies;
4. the binding.

License for Use of Physically Handicapped. Form TX provides a section whereby the applicant may elect to grant the Library of Congress the right to reproduce and distribute braille copies of the work, or phonorecords, for the use of those unable to read normal printed material.

Deposit Accounts. For convenience, people who frequently make payments to the Copyright Office may choose to pay a lump sum deposit account in advance against which the Copyright Office charges its fees. The application form calls for account identification information for any such account.

Correspondence. The applicant should provide a name and address for Copyright Office correspondence about the application.

Certification. The application calls for a signed certification of the signator's relation to the work to be registered and of the application statement's correctness (to the best of the signer's knowledge).

Address for Mailing of Certificate. The address provided in this section will be the one to which the Copyright Office will mail the certificate of registration.

Deposit Requirements for Registration

General Rules. The general deposit rules for registration purposes are as follows [408(b)]:

Unpublished work	One complete copy or phonorecord
Published work	Two complete copies or phonorecords of the best edition
Work first published outside of the United States	One complete copy or phonorecord as published outside of the United States.

| Contribution to a collective work | One complete copy or phonorecord of the collective work |

The "best edition" of a work is defined as the edition, published in the United States at any time before the date of deposit, that the Library of Congress determines to be most suitable for its purposes [101 "best edition"]. This will not always be the edition published by the person filing for registration. For example, the owner of exclusive paperback rights in a work might, when registering, be depositing two hardbound copies of the work.

Exceptions. The Register of Copyrights may, by regulation: (1) exempt certain classes of works from the deposit requirement, or (2) require only one copy where two would otherwise be required, or (3) require or permit identifying material to be submitted in lieu of copies [408(c)]. Regulations concerning deposits are included in Appendix 9.

Deposits: Section 407. As discussed in Chapter 4, there are deposit requirements, for Library of Congress purposes, that apply to published works whether or not the work is being registered [407]. However, the deposits made pursuant to section 407 also may be used to satisfy the deposit requirements for registration if they are accompanied by the registration application and fee [408(b)].

Rights in Material Deposited. The material deposited becomes the property of the United States. The disposition of *published* material was considered in Chapter 4. In the case of unpublished works, the Library of Congress may, subject to regulations, select materials for its collections or for transfer to the National Archives or to a federal records center [704(b)]. During the work's term of copyright, a deposited unpublished work is not supposed to be destroyed unless a facsimile has been made a part of the Copyright Office records [704(d)].

Depositors of published or unpublished works, and copyright owners, may request that one or more deposited copies be retained, under control of the Copyright Office, for the full term of copyright [704(e)]. The law provides that Copyright Office regulations govern such requests.

Fees

The application fee for a registration is $10 [708(a)(1)]. For those who have frequent dealings with the Copyright Office that call for the payment of statutory fees, it is possible to establish a deposit account for convenience in handling payments.

As for mailing costs, publishers and distributors can qualify for a special rate when the registration calls for deposit of books.[1]

SUPPLEMENTARY REGISTRATIONS

Once a registration or renewal registration has been made for a work, an author or other copyright claimant, or an owner of any exclusive right in the work, may apply for a supplementary copyright registration to correct or amplify the information given in the registration.

Copyright Office form CA is used to apply for a supplementary registration. A copy of the form, including the instructions for its use, is included in Appendix 8 in reduced format.

There are separate provisions in the law for recording transfers of copyright ownership and statements relating to the death of an author [205; 302(d)]. These are considered in Chapters 6 and 9. Form CA is not used for ownership transfers.

RENEWAL REGISTRATIONS

The new law generally provides for a single term of copyright duration. However, as considered later in this chapter, for federal copyrights that were secured prior to 1978, there is an initial term of copyright and a renewal term. The renewal term must be applied for during the last year of the initial term.

Ordinarily, a renewal registration is for one work. However, under defined circumstances, a single renewal registration may be made for a group of works by the same individual author, all published as contributions to periodicals [408(c)(3)].

Copyright Office form RE is used to apply for a renewal registration. A copy of the form, including the instructions for its use, is included in Appendix 8 in reduced format.

The fee for a renewal registration is $6 [708(e)(2)].

CERTIFICATES OF REGISTRATION

The effective date of a basic registration is the date when an application, deposit, and fee—acceptable for registration—all have been received in the Copyright Office [410(d)]. A comparable rule, excluding the deposit, presumably is applicable in cases where no deposit is required.

There is a common misconception about "registrations" and certificates of registration—the idea that they are copyrights. Neither one is. Under the old law, a copyright ordinarily was obtained by publishing a copyrightable work with notice of copyright.[2] Under the new law a copyright is obtained by developing an original work of authorship and setting it down in a sufficiently tangible form. As we shall see, the registration of a copyright can be very important and, on some occasions, can be essential to having copyright protection. But a valid copyright ordinarily can exist even if there has been no registration.

ADVANTAGES OF REGISTRATION

The new copyright law does not legally compel you to apply for a registration (although you may take on such an obligation contractually). And only in a few situations, which we will consider shortly, is the application necessary to preserve a copyright. Why, then, should you apply for registration when you are not in one of those situations?

One reason is that it makes information about your copyright available to the public. Some people interested in your works might well search for that information in Copyright Office records, rely on it, and respect your rights that it reveals. Thus, the registration might give you some practical benefit regardless of its legal necessity or desirability. However, the legal points are also important. Early registration of a copyright claim captures many legal benefits that might be unavailable if you withhold registering until a problem, such as infringement of your copyright, arises.

Essential Registration

Renewal Term.   There are two categories of works that have a maximum copyright duration of 75 years, but for which the last 47 years are available only if applied for by timely application to the Copyright Office [304(a)].

Works published before 1978 constitute one category. If the renewal term was properly applied for before 1978, no new application need be made. The new law's longer renewal term (47 rather than 28 years) automatically applies [304(b)]. Where a renewal term was not applied for before 1978, it may be applied for, under the new law, within one year prior to the expiration of the original term of copyright [304(a)]. For works still in their initial term on January 1, 1978, that initial term lasts for 28 years from first publication and to the end of that last calendar year in which the 28th anniversary of first publication falls [304, 305].

The second renewal category applies to a work for which the copyright owner elected, under the old law, to obtain a federal copyright registration in the work in its unpublished form [304(a)]. For such registration still in initial term on January 1, 1978, a renewal term is obtainable if applied for prior to the expiration of the initial term. For works still in initial term on January 1, 1978, the initial term lasts for 28 years from the initial registration and to the end of that last calendar year in which the 28th anniversary of the initial registration falls [304(a); 305].

Commencing Infringement Suit.   The new law generally provides that no lawsuit for an infringement of the copyright in any work shall be instituted until registration of the copyright claim has been made [411]. (If, in the lawsuit, you are claiming to be owner of copyright, or of an exclusive right of copyright by virtue of a transfer from another, then the transfer document also should be recorded prior to bringing suit [250(d)].[3]

Compensating for Notice Omissions. As considered in Chapter 3, there can be circumstances where the omission of the copyright notice on publicly distributed copies will result in loss of copyright. One of the ways to "save" a potentially fatal omission, when it has occurred after 1977, is to register the claim of copyright within five years after the omission or to have already registered earlier. In either case, a reasonable effort must be made to add the notice to all copies publicly distributed in the United States after discovery of the omission [405(a)(2)].[4]

A registration before any omission has occurred has the slight advantage of making the copyright owner eligible to use the above procedures even if, later, a seemingly fatal notice defect occurs and remains unnoticed for five years. This is not quite as unlikely a situation as it seems since copyright notice *errors* are sometimes equated with omissions.

Other Advantages

To Recover Statutory Damages. When a copyright is infringed, there sometimes will be considerable difficulty proving the extent of the economic injury that the infringement caused. For example, if only a part of your work was used as only a part of the infringing work, the extent of the damages may be difficult to establish. The new law recognizes this problem and provides a system whereby the copyright owner may elect to receive statutory damages—generally, an amount the court considers just—rather than actual damages [504(c)].

If the infringement is of an unpublished work, the right to elect statutory damages is not available unless the work was registered prior to the time the infringement commenced. If the infringement commenced after first publication of the work, the remedy is available if the work is registered within three months of its first publication. Otherwise, it is available only if registration occurred prior to the time the infringement commenced [412].[5] (In these and other situations concerning infringement suits, we are considering infringements in 1978 or later. Pre-1978 infringements are governed by the old law [Transitional and Supplementary Provisions, Sec. 112].)

To Recover Attorney's Fees. One of the copyright owner's potential remedies for infringement is the recovery of reasonable attorney's fees in the infringement litigation [505]. However, if the infringement is of an unpublished work, this remedy is not available unless the work was registered prior to the time the infringement was commenced. If the infringement commenced after first publication of the work, the remedy is available if the work is registered within three months of its first publication. Otherwise, it is available only if registration occurred prior to the time infringement commenced [412].[6]

A court is not required to award reasonable attorney's fees and is authorized to do so only for the prevailing party [505].

Since the remedies of attorney's fees and statutory damages are often significant in infringement litigation, many copyright owners of published works will find the potential benefit of a registration well worth its inconvenience and expense. However, copyright owners who generate a great deal of certain types of copyrightable works (e.g., brochures and other promotional material) might conclude that the cumulative inconveniences and costs of registration outweigh the potential benefits when judged in light of the probability of an infringement arising and the other remedies available, e.g., an injunction.

As for unpublished works, many may elect not to register them despite the potential advantages. This may be particularly true where the unpublished work is not in final form and where the copyright owner retains control of the original (and any copies) to a sufficient degree that infringement opportunities are unlikely. It should be kept in mind, however, that some works are accessible to the public even though unpublished in the copyright sense. For example, the public performance of a play is not by itself a publication [101 "publication"]. Thus a copyright owner might choose to register a particular unpublished work even though that owner might choose not to register unpublished works as a general practice.

Prima Facie Evidence. If a claim of copyright is registered either before publication or within five years after publication, the certificate of registration constitutes prima facie evidence of the validity of the copyright and of the facts stated in the certificate [410(c)]. Although such evidence is rebuttable, the prima facie status nonetheless is valuable. This is especially true in infringement suits that arise years after the work was first created or published, when the facts of years earlier are sometimes difficult to ascertain and prove.

The language of section 410 (c)'s prima facie–evidence rule is consistent with its application to supplementary as well as basic registrations and that appears to be the intent.[7]

Since all of the prima facie facts will have been provided by the applicant for the registration, a moral obligation exists for the applicant to try to be accurate. The need to be honest goes without saying. Nonetheless, Congress has said that it is a criminal offense knowingly to make a false representation of a material fact in a registration application [506(c)].

If a certificate does not quality for prima facie–evidence status, the evidentiary weight to be given it is within the discretion of the court

[410(c)]. Ordinarily, a certificate will have more inherent credibility if it is obtained soon after the work is first published.

Avoiding Double-Deposit Requirement. As pointed out in Chapter 4, there is an obligation to deposit certain published works with the Copyright Office within three months after first publication. This deposit requirement, under section 407 of the new law, is separate from the deposit for registration purposes. However, a single deposit can serve both purposes [408(b)].

Protection against Conflicting Transfers of Ownership. If ownership of a right under copyright is transferred to you, you maximize your protection against a later inconsistent license or transfer (by the prior owner or owners) if you record your transfer with the Copyright Office promptly (and in any event no later than within one month after its execution) and if the work is also registered by then. (A two-month period is applicable if your transfer was executed outside of the United States.) Even if you do not take those steps within the specified period, you will prevail over the later transferee if you follow that recording-registration procedure before he or she does [205(e)].[8]

Just as the record-and-register rule permits you to prevail over a later ownership transferee, it may permit an earlier such transferee to prevail over *you.* Early registration of the work and recordation of the ownership transfer to *you* provide the maximum protection available under the copyright law, but because of the "one-month or two-month" rule, there is some exposure. For some protection covering that period, your agreement with your transferor might provide for payment not to be made until the period has passed when you have had an opportunity to learn from the Copyright Office records, that no earlier transfer has been recorded that will take priority. You may well find that it is not always practical or desirable to provide for a delayed payment, but you should keep the possibility in mind.

The registration benefits about conflicting transfers that are discussed in this section are important, but keep in mind that they are designed to cover an unlikely situation—an improper transfer of ownership or license by someone. However, also keep in mind that such an event can happen inadvertently and the precautions you may take need not necessarily reflect a distrust of your transferor.

In light of the new law's advantages for recording transfers of ownership, transfers may be reflected not only in formal contracts, but also in contemporaneous and brief transfer documents. In that way, it may be possible to record the transfer without disclosing all of the business arrangements. Incidentally, more than one title may be recorded in a single transfer document [708(e)(4)].

In making judgments as to whether transfer documents will be recorded, keep in mind that savings in recording expenses may be achieved in the case of works made for hire, a category considered in Chapter 6. For such a work, the employer, or the one who commissioned the work, has the status of an initial owner and thus has no need to record ownership transfer documents. In the case of works prepared through the creative efforts of many individuals, the savings in recording fees can be considerable if the work-made-for-hire approach is available and used.

Protection against Notice Inaccuracies. If a copyright notice is incorrect as to the name of the copyright owner, a section of the new law allows, under defined circumstances, an infringement defense to a person who innocently acquired rights from the person named in the notice [406(a)]. This defense is precluded if, before the infringing undertaking begins, the work has been registered in the name of the true owner of copyright [406(a)(1); see also 406 (a)(2)].

As considered in Chapter 3, an *omission* of a copyright notice from publicly distributed copies can be damaging even when loss of copyright does not result. Persons misled by an omission have an infringement defense under defined circumstances. However, that defense principally applies only to infringing acts committed before receiving actual notice of registration of the work [405(b)].

Constructive Notice. The new law has a general provision that documents pertaining to a copyrighted work may be recorded in the Copyright Office [205(a)]. If the work is also registered, others ordinarily cannot use ignorance of the facts recorded as an excuse; i.e., they are said to have "constructive notice" of the information [205(c)]. (In some situations, they must have actual notice of the information before the knowledge will be attributed to them [405(b)].)

In some of the transfer situations already considered we have made use of this constructive-notice rule.

Manufacturing Clause. When certain types of works not manufactured in the United States or Canada are imported into the United States in violation of the new law's manufacturing clause, a consequence is that certain infringements of the works by others will be allowed under defined circumstances. The copyright owner can minimize these "lawful infringement" possibilities by publishing in compliance with the manufacturing clause and also registering the work [601(d)(3)]. Incidentally, the Copyright Office has indicated that, under exceptional circumstances, a second basic registration for a work may be allowed in situations involving the subsection just cited.[9]

6

COPYRIGHT OWNERSHIP, TRANSFERS, AND LICENSES

INITIAL OWNERSHIP

Individual Works

The author of an original work of authorship is the initial owner of the copyright in the work and thus initially owns the exclusive rights of copyright: reproduction, preparation of derivative works, public distribution, public performance, and public display [106; 201(a)]. In the case of a work that qualifies as a work made for hire, the employer or the one who commissioned the work is considered to be the author [201(b)]. (Works made for hire are addressed later in this chapter.)

Joint Works

A joint work is a work prepared by two or more authors with the intention that their contributions be merged into inseparable or interdependent parts of a unitary whole [101 "joint work"]. The key point is the intent of the authors at the time the work is prepared. The authors of a joint work are co-owners of copyright in the work [201(a)].

As co-owners of copyright in a work, each joint author potentially has an independent right to license the use of the work (with a duty to account for the profits received).[1] Those who collaborate in the preparation of copyrighted works should reach a clear understanding of whether they intend to create a joint work and as to their respective rights in the work. An ambiguous agreement may destroy an amicable one.

Collective Works

A collective work is a work in which a number of contributions, constituting separate and independent works in themselves, are assembled into a collective whole. Anthologies, periodicals, and encyclopedias are examples [101 "collective work"].

In considering collective works, it is necessary to distinguish between the work as a whole and each individual contribution. The work as a whole is one work. Each contribution ordinarily is a separate work.

The owner of copyright in the work as a whole is not automatically the owner of copyright in each contribution [201(c)]. Under the old law there was some support for the position that, absent sufficient evidence to the contrary, the owner of the collective work acquired copyright ownership in the individual contributions submitted for the collective work.[2] That position may still be relevant in considering ownership of pre-1978 contributions.[3]

When the new law applies, there is a specific rule. In the absence of an express transfer of the copyright, or of any rights under it, the owner of copyright in the collective work is presumed to have acquired only the privilege of reproducing and distributing the contribution as part of:

1. that particular collective work;
2. any revision of that collective work;
3. any later collective work in that same series [201(c)].

Thus, when the new rule applies, the publisher of a magazine may, absent an agreement to the contrary, publish the separate contribution in a later issue of the same magazine, but not in a different magazine or in a book. Similarly, the copyright owner of an encyclopedia may publish the contribution in a revised edition but not in a different work unless that was expressly agreed to. In this discussion we have assumed that the contribution was not a work made for hire, a category to be examined later in this chapter.

Derivative Works

A derivative work is a work based upon one or more preexisting works. Examples are: translations, abridgements, condensations, dramatizations, fictionalizations, musical arrangements, sound recordings, art reproductions, and motion picture versions [101 "derivative work"].

The owner of copyright in a derivative work does not, by creating the derivative work, acquire ownership of copyright in the underlying work. Consequently, when acquiring rights from the author of a derivative work, you must consider whether it also is necessary to acquire related rights in the underlying work. The author of the derivative work, of course, had the same problem. That author may, however, have acquired only rights covering the objectives then in mind. He or she may not have acquired the right to pass on the particular rights in the underlying work in which you are interested.

In a few situations, the new copyright law allows the preparation of a derivative work without the consent of the owner of rights in the underlying work. For example, once the author of a nondramatic musical work has allowed the music to be recorded and publicly distributed on phonorecords in the United States, others may obtain a compulsory license to record their own rendition of the music for similar public distribution [115]. In these situations, the licensee's arrangement of the music is not copyrightable as a derivative work except with the express consent of the copyright owner of the underlying work [112(e); 115(a)(2)].

Works Made for Hire

In the case of works made for hire, the employer or the one who commissioned the work is considered to be the author [201(b)].

A work-made-for-hire category has been part of U.S. copyright law for a long time. Congress wanted to retain the concept in the new law, but decided to limit specifically the types of works that can fall within it. The new law provides for two categories.

Works by Employees.   A work prepared by an employee within the scope of his or her employment is a work made for hire [101 "work made for hire"]. The employer owns all of the rights of copyright in the work unless the employer and employee have agreed otherwise in a written instrument signed by them [201(b)].

Often, the employer–employee relationship is clear as is the "scope of employment" issue. Sometimes, however, there is room at least for argument. The employer, for example, could consider preserving a record of the facts, establishing the employment and its scope. The employer should also consider, in some cases, drawing up a formal agreement that reflects the work-made-for-hire status of the work.[4]

Theoretically, an employer's work made for hire can be any type of work since the employer–employee relationship can cover just about anything. Two of the most frequent types of "employer" works made for hire are periodicals (as collective works) and periodical contributions prepared by employees of the publication. Of course, they do not *have* to be works made for hire, but they very often are.

Specially Ordered or Commissioned Works.   The new law's second category of a work made for hire relates to works that are specially ordered or commissioned [101 "work made for hire"]. There are two requirements for this category. First, the parties must expressly agree in a written instrument signed by them that the work shall be considered a work made for hire. Second, the work must be specially ordered or commissioned for use as one or more of the following:

1. translation;
2. atlas;
3. contribution to a collective work;
4. compilation;
5. part of a motion picture or other audiovisual work;
6. test;
7. answer material for a test;
8. supplementary work;
9. instructional text.

A "supplementary work" is a work prepared for publication as a secondary adjunct to a work by another author for the purpose of introducing, concluding, illustrating, explaining, revising, commenting on, or assisting in the use of the other work. Examples are forewords, afterwords, illustrations, maps, tables, editorial notes, bibliographies, appendices, and indexes [101 "work made for hire"].

An "instructional text" is a literary, pictorial, or graphic work prepared for publication and with the purpose of use in systematic instructional activities [101 "work made for hire"].

Practical Significance of Works Made for Hire. Why does it matter whether a work is or is not a work made for hire? The work-made-for-hire status gives the employer or the person who specially commissioned the work the maximum possible rights under copyright. The status of the work sometimes can be legally determinative on five points: initial ownership, rights after 28 years, rights after 35 years, rights after 56 years, and copyright duration.

The last four points are of practical consequence only for works of value 28 or more years after their creation. Motion pictures come to mind as potentially having such durability. Other works, however, are sometimes as vigorous at a late age.

The "work-made-for-hire-or-not" issue is determinative of the *initial ownership* of copyright. If, for example, a specially commissioned work is a work made for hire, the one who commissioned it has that initial ownership. If it is not a work made for hire, the scope of rights in the one who commissioned the work will depend on what rights can be shown to have been transferred [201(a), (b); 204(a)]. Initial ownership of the work is important not only to the first parties involved in a transfer of rights but also to any later transferees. They will want to be confident that the rights indeed trace back to the true "initial" owner.

Let us assume that a person who created the original work of authorship transfers all rights of the copyright to a second person in a properly signed document. Could it *then* matter to that second person whether or not the work was or could have been a work made for hire? (After all, that second person now has ownership in any event.) Yes, it could matter in the four areas previously mentioned—copyright duration and the 28-, 35-, and 56-year situations.

The duration of copyright can be affected by whether or not a work is a work made for hire.

In the dual-term-of-copyright situations still in force for works under federal copyright protection prior to 1978, the maximum copyright duration is 75 years regardless of whether a work is one for hire.

For works subject to *other* duration rules, the copyright generally is either the life of the author plus 50 years or—and this includes the work-for-hire category—75 years from the work's first publication or 100 years from its creation, whichever expires first. You can hypothesize situations where the classification of the work can affect the copyright duration by 25 years or more either way. However, a very long copyright duration—50 years or more—is present no matter what the classification.

The 28-, 35-, and 56-year situations will be discussed later on in this chapter. We now will consider transfers of ownership for all types of works.

TRANSFERS OF OWNERSHIP

The initial owner of a copyright owns the exclusive rights of reproduction, preparation of derivative works, public distribution, public performance, and public display [106].

The new law states that any one of those rights and any subdivision of one of those rights may be transferred and owned separately [101 "transfer of copyright ownership"; 201(d)(2)]. If an exclusive right is transferred, the transferee is a copyright owner to the extent of the exclusive rights transferred [101 "copyright owner"; 201(d)(2)]. For instance, the transferee is entitled to sue for an infringement committed during the period when the transferee owns the right that was infringed [501(b)].

The idea that the exclusive rights of a copyright can be split up and owned separately is a feature of the new law that was not explicit in the old law. Under the old law, ownership was sometimes considered to be indivisible, and those who held an exclusive license were not, by that fact alone, always in the position of owners.

When a right under copyright is licensed on a nonexclusive basis, the licensee is not an owner of a right of copyright and the copyright law does not give the licensee the right to sue for infringement [101 "transfer of ownership," "copyright owner"; 201(d)(2); 501(b)].

A transfer of copyright ownership is ordinarily not valid unless there is a record of the transfer signed by the owner of the rights conveyed or by that person's authorized representative [204(a)].

A transfer of copyright ownership may be recorded in the Copyright Office. The document submitted should either bear the actual signature of the person who executed it or should be accompanied by a sworn certificate that it is a true copy of the original, signed document [205(a)]. For a document of six pages or less (one title), the fee for recordation is $10. The fee goes up thereafter by $.50 per additional page and by $.50 per additional title [708(a)(4)].

The prompt recording of a transfer of ownership in the Copyright Office can protect the transferee against the possibility of conflicting transfers of ownership if the work is also registered [205(e)]. This is important if you are already a transferee and wish to seek maximum protection. It is also important if you are a prospective transferee since you may wish to confirm from Copyright Office records that no inconsistent transfer has been recorded. The records are open to public inspection. Alternatively, upon payment of a $10 per hour search fee to the Copyright Office, the Office will report to you the information that its records disclose [705(c); 708(a)(10)].

Recording a transfer of ownership is most beneficial if the work is also registered. However, recording of the transfer alone may serve legally to protect the transferee against later inconsistent nonexclusive licenses [205(f)(2)].

OWNERSHIP OF COPYRIGHT-RELATED OBJECTS

Copyright Ownership–Object Ownership

The rights of copyright are intangible. Ownership of them is distinct from ownership in the related material or physical object. Consequently, when transferring copyrights, one should consider to what extent rights in the physical object will also be transferred. Similarly, when transferring ownership in a physical object that includes copyrighted work, one should consider to what extent rights of copyright will also be transferred. The new law provides that, absent an agreement, the transfer of rights of copyright does not convey ownership in the related physical object. Similarly, the transfer of ownership of a physical object does not of itself convey rights of copyright in the copyrighted work represented by the object [202]. For example, when you acquire ownership of unpublished letters you do not automatically acquire also the right to publish them. Similarly, when you buy a painting you do not automatically acquire reproduction rights. (Under the old law, there was some authority for a legal presumption that sale of a painting included publication rights unless those rights were specifically reserved.[5] The new law reaches the opposite result, at least for post-1977 transactions.)

Object Ownership–Display Rights

Although the owner of, say, a painting may not be a copyright owner, he or she nonetheless may, in the absence of a contrary agreement, display the object publicly to viewers present at the place where the copy is located. (This limitation on the copyright owner's right of public display would not apply if the painting had been merely acquired by loan or lease [109(b), (c)].)

Object Ownership–Sale Rights

If someone acquires ownership of a lawfully made copy (or original) of a work, e.g., a book or manuscript, he or she may, without the copyright owner's permission, sell that work without infringing copyright in the work.[6] (This limitation on the copyright owner's right to distribute copies publicly does not apply to material acquired by loan or lease [109(a), (c)].)

NONEXCLUSIVE LICENSES

When a right under copyright is granted on a nonexclusive basis, no transfer of ownership of the copyright is involved, and the licensee, not being a copyright owner, does not, for example, have the statutory right to sue for copyright infringement [501(b)].

Another difference between ownership and a nonexclusive license is that a transfer of copyright ownership must be in writing while there is no similar requirement for a nonexclusive license [204(a)]. A signed agreement, of course, has advantages whether required by copyright law or not. Even under the copyright law, it has advantages. If the license is in writing and signed by the owner of the rights licensed, the license will remain valid under its terms despite a later inconsistent transfer of ownership by the copyright owner. It will even remain valid as against an inconsistent *prior* transfer if the license was taken in good faith before the ownership transfer was recorded and without notice of the transfer [205(f)].

PERMISSIONS LICENSES

A very common nonexclusive license is the so-called permission which, properly enough, is rarely called anything so awkward as a "nonexclusive license." The term "permissions" generally is used in instances where an author, for his or her work, obtains the right to include excerpts, or the complete text, or an adaptation, of another's work. Permissions also relates to rights that users such as educators obtain to copy and distribute a work. Permissions are sought as a matter of courtesy, or when the copying would be beyond fair use, or when the requestor would like to avoid having to decide whether the copying would be legally all right without the copyright owner's consent.

Permissions requests are not as easy to administer as might first appear. For example, a permission request to a publisher potentially raises these questions for the publisher:

1. Would the granting of permission be consistent with the language of my agreement with the author?
2. Is the material to be copied something that "my" author prepared or was my author using the material by permission? If the latter, did the permission my author received go so far as to authorize the granting of this permission?
3. Exactly what portion of the work does the requesting person want to use and in what manner?
4. Will a quantity limitation be acceptable? Are copies to be sold? Will a time limitation be acceptable? Will a geographic limitation be acceptable or must world rights be considered?

The answers to these questions can determine whether the publisher has the right to grant permission and, if so, whether it should be granted on a gratis basis or for a fee, and, if the latter, the amount of the fee. People requesting permissions can minimize the potential complexities and delays of back-and-forth communications by specifying precisely what he or she wants to copy and from what source, and by describing what use is planned for the copies. Concerning the description of the proposed use, the more limited it is in scope, the more likely it is that the person receiving the request will say yes, will not need to ask for further information, and will not seek to obtain a fee or will seek to obtain only a minimum fee.

The subject of permissions is so integrally related to the doctrine of fair use that a few words about fair use are in order here even though it is the subject of Chapter 11. For convenience, we will speak here in the context of book publishing. The concept in book publishing is a little more settled than in fields such as teaching or in contexts such as photocopying, areas given special attention in Chapter 11.

In deciding whether the obtaining of permission to copy copyrighted material is essential in a particular case, you usually have to make a judgment whether your use, without permission, would be a fair use. In the field of book publishing, there will be some situations where you will *know* that your planned use will fall within the fair-use doctrine. For example, the material to be used will be a very brief excerpt from a lengthy published narrative. It will comprise only a very minor part of your work and will be used to illustrate a point. It will not be used out of its context nor to distort the original meaning. The use will not be in such a manner as to injure the sale of the original work (or, if it might do so, it will not be because of the copying but because of permissible criticism).

There will be many situations where fair use is clear. However, there will be others where it is not so clear. Unless you are going to deliberately operate with excessive caution, you will have to tolerate some uncertainty as to whether your honest, carefully considered judgment would definitely prevail in court. Uncertainty is sometimes inevitable, for fair use is intentionally general so that it can have equitable application to myriad cases without its being encumbered by a "tax code" of detailed rules.

At least in traditional publishing contexts, if you are confident that a use is a fair use, it is likely to be so if you have good judgment and if you have looked at the proposed use from the perspective of how you would feel if you were the author of the work.

Even with a high degree of self-confidence, there may be times when you will conclude the use is fair but also will conclude that your judgment might be contested. In these situations, you may have to be very practical. Would the prospective contestant have a respectable position (even though an incorrect one in your view)? Do you want to risk the possible time and expense of a dispute? Are the consequences of various possible adverse decisions, or settlements, tolerable? Could you obtain permission within a reasonable time under reasonable terms (even though you don't think you need it)? Can the use be avoided without substantial harm to your work?

TERMINATION OF TRANSFERS AND LICENSES

Ordinarily, a transfer of ownership or a nonexclusive license is governed by the terms of the license agreement. There are three exceptions where the copyright law in effect can override the agreement. These exceptions are the three "number rules" mentioned earlier in this chapter under works for hire—the 28-year rule, the 35-year rule, and the 56-year rule—and are discussed in the following sections.

The 28-Year Rule

For works subject to federal copyright protection prior to 1978, there was a dual term of copyright protection, and, for those works, that dual-term concept continues. To obtain the second term, one must apply for it before the expiration of the first term, which is approximately 28 years. The work's status is determinative as to who is entitled to own the renewal copyright. If the work is a work made for hire, the proprietor has the right. If initial ownership in the work rested in an individual author, he or she is entitled to the renewal copyright [304(a)]. If the author is deceased, his or her statutory successors are entitled to the renewal term, even if the author had contractually agreed that another would have the renewal right.[7]

Under the new law, we will not be establishing any additional dual-term copyright situations. However, there will be quite a carry-over of those already established under the old law. Renewal copyrights will be applied for even after the turn of the century.

The 35-Year Rule

General. The 35-year rule applies to all copyrights, dual term and otherwise [203] except with regard to works made for hire [203(a)].

This rule relates only to the termination of those transfers of ownership or nonexclusive licenses (of U.S. copyright) that were executed by the author in 1978 or later. It relates to each such transfer or license (other than by will and other than in the case of a work made for hire [203(a)]). It applies even if the transfer or license says that it does not [203(a)(5)].

The 35-year rule gives the author (or his or her statutory successors) the right to terminate the transfer or license only insofar as rights arising under U.S. copyright law are concerned [203(b)(5)]. The transfer or license of those U.S. copyrights remains unaffected if the termination right is not exercised [203(b)(6)].

A derivative work, prepared under the authority of a grant before the grant's termination, may continue to be utilized under the terms of the grant after its termination [203(b)(1)].

The rationale for the 35-year rule comes from the judgment that authors, while in the stages of initial negotiations for their works, are generally not in a very good position, when they grant rights in works, to have the prospective value of their works, 35 or more years later, reflected in the transaction.

Time and Notice of Termination. The 35-year rule sets up two timetables for termination: In the case of a grant that does not cover the right of publication, the termination may occur at any time during a five-year period beginning at the end of 35 years from the date of execution of the grant. In the case of a grant that does cover the right of publication, the five-year period begins at the earliest of these two dates: (a) the end of 40 years from execution of the grant or (b) the end of 35 years from the date of publication under the grant [203(a)(3)].

In any case, the notice of termination must be served at least two years before the selected termination date, and it may be sent as many as ten years before that date [203(a)(4)(A)].

Here is an example of the rule in operation:

April 10, 1980	Book contract execution.
August 23, 1988	Book published.
April 10, 2020	Five-year right of termination period begins (40 years from execution being earlier than 35 years from publication).
January 1, 2021	Assumed date of selected termination.

| January 1, 2019 | Last date for notice of termination if the termination is to be on January 1, 2021. The notice could have been served, for that termination date, as early as January 1, 2011. |

Notice Standards, Filing Requirements. The notice of termination, and the service of it, must comply with Copyright Office regulations. Moreover, prior to the effective date of the termination, a copy of the notice must be recorded with the Copyright Office [203(a)(4)(A), (B)].

Multiple Authors. When authors of a joint work have executed a grant of U.S. copyrights, termination of the grant may be carried out by a majority of the authors who executed it. If one of the authors is dead, his or her termination interest may be exercised as a unit by those of the author's statutory successors who own and are entitled to exercise a total of more than one half of that author's interest [203(a)(1)]. The rules that determine an author's statutory successors are considered below.

Author's Statutory Successors. If a termination right arises when an author is dead, it may be exercised by those statutorily designated classes of persons who own and are entitled to exercise a total of more than one half of the author's termination interest [203(a)(1)].

The deceased author's spouse owns the termination interest unless there are surviving children or grandchildren of the author. In that event, the spouse owns one half of the author's interest [203(a)(2)]. The children each own an equal share of the other half. If one of the children is dead, his or her children—the author's grandchildren—would own their parent's share [203(a)(2)].

Current Significance. The earliest termination notice under the 35-year rule will not be served until after the turn of the century. Nonetheless, there are several reasons why the rule is of interest now.

If you are an author, you should be aware of the rule's existence for possible future use. Equally important, you should be aware that if you are dead when a termination right arises, it will belong to people designated in the statute (e.g., your spouse or children); they are not necessarily those whom you would think it best to have this particular right. You cannot change the statutory distribution rules. However, you can limit their practical effect, from time to time, by voluntarily agreeing with your existing transferee or licensee to terminate the existing grant and substitute a new one.[8] This possibility permits you to have a "younger" transfer outstanding, and thus delays the time that the 35-year rule will have a practical effect. It is also consistent with the object of the 35-year rule, i.e., to let you negotiate anew as to the later term value of rights in your work.

Just as the author may be interested in negotiating new licenses well ahead of time, so too may a publisher negotiate new licenses if he or she wishes to postpone or avoid the possible complexities of negotiating new arrangements with the statutory successors. Also, the publisher should keep the 35-year rule in mind so as not to sublicense rights in such a way that the obligations to the sublicensee may seem to apply even should the publisher's underlying right be terminated by the author.

The 56-Year Rule

This rule relates only to the termination of those transfers (of ownership or licenses of U.S. copyrights) executed *before* 1978. Moreover, it relates only to works that *on* January 1, 1978, were under the dual-term copyright system of an initial term and a renewal term. Within that confined scope, the 56-year rule applies to each transfer or license (other than by will and other than in the case of works made for hire) [304(c)]. It applies even if the transfer or license says that it does not [304(c)(5)].

The rationale for the 56-year rule comes from the fact that, by the new law, Congress generally was extending the maximum life of these dual-term copyrights from 56 to 75 years. Congress concluded that the author should be able to control these extra 19 years.[9] The 56-year rule gives the author (or his or her statutory successors) the right to terminate the pre-1978 transfer or license insofar as rights under U.S. copyright are concerned. The transfer or license remains unaffected if the termination right is not exercised [304(c)(6)(F)].

Here is the 56-year rule in operation in a relatively simple case.

In 1925 you, the author, executed a transfer of ownership in your work to a publisher who published the work, with notice of copyright, on January 2, 1926. You renewed your copyright in 1953, the renewal term to begin on January 2, 1954. On January 2, 1979, you serve a written, and signed, notice on the publisher that the 1925 grant will terminate on January 3, 1982, insofar as U.S. copyrights are concerned. The notice and its service upon the grantees are such that they conform with Copyright Office regulations [304(c)(4)(B)]. Prior to the effective date of termination, you record a copy of the notice with the Copyright Office [304(c)(4)(A)].

When January 3, 1982, arrives, the grant terminates insofar as those rights arising under U.S. copyright are concerned. The termination does not affect rights arising under other laws—federal, state, or foreign [304(c)(6)(E)]. Moreover, a derivative work prepared under authority of the grant before its termination may continue to be utilized under the terms of the grant after its termination [304(c)(6)(A)].

The notice and termination dates used above were not the only ones that could have been selected. The statutory rule is that termination may be effected at any time during a period of five years, beginning at the end of 56 years from the date copyright was originally secured or beginning January 1, 1978, whichever is later [304(c)(3)]. The notice of termination may be served not less than two nor more than ten years before the effective date of termination [304(c)(4)(A)].

The statutory succession rules that apply when the author is deceased are similar to those applicable under the 35-year rule [304(c)(2)]. In addition, there are rules that take into account the fact that some of the basic grants that ordinarily would have been made by an author may instead have been made by his or her statutory successors under the 28-year rule, i.e., those who became the initial copyright owners of the renewal copyright [304(c)]. When a grant was made by such statutory successors and they are deceased, termination can be effected only by the unanimous action of the survivors of those who executed the grant.

The 56-year rule is quite complex. The major points have been covered in this chapter though not fully developed. While you may wish to make specific plans to implement the rule yourself, I suggest you consult an attorney at least before you actually carry them out.

7

EXCLUSIVE RIGHTS OF COPYRIGHT

FIVE EXCLUSIVE RIGHTS

The owner of copyright generally has the exclusive right to do and authorize the following with respect to the copyrighted work:

1. reproduce it in copies;
2. prepare derivative works based upon it;
3. distribute copies of it to the public;
4. perform the work publicly;
5. display the work publicly [106].

The ownership of these exclusive rights may be transferred in whole or in part. A transferee who obtains a right on an exclusive basis stands in the position of a copyright owner, insofar as that right is concerned, for the period he or she owns it [201(d)(2); 501(b)]. This is true even if the transfer of ownership is for only a limited time [101 "transfer of copyright ownership"]. A transferee who obtains a right on a nonexclusive basis is referred to as a nonexclusive licensee or as a licensee. Such person has authority to exercise rights under copyright but is not considered to be a copyright owner.

Each of the five rights of copyright will be considered here together with some of the limitations on each right that are of general applicability. There are also a number of limitations that apply to particular situations, e.g., the right of teachers publicly to perform a work during the course of face-to-face teaching activities [110(1)]. A table listing specific limitations is found in Appendix 6 of this book. The principal limitations, including the broadly applicable fair-use doctrine, are discussed in Chapters 11 through 14.

Reproduction

The reproduction rights of copyright relate to the making of copies or phonorecords of a work. There is no copy or phonorecord unless the physical object holds the work for more than a transitory duration [101 "copy, phonorecord, fixed"]. To illustrate, the duplication of a videotape would be the reproduction of a copy but the continuous playback of the tape would not result in a copy being made on the screen. In the copyright sense, the playback would be a "performance" or a "display" of the work [101].

Two of the principal limitations on the exclusive right of reproduction are the fair-use doctrine and the library reproduction rights provisions. For further discussion of these two sections of the law, see Chapters 11 and 12.

Preparation of Derivative Works

The copyright owner has the exclusive right to prepare derivative works based upon the copyrighted work [106(a)(2)]. A derivative work is a work based upon one or more preexisting works. The statutory definition includes translations, condensations, abridgments, dramatizations, motion picture versions, art reproductions, musical arrangements, and sound recordings [101].

Public Distribution

The third exclusive right of copyright in the statute is the right to distribute copies (or phonorecords) of the copyrighted work to the public by sale or other transfer of ownership, or by rental, lease, or lending [101 "publication"; 106(a)(3)]. An appearance of a work on television or on stage ordinarily would not, by itself, be a public distribution, the appearance being too transitory to qualify as a copy. Of course, public display or performance rights might be involved, depending upon the circumstances.

According to the legislative history, distribution to the public means, generally, distribution to persons under no explicit or implicit restrictions with respect to disclosure of the contents of the work.[1]

Once a person obtains *ownership* of a copy, he or she may, without the authority of the copyright owner, sell or otherwise dispose of that copy and he or she will not infringe the copyright by so doing [109(a)]. Although this does not mean that there can never be valid *contractual* restrictions on resale,[2] such restrictions in the case of published works may be found unreasonable and invalid in many circumstances.

Public Performance

The owner of copyright has the exclusive right to perform the copyrighted work publicly, except in the case of pictorial, graphic, or sculptural works [106(4)]. This right also does not apply to sound recordings, but keep in mind that copyright in the underlying work is separate from copyright in the sound recording as such [114(a)]. Thus if some-one publicly plays your hit recording of someone else's copyrighted song, *you* have no copyright case, but the copyright owner of the song may have one.

Performances may occur in a variety of situations, e.g., singing, dancing, acting, reciting, or broadcasting. Even you, when you turn on your television set, are engaged in a performance of the work (at least if someone is listening) [101 "perform"]. However, the copyright owner's exclusive right covers no more than public performances.

The definitions of public performances and public displays are combined in the statute. To perform or display a work publicly includes any of the following:

1. performance or display at a place open to the public;
2. performance or display at any place where are gathered a substantial number of persons outside of a normal circle of family and its social acquaintances;
3. transmitting or otherwise communicating a performance or display of the work to the public or to one of the places described in (1) or (2) above.

Under the third clause, there can be a public performance or display even if the viewers or hearers are not present in the same place or seeing or hearing the material at the same time [101 "publicly"].

Under the old law, many of the copyright owner's exclusive performance rights were limited to public performances for profit. Although the new law does away with that broad for-profit distinction, it replaces it with a number of other limitations on the owner's public performance rights. These limitations are considered in Chapters 13 and 14.

Public Display

The fifth exclusive right of copyright is the right to display the copyrighted work publicly [106(5)]. Like the public performance right, it is not applicable to sound recordings [114(a)].

The public display right is new statutory language. The status of the right under the old law was uncertain.[3]

To display a work means to show the original, or a copy of it, either directly or with mechanical aids, such as a projector. In the case of a motion picture or other audiovisual work, one "displays" the work by showing individual images nonsequentially [101 "display"]. One "performs" such a work by showing it in sequence or by making the accompanying sounds audible [101 "perform"].

The owner of the original work, or of a lawfully made copy of it, is entitled (without the authorization of the copyright owner) to display that copy publicly to viewers present at the place where the copy is located. This may be done directly or by the projection of no more than one image at a time [109(b)].

Notwithstanding the five exclusive rights of copyright applicable under the new law, the owner of copyright in a work generally has no greater or lesser rights than he or she had on the day before the new law took effect, with respect to the use of the work in conjunction with computers [117]. This preserves the *status quo ante* until Congress considers the matter in light of a report it has requested from CONTU (the National Commission on New Technological Uses of Copyrighted Works).

The *status quo ante*, although preserved, is unclear. Was the input of copyrightable material into a computer the exercise of a right of copyright under the old law? Assuming that it was, are there circumstances when it would have been fair use? Is the search of computerized data an exercise of a right of copyright under the old law? If so, under what circumstances would permission have been implied or would fair use have been considered applicable? You won't find the answers spelled out in the old law and judicial expositions on these issues are scarce. That's part of the reason CONTU was created.

EXCLUSIVE RIGHTS OF COPYRIGHT VS. RIGHTS UNDER OTHER LAWS

Federal Statutes

The new copyright law does not annul or limit any rights or remedies under any other federal statutes [301(d)]. Five of the federal statutory areas that should be kept in mind in this context are: utility patents, design patents, trademarks, antitrust law, and federal communications law. Although none of these areas are within the scope of this book, some remarks are presented below.

Patents. The federal patent law concerns new and nonobvious useful inventions. Patent protection covers a period of 17 years. An owner of a valid patent obtains the exclusive right to make, use, or sell the patented invention. This right may apply even as against another who independently developed the same invention.[4]

Design Patents. Federal design patent law concerns new, original, and ornamental designs for articles of manufacture. Design patent protection can extend as long as a 14-year period. Design patents are issued only after a search is made to determine that the design is novel.[5]

Trademarks. The federal trademark law—the Lanham Act—provides a registration and protection system for those words, names, symbols, and devices that identify the trademark owner's goods and services, and distinguish them from others. Trademark protection can last as long as the mark retains its identifying and distinguishing function. The federal law generally relates to federally registered trademarks. However, it also contains a provision that prohibits false designations of origin and false descriptions of goods and services even when federally registered trademarks are not involved.[6]

Antitrust Laws. The federal antitrust laws prohibit, under defined circumstances, such things as: contracts in unreasonable restraint of trade, unfair trade practices, certain kinds of price discrimination, and monopolization and attempts to monopolize.[7]

Federal Communications Law. The Federal Communications Act of 1934 governs broadcast and certain cablecast activities.[8]

State and Local Laws

The new copyright law aims for a uniform national policy on copyright matters and seeks to accomplish this through what are called the "preemption" provisions of section 301. That section provides the authority for the new law to override state and local laws—called here "state laws" for convenience—that provide rights equivalent to the exclusive rights of the new law with respect to tangibly fixed original works of authorship [301(a)].

State laws are not limited by the new federal law insofar as the state laws cover rights and remedies with respect to subject matter that does not come within the new law's "subject matter of copyright" [301(b)(1)]. For example, state law can protect original works of authorship that have not yet been set down in a fixed tangible form [101, 301]. Sound recordings first fixed before February 15, 1972, may also be protected by state law [301(c)]. (Federal protection for sound recordings, as such, began with those first fixed on that date and after.)

Rights and remedies under state law are also not limited by the new copyright law insofar as the rights and remedies relate to any cause of action arising from undertakings commenced before January 1, 1978 [301(b)(2)].

Finally, state law rights and remedies are not limited by the new copyright law with respect to activities violating legal or equitable rights "that are not equivalent to any of the exclusive rights within the general scope of copyright as specified by section 106" [301(b)(3)]. Section 106 sets forth the five exclusive rights of copyrights—reproduction, preparation of derivative works, public distribution, performance, and display—and notes that those rights are subject to the limitations of the 12 subsequent sections, 107 through 118.

The full scope of the not-equivalent standard of subsection 301(b)(3) is likely to remain unclear for some time to come. This is especially true because, just prior to the passage of the new law, the then copyright revision bill mentioned examples of types of state laws that potentially could meet the not-equivalent test. These examples were deleted in the final days before enactment, but the legislative history leaves the rationale for the deletion somewhat unclear. We will mention here only some of the main points of the legislative history.

As of the beginning of September 1976, the copyright revision bill included these not-equivalent rights as examples:

> . . . including rights against misappropriation not equivalent to any such exclusive rights [of section 106], breaches of contract, breaches of trust, trespass, conversion, invasion of privacy, defamation, and deceptive trade practices such as passing off and false representation.[9]

On September 22, the House deleted this language. There was expressed concern by the proposer of the deletion amendment that the reference to "misappropriation" might be construed as authorizing states to pass misappropriation laws, and that a misappropriation law could be so broad as to render the general preemption approach of the new law meaningless. At the same time, however, the same congressman concurred with the view that, by the step of striking "misappropriation," there was no intent to change the existing state of the law relating to misappropriation. This was all reported in the *Congressional Record*[10] and the language of the reported remarks suggests that the congressmen who were addressing each other may not have had a complete meeting of minds, but only thought they did. Thus, it is difficult to attach any firm conclusion, from the remarks, as to what Congress intended by the deletion. Although the answers may affect only what nuances will be given to the statute's not-equivalent phrase (even the deleted language did not authorize any and all state laws dealing with misappropriations), the nuances may have significant practical consequences.

The accompanying table summarizes the preemption provisions in the new law.

Although the full scope of the preemption provisions is unclear, that is no reason not to continue to pay attention to state defamation and invasion-of-privacy laws. Those laws reflect some different policy interests than copyright law does and ordinarily will readily survive a copyright preemption argument. Thus, for example, photographers should continue to obtain model releases, for "privacy law" purposes, in circumstances where that was appropriate before the new law.

TABLE OF NEW LAW'S PREEMPTION PROVISIONS

Subject or Activity	Preemption by the New Law?	Reference*
Subject matter not within section 102–103's scope of copyright	No	301(b)(1)
Claims arising from undertakings commenced prior to 1978	No	301(b)(2)
Sound recordings first fixed prior to February 15, 1972	No (until 2047)	301(c)
Rights, remedies under federal statutes	No	301(d)
Activities violating rights not equivalent to any of the exclusive rights of copyright within the general scope of copyright as specified by section 106	No	301(b)(3)
Rights equivalent to any of the exclusive rights of copyright as specified in section 106 in tangibly fixed works of authorship within the subject matter of copyright as specified by sections 102 and 103	Yes	301(a)
Rights of owner of copyright in a work that portrays a useful article as such	New law incorporates pre-1978 state and federal standards	113(b)
Rights of owner of copyright with respect to use of the work in conjunction with computers	New law incorporates pre-1978 state and federal standards	117

*Denotes sections of the new copyright law.

8

COPYRIGHT INFRINGEMENT REMEDIES

The principal remedies in a civil action for copyright infringement under the new law are: (1) an injunction against the infringing activity, (2) recovery of actual damages, (3) recovery of the infringer's profits arising from the infringement, (4) recovery of statutory damages, and (5) recovery of attorney's fees in the infringement action.

We will consider each such remedy in this chapter. At the end of the chapter are two tables listing these and other remedies and sanctions (civil and criminal) provided by the new copyright law.

Under the new law, the owner of an exclusive right of copyright is entitled to sue for any infringement of that particular right committed while he or she is the owner of it [501]. The legal or the beneficial owner of such a copyright right is entitled to bring suit. The legislative history states that a "beneficial owner" would be, for example, an author who parted with legal title in exchange for percentage royalties based on sales or license fees.[1]

REQUIREMENTS FOR COMMENCEMENT OF SUIT

To commence a copyright infringement action, a claim of copyright in the work ordinarily (almost always) must first have been registered [411]. Further, if the owner of the infringed exclusive right became such as the result of a transfer of ownership from another, the instrument of transfer must also be recorded in the Copyright Office before the suit may properly commence [205(d)].

Another formal requirement for the lawsuit exists when the so-called manufacturing-clause requirements apply and the suit is for infringement of reproduction and distribution rights. In such situations manufacturing data about the work infringed should be included in the complaint filed with the court in order to begin the lawsuit [601(e)].

The manufacturing-clause provisions apply only to a narrow class of works. The threshold test for the manufacturing clause is that the work consists preponderantly of nondramatic literary material that is in the English language and is protected by U.S. copyright [601(a)]. However, that entire category is not covered by the manufacturing clause, there being a number of works that may be excluded. Oversimplifying somewhat, the manufacturing clause covers only English-language nondramatic literary material by an American author who is not a permanent foreign resident. The manufacturing clause is taken up further in Chapter 10.

Suits for copyright infringement under the new law may be brought only in federal court. They must be commenced within three years after the claim for infringement accrued [507(b)].

If another person has a claim or interest in the copyright being sued upon, the court may order the person bringing the suit to serve written notice of it on that person [501(b)].

INJUNCTIONS

The copyright law gives the court the power to grant temporary and final injunctions to prevent or restrain infringement of a copyright [502(a)]. Temporary injunctions are usually sought early in the case, before it is fully ready for trial. In determining whether to grant temporary injunctions, the court takes into account the strength of the proof that infringement has indeed occurred and, in some cases, the relative harm that will be caused the respective parties should the temporary relief be granted (or denied) pending the final outcome of the litigation.

The injunction remedy is not available against the U.S. government or, in some circumstances, against infringements arising under federal contracts. When these circumstances apply, the copyright owner's remedy is for recovery of reasonable compensation.[2]

ACTUAL DAMAGES

The court may award the copyright owner an amount equal to the actual damages caused the owner as a result of the infringement [504(a)].

DEFENDANT'S PROFITS

One of the remedies for copyright infringement is the right to recover any profits of the infringer that are attributable to the infringement and are not taken into account in computing the actual damages. The copyright owner's obligation is merely to prove the infringer's gross revenue. It is the infringer's burden to prove what the deductible expenses were and also to prove the elements of profit, if any, that were attributable to factors other than the infringed work [504(b)].

STATUTORY DAMAGES

It is often difficult to establish what the actual damages in a case are. Also the infringer's profits attributable to the infringement may be uncertain or nonexistent. Recognizing these possibilities, the law allows the copyright owner to elect to recover "statutory" damages instead of actual damages and the infringer's profits. The statutory-damages provisions allow the court to make an award of from $100 to $50,000 depending, as we shall see, on the circumstances [504(c)]. The election of the statutory-damages remedy may be made at any time before final judgment is rendered [501(c)(1)]. However, no statutory-damages award will be made for any infringement of copyright, in an unpublished work, commenced before registration of the claim of copyright. And none will be made for any infringement commenced after first publication of the work infringed unless registration of that work was made either (a) before commencement of the infringement or (b) within three months after first publication [410(d); 412].

For statutory-damage purposes, there are, in a sense, four types of infringements, which we will informally label regular, willful, innocent, and privileged.

The "regular" type is the catchall one, i.e., an infringement where the other three types do not come into play. For all the infringements in the lawsuit with respect to any one work, the statutory-damage award may be between not less than $250 and not more than $10,000. The court has wide discretion [504(c)(1)].

A single infringer is liable only for a single statutory-damage award in a suit for infringement of a single work. This is true even if several infringing acts are involved and even if there are several owners of the various rights of copyright involved in the suit [504(c)(1)]. Similarly, if there are joint infringers, only a single statutory-damage award would be called for, not a separate one against each joint infringer [501(c)(1)]. In the case of separate infringements by persons who are not jointly liable, separate statutory-damage awards may be made.[3]

If more than one work is infringed, there can be more than one statutory-damage award. However, for the purposes of the statutory-damage rule, all the parts of a compilation or derivative work are considered one work [504(c)(1)].

If the copyright owner proves that infringement was committed "willfully," the amount of the statutory-damages award may be increased to as much as $50,000 [504(c)(2)]. If the infringer proves that he or she was not aware, and had no reason to believe, that his or her acts constituted an infringement, the court, in its discretion, may reduce the award of statutory damages to as low as $100 insofar as that "innocent" infringer is concerned [504(c)(2)].

The "privileged" infringer—insofar as statutory damages are concerned—is one who (a) was an employee or agent of a nonprofit educational institution, library, or archives, acting within the scope of his or her employment, who infringed the work by reproducing it and who (b) believed and had reasonable grounds for believing that his or her use of the copyrighted work was a fair use under section 107. The court will not order that person to pay statutory damages. The same is true if it is the institution itself that is being sued, rather than or in addition to the individual.

Another category of privileged infringer—insofar as statutory damages are concerned—is a public broadcasting entity (or a person acting as a regular part of the entity's nonprofit activities) that infringed copyright by performing a published nondramatic literary work or by reproducing a transmission program of such a work. If the infringer believed, and had reasonable grounds for believing, that the use was a fair use, statutory damages will be remitted [504(c)(2)].

ATTORNEY'S FEES

In an infringement suit, the court may, in its discretion, award a reasonable attorney's fee to the prevailing party [505]. However, no such award is made for any infringement, in an unpublished work, commenced before registration of the claim of copyright. And none is made for any infringement commenced after first publication of the work unless registration is made either within three months after first publication or before the commencement of the infringement [410(d); 412].

Attorney's fees are not recoverable in an infringement suit against the United States [505].

PRE-1978 INFRINGEMENTS

All causes of action for copyright infringement that arose prior to 1978 are governed by the old law as it existed when the cause of action accrued. [Transitional and Supplementary Provisions, Sec. 112.]

The two accompanying tables list civil remedies and criminal sanctions provided under the new copyright law.

TABLE OF CIVIL REMEDIES

Remedy	References*
1. Injunction	502; 510(a)
2. Actual damages	504(a), (b); 510(a)
3. Infringer's profits from the infringement	504(a), (b); 510(a)
4. Statutory damages	504(a), (c); 510(a)
5. Costs of suit	505; 510(a)
6. Attorney's fees	505; 510(a)
7. Impoundment of infringing material	503(a); 510(a)
8. Destruction or disposition of infringing material	503(b); 510(a)
9. Suspension of right to compulsory license (Cable System)	510(b)
10. Importation exclusions	602(b); 603
11. Limited remedies against the U.S. Government	505; 28 U.S.C. 1498

*Denotes sections of the new copyright law except for item 11 which is to Title 28 of the *U.S.C.* (*United States Code*).

TABLE OF CRIMINAL LAW SANCTIONS

Sanction	References*
1. Copyright infringement generally	
Fine	506(a)
Imprisonment	506(a)
Forfeiture	506(b)
Destruction or disposition of infringing material	506(b); 509; 603
2. Fraudulent copyright notice—a fine	506(c)
3. Fraudulent removal of copyright notice—a fine	506(d)
4. False representation—copyright registration applications—a fine	506(e)
5. Fraudulent activity, jukebox licenses—a fine	116(d)
6. Phonograph records, counterfeit labels	18 U.S.C. 2318

*Denotes sections of the new copyright law except for item 6 which is to Title 18 of the *U.S.C.* (*United States Code*).

9

COPYRIGHT DURATION

Under the old copyright law, unpublished works generally were not protected by federal copyright law.[1] Protection was available under state law, ordinarily for as long as the work remained unpublished.[2] In effect, this provided the author an indefinite right of first publication.

Once a work was published, the federal copyright law generally controlled. Copyrighted works had an initial term of copyright of 28 years from first publication. A renewal term of another 28 years was available if properly applied for before the expiration of the initial term.[3]

Beginning in the 1960s, Congress recognized—prematurely, as it turned out—that it would probably soon change the law concerning copyright duration. To give the existing published works (and federally copyrighted unpublished works) the opportunity to benefit from any lengthened term, Congress from time to time extended the renewal term of such works by two-year periods.[4] These extensions protected works published as early as September 19, 1906, provided that the renewal term had been properly applied for before the expiration of the initial term.

The new law preserves the dual-copyright term arrangement for these works [304]. The renewal term, which still must be applied for before the expiration of the initial term, is now for 47 years [304(a)]. Details about pre-1978 published or federally copyrighted works are given later in this chapter.

Under the laws of many countries, the period of copyright duration is for the life of the author plus 50 years.[5] By the new law, Congress adopted the same general rule for U.S. copyright protection for copyrightable works *not* published or federally copyrighted before 1978 [302(a)]. There are exceptions. One, as discussed in Chapter 6, is a work made for hire. The author of a work made for hire usually is not an individual but a corporation. The new law's copyright duration for a work

made for hire is 75 years from first publication or 100 years from creation, whichever expires first [302]. Other exceptions relate to anonymous and pseudonymous works, considered later in this chapter.

In addition to providing new duration rules, the new copyright law
takes over copyright control from the 50 states for all unpublished works
set in a suitably tangible form [102(a); 301(a)]. Under the old law, unpublished works were covered by federal copyright only if they were
registered, and not all could qualify. The usual new duration rules—
"life plus 50" or "75-100"—apply. However, copyright protection, even
in a very old unpublished work, will not expire before the end of 2002
at the earliest if it remains unpublished and not before the end of 2027
if the work becomes published by December 31, 2002 [303].

In considering the copyright-duration rules, keep in mind that we
are concerned with a copyright's "normal" life. Copyrights can expire
prematurely, e.g., in certain circumstances by publishing without notice
of copyright [405].

Following is a more detailed discussion of the new copyright-duration
rules, the most significant points of which are also presented in tabular
form at the end of this chapter.

1978 AND LATER WORKS; PRE-1978 WORKS NOT FEDERALLY COPYRIGHTED BEFORE 1978

Individual Author

The rule here is that federal copyright protection begins at the time
the work is created and lasts for the life of the author plus 50 years and
to the end of that last calendar year [302(a); 305]. Example: you write a
novel in 1979 at the age of 22. It is published in 1985. You die in 2038,
at the age of 81. The copyright commenced in 1979 and will expire at
the end of 2088. (The date of publication, being after 1977, was irrele-
vant.)

Federal copyright protection begins when the work is "created."
That occurs when the work is set in a tangible form from which it can
be perceived for more than a transitory duration [101 "created,"
"fixed"]. Thus, a final manuscript is created when the author has fin-
ished writing or typing it. As he or she went along, copyrighted works
(i.e., partial manuscripts) were continually being created. Since copyright duration generally depends on the author's life span, we, fortunately, will not often need to know when an individual portion of a
particular work was created.

Even if a copyrightable work was created before 1978, the life-plus-50
rule applies if the work was neither published nor federally copyrighted
before 1978 [303]. The 2002-2027 rule mentioned above is also applicable. It was included by Congress for old unpublished works because,

prior to the new law, they had an open-ended protection period so long as they remained unpublished.

Joint Works

A "joint work" is a work prepared by two or more authors with the intention that their contributions be merged into inseparable or inter-dependent parts of a unitary whole [101 "joint work"].

Federal copyright protection for a post-1977 joint work begins when the work is created and lasts for the life of the last surviving author plus 50 years and to the end of that last calendar year [302(b); 305]. The same is true for joint works that were created before 1978 but were neither published nor federally copyrighted before then. The 2002–2027 rule, described above, also applies [303].

Works Made for Hire

A work made for hire includes a work prepared by an employee within the scope of his or her employment. It also includes enumerated types of works, e.g., an instructional text, if specially ordered or commis-sioned and if the parties expressly agree in a signed writing that the work shall be considered a work made for hire [101 "work made for hire"]. See a general discussion of work made for hire in Chapter 6.

Federal copyright protection for a post-1977 work made for hire begins when the work is created and lasts for 100 years after that time or for 75 years after first publication, whichever period expires first [302(c)]. In either case, the copyright extends to the end of the last calen-dar year [305]. The same duration rules apply to works made for hire that were created before 1978 but that were neither published nor federally copyrighted before then; the 2002–2027 rule also applies [303].

Anonymous and Pseudonymous Works

An "anonymous work" is a work on the copies or phonorecords having no natural person identified as author. A "pseudonymous work" is a work on the copies or phonorecords having the author identified under a fictitious name [101].

The "75 or 100" years rule applies to post-1977 anonymous and pseud-onymous works. If, prior to the expiration of the applicable time, the identity of the author is revealed in appropriate Copyright Office rec-ords, the copyright duration period shifts to the life of the author plus 50 years standard previously discussed [302(c)]. The same rules apply to anonymous and pseudonymous works created before 1978 but neither published nor federally copyrighted before then; the 2002–2027 rule also applies [303].

Author's Life Span

Any person having an interest in a copyright may, by following designated Copyright Office procedures, have recorded in the Copyright Office a statement as to the author's death or a statement that he or she is still living. The Copyright Office also may use other reference sources for such information [302(d)]. The information can be relevant in estimating copyright duration and, sometimes, in determining when an author may be presumed to have died.

Presumption of Author's Death

If, at any time, a work is either 100 years old, or was published at least 75 years earlier, the author may, for copyright purposes, be presumed to have died more than 50 years before if a certificate is obtained from the Copyright Office stating that its records indicate nothing to the contrary. One must rely on the presumption of good faith for it to have legal value [302(e)].

Works Not in Tangible Form

The new copyright law protects only works that have been fixed in a sufficiently tangible form [101 "created," "fixed," "publication"; 102(a); 302(a)]. State law governs protection of works not yet so fixed [301]. (Tangible form was reviewed in Chapter 2.)

PRE-1978 PUBLISHED OR FEDERALLY COPYRIGHTED WORKS

General

Under the old law, federal copyright was obtained by publishing a copyrightable work with notice of copyright. For certain classes of works, e.g., a drama, a federal copyright could also be obtained in the work as unpublished; this type of copyright was secured through a registration with the Copyright Office.[6] In each case, the copyright's initial term was for 28 years (from date of first publication or date of registration, depending on which of the categories was involved).

The 28-year rule basically continues to apply to such pre-1978 federally copyrighted works [304(a)]. However, now the copyright continues to the end of the last calendar year in which its 28th year expires [305].

In addition to the initial term, a renewal term of copyright could be obtained, but only by applying for it in accordance with Copyright Office requirements. For those who applied for a renewal term before 1978, the renewal term automatically lasts for 47 years (assuming, of course, that the application was proper and timely) and to the end of that last calendar year [304(b); 305].

Example: You published your work, with copyright notice, in 1920 and applied in 1947 for a renewal copyright, which began in 1948. The copyright expiration date is the end of 1995.

Example: You published your work, with copyright notice, in 1920 and did not later apply for a renewal copyright. Your copyright expired at some time in 1948.

Even a work published as far back as September 19, 1906, can still be in copyright if a renewal term was obtained. Works published before then have gone out of U.S. copyright. The expiration date for 1906-renewed works is the end of 1981, for 1907-renewed works the date is 1982, and so on. For unrenewed works the 1949 U.S. copyrights expired in 1977. Without renewal by the end of 1979, the 1951 copyrights expire at the end of that year.

Sound Recordings

The old law did not provide federal copyright protection in a sound recording, as such, until February 15, 1972. That remains a key date under the new law. Sound recordings that were first fixed before then are protected under state law for a long transitional period that the new copyright law permits the states, namely up to February 15, 2047.

Sound recordings first fixed on or after the 1972 date are directly protected by federal copyright law, and the normal duration rules apply to them. These rules, of course, turn on the usual factors, such as whether or not the work was published before 1978.

Ad Interim Copyrights

Under the old law, certain English-language works manufactured abroad were entitled to U.S. copyright protection only if the work was registered with the Copyright Office within a brief time after publication. This was called "ad interim" copyright. If that was obtained, the U.S. copyright protection was only for a short period—five years under the most recent terms of the old law. To obtain the normal U.S. copyright (i.e., a 28-year initial term subject to an additional renewal term), the work had to be manufactured in the United States within a short period of the ad interim copyright.[7]

The new law does not use this ad interim system for works first published on or after July 1, 1977; copyright durations for such works are the same as for other pre-1978 copyrighted works. Further, if an ad interim copyright was obtained anytime after 1972, the normal duration rules for pre-1978 copyrighted works automatically apply even though the work was not (or will not be) manufactured in the United States within the subsequent five-year period [Transitional and Supplementary Provisions, Sec. 107].

Notwithstanding the provisions just mentioned, the ad interim rules continue to be of significance under the new law, in judging the copyright status of English-language works first published in foreign countries before July 1977. If an ad interim copyright was required and not obtained, the work went out of copyright in the United States. If the ad interim copyright was obtained (prior to 1972) and the work was not timely manufactured in the United States, the U.S. copyright also expired. The new copyright law does nothing to revive these lost copyrights [Transitional and Supplementary Provisions, Sec. 103].

COPYRIGHT NOTICE DATE INFORMATION

In Chapter 3 on copyright notices, we considered the legal information that could be derived from a copyright notice apart from the notice date. Since the copyright duration rules have been reviewed, we can now look at copyright notices from the standpoint of what legal information the date reveals.

Let us assume that a single date is given in the notice. If more than one date is given (e.g., © 1940, 1945 Your Name) in a real situation, there is usually more than one of the owner's copyrights involved, such as an original and a revised edition. The following discussion will be relevant to each such copyright. We assume below that the date in the copyright notice is the true date of first publication of the copyrighted work, that it was first published in the United States, and that the copyright claim for the publication is valid.

As we discuss the legal significance of the notice date, remember that the information will relate to the *author's* copyright in the work as published. It will not necessarily relate to the copyright status of someone else's copyrighted material used in the author's work, or to earlier editions of the author's work. Also, the information will relate to the U.S. copyright; we are not considering here the life of the copyright in other countries. Finally, it should be pointed out that some think it appropriate, at least under certain circumstances, to seek an author's consent when a copyright has expired short of its maximum term, even though the author's consent is not legally required.

At the end of the following discussion concerning works first published during the 1906–1977 period, a table is presented summarizing copyright expiration information.

Pre-September 19, 1906

An author's U.S. copyright in a work published before September 19, 1906, has expired.[8]

September 19, 1906, to 1950

An author's U.S. copyright in a work published after September 18, 1906, but before the end of 1949, expired before 1978 unless copyright was renewed within the last year of the initial copyright term. The initial copyright lasted for 28 years from first publication.

The copyright owner had a full year within which to obtain a renewal registration and that full year almost always covered parts of two different calendar years. Ordinarily you will not know *which* parts because the notice usually will give only a year, not a month and date. Consequently, if you wish to check renewal registration records, you must be concerned about the records for two calendar years. Here is the formula to use:

1. Take the year date of publication (e.g., 1907).
2. Add the number 27 (1934).
3. Separately add the number 28 (1935).
4. Check the renewal registrations for those two years (1934 and 1935).
5. If registration was not renewed, the U.S. copyright has expired.
6. If registration was renewed, the copyright will expire at the end of the calendar year of the first publication's 75th anniversary (1982).

The Copyright Office publishes renewal registration data and some libraries carry these publications. The Copyright Office will also provide renewal registration information upon request [705(c)]. It charges $10 an hour for its search-report activities and thus it makes sense to give the Copyright Office as much relevant information about the copyright as possible when you ask for a search and to say precisely what you want to know.

1950 Publications

The above formula is applicable here as well. In the case of works first published in 1950 you *must* check in two calendar years even if you know the date and month of first publication. That is because a renewal can be obtained for such a work either during the part of 1977 when it was in its 28th year *or* at any time in 1978 [304(a), (b); 305].

1951 to 1977 Publications

Works first published in 1951 fall into the public domain at the end of 1979 unless copyright is renewed during 1979. In the event of renewal, copyright will not expire until the end of 2026 [304(a), (b); 305]. Here is the formula to use:

1. Take the year date of publication (e.g., 1955).
2. Add the number 28 (1983).
3. Check the renewal registrations for that year (1983).
4. If registration is not renewed, the copyright expired at the end of that year (1983).
5. If registration was renewed, the copyright will not expire until the end of the calendar year of the 75th anniversary of first publication (2030).

This is a more simple formula since only one year need be checked for renewals. That is because, for works first published in 1952 or later, renewals must be made within one year prior to the expiration of the initial term of copyright *and* the initial term always expires at the end of a calendar year [304(a); 305]. There is one situation where perhaps two years should be checked—when December 31 of the renewal year falls on a Saturday, Sunday, holiday, or other nonbusiness day. If a registration application is completed on the next succeeding business day of the new year, it might be timely [305; 410(d); 703]. If so, the registration will probably nonetheless be reported for the prior year, but caution suggests a double check.

TABLE OF COPYRIGHT EXPIRATION INFORMATION

Date of First Publication	Year during Which Initial Term of Copyright Expires(ed)	Year during Which Renewal Term of Copyright, if any, Expires(ed)
9-18-06 or earlier	1934 or earlier	1962 or earlier
9-19-06 through 12-31-06	1934	1981
1907	1935	1982
1908	1936	1983
—	—	—
1948	1976	2023
1949	1977	2024
1950	1978	2025
1951	1979	2026
1952	1980	2027
—	—	—
1977	2005	2052

Post-1977 Publications

For works first published in 1978 or later (and not federally copyrighted before 1978), the required copyright notice will not tell you much at all about copyright expiration. The reason is that copyright duration for many of these works depends not on the year of first publication but on the date when the author dies. However, your lack of precise duration knowledge is not too important. An author's copyright in a work first published in 1978 will not expire before the end of 2027 at the earliest and usually not for decades thereafter [302, 303].

Since copyright notice dates for new works are not as legally relevant under the new law as notice dates were under the old law, you may wonder why they are still called for in the notice. There are at least two reasons. First, the date provides some helpful information for users, i.e., it is one of the indicia of how current the work is. Second, the year date continues to be legally relevant in some situations as to copyright duration, even for new works if they are anonymous, pseudonymous, or works made for hire [302(c), (e)].

The following table summarizes periods of copyright duration under the new law for works not in the public domain.

TABLE OF NEW U.S. COPYRIGHT DURATION STANDARDS FOR WORKS NOT IN PUBLIC DOMAIN

Category of Work	Period of Copyright Duration
1. Works created in 1978 or later	
a. Individual author	a. Author's life plus 50 years [302(a)].
b. Joint work	b. Last surviving author's life plus 50 years [302(b)].
c. Work made for hire	c. Shorter of: 75 years from first publication or 100 years from creation [302(c)].
d. Anonymous, pseudonymous work	d. 75 or 100 years as in (c) but shifts to author's life plus 50 years if author's name is timely revealed in Copyright Office records [302(a)].
e. All works	e. Copyright lasts to end of the last calendar year involved [305].
2. Works created before 1978	
a. Works not federally copyrighted before 1978	a. Same rules as in 1(a)–(e) except copyright duration lasts through at least 2002 and, if published by then, through at least 2027 [303].
b. Works federally copyrighted before 1978	b. Initial term of copyright of 28 years from when copyright was secured. Renewal term of 47 years if renewal term is (or was) obtained in last year of initial term [304(a)]. For both initial and renewal term, copyright lasts to the end of the last calendar year involved [305].
3. Sound recordings	
a. Sound recordings first fixed before February 15, 1972	a. State law applies and may provide protection through 2047 [301(c)].
b. Sound recordings created on or after February 15, 1972, but before 1978	b. Applicable rules in 2 above apply [303, 304(a)].
c. Sound recordings created after 1977	c. Applicable rules in 1 above apply [302].

10

INTERNATIONAL CONSIDERATIONS

PROTECTION FOR NON-U.S. CITIZENS

Unpublished Works

If an unpublished work is subject to U.S. copyright protection under general copyright criteria, it has that protection, while it remains unpublished, regardless of the citizenship or domicile of the author [104(a)].

Published Works

For published works, we look at our international copyright relations, and at the status of the author, at the time the work is first published. The work is subject to U.S. copyright protection if, at the time the work is first published, any of the following are true:

1. The work is first published in the United States.
2. One or more of the authors is a national or domiciliary of the United States.
3. One or more of the authors is a stateless person.
4. One or more of the authors is a national or a domiciliary, or a sovereign authority, of a foreign nation that is a party to the Universal Copyright Convention or to another copyright treaty to which the United States is a party.
5. The work is first published in a foreign nation that is a party to the Universal Copyright Convention.
6. The work is first published by the Organization of American States or by the United Nations or any of its specialized agencies.
7. The work comes within the scope of a presidential proclamation extending U.S. copyright protection to nationals, domi-

ciliaries, or the sovereign authority of a foreign nation (or to works first published in that nation) [104(b)].

Appendix 5 lists the treaty and proclamation countries.

By the time all of the above seven possibilities have been considered in the context of all of the countries involved, there is not a great deal that will be excluded from U.S. copyright protection because of nationality considerations, or, to put it in a more relevant context, because of an absence of the necessary copyright relations between our country and the other country in question.

The new law does not bring into U.S. copyright a work that previously had gone into the public domain [Transitional and Supplementary Provisions, Sec. 103]. However, we have had extensive international copyright relations for many years, and thus many older foreign published works by foreign authors continue to be eligible for U.S. copyright protection.[1]

In addition to presenting information about our copyright relations with other countries, Appendix 5 sets forth brief descriptions of the principal multinational copyright agreements to which the United States is a party and of one major set of agreements (the Berne conventions) to which the United States is not a party. All of the information is taken from Copyright Office circulars. The Copyright Office also makes available the texts of our leading international copyright agreements—the 1952 and 1971 Universal Copyright Conventions, the 1971 Convention concerning phonograms, and the Buenos Aires Convention of 1910. The texts are contained in the Copyright Office circular 38c, which may be ordered free from the Copyright Office, Library of Congress, Washington, D.C., 20559.

FOREIGN COPYRIGHT LAWS

The copyright laws of other countries are not within the scope of this book. Copyright law is a territorial concept and each nation has its own rules. Nonetheless, the concepts and rights are often similar to or compatible with U.S. standards.

The Bureau of National Affairs and UNESCO publish an English-language compilation of copyright statutes and treaties—*Copyright Laws and Treaties of the World*—for reference purposes. An updated supplement is generally published every year.

MANUFACTURING CLAUSE

The new law's manufacturing clause—much less severe than its predecessors—restricts the importation into the United States of certain works [601(a)]. (Aspects of the manufacturing clause were discussed in Chapter 5.)

Works Covered

To be subject to the manufacturing clause, the work must at least consist preponderantly (in terms of importance) of *nondramatic literary material that is in the English language and is protected by U.S. copyright law* [601(a)].

Even so, the manufacturing clause is inapplicable if the work is not a work made for hire and if the author of any substantial part of that "nondramatic, etc." material is not a citizen or domiciliary of the United States. The manufacturing clause is also inapplicable if the author of any substantial part of that nondramatic, etc., material *is* a citizen of the United States, but has been domiciled outside of the United States continuously for a year or more. (These judgments about the author's status are made at the time importation of the work is sought or when public distribution is made in the United States [601(b)(1)].)

In the case of a work made for hire, the exceptions in the above paragraph apply only if a substantial part of the work was prepared for an employer (or other person) who is not a national or domiciliary of the United States or a domestic corporation or enterprise [601(b)(1)]. The term "domestic corporation or enterprise" is intended to cover something such as a foreign subsidiary formed primarily for the purpose of obtaining the exemption.[2]

Manufacturing Criteria

To meet the manufacturing criteria when the manufacturing clause is applicable, the sine qua non is that the printing (or other final process of producing copies) and any binding of the copies of the nondramatic, etc., material be performed in the United States or Canada [601(c)(3)].

If the copies of the nondramatic, etc., material are printed directly from type that has been set, or directly from plates made from such type, the setting of type and the making of the plates must be performed in the United States or Canada [601(c)(1)]. Alternatively, if the making of plates by a lithographic or photoengraving process is a final or intermediate step preceding the printing, the making of the plates must have been performed in the United States or Canada [601(c)(2)]. By virtue of this latter clause, reproduction proofs may be imported, without incurring manufacturing-clause problems, as long as the plates from which the copies of the nondramatic, etc., materials are printed are made here or in Canada and the printing and binding takes place here or in Canada.[3]

Import Restrictions

The general rule is that copies of a work that fail to meet the manufacturing requirements may not be imported or publicly distributed in the United States [601(a)]. However, the copyright owner may—once the work is registered—obtain an import statement from the Copyright Office that authorizes the import of up to 2,000 copies [601(b)(2)].

Numerous other exemptions are made by further subsections and sub-subsections [601(b)(3)–(7)].

Effect on Copyright

Violation of the importation or U.S. public-distribution limitations does not result in loss of copyright. However, an infringer whose infringing copies are manufactured in the United States or Canada can, under defined circumstances, have a defense against the infringement suit if the import or distribution limitations have been violated by the copyright owner [601(d)].

Expiration Date

The expiration date for the manufacturing clause is July 1, 1982 [601(a)]. Prior to that, the Register of Copyrights is to report to Congress about the economic ramifications of the expiration on the U.S. printing industry.[4]

Prior Law

The manufacturing clause in the old law, when considered together with other provisions of that law, could cause loss of copyright.[5] If loss occurs, the new law does not revive the copyright [Transitional and Supplementary Provisions, Sec. 103].

OTHER IMPORT RESTRICTIONS

In a case where the making of copies or phonorecords abroad would have been an infringement of U.S. copyright law had it been applicable, their importation is prohibited [602(b)]. But suppose the work has been lawfully reproduced? Will there be an infringement of U.S. copyright if the copies or phonorecords are imported into the United States without authorization? The general answer is yes [602(a)]. However, there are three exceptions. For convenience we will call them personal, governmental, and educational-religious exceptions.

Personal-Use Exception

This applies where the importation is for the private use of the person doing the importing and not for distribution. For a person arriving from outside of the United States, the exception covers copies or phonorecords forming part of his or her personal baggage. Where the person doing the importing is already here, the exception covers no more than one copy or phonorecord of any one work at any one time [602(a)(2)].

Governmental Exception

This exception generally covers copies or phonorecords imported under the authority of, or for the use of, a local or state government or the federal government. It does not go so far as to include copies or phonorecords for use in schools; nor are copies of audiovisual works covered by this exception if they are imported for purposes other than archival use [602(a)(1)].

Educational-Religious Exceptions

These relate to copies or phonorecords imported by or for an organization operated for scholarly, educational, or religious purposes and not for private gain [602(a)(3)].

With respect to audiovisual works, the exception applies to no more than one copy for the organization's archival purposes. With respect to other works, the exception applies to no more than five copies of phonorecords for the organization's library lending or archival purposes. Even then, the exception does not apply if the importation is part of an activity consisting of a systematic reproduction or distribution engaged in by such organization in violation of the library reproduction and distribution provisions of subsection 108(g)(2) [602(a)(3)]. Subsection 108(g)(2) is considered in Chapter 12.

11

FAIR USE: SECTION 107

GENERAL RULES

The fair use of a copyrighted work is not an infringement of copyright. In determining whether a use is a fair use, you must take into account the nature of the copyrighted work, the character of the use, the purpose of the use, the amount used, and the effect of the use upon the value of the copyrighted work [107].

A fair-use doctrine has been part of our copyright law as a judicial interpretation for many years, but the new law represents the first formal statement of it in U.S. copyright legislation. The legislative history notes that the section is intended to state the present judicial doctrine and not to change it in any way or to restrict its development.[1] Whatever the general intent, Congress has said—in the legislation and legislative history—such a great deal concerning fair use that the section may well be interpreted to have a meaning different in certain situations than under the pre-1978 judicial doctrine. Nonetheless, the main point—an adoption of the judicial doctrine—remains valid in a general sense.

Following are some of the fair-use examples from a 1961 report of the Register of Copyrights[2]:

1. quotations of excerpts in a review or criticism, for purposes of illustration or comment;
2. quotations of short passages, in a scholarly or technical work, for illustration or clarification;
3. summary of an address or article, with brief quotations, in a news report;
4. incidental and fortuitous reproduction, in a newsreel or broadcast, of a work located on the scene of an event being reported;

5. reproduction by a library of a portion of a work to replace part of a damaged copy;
6. reproduction by a teacher or student of a small part of a work to illustrate a lesson;
7. reproduction of a work in legislative or judicial proceedings or reports.

Although these examples are fairly clear cut, fair use is not always so.

The application of the fair-use doctrine to a particular situation depends upon just about *all* of the circumstances. For example, let us assume you are the copyright owner of a motion picture. Someone else publishes a book on the same subject as your film and uses many drawings derived from your photographs. That certainly does not sound like fair use. But suppose the subject of the book was the assassination of President Kennedy; the copyrighted film was of the actual scene of the assassination; the film was the most important primary source material on the subject; the book was an analysis of what happened that day; and the analysis depended a good deal on exactly who was located where and at what instant and in what posture, *all* of which were shown in the film. In such circumstances, the use of the drawings could be fair use.[3]

Let's consider another example. Your financial house publishes, for your customers generally, copyrighted financial reports. It would ordinarily be fair use for a newspaper to report the general conclusion of one of your reports and a brief quotation reflecting that conclusion. If your report was issued a few years ago and presented a startling conclusion about, say, the financial health of New York City, a contemporary news report about it presumably could have been fair use even if it made more-than-minor use of copyrighted excerpts. But suppose instead that a financial newspaper was regularly using your reports, regularly excerpting significant portions of the copyrighted material, and the newspaper reports were a reasonable substitute for your own reports. That would be going beyond fair use.[4]

In short, it all depends upon the circumstances. The four principal factors are: extent of the use, the purpose and character of the use, the nature of the copyrighted work, and the effect of the use on the potential market for, or value of, the copyrighted work [107]. When you are a prospective fair user, it usually makes sense to try to look at the use from the other person's perspective and then make your own judgment as to whether any likely complaints would make sense to you. Of course, if your familiarity with the fair-use doctrine is limited, you should consider consulting an attorney, especially if potential adverse consequences of an error are substantial.

Extent of Use

In considering the extent of the use, you, of course, consider the amount used in an absolute sense, e.g., the number of words or the number of pages. You also consider "extent" in terms of the proportion the material represents of the "borrowing" work and of the work that is borrowed from. For example, the borrowing work may be very long and the amount used may be less than 1 percent of that work. But it may be 30 percent of the work borrowed from.

Except in the case of some "fair use in education" guidelines, to be considered later in this chapter, there are no mathematical formulas that determine how much may be fairly used. It all depends upon the context and the circumstances.

In addition to a quantitative comparison, the substantiality of the portion used is judged in a qualitative sense. How important, to the borrowing work and the work borrowed from, was the portion that was used? It is also relevant to consider whether the borrowing work only reiterates the borrowed work or whether additional contributions have been added by the borrower so as to augment the contribution made by the work borrowed from.

Purpose of Use

In considering the purpose, the following have been cited with favor in the statute as some of the purposes for which a use may be considered a fair use (after the other factors have been considered): criticism, comment, news reporting, teaching, scholarship, and research. The legislative history adds three additional examples:

1. an audiotape, of a book, made by an individual as a free service for a blind person;
2. the copying, for preservation purposes, of deteriorating and irreplaceable motion pictures;
3. the copying, by a calligrapher for one client, of a single excerpt from a copyrighted work.[5]

Whether a use is for a commercial purpose is often a significant factor in determining fair use, but the fact that a work is designed for sale to a wide audience is not, taken by itself, a conclusive point against the possibility of fair use within the work.

Nature of Copyrighted Work

Some types of works "invite" a degree of fair use—e.g., reference works and public speeches. Other types of works almost implicitly contain a warning that fair use should proceed with caution. For example, the application of fair use to unpublished letters would, under ordinary circumstances, be very narrow. The copyright owner's right would ordinarily have great weight. Still other works, because of their compactness, suggest narrow limits of fair use—poems and songs are examples. But, again, there are no absolute rules.

Effect of Use on Work's Value

The more that use in a work is likely to adversely affect the market or potential for the work being copied, the more likely it is that fair use will not be available, e.g., the more likely it is that the borrowing work may become a substitute or partial substitute for the copyright work or a potential derivative work. This factor (of an adverse effect on the work's value) is not meant to apply so as to narrowly restrain adverse criticism or parody.

The regular practice of photocopying an entire newsletter is an example where the "effect on the market" would come into play against a fair use. An example to the contrary is the use of a small portion of a copyrighted work that is long out of print and is likely to remain so. Of course, the fact that a work is long out of print is not *conclusive* as to fair use.

In considering the effect of use, you must consider whether, and to what extent, the borrowing work will compete directly with the borrowed work. The Senate Judiciary Committee report on the new law states that a use that supplants any part of the normal market for a copyrighted work would ordinarily be an infringement. The extent to which the borrowing work harms a *potential* use for the other work can also be relevant.

EDUCATIONAL CONTEXTS

Much of congressional attention to fair use was in the context of teaching activities, principally those in not-for-profit educational institutions. The legislation itself makes mention of fair use in education and the legislative history presents many comments approving fair use in educational contexts. In addition, with the encouragement of Congress, fair-use guidelines for educational activities were developed by representatives of authors, educators, and publishers.

Congress enacts *statutes*, not legislative history, and the latter does not have the force of law. It is merely a context for the law. Nonetheless, fair use is a sufficiently nebulous concept that the Senate and House Judiciary Committees' remarks concerning fair use are likely to be relied upon by educators and others as a practical matter and to be given considerable respect by the courts.

Legislative Examples

Multiple Copies for Classroom Use. Section 107 specifically notes that it is possible for the making of multiple copies for classroom use to constitute fair use. The House Judiciary Committee report on the new law (referred to here as the "House Committee report") puts that statutory language in context by first noting that the reference to fair use by reproduction in copies is mainly intended to make clear that the doctrine has as much application to photocopying as to older forms of use but is not intended to give that type of use any special status or to sanction any reproduction beyond the normal and reasonable limits of fair use. The report then goes on to say: "Similarly, the newly added reference to 'multiple copies for classroom use' is a recognition that, under the proper circumstances of fairness, the [fair-use] doctrine can be applied to reproductions of multiple copies for members of a class."[6]

Nonprofit Educational Purposes. One of the factors in determining fair use is the purpose and character of the use "including whether such use is for nonprofit educational purposes"[107]. The House Committee report states that the quoted language was not intended to limit fair use to not-for-profit institutions. Rather it was an express recognition that the commercial or nonprofit character of an activity should be weighed along with other factors.[7]

The Senate Judiciary Committee report contains numerous fair-use statements in the context of reproductions of works for classroom purposes:

Entire Works. "In general terms it could be expected that the doctrine of fair use would be applied strictly to [i.e., against] the classroom reproduction of entire works, such as musical compositions, dramas, and audiovisual works including motion pictures, which by their nature are intended for performance or public exhibition."[8]

Extracts. "In general, and assuming the other necessary factors are present, the copying for classroom purposes of extracts or portions, which are not self-contained and which are relatively 'not substantial in length' when compared to the larger, self-contained work from which they are taken, should be considered fair use. Depending on the circumstances, the same would also be true of very short self-contained works such as a brief poem, a map in a newspaper, a 'vocabulary builder' from a monthly magazine, and so forth. This should not be construed as permitting a teacher to make multiple copies of the same work on a repetitive basis or for continued use."[9]

Textbooks. "Textbooks and other material prepared primarily for the school markets would be less susceptible to reproduction for classroom use than material prepared for general public distribution."[10]

Consumables. "Where the copyright work is intended to be 'consumable' in the course of classroom activities—workbooks, exercises, standardized tests, and answer sheets are examples—the privilege of fair use by teachers or pupils would have little if any application."[11]

Periodicals. "With respect to material in newspapers and periodicals, the doctrine of fair use should be liberally applied to allow copying of items of current interest to supplement and update the students' text-books, but this would not extend to copying from periodicals published primarily for student use."[12]

Off-Air Recordings. "The committee's attention has been directed to the special problems involved in the reception of instructional television programs in remote areas of the country.... A particular difficulty exists when such transmissions extend over several time zones within the same state, such as Alaska. Unless individual schools in such states may make an off-air recording of such transmissions, the programs may not be received by the students during the school's daily schedule. The committee believes that the making, by a school located in such a remote area, of an off-the-air recording of an instructional television transmission for the purpose of a delayed viewing of the program by students of the same school constitutes a fair use. The committee does not intend to suggest, however, that off-the-air recording for convenience would, under any circumstances, be considered 'fair use.' To meet the requirement of temporary use the school may retain the recording for only a limited period of time after the broadcast."[13]

The later House Committee report commented more generally on the subject of off-the-air taping for nonprofit classroom use. The committee stated its belief that the fair-use doctrine had some limited application in this area, that study would be needed to develop guidelines, and that nothing in the bill was intended to prejudge the law on this point. The committee urged representatives of the various interests to have discussions on this matter "actively and in a constructive spirit."[14]

Hearing-Impaired. The Senate–House Conference Committee endorsed the view that, assuming there are no other factors that would make the use "unfair," the doctrine of fair use is broad enough to permit the making of an off-air copy of a television program by a nonprofit educational institution for the deaf and hearing-impaired, and (a) the making of a captioned version, (b) the performance of that version, solely for educational purposes, within the institution for its students, and (c) the sharing of the captioned version among other such institutions.[15] Emphasis was placed on the point that the activity would have to be noncommercial in every respect, and that each of the institutions involved would have to assure against unauthorized reproduction or distribution, and against performance or retention for other than educational purposes.[16]

Calligraphy. "A single copy reproduction of excerpts from a copyrighted work by a student calligrapher or teacher in a learning situation would be a fair use of the copyrighted work."[17]

Supplemental Nature of Fair Use. "Fair use is essentially supplementary by nature, and classroom copying that exceeds the legitimate teaching aims, such as filling in missing information or bringing a subject up to date, would go beyond the proper bounds of fair use. Isolated instances of minor infringements when multiplied many times, become in the aggregate, a major inroad on copyright that must be prevented."[18]

FAIR USE GUIDELINES

With the encouragement of Congress, representatives of authors, educators, and publishers developed guidelines stating certain educational uses of copyrighted materials that they agreed would ordinarily constitute fair use. There are two sets of guidelines: books and periodicals excluding musical works, and musical works. These guidelines were developed in time for incorporation into the House Judiciary Committee's report, which preceded the new law. The committee thought they were a reasonable interpretation of what fair use minimally allows at the present time.[19] The texts of the guidelines are included in Appendix 3 and are discussed next. You should also keep in mind that, in addition to fair use, nonprofit educational institutions have some explicit statutory rights of performance and display. These are considered in Chapter 13.

BOOK AND PERIODICAL GUIDELINES

Teacher Copies

Under these guidelines, which relate only to not-for-profit educational institutions, a teacher may, under defined conditions, make or acquire single copies of any of the following for scholarly research or for preparation for teaching or for use in actual classroom teaching: (1) an article from a periodical; (2) a short story, essay, or poem; (3) an illustration from a periodical or book; and (4) a chapter from a book. The concept of "teacher" is broad enough to include institutional specialists working in consultation with actual instructors.[20] The guidelines do not purport to define the maximum that may be done under fair use. To be within the guidelines, the copy must be made either by the teacher or at the teacher's individual request. There are some other general caveats restricting the scope of the teacher's-copies portion of the guidelines. These caveats also apply to the classroom-use guidelines and are included at the end of the following discussion.

Classroom Uses

These guidelines relate to multiple copies for classroom use in not-for-profit educational institutions. The number of copies should not exceed the number of students in the course. The copies must be made by or for the teacher giving the course, for classroom use or discussion. Each copy must include a notice of copyright.

For the copying to be within the guidelines, it must also be spontaneous, and the amount copied must meet the guideline's brevity standards. Moreover, the copying activities, taken together, must not exceed the cumulative-effect standards and must not run afoul of what we will call the general caveats, to be taken up shortly. Each category of restrictions is considered below.

At first reading, the rules may seem overwhelming in their number. But if you seldom use the guidelines, it is not much trouble to look them up. If you use them often, you will absorb them quickly.

Cumulative Effect. The classroom-use guidelines authorize no more than nine instances of multiple copying for one course during one class term.

With respect to any one author, the guidelines authorize no more than one complete item (short poem, article, story, essay) or two excerpts during one class term.

For any one collective work or periodical volume, the guidelines authorize no more than three excerpts during one class term. (Note: These three restrictions do not apply to newspapers, current news periodicals, or current news sections of periodicals.)

The copying of any particular material is authorized by the guidelines "for only one course in the school in which the copies are made."

Spontaneity. To conform to classroom-use guidelines, the copying must be at the "instance and inspiration" of the teacher. Moreover, the inspiration and decision to use the work must be so close in time to the moment of its use for maximum teaching effectiveness that it would be unreasonable to expect a timely reply to a permission request.

Brevity. To be within the classroom-use guidelines, the amount copied from any particular material must be sufficiently brief. The guidelines provide the following quantitative brevity standards:

> For *illustrations*, the standard is one illustration per book or periodical issue.
>
> For *poetry* the standards include a complete poem if less than 250 words and if printed on not more than two pages. From a longer poem, an excerpt of not more than 250 words is permissible. (If that leaves you in the middle of a line, you may complete the line.)
>
> For *prose* (other than a "special work") the brevity standards permit an excerpt of 10 percent from a prose work provided you do not copy more than 1,000 words. A 500-word minimum, however, is allowed. (If the applicable standard leaves you in the middle of a paragraph, you may complete the paragraph.) The guideline's brevity standards also sanction copying a *complete* article, story, or essay if less than 2,500 words.
>
> The guidelines describe *special works* as: "Certain works in poetry, prose or 'poetic prose' which often combine language with illustrations and

which are intended sometimes for children and at other times for a more general audience [and which often] fall short of 2,500 words in their entirety."

Under the guidelines, special works may not be reproduced in their entirety. Up to two of the published pages may be reproduced, but only if that would reproduce no more than 10 percent of the text.

General Caveats

The guidelines specifically do not sanction: (1) copying from works intended to be "consumable," e.g., workbooks, standardized tests; (2) copying used to substitute for the purchase of books, publishers' reprints, or periodicals; or (3) copying to create anthologies or compilations or to replace or substitute for them.

Reactions to the Guidelines

When the National Education Association supported the copyright revision bill, it took the position that, in the context of the legislative history, the bill represented "a major breakthrough in establishing equitable legal guidelines for the use of copyright materials for instructional and research purposes."[21]

Representatives of the American Association of University Professors and of the Association of American Law Schools wrote to the House Judiciary Committee strongly criticizing the guidelines in the context of university teaching. The committee's report, noting the objection, made these points: (1) Representatives of higher education helped to develop the guidelines, (2) the purpose of the guidelines was to state the minimum and not the maximum standards of educational fair use, and (3) the guidelines themselves acknowledged that there may be instances not within the guidelines that nonetheless are within fair use.[22]

MUSIC GUIDELINES

The music guidelines are less complex than the books and periodicals guidelines. Music guidelines, which do not relate solely to not-for-profit institutions, cover some copying and some recording as well.

Copies of Sheet Music

The guidelines authorize emergency copying to replace purchased copies when they are not available for an imminent performance, so long as purchased replacement copies are substituted in due course. Other than in this specific situation, the guidelines do not authorize copying sheet music for the purpose of performances.

For academic purposes other than performances, single or multiple copies of excerpts of musical works may be made (not to exceed one copy per pupil) so long as the excerpts do not comprise a part of the whole that would constitute a performable unit such as a selection, movement, or aria and do not total more than 10 percent of the whole work. Other than this rule and the one preceding, the guidelines do not authorize copying sheet music for a class. For purposes of a teacher's scholarly research or class preparation, the guidelines permit a single copy of an entire performable unit (e.g., section, movement, aria) to be made if it is (1) confirmed by the copyright proprietor to be out of print or (2) unavailable except in a larger work.

Recordings

A single phonorecord of recordings of performances by students may be made for evaluation or rehearsal purposes.

The phonorecord may be retained by the educational institution or individual teacher. (This applies to the next standard as well.)

A single phonorecord of a sound recording of copyrighted music may be made from sound recordings owned by an educational institution or an individual teacher for the purpose of constructing aural exercises or examinations. (This standard relates only to the underlying copyrighted music, e.g., the sheet music. There are no guidelines with respect to duplication rights concerning the sound recording itself.)

General Caveats

The guidelines call for the copying to include the copyright notice that appears on the printed copy.

The guidelines do not authorize copying to create, or replace, or substitute for anthologies, compilations, or collective works, nor copying from works intended to be consumable.

The guidelines recognize that there may be instances in which copying not within the guidelines may nonetheless be allowed under fair use.

PHOTOCOPYING

There is a 1962 case of a choir director who, without copyright authorization, adapted a copyrighted religious song, reproduced 48 copies of the arrangement on a duplicating machine, and had the arrangement performed once each by a school and church choir. He was held to have infringed.[23] A decade later came the vastly more complex *Williams & Wilkins* case in the United States Court of Claims in which that publisher of medical journals sought copyright infringement damages with respect to the article photocopying practices of NLM (the National Library of Medicine) and NIH (the National Institutes of Health). The initial judge's decision—infringement; the full Court of Claims' decision—no infringements by a 4–3 vote.[24] The case went to the U.S. Supreme Court where the appellate result was anticlimactically affirmed by an equally divided court—4-4 with no opinions issued. (In such a situation the affirmance is not a binding precedent for other cases. In any event, we wouldn't know what principles the precedent stood for because no opinions were issued and various combinations of several different rationales may have supported the 4–4 vote.)

The *Williams & Wilkins* case involved a combination of numerous facts and theories and does not point unequivocally to a particular result, one way or the other, in a future case. The Court of Claims majority intended it that way. It said its fair-use conclusion rested on all of the elements and not upon any combination less than all. Some of the conclusions underlying the majority's decision were: (1) the publisher did not show it was being "harmed substantially"; (2) NIH and NLM are nonprofit institutions; (3) both libraries enforced "reasonably strict" limitations that keep the duplication "within appropriate confines"; and (4) the problem of accommodating the competing interests calls fundamentally for legislative guidance and, in the period before that is forthcoming, risk of harm upon medicine should not be placed.

The *Williams & Wilkins* decision predates the enactment of the new copyright law and you might, quite reasonably, surmise that Congress probably had a great deal to say about the case in the context of the new statute. However, that did not happen. The Senate Committee report noted: "As the Court of Claims opinion succinctly stated, 'there is much to be said on all sides.'" The report also remarked that the court's opinions "provide additional support for the balanced resolution of the photocopying issue" in the library reproduction provisions of section 108.[25]

The quoted Senate report language may be construed to mean no more than that the scope of fair-use copying is subject to conflicting good arguments, and thus it is desirable to have a provision, section 108, which, apart from the generalities of fair-use criteria, deals with certain library photocopying practices with some specificity. That would be literally consistent with a provision in section 108 (regarding library reproductions) which says that nothing in the section affects the right of fair use [108(f)(4)]. However, section 108, which is discussed in the next chapter, is sometimes detailed, quite complex, and occasionally quite ambiguous. The presence of the combination of these three factors suggests correctly that the section is the result of a difficult-to-reach political compromise. It is not easy to believe that section 108 will be ignored completely by a court seeking to resolve fair-use issues in a context involving facts of the type that are addressed by section 108. Thus, while nothing in section 108 literally affects the right of fair use, the practicalities are that the provisions of section 108 are likely to play at least some role—admitted or otherwise—in interpreting the scope of fair use in the context of libraries that have section-108 eligibility.

CONTU (the National Commission on New Technological Uses of Copyrighted Works) was directed to report to Congress on the subject of photocopying of copyrighted materials. While CONTU may recommend changes to the new law, considerable time may pass before congressional action is taken.

Meanwhile, marketplace developments are taking place with respect to photocopying. Some companies, who have article duplication rights, are seeking to expand their marketing effort. Other companies, with a continuing need for many article copies, are seeking to obtain licenses from periodical publishers to cover in-house copying. Some publishers of periodicals are revising their agreements forms so as to clearly obtain article reproduction rights and are considering how best to meet the demand for article copies. And the Association of American Publishers and the Information Industry Association have formed a Copyright Clearance Center. The center is designed to serve an administrative function. Participating publishers authorize users to copy articles for a publisher-designated fee. Participating users make their authorized copies themselves, pay the fees to the center, and provide the center with data as to what was copied. The center distributes the fees to the publisher based on the user-supplied data.

If some or all of the above practices flourish, it may be that owner-authorized copies will eventually become quickly available, without undue administrative burdens, for a high percentage of articles. Opinions differ about the prognosis. If it should happen, then, when it is clear that it has, fair use will operate in a somewhat different environment in the context of article copying. The impracticality of obtaining owner-authorized copies fast and efficiently has been used as a major argument for fair use being applicable in many article-copying circumstances. Should that rationale cover a significantly narrower field, there will be more focus on the underlying issue of when free copies should be fair copies.

There are divergent views as to how fair use, under the new law, will be interpreted by the courts with respect to various photocopying activities within organizations. Well-informed and competent people sometimes disagree sharply as to particulars. Organizations that frequently confront the issue should consider seeking general guidance from a person who is familiar not only with this area of law but also with the particular contexts in which the issue arises within the organization.

It is to be expected that, from time to time, organizations representing authors, or publishers, or educators, or librarians will be disseminating facts or viewpoints concerning the scope of fair use in the context of photocopies or other document reproductions. Among the organizations to which you might inquire are the American Library Association (Chicago), the Association of American Publishers (New York), the Authors League of America (New York), the National Education Association (Washington, D.C.), and the Special Libraries Association (New York).

12

LIBRARY REPRODUCTIONS: SECTION 108

The right to reproduce and distribute copies of copyrighted works are two of the copyright owner's five "exclusive" rights [106]. However, there are statutory limitations on those rights. For libraries and librarians, two of the most significant limitations are the fair-use provisions of section 107 and the library reproduction and distribution rights of section 108.

Under section 108 an eligible library (and its employees acting within the scope of their employment) may reproduce and distribute a copy or phonorecord of designated types of works without the permission of the copyright owner and without infringing copyright. The activities covered (with limitations to be discussed later in this chapter) include such as the making of an entire copy or phonorecord of a work for preservation or replacement purposes, the taping of audiovisual newscasts, and the reproduction and distribution of an article from a periodical.

In discussing section 108, we will first consider its relationship with fair use in section 107. Next, we will consider the general eligibility criteria a library must meet to exercise section-108 rights. Then we will take up each of the particular activities that section 108 authorizes.

Section 108 covers both libraries and archives. For convenience, we will use "libraries" to refer to each. Section 108 also covers library employees when acting within the scope of their employment [108(a)]. For convenience, we will generally not mention employees separately.

Section 108 relates to both copies in the traditional sense and to phonorecords, e.g., records and audiotapes. We will use "copies" to refer to all of these and will note distinctions where appropriate.

RELATION TO SECTION 107

Effect on Library Activities

When a law contains one provision covering an area of activity in general terms and a second provision covering some of that same area in detailed terms for a particular group, an interpretive issue can arise of whether, for the particular group, only the detailed terms are applicable. That issue is potentially present in section 107, covering fair-use copying, and section 108 and its subdivisions, covering copying by libraries. Congress addressed the issue by stating that nothing in section 108 ". . . in any way affects the right of fair use as by section 107" [108(f)(4)]. This means that libraries are not precluded from using section 107 where it is applicable.

However, it may not also mean that a library's copying activities under section 107 are to be judged without regard to those same activities under section 108. In other words, it is likely that one of the circumstances to be considered in determining the application of a library's "right of fair use as provided by section 107" will be the scope of the library's copying activities undertaken through the use of section 108.

Differences between 107 and 108

Section 107 has no restriction as to who may utilize it; section 108 relates only to libraries. (When a library uses section 108 as authority for the making of, for example, a copy of an article for someone other than another library, the person receiving the copy does not have explicit section-108 rights. He or she ordinarily must rely on fair use or some other justification for the copy.)

Section 108's coverage of copying activities is sometimes narrower and sometimes broader than section 107's. For example, section 108 does not ordinarily cover more than one copy of something at any one time whereas section 107 sometimes permits multiple copies on a single occasion [107; 108(a)–(e); (g)]. An example of where section 108 may be broader is in the rights it gives to copy from unpublished works for deposit in another library [108(b)]. Fair use might not cover such activities to the degree that section 108 does.[1]

Since the scope of 107's coverage is often vague, it may be difficult to say whether a particular right of section 108 is broader or narrower than fair use would allow. One of section 108's attractive features is that it allows a library, at least on occasion, the luxury of not worrying about whether section 107's fair use does or does not apply. Although there will be cases where a librarian will worry about whether *section 108* does or does not apply, nonetheless, for many libraries, in many situations, section 108 does resolve legal uncertainties.

In considering the material that follows, you will see that section 108 is often ambiguous and complex. Fortunately, if you are in a library in a not-for-profit organization, many of the ambiguities may be over-looked. If you are in a library in a for-profit organization, you may over-look all of the ambiguities if your library decides it does not and will not meet the first standard discussed below.

ELIGIBILITY STANDARDS: COLLECTIONS ACCESSIBILITY

A library is eligible to exercise section-108 rights if its collections are open to the public. Even when that is not the case, a library is eligible to exercise section-108 rights if its collections are available, not only to researchers affiliated with the library or with the institution of which it is a part, but also to others doing research in a specialized field [108(a)(2)]. The collections-accessibility criteria may rule out section-108 eligibility for many libraries in for-profit institutions.

GENERAL COPYING STANDARDS

Notice of Copyright

Copies made under section 108 are required to bear a notice of copy-right [108(a)(3)]. A notice repeating the original notice will ordinarily suffice, although section 108 does not state that such a complete notice is required. (Failure to use that kind of notice will ordinarily not jeopar-dize the copyright owner's copyright since section-108 copies are not copies publicly distributed by authority of the copyright owner [405(a); 406].)

No Commercial Advantage

General. The rights under section 108 apply only to copies made or distributed "without any purpose of direct or indirect commercial advantage" [108(a)(1)]. This means that a library cannot use section 108 as a basis for operating a for-profit copying center. It also means that a library cannot use section 108 when obtaining copying services from a for-profit copy center.[2] Of course, if that copy center happens to have permission from the copyright owner, section 108 is not needed.

Profit Organization Libraries. Does the no-commercial-advantage restriction mean that a library in a for-profit organization may not avail itself of section 108 to provide copies to the organization's employees for their research activities?

As we shall see, the answer is not clear. Moreover, even if the general answer is yes, the practical utility of section 108 may be limited both for libraries in for-profit organizations and for the organizations them-selves. All of these issues will be discussed in this chapter, but it is advisable for libraries in for-profit institutions to obtain legal advice from their own attorneys as to the interpretation of the law that should be followed.

First, let us look at some legislative history. The November 1975 Senate Judiciary Committee report stated that the no-commercial-advantage clause was

> intended to preclude a library or archives in a profit-making organization from . . . [using section 108 to provide] . . . photocopies of copyrighted materials to employees engaged in furtherance of the organization's commercial enterprise unless such copying qualifies as a fair use.[3]

Clear enough. But the later (September 3, 1976) House Judiciary Committee report concluded otherwise. The committee recognized that section 108 covers only a copy that is made and distributed "without any purpose of direct or indirect commercial advantage." But, said the committee's report:

> . . . the "advantage" referred to in this clause must attach to the immediate commercial motivation behind the reproduction or distribution itself, rather than to the ultimate profit-making motivation behind the enterprise in which the library is located.

The House Committee concluded that a library in a for-profit institution can have section-108 rights.[4]

The Senate–House Conference Committee report (September 29, 1976) generally went along with the House interpretation:

> As long as the library or archives meets the criteria in section 108(a) and the other requirements of the section . . . , the conferences consider that the isolated, spontaneous making of single photocopies by a library or archives in a for-profit organization without any commercial motivation, or participation by such a library or archives in interlibrary arrangements, would come within the scope of section 108.[5]

It seems a good possibility that the conference report will be considered to represent the legal outcome of the interpretive conflict between the House and Senate reports and that a court would follow the report so long as that court concluded that the statutory phrase "commercial advantage" could reasonably be given the House report's narrow interpretation. Right now, the outcome is unknown.

Assuming that a library in a for-profit organization may use section 108, that right may be less significant than at first appears. In the case of article copying, the availability of section-108 rights calls for a library to have had no notice that the copy would be used for any purpose other than "private study, scholarship, or research" [108(d)(1); see also 108(e)(1)]. Would a library in a for-profit institution have "no notice" when, say, the employee is a research chemist and requests a chemistry article? If it is concluded that the library *has* notice that the purpose is for the organization's research purposes, is such a purpose one for "private study, scholarship, or research" [108(d)(1); see also 108(e)(1)]? If it is not, then section 108 would not apply to the copy made. None of the above congressional reports directly interpret the "private study, scholarship, or research" phrase. However, the House report, interpreting the no-commercial-advantage clause, reflects a clear intent, on the committee's part, to make section 108 capable of covering an article copy made by a library in a for-profit organization for research activities, on behalf of the organization, by one of its employees. Consequently, it is possible, but not certain, that the word "private" in "private study, scholarship, or research" will be construed not to modify "research" nor that the employee's research will be considered "private research." Either interpretation would also affect a library in a not-for-profit institution. Such a library (assuming compliance with section 108 in other respects) could rely on section 108 to fulfill an article copy request for a for-profit organization even when the library happens to have had notice that the article would be used for the organization's research purposes.

Even assuming that the "no commercial advantage" and "private study, scholarship, or research" clauses are construed favorably to the library in a for-profit organization, the remainder of the organization, and thus the organization itself, nonetheless may need a legal justification for the copy, in addition to section 108. Nothing in section 108 "excuses a person who requests a copy under subsection (d) [which covers article copies] from liability for copyright infringement for any such act . . . if it exceeds fair use as provided by section 107" [108(f)(2)].

Multiple Copies Restriction

Section 108 ordinarily authorized only the making of a single copy of something on any one occasion [108(a)–(e), (g)]. Shortly, we will cover the fact that a second or subsequent copy may be made on one or more "separate" occasions. Nonetheless, the fact that section 108 did not authorize multiple copies of any particular thing at any one time should be kept in mind as one of its significant limitations.

The rights of reproduction and distribution under section 108 extend to the "isolated and unrelated" reproduction or distribution of a single copy of the same material on separate occasions. However, they do not extend to cases where the library, or its employee, has substantial reason to believe that it is engaging in the "related or concerted" reproduction of multiple copies *of the same material* (1) whether made on one occasion or over a period of time, and (2) whether intended for aggregate use by one or more individuals or for separate use by the individual members of a group [108(g), (g)(1)].

All that complex language—"isolated and unrelated," "related or concerted"—may well cause baffling problems at some time. However, keep in mind that 90 percent of the point might be covered in this manner: Section 108 authorizes only one copy of something at any particular time. You can sometimes use section 108 properly to make a later copy of that material. But do not use that as an open door. Do not make one copy, walk around the copying machine, and then make another.

Conflicting Agreements

The fact that section 108 may generally authorize a copy of a work to be made does not "in any way" affect any contractual obligations assumed at any time by the library when it obtained a copy of the work in its collections [108(f)(4)]. In the case of unpublished works and works only leased (e.g., sometimes, films) contractual restrictions against copying may have a broad and legally valid scope. Contractual restrictions as to copying, under section 108, published works purchased by the library might also be valid in particular circumstances, but perhaps not in as many cases as for unpublished or leased materials.

UNPUBLISHED WORKS: COPYING FOR PRESERVATION, SECURITY

A library that is eligible to exercise section-108 rights may use them to copy an unpublished work for purposes of preservation and security or for deposit for research use in another library that has section-108 eligibility. The work must be duplicated in facsimile form, e.g., a manuscript could not be converted into computer data. In addition, the library making the copy must have the unpublished work in its current collection [108(b)].[6]

PUBLISHED WORKS: REPLACEMENT COPYING

Section 108 applies to an eligible library's making a copy, in facsimile form, of a published work where the copy is made solely for the purpose of replacement of a copy that is damaged, deteriorating, lost, or stolen. However, the library must first have determined, after a reasonable effort, that an unused copy cannot be obtained at a fair price [108(c)].

The reasonable effort may vary with the circumstances but, according to the legislative history, will

> always require recourse to commonly known trade sources in the United States and in the normal situation also to the publisher or other copyright owner (if such owner can be located at the address given in the copyright registration), or to an authorized reproducing service. . . .[7]

USER REQUESTS: COPYING ENTIRE WORKS

An eligible library under section 108 may, under defined circumstances, make and distribute a copy of an entire work (or a substantial part of it) pursuant to a user's request made at the same or another library [108(e)].

This right does not apply to a musical or a sculptural work. It is also inapplicable to audiovisual works (including motion pictures) other than an audiovisual work dealing with news. Finally, it does not apply to pictures or graphic arts except where they are published as illustrations to material that is eligible to be copied and is copied [108(h)].

Before making a copy authorized by section 108(e), the library must first have determined, on the basis of a reasonable investigation, that a copy cannot be obtained at a fair price [108(e)]. The previously quoted reasonable-effort standard is also applicable here to the reasonable-investigation standard.[8]

A requirement of the section is that the copy must become the property of the user [108(e)(1)].

The library must have had no notice that the copy would be used for any purpose other than "private study, scholarship, or research" [108(e)(1)]. Also, the library must include a "warning of copyright" on its order forms and prominently display a warning of copyright at the place where orders are accepted [108(e)(2)]. The warning-of-copyright criteria are covered in Copyright Office regulations set forth in Appendix 9.

The material that follows concerns the rights that relate, among other things, to journal articles. But at least in one copyright sense, a typical journal article could be considered an "entire work." This is because an article, while within a "collective work" comprising the journal issue, may itself be a separate and independent work [101 "collective work"; 201(c)]. In that case, does a library follow section 108(e), or 108(d), or may it choose whichever one it prefers? It seems likely that the provision applicable to journal articles will ordinarily be section 108(d), because its language and legislative history is so specifically directed to journal articles.

USER REQUESTS: COPYING ARTICLES AND EXCERPTS

General Coverage

An eligible library under section 108 may, under defined circumstances, make and distribute a copy of an article (or other contribution to a copyrighted collection or periodical issue) pursuant to a user's request. The same is true for a copy or phonorecord of a small part of any other copyrighted work [108(d)]. Some of the rules applicable to user requests for a copy of an entire work, considered in the previous section, also apply here; i.e., the written warning-of-copyright statements are necessary and the library must have no notice that the material would be used for any purpose other than "private study, scholarship, and research" [108(d)(1), (2)].

The section-108(d) right does not apply to a musical or a sculptural work. Pictures and graphic art are also not included except where they are published as illustrations to material that is eligible to be copied and is copied. Section 108(d) is inapplicable to a motion picture and other audiovisual work except for an audiovisual work dealing with news [108(h)].

Isolated and Unrelated Copies

As was the case for the other types of section-108 rights, the section-108(d) right: (1) extends to the isolated and unrelated reproduction or distribution of a single copy of the same material on separate occasions but (2) does not extend to cases where the library or its employee has substantial reason to believe that it is engaging in the related or concerted reproduction or distribution of the same material [108(g), (g)(1)].

No Systematic Copying

Section 108(d)'s rights of reproduction and distribution do not extend to cases where the library "engages in the systematic reproduction or distribution of single or multiple copies . . . of material described in subsection (d). . . ."

The "systematic" clause does not seem intended to preclude a library from using section 108(d) solely because the library receives enough requests from its own patrons to warrant having a "system" for handling them efficiently. Rather, the clause was apparently intended primarily to preclude substitutions of photocopying arrangements for subscriptions or purchases. At the time of the Senate Judiciary Committee report, the focus was on interlibrary transactions:

> Systematic reproduction or distribution occurs when a library makes copies of such materials available to other libraries or to groups of users under formal or informal arrangements whose purpose or effect is to have the reproducing library serve as their source of such material. Such systematic reproduction and distribution, as distinguished from isolated and unrelated reproduction or distribution, may substitute the copies reproduced by the source library for subscriptions or reprints or other copies which the receiving libraries or users might otherwise have purchased for themselves, from the publisher or the licensed reproducing agencies.[9]

As we shall see, this problem received special attention in a proviso subsequently added to section 108(g)(2). The point here is that the basic clause seems to derive from a concern about subscription or purchase substitutions; that seems to be its primary relevance, even in a situation not involving interlibrary arrangements, but since systematic is not formally defined it may be argued that it has a broader scope.

Interlibrary Arrangements

The Statute.   The anti-systematic clause provided a storm of controversy concerning the extent to which restrictions would prevent the continuation and development of interlibrary networks and other arrangements involving the exchange of photocopies. When the storm cleared, the statute said that the exclusion of systematic copying or distribution did not prevent a library, under section 108(d), from

> participating in interlibrary arrangements that do not have, as their purpose or effect, that the library . . . receiving such copies or phonorecords for distribution does so in *such aggregate quantities as to substitute for a sub-scription to or purchase of such work* [108(g)(2)]. [Italics added.]

The Guidelines.   CONTU (the National Commission on New Technological Uses of Copyrighted Works), with the concurrence of representatives of authors, librarians, and publishers, developed guidelines interpreting the above italicized words. The legislative history states that the guidelines are not intended as, and cannot be considered, explicit directions covering all cases but nonetheless are a reasonable interpretation of the aggregate-quantities standard in the most common situations to which the standard applies today.[10] These 108(g)(2) guidelines are found in Appendix 4.

Concerning article copies, the guidelines consider only what we might call "recent" articles and issues, i.e., articles published in issues within five years prior to the date of a library's request for a copy from another library. The guidelines leave "to future interpretation" the application of the aggregate-quantities standard to copies of older articles from older issues.

A calendar year is the base period for applying the guidelines. If, during such a period, the requesting library receives a total of no more than five copies of articles from recent issues of the same publication, the library is within the guidelines. The sixth copy is beyond the guidelines. The five copies may be of the same article or a combination of different articles from the publication. (As previously considered, section 108 does not authorize multiple copies of the same article being obtained on the "same occasion.")

It may sometimes happen that the interlibrary request will be made even though the requesting library has a subscription in force or on order. If that is the case, the copy requested will not count as one of the five copies when the material to be copied was not reasonably available for use by the requesting library itself. (This part of the guidelines theoretically allows abuses but, as noted, the guidelines are not intended as explicit directions covering all cases.)

In addition to the quantitative "rule of fives" (five copies, five years of issues), the guidelines have some procedural rules. The copy request is not supposed to be made unless the requesting library could have made and supplied the copy under section 108 had the article been in its own collections.

Under the terms of the guidelines, the supplying library is supposed to fulfill another library's recent-article requests only if the requesting library represents that the request conforms with the guidelines. The requesting library is supposed to maintain a record of its interlibrary requests for section-108(d) materials and of fulfillments of such requests. These records are supposed to be kept during the calendar year of the recorded event and for three calendar years thereafter.

It should be noted that while the guidelines speak in mandatory terms ("no request may be fulfilled" or "the requesting entity shall maintain"), they are only guidelines, not a statute. Compliance is necessary only to be fully operating within the guidelines—beneficial, to be sure, but not explicitly mandated by the statute.

The guidelines do not deal with the subject of requests for articles from journal issues that are more than five years old (judged at the time of the library's interlibrary request).

There are interlibrary guidelines for other section 108(d) materials, i.e., copies or phonorecords of a small part of any other copyrighted work covered by section 108(d). A library may fulfill requests for such materials through interlibrary "loans" or transactions. However, the guidelines state that during any calendar year the copies to be provided should not total more than five interlibrary copies from any given work. Unlike the portion of the guidelines dealing with articles, this guideline standard applies not merely to material published within five years prior to the request but to the entire copyright period. The procedural standards discussed above apply here as well. The requested copy does not count as one of the five copies if the requesting library has the material or has it on order but it is not reasonably available.

Libraries in For-Profit Organizations. As mentioned earlier in this chapter, the Senate report concluded that a library in a for-profit institution could not use section 108 at all for its employees' research needs; the House report concluded that the library could; and the Senate-House Conference report sided with the House. However, the Conference report, while appearing to agree with the House report on this point in a general way, sanctioned the for-profit library's use of section

108 if that was done without "participation by such a library . . . in inter-library arrangements. . . ."[11] The House report explicitly stated such participation was permissible under 108.[12]

The issue of how section 108 applies is significant enough that perhaps authoritative guidance will develop before too long. Meanwhile, libraries in for-profit institutions that plan to use section 108 should, at the very least, be sensitive to the following examples, from the Senate report, of subscription-substitution situations.[13] The examples were developed before the interlibrary-arrangements proviso came into the new law, but they are nonetheless worth noting.

> A library with a collection of journals in biology informs other libraries with similar collections that it will maintain and build its own collection and will make copies of articles from these journals available to them and their patrons on request. Accordingly, the other libraries discontinue or refrain from purchasing subscriptions to these journals and fulfill their patrons' requests for articles by obtaining photocopies from the source library.
>
> Several branches of a library system agree that one branch will subscribe to particular journals, in lieu of each branch's purchasing its own subscriptions, and the one subscribing branch will reproduce copies of articles from the publication for users of the other branch.

The Supplying Library. The section-108(g)(2) proviso speaks in terms of sanctioning a library's participation in interlibrary arrangements if the *receiving* library is within the aggregate-quantity rule. Thus the supplying library would seem to be protected, as a literal matter, when the receiving library is. It remains to be seen whether that interpretation will prevail. An unequivocal resolution favorable to the supplying library does not necessarily leave that library without other potential problems. Some concern would have to be given to section 108(g)(1)'s exclusion of related and concerted copying of the same material on separate occasions. Also, the following remark by CONTU, prefatory to the guidelines themselves, should be kept in mind:

> The point has been made that the present practice on . . . use of photocopies in lieu of loans may be supplemented or even largely replaced by a system in which one or more agencies or institutions, public or private, exist for the specific purpose of providing a central source for photocopies. Of course, these guidelines would not apply to such a situation.[14]

UNSUPERVISED REPRODUCING EQUIPMENT

Nothing in section 108 is to be construed to impose library liability for copyright infringement for the unsupervised use of reproducing equipment located in the library's premises *if* such equipment displays a notice that the making of a copy may be subject to the copyright law [108(f)(1)].

As a literal matter, the subsection does not relieve a library from liability since the provision just relates to the impact of section 108. However, the House and Senate Judiciary Committee reports on the law state that the clause "specifically exempts" the library.[15] (Note that only the library and its employees are covered.)

The House Judiciary Committee report states that a library in a for-profit organization could not avoid obligations under section 108 by installing reproducing equipment on its premises for unsupervised use by the organization's staff.

IMPORT PROVISIONS

The import provisions of the new law generally provide that it is an infringement of copyright to import a work (that is protected by U.S. copyright) without the copyright owner's consent [602].

We will consider two exceptions relating to libraries. They relate only to imported copies made under circumstances where, had U.S. copyright law been applicable, there would have been no infringement in the making of the copies [602(b)]. So-called piratical copies are not covered by the exceptions.[16]

One exception allows importation of one copy of an audiovisual work for archival purposes and up to five copies of other works for library lending or archival purposes. This exception applies to importations by or for an organization operated for scholarly, educational, or religious purposes, and not for private financial gain. The exception is not applicable if the importation is part of an activity consisting of systematic reproduction or distribution engaged in by the organization "in violation" of section 108(g)(2) [602(a)(3)].

Another exception allows the importation of copies under the authority of or for the use of the U.S. government or of any state or political subdivision [602(a)(3)]. (The provision does not apply to copies for use in schools and it applies to audiovisual works only when imported for archival use.) This provision does not contain any qualifying language about section 108 as did the first exception. It nonetheless may be true that, in the case of a library, the copies imported are relevant in any analysis of the library's section-108 activities and that section 602(a)(1) may authorize merely the importation as such.

AUDIOVISUAL NEWS PROGRAMS

Library of Congress

At the time the new copyright law was passed, Congress also passed the American Television and Radio Archives Act [Transitional and Supplementary Provisions, Sec. 113].

Under that act, the Librarian of Congress is authorized, among other things, to record broadcasts of news programs and to make compilations of them according to subject matter. The Librarian of Congress is also authorized to distribute a reproduction of such a newscast or compilation for deposit in a library whose collections meet the eligibility criteria of section 108(a). This distribution should be for use by researchers only in their research and not for further reproduction or performance. The library providing the recording to the researcher is supposed to lend it, not sell it.

Other Libraries

As a companion provision to the American Television and Radio Archives Act, section 108 of the new copyright law provides that nothing in that section shall be construed to limit the reproduction and distribution (through the lending of a limited number of copies and excerpts) of an audiovisual news program by a library [108(f)(3)]. According to the House Judiciary Committee report, the clause is intended to permit libraries to make off-the-air recordings of daily network newscasts for limited distribution for use in research. The later Senate-House Conference report added that the term "audiovisual newscast program" is intended to include local, regional, and network newscasts and also on-the-spot coverage of news events and interviews concerning news events.[17] The copying and lending right is available to libraries that meet the collections-availability criteria of section 108. Any reproduction should include a notice of copyright and copies should be loaned without any purpose of commercial advantage.

FUTURE DEVELOPMENTS

Section 108 is in the nature of a legislative experiment. The Register of Copyrights is supposed to report on it to Congress by 1983 [108(i)]. The related interlibrary transaction guidelines, by their own terms, are also supposed to be reconsidered by that time.

13

LIMITS ON EXCLUSIVE PERFORMANCE AND DISPLAY RIGHTS

Two of the copyright owner's exclusive rights of copyright are the rights of public performance and public display of the copyrighted work [106]. A public performance or display may take place not only at locations open to the public but also anywhere a substantial number of people, outside of a normal circle of a family and its social acquaintances, is gathered. It may take place by a live performance in one of those places or by a transmission of a performance from somewhere else [101 "publicly"].

There are a number of exceptions to the copyright owner's public performance and display rights. Specific ones are considered in this chapter under three broad categories: (1) educational, charitable, and religious; (2) aid to the handicapped; and (3) miscellaneous. In addition, the general fair-use doctrine will sometimes be applicable as will some other exemptions previously considered, relating to useful articles, displays of owned works, and computer applications [107, 109, 113, 117].

EDUCATIONAL, CHARITABLE, AND RELIGIOUS EXEMPTIONS

Face-to-Face Teaching

Nonprofit educational institutions may generally perform or display works in the course of face-to-face teaching activities. The activities are to be carried out by the instructors or pupils and in the classroom or similar place devoted to instruction [110(1)].

As part of this exemption, the provision states that in the case of an audiovisual work, the performance or display of an unlawfully made copy is not authorized if the person responsible for the performance had reason to believe the copy was not lawfully made.

The legislative history provides interpretations of the face-to-face teaching activities provision, e.g., (1) the exempted activities cover a wide area of performances but not performances given for recreation or entertainment; (2) the section does not cover the case of performers brought in to put on a program, but an "instructor" can be a guest lecturer whose instructional activities remain confined to classroom situations and who performs a copyrighted work; (3) "pupils" means, in general, the enrolled members of a class; and (4) "classroom or similar place devoted to instruction" can include places such as an auditorium or gymnasium, when used in the context of instructing a class but not where the audience is broader in scope, e.g., a school assembly or a general athletic event.[1]

Instructional Transmissions

Nonprofit educational institutions may perform or display works, under defined circumstances, by transmissions primarily to students [101 "transmit"; 110(2)]. There is no limit as to the types of works that may be displayed. However, only nondramatic literary or musical works may be performed [110(2)]. Under defined circumstances, copies of the transmission program may be made and distributed to other parties eligible to use section 110(2) and they can use them for section-110(2) purposes [112(b)].[2] Ordinarily, the program could not be separately copyrighted [112(e)].

Because of the confined scope of the performance exception—nondramatic literary or musical works—works such as operas, musical comedies, motion pictures, and filmstrips are not covered. Moreover, since the exemption covers only performances and displays, it does not authorize the development of a derivative work from a copyrighted work.[3]

A performance or display by transmission is covered by this section only if it is a regular part of the *systematic instructional activities* of a governmental body or of a nonprofit educational institution. The italicized phrase is equated in the legislative history with curricula and, in the case of institutions that systematically use teaching methods not related to specific course work, with such methods.[4]

Another standard of the section is that the performance or display must be directly related to and of material assistance to the teaching content of the transmission.

A third standard is that the transmission be made primarily (not solely) for one of these three purposes: (1) reception by government employees as part of their official duties; (2) reception in classrooms or similar places normally devoted to instruction; or (3) reception by persons to whom the transmission is directed because special circumstances, such as their disabilities, prevent their attendance at class. "Primary purpose" can depend on such facts as subject matter and the time of transmission. "Special circumstances" can include not only the case of the handicapped but also the case of those that "cannot" attend class for other reasons, e.g., preschool children.[5]

Free Performances

Section 110(4) of the new law authorizes noncommercial, nonprofit free performances (other than by transmission) of certain types of works under defined circumstances. The types of works involved are nondramatic literary or musical works. For the performance to qualify, the performers and promoters must receive no compensation and no admission must be charged. There must be no purpose of direct or indirect commercial advantage, thus excluding from the section free public performances given or sponsored in connection with a commercial or profit-making organization [110(4)].[6]

Fund-Raising Performances

In addition to covering certain free performances, section 110(4) also covers noncommercial fund-raising performances (other than by transmission) if the funds, after reasonable production expenses, are used exclusively for educational, religious, or charitable purposes and not for private financial gain. If the performers, promoters, or organizers are to be compensated, this exemption does not apply. Only nondramatic literary or musical works are covered.

By following certain procedures, the copyright owner has the power to remove his or her work from this exemption as to a particular performance [110(4)]. The no-compensation-to-the-performers rule is not considered violated if, for example, the performance is by a school orchestra conducted by a music teacher who receives an annual salary or if it is by members of a service band whose performance is part of their assigned duties and who receive military pay.[7]

Religious Services

A section of the new law allows, without the necessity for copyright-owner consent, the display of a copyrighted work, and the performance of certain classes of works, in the course of services at a place of worship or other religious assembly.

The classes of works subject to the performance rights are nondramatic literary works (thus excluding, among others, motion pictures and other audiovisual works), nondramatic musical works, and dramatico-musical works of a religious nature. The latter phrase is designed to exclude such things as secular operas even though they may have a religious or philosophical theme, and yet to include sacred music, even though it might be perceived, in some cases, as a dramatic work. The "in the course of services" phrase of the section is intended to exclude performances that happen to be at a place of worship but are for social, entertainment, educational, or fund-raising purposes.[8] Under some circumstances performances for such purposes might be authorized under one of the provisions discussed earlier in this chapter.

Public Broadcasting

The new law provides for a compulsory license for public broadcasting entities with respect to published nondramatic musical works and with respect to published art. This is considered in Chapter 14.

AID FOR THE HANDICAPPED

Nondramatic literary works may be transmitted on a noncommercial basis by specified types of noncommercial entities, e.g., educational broadcasters, when the transmission is specifically designed for and primarily directed to the blind, the deaf, or those seriously handicapped in sight or hearing. The performance must be made without any purpose of direct or indirect commercial advantage. The transmission must be made through the facilities of a governmental body or through certain other facilities described in federal communication law or regulations [110(8)]. Under defined circumstances, up to ten copies may be made and distributed to other institutions eligible under this section 110(8) for their use under this section [112(d)].

A dramatic literary work, at least ten years old, may be performed by transmission, through specified types of noncommercial entities, on a not-for-commercial-advantage basis when the transmission is primarily designed for the blind or visually handicapped. This section would not authorize the performance of the same work by the same performers more than once, or more than once by or under the auspices of the same organization. [110(9)].

In addition to the two provisions discussed under this heading thus far, the previously mentioned provisions regarding instructional activities also take the needs of the handicapped specifically into account. Furthermore, there is a new provision in the law by which the Copyright Office is authorized to ask copyright owners to voluntarily license certain rights in nondramatic literary works to the Library of Congress for the benefit of the physically handicapped [710].

MISCELLANEOUS

Sound Recordings

The public performance right is not applicable to sound recordings as such [114(a)]. However, the public performance of a sound recording ordinarily will also involve the public performance of a copyrighted work underlying the sound recording. Thus usually a license will be required with respect to that underlying work or the public performance will need to come within one of the statutory exemptions.

Compulsory Licenses

In addition to the compulsory-license system for certain noncommercial broadcast activities, there are compulsory-license systems covering performances by cable television systems and by jukebox operators. These compulsory-license systems are considered in Chapter 14.

Record Shops

The performance of a nondramatic musical work by a record shop, solely to promote retail sales of copies of the work or phonorecords of it, is authorized by the new law if the sounds are not broadcast elsewhere by the shop, if the place is open to the public, and if there is no admission charge [110(7)].

Home Receiving Apparatus

The ordinary use of home radio and television receivers is not a public performance and thus creates no special issues. A provision of the new law also allows the use of such receivers in public places if no charge is made to see or hear the performance and if the received transmission is not further transmitted [110(5)].

Annual Agricultural Fairs

Performances of a nondramatic musical work by a nonprofit agricultural or horticultural organization in the course of its annual agricultural or horticultural fair are allowed. This section of the new law protects the organization but does not extend to such people as concessionaires who exercise a performance right in a work [110(6)].[9]

14

COMPULSORY LICENSES

Under the new law and under prescribed circumstances, a person has a statutory right, in four copyright areas, to make use of a copyrighted work if certain procedures are followed and fees defined by statute are paid. These four areas of compulsory licenses relate to: (1) recording rights in nondramatic musical compositions; (2) jukebox performances of nondramatic musical compositions; (3) noncommercial broadcasters' transmissions of published nondramatic musical works and of published pictorial, graphic, and sculptural works; and (4) cablecasts of broadcast transmissions.

MUSICAL COMPOSITIONS: RECORDING RIGHTS

General

This category of compulsory license covers rights to reproduce and distribute phonorecords of *nondramatic* musical compositions [115]. The license does not include the right of public performance [106, 115]. The license also does not include the right to duplicate the sound recording made by others [115(a)].

The compulsory license may be obtained only if the primary purpose in making the phonorecords is to distribute them to the public for private use rather than, for example, to distribute them primarily for commercial uses, such as jukebox or broadcast uses or for background music services.[1]

The license includes a right of making musical arrangements of the work for recording purposes, but the arrangement may not change "the basic melody or fundamental character of the work." Although the arrangement may be a derivative work, it is not protected as such under the copyright law except with the express consent of the copyright owner of the underlying work [115(a)(2)].

When Available

The right to the compulsory license becomes available once phonorecords of the work have been distributed to the public in the United States by authority of the copyright owner [115(a)(1)]. (Note: The sound track on a motion picture or other audiovisual work is not a "phonorecord" [101].)

How Obtained

The compulsory license is obtained by serving notice of intention to do so on the copyright owner or, under certain circumstances (i.e., if registration or public records of the Copyright Office do not identify copyright owner and include an address at which the notice can be served), on the Copyright Office. The latter's regulations prescribe the form, content, and manner of service. The notice must be served before, or within 30 days after, making the phonorecords but, in any event, before distributing them [115(b)].

Royalties

The licensee is obligated to pay royalties with respect to phonorecords made and distributed under the license any time after the copyright owner is identified in the registration or other public records of the Copyright Office [115(c)].

The statutory royalties apply to those phonorecords made and distributed under the license. For each work embodied in the phonorecord the royalty typically will be two- and three-quarters cents ($.0275). However, if the phonorecord playing time for the work is over five minutes, the royalty is one half of one cent ($.005) per minute or fraction thereof [115(c)(2)]. Thus, playing time of five minutes or less calls for 2.75 cents per recording of the work and playing time of more than five, but not more than six, minutes calls for 3.0 cents.

Royalty payments are due monthly (by the 20th) for the month next preceding and are required to be made under oath. Copyright Office regulations govern the monthly and annual statements of account that are required [115(c)(3)].

If the payments and statements are not timely provided, the copyright owner may give notice of default and a 30-day termination notice to the compulsory licensee. If the default is not remedied within 30 days of the date of the notice, the compulsory license terminates. Those phonorecords not covered by the paid royalties are infringing phonorecords [115(c)(4)].

The Copyright Royalty Tribunal, established under the new law, may make periodic determinations concerning the adjustment of the general royalty rates [801(b)(1); 804(a)(2)(B)].

Related Voluntary Licenses

The old copyright law had a compulsory license arrangement similar to the above, one of the principal differences being that it had no royalty rate adjustment provision.[2]

Nothwithstanding the availability of the compulsory license, many licenses were arranged voluntarily by the parties or their representatives, the Harry Fox Office being the leading representative of copyright owners in this area of licensing activity. The private licensing arrangements permitted greater flexibility in administration, in the definition of when royalties were due and, sometimes, in the royalty rate. Of course, the terms of these private licenses were greatly influenced by the terms of the available compulsory license. It appears that these private arrangements will continue to be made under the new copyright law.

JUKEBOX PERFORMANCES

General

This new category of compulsory license relates to nondramatic musical works and the public performance of them by means of a coin-operated phonorecord player [116(a)]. That latter term is defined so as to exclude from the compulsory license record players that are located in establishments making a direct or indirect charge for admission. The definition also excludes record players that do not permit the patrons of the establishment to make the playing choices from among the works available [116(e)(1)].

Eligibility

The compulsory license is obtained by the "operator" of the coin-operated record player (henceforth, here, the jukebox). The operator can be the person who owns the jukebox or has the power to make a jukebox available for placement (e.g., a jukebox distributor) or who has the power to exercise primary control over the selection of musical works to be included in the jukebox repertoire [116(e)(2)]. The proprietor of the establishment where the jukebox is located will not ordinarily be a jukebox operator (within the meaning of the compulsory license provisions) and ordinarily will not be liable for any infringement by the jukebox performances when the compulsory license provisions are not followed [116(a)(1); 116(b)(2)].

How Obtained

A jukebox operator obtains an annual jukebox license by: (1) filing an application with the Copyright Office; (2) affixing to the jukebox the certificate that the Copyright Office issues pursuant to the application; and (3) by paying a royalty fee to the Copyright Office [116(b)(1)].

Royalties

A full-year fee is $8, payable each January. For new licenses in mid-year or later, the fee for the remainder of that year is $4 [116(b)(1)(A)].

The royalty payments are per jukebox, but the royalty recipients are the copyright owners of the musical works underlying the recordings. This statutory setup presumes that most of the royalty claimants will be represented by performance rights societies such as ASCAP (the American Society of Composers, Authors, and Publishers), BMI (Broadcast Music Inc.), and SESAC, Inc.[3] There is the hope that these societies will work out a fair distribution of the royalties among themselves, with the Copyright Royalty Tribunal deciding the fair share of others. However, the Tribunal can resolve the allocations among the societies if they do not agree among themselves [116(c); 801(b)(3)]. The allocations are made annually.

The Copyright Royalty Tribunal may periodically consider adjustments to the jukebox royalty rates, the first such review being not before 1990 [804(a)(2)(c)].

NONCOMMERCIAL BROADCASTING

This new category concerns program productions by public broadcasting entities and relates to published nondramatic musical works and to published pictorial, graphic, and sculptural works [118(d)]. Excluded from the compulsory-licensing area are *dramatizations* of nondramatic musical works, the unauthorized use of any portion of an audiovisual work, and the production of a transmission program drawn to any substantial extent from a published compilation of pictorial, graphic, or sculptural works [118(f)]. (While nondramatic literary works are not governed by the compulsory license, voluntary agreements establishing licensing rates and terms for public broadcasting are encouraged by the statute. The Register of Copyrights is to report to Congress in 1980 on the extent to which such voluntary agreements have been reached and on any legislative or other recommendations that may be warranted [108(e)(2)].)

To return to the compulsory license, it covers the use of the included works as part of programs for noncommercial educational broadcast station transmissions and also authorizes reproductions, distributions, and performances of those programs under defined circumstances [118(d)].

When the new law was enacted, no licensing rates had been established for these compulsory licenses. The statute encouraged voluntary agreements to be reached and, for other cases, provided for the Copyright Royalty Tribunal to determine a schedule of reasonable terms and rates of royalty payments [118(b)]. These rates will be subject to adjustment in 1982 and at five-year intervals thereafter [118(b), (c); 804(c)].

Until the publication of the rates and terms in the *Federal Register*, the copyright law, as it was in effect on December 31, 1977 controls the rights covered by section 118 [118(b)(4)]. It seems unlikely at present that there will be any significant litigation as to how the old law should be interpreted concerning the activities now within section 118.

CABLE TELEVISION

This new compulsory license is the fruit of much controversy that prevailed when the new law was developing. It is very complex, both in its own provisions and in its interaction with complex regulations of the FCC (Federal Communications Commission). The complexities will not be covered in detail in this book but the license system's general structure will be considered.

The compulsory license relates to a subscription service cable system and to its carriage of broadcast signals [111(c), (f)]. (Certain transmissions are given a general exemption from copyright liability under prescribed conditions. These exemptions relate to such activities as relays of broadcast signals by a hotel or an apartment house to the residents' lodgings, to secondary transmissions by nonprofit "booster-signal" stations, and to so-called passive carriers who provided communications channels for the use of others [111(a)(1), (3), (4)].)

Generally speaking, a cable system subject to a compulsory license obtains the right to carry broadcast signals as a result of FCC regulations. Some of these signal-carriage rights relate to broadcasts that are, roughly speaking, "local" broadcasts from the standpoint of the cable system's location. Others are "distant-signal" broadcasts.

Although the compulsory copyright license does not give the cable system the absolute right to carry broadcast signals, the FCC having that role, the license does give certain rights to the system to carry the signals free of liability for copyright infringement.

A percentage fee is called for to cover the right, under copyright, to carry distant signals. In addition to this base percentage fee, there are also separate percentage fee calculations that depend upon the distant signals actually carried. The base fee is applied against the second fee, if any. Both types of fees are determined by statutorily established percentages of the system's semiannual gross receipts from the subscribers to the basic cable service [111(d)(2)(B)]. When such gross receipts are less than $160,000, reductions from the normal percentage rates are provided for [111(d)(2)(C), (D)]. At the time of the House Judiciary Committee's report on the compulsory-license provisions (September 1976), it was estimated that the first year's fees would equal approximately $8.7 million, or about $.81 per subscriber.[4]

The licensed cable system pays fees to the Copyright Office and also files with it accounting statements and statements of signal-carriage activity [111(d)(1), (2)]. Each July, claims are to be filed with the Copyright Royalty Tribunal by persons claiming to be entitled to share in the compulsory-licensing fees. The Tribunal resolves the controversies that cannot be resolved by agreement [111(d)(5)].

The initial royalty rates are set by the statute. They are subject to possible adjustments should the FCC make a change in its signal-carriage rules [801(b)(2)(B), (C)]. They also are subject to possible adjustments at five-year intervals beginning in 1985 [804(a)(2)(A)].

NOTES AND REFERENCES

The notes and references that follow are cited in thirteen of the book's fourteen chapters. Listed below are abbreviated forms of items found in the notes and references themselves.

"The 1909 Act." The Copyright Act of 1909, as amended up to the enactment of the new law October 19, 1976.

"1975 Senate Report." The November 20, 1975 copyright law revision report of the Senate Committee on the Judiciary, 94th Cong., 1st sess., 1975, S. Rept. No. 94-473.

"1976 House Report." The September 22, 1976 copyright law revision report of the House Committee on the Judiciary, 94th Cong., 2d sess., 1976, H.R. Rept. No. 94-1476.

"1976 Conference Report." The September 29, 1976 Senate–House Conference Report on the new copyright law, 94th Cong., 2d sess., 1976, H.R. Rept. No. 94-1733.

CONTU—National Commission on New Technological Uses of Copyrighted Works.

CHAPTER 1

1. Title 17 of the *United States Code, Annotated* (1952 ed.) and its *Cumulative Annual Pocket Part* (1976 ed.) include historical notes for each amended section of the 1909 Act.
2. Appendix 7 cross-references the new law's provisions to the 1909 Act.
3. Ibid.
4. 1976 House Report, p. 51.
5. See also Beckett, "The Copyright Act of 1976: When Is It Effective?," *Bulletin of the Copyright Society of the USA* 24 (1977): 391–426.
6. 1976 House Report, pp. 62–63.
7. 1976 House Report, p. 51.
8. Section 1(e), 1909 Act.
9. Ibid.
10. See 1976 House Report, p. 89.

11. 88 Statute 1873 (1974), Title 17 *United States Code, Annotated* Sec. 201 (1976 Supplement).

12. 1976 Conference Report, p. 69.

13. For comments on the Senate's design protection concepts, see the 1975 Senate Report, pp. 162–167.

14. 1976 House Report, p. 50.

CHAPTER 2

1. 1976 House Report, pp. 51–52.

2. 1976 House Report, p. 51.

3. Donald v. Zack Meyer's T.V. Sales and Services, 426 F.2d 1027 (5th Cir. 1970), *cert.* denied, 400 U.S. 992 (1971).

4. Morrissey v. Proctor & Gamble Co., 379 F.2d 675 (1st Cir. 1967).

5. See 1976 House Report, pp. 52–53.

6. 1976 House Report, p. 54.

7. 1976 House Report, pp. 53–54.

8. 1976 House Report, pp. 54–55.

9. Most states have such protection. See *Bulletin of the Copyright Society of the USA* 23 (1976): 321–334.

10. 1976 House Report, p. 56.

11. 1976 House Report, p. 57.

12. Ibid.

13. The most direct authority for federal copyright legislation is in Article I, section 8 of the *Constitution* and grants Congress the power "To promote the Progress of Science and useful Arts, by securing for limited Times to Authors and Inventors the exclusive Right to their respective Writings and Discoveries."

14. Nichols v. Universal Pictures Corp., 45 F.2d 119 (2nd Cir. 1930), *cert.* denied, 282 U.S. 902 (1931).

15. See *Nimmer on Copyright*, vol. 1, sec. 29.2–29.5 (New York: Matthew Bender & Co., Inc. 1976).

16. See Gorman, "Copyright Protection for the Collection and Representation of Facts," *Harvard Law Review* 76 (1963): 1569.

17. Neither the 1976 House Report nor the 1975 Senate Report specifically refer to these three categories; the general intent was continuity of concept (1976 House Report, pp. 51–52). The categories were not covered by copyright under the 1909 Act. For protection of titles generally, see *Nimmer on Copyright*, vol. 1, sec. 34 (1976 ed.).

18. 1976 House Report, p. 59.

19. 1976 House Report, pp. 52, 54, 57.

20. In 1977 the CONTU Data Base Subcommittee concluded that, for data bases (a) the new law's notice requirements are suitable, and (b) that Copyright Office deposit regulations might appropriately call for deposit of identifying material rather than full copies.

21. In 1977 the CONTU Data Base Subcommittee concluded that existing copyright principles were generally suitable.

22. In 1977 the CONTU Software Subcommittee supported copyright protection for computer programs and continuation of the copyright law's standards that ideas, etc., are not protected by copyright. One commissioner strongly opposed copyright protection as such but, nonetheless, favored some comparable protection.

23. The 1977 CONTU Software Subcommittee report seemed to conclude that it would be appropriate for the normal copyright law preemption rules to apply to data bases, but also that this would not preclude some trade secret or similar protection in limited circumstances.

CHAPTER 3

1. 1976 House Report, p. 52.

2. 1976 House Report, p. 138.

3. See Appendix 5 introductory material.

4. Ibid.

5. But see Rinaldo, "The Scope of Copyright Protection in the United States Under Existing Inter-American Relations: Abrogation for the Need for U.S. Protection Under the Buenos Aires Convention by Reliance Upon the UCC," *Bulletin of the Copyright Society of the USA* 22 (1975): 417.

6. A specific statement about "copies" is in the new law in the notice section, but a comparable statement is not included in the notice section about "phonorecords." See sections 401(a)(2); 402(a)(2).

7. See 1976 House Report, p. 145.

8. See *Nimmer on Copyright*, vol. 1, sec. 82 (1976 ed.).

9. See 1976 House Report, pp. 147–148.

10. See Copyright Office, *Compendium of Copyright Office Practices*, sec. 4.2.2 (1973 ed.).

11. Direct contiguity of copyright notice elements is not absolutely necessary under the new law (1976 House Report, p. 150).

12. 1976 House Report, pp. 145–146.

13. 1976 House Report, pp. 149–150.

CHAPTER 5

1. A statement explaining the procedures is available from the Copyright Office. Ask for the December 1977 Announcement entitled *Postage for Books Mailed to the Copyright Office* (ML176). Section 15 of the old copyright law, which allowed for postage-free mailings, was not carried over into the new law.

2. Sections 10 and 12, 1909 Act.

3. The Register of Copyrights, in a statement preceding the issuance of its registration forms, took the position that "A basic registration made by any author or copyright owner will be sufficient to allow an action to be brought

by any author or other copyright owner of the work, provided that the plaintiff has recorded an appropriate document under section 204(d)" (*Federal Register* 42 [Sept. 26, 1977]: 48946). The statement was in the context of basic and supplementary registrations. A renewal registration, when applicable, will of course have been made if there is to be a valid claim for infringement of a renewal copyright.

4. In the *Federal Register* citation given in note 3, the Register of Copyrights also took the position that a single basic registration made by any author or copyright owner will suffice for purposes of section 405(a)(2).

5. In the *Federal Register* citation given in note 3, the Register of Copyrights took the position that "A timely registration by any author or copyright owner will preserve the possibility of such remedies [i.e., statutory damages and attorney's fees] for any other author or copyright owner of the work."

6. See note 5.

7. In the *Federal Register* citation given in note 3, the Register of Copyrights stated that "The language and history of the act indicate that certificates of both basic and supplementary registration may be given such [i.e., prima facie] effect."

8. The priority rules considered in the text are based on the constructive notice provisions of section 205(c), which call for registration of the work. In the *Federal Register* citation given in note 3, the Register of Copyrights took the position that "One basic registration will suffice for this purpose [i.e., 205(c) purposes], and that basic registration need not be in the name of a party to the document [to which the constructive notice rule will apply]."

9. *Federal Register* 42 (Sept. 26, 1977): 48946.

CHAPTER 6

1. 1976 House Report, p. 121.

2. See Best Medium Pub. Co. v. National Insider Inc., 259 F. Supp. 433 (N.D. Ill. 1966), *aff'd.* 385 F.2d 384 (7th Cir. 1967), *cert.* denied, 390 U.S. 955 (1968).

3. The new law's different position on this issue may, as a practical matter, influence close cases involving pre-1978 facts, particularly since blind acceptance of the presumption was not a set pattern even before the new law.

4. For a discussion of when a person is considered an "employee" for work made for hire purposes, see Angel and Tannenbaum, "Works Made for Hire Under S.22," *New York Law School Law Review* 22 (1976): 209; 221–225.

5. See 1976 House Report, p. 124.

6. See 1976 House Report, p. 79.

7. Section 24, 1909 Act.

8. 1976 House Report, p. 127.

9. 1976 House Report, p. 140.

CHAPTER 7

1. 1976 House Report, p. 138.

2. 1976 House Report, p. 79.

3. 1976 House Report, p. 63.
4. Both utility patents and design patents are covered by Title 35 of the *United States Code*.
5. Ibid.
6. The Lanham Act is included in Title 15 of the *United States Code*. The false designations of origins section of the Act is set forth in Title 15 of the *United States Code*, sec. 1125.
7. The federal antitrust laws are set forth in Title 15 of the *United States Code*, principally in the first 77 sections.
8. Federal communications law is covered in Title 47 of the *United States Code*.
9. 1976 House Report, p. 24.
10. *Congressional Record* 122 (daily ed., Sept. 22, 1976): H10910.

CHAPTER 8

1. 1976 House Report, p. 159.
2. Title 28 *United States Code* sec. 1498.
3. See 1976 House Report, p. 162.

CHAPTER 9

1. See sections 10 and 12, 1909 Act.
2. See 1976 House Report, pp. 138–139.
3. Section 24, 1909 Act.
4. See note to section 24 in Appendix 2.
5. 1976 House Report, p. 135. A compilation of various nations' copyright duration rules appears on pp. 123–124 of the *Hearings Before the Subcommittee on Court, Civil Liberties, and the Administration of Justice of the House Committee on the Judiciary*, 94th Cong., 1st sess., 1975, ser. 36, pt. 1. The adoption of the life-plus-50 rule removes a barrier that precluded the U.S. from joining the Berne Convention (described in Appendix 5). A committee of the American Bar Association's section of Patent, Trademark, and Copyright Law has recommended that a subcommittee study this issue and report on the study of the section in 1978. See *1977 Committee Reports, Section of Patent, Trademark, and Copyright Law*.
6. Section 12, 1909 Act.
7. Sections 16, 17, 22, and 23, 1909 Act.
8. See note to section 24 in Appendix 2.

CHAPTER 10

1. See Appendix 5.
2. 1976 House Report, p. 167.
3. 1976 House Report, p. 168.
4. *Congressional Record* 122 (daily ed., Sept. 30, 1976): S17253.
5. See sections 16, 17, 21, and 22, 1909 Act.

CHAPTER 11

1. 1976 House Report, p. 66.
2. These are incorporated into the 1976 House Report, p. 65.
3. Cf.. Time Inc. v. Bernard Geis Assoc., 293 F. Supp. 130 (S.D.N.Y. 1968). The text remarks are based on the case just cited only to make a general point. They should not be construed to represent the court's exact holding in the case.
4. See H. C. Wainsright & Co. v. Wall Street Journal Transcript Corp., 418 F. Supp. 620 (S.D.N.Y. 1976), aff'd.558 F.2d 91(2nd Cir. 1977). The text remarks are based on the case just cited only to make a general point. They should not be construed to represent the court's exact holding in the case.
5. 1975 Senate Report, pp. 66–67.
6. 1976 House Report, p. 66.
7. Ibid.
8. 1975 Senate Report, p. 64.
9. 1975 Senate Report, p. 65.
10. 1975 Senate Report, p. 64.
11. Ibid.
12. Ibid.
13. 1975 Senate Report, pp. 65–66.
14. 1976 House Report, pp. 71–72.
15. 1976 Conference Report, p. 70.
16. Congressional Record 122 (daily ed., Sept. 22, 1976): H10875; 1976 Conference Report, p. 70.
17. 1975 Senate Report, p. 67.
18. 1975 Senate Report, p. 65.
19. 1976 House Report, p. 72.
20. Congressional Record 122 (daily ed., Sept. 22, 1976): H10875; 1976 Conference Report, p. 70.
21. Congressional Record 122 (daily ed., Sept. 22, 1976): H10875.
22. Congressional Record 122 (daily ed., Sept. 22, 1976): H10881; 1976 House Report, p. 72.
23. Wihtol v. Crow, 309 F.2d 777 (8th Cir. 1962).
24. Williams & Wilkins Co. v. U.S., 487 F.2d 1345 (Ct. Claims 1973), 420 U.S. 376 (1975).
25. 1975 Senate Report, p. 71.

CHAPTER 12

1. See 1975 Senate Report, p. 64.
2. 1976 House Report, p. 74.
3. 1975 Senate Report, p. 67.
4. 1976 House Report, p. 75.
5. 1976 Conference Report, p. 73.

6. 1976 House Report, p. 75.
7. 1976 House Report, p. 76.
8. 1976 House Report, pp. 75–76.
9. 1975 Senate Report, p. 70.
10. 1976 Conference Report, pp. 71–72.
11. 1976 Conference Report, p. 74.
12. 1976 House Report, p. 75.
13. 1975 Senate Report, p. 70.
14. 1976 Conference Report, p. 72.
15. 1976 House Report, p. 76; 1975 Senate Report, p. 69.
16. 1976 House Report, p. 169.
17. 1976 Conference Report, p. 73.

CHAPTER 13

1. 1976 House Report, p. 82.
2. 1976 House Report, p. 103.
3. 1976 House Report, p. 83.
4. Ibid.
5. 1976 House Report, p. 84.
6. 1976 House Report, p. 85.
7. Ibid.
8. 1976 House Report, p. 84.
9. 1976 House Report, p. 87.

CHAPTER 14

1. 1976 House Report, p. 108.
2. Section 1(e), 1909 Act.
3. See 1976 House Report, p. 115.
4. 1976 House Report, p. 91.

APPENDIX 1
TEXT OF THE COPYRIGHT ACT OF 1976—PUBLIC LAW 94-553

TITLE I—GENERAL REVISION OF COPYRIGHT LAW

SEC. 101. Title 17 of the United States Code, entitled "Copyrights", is hereby amended in its entirety to read as follows:

TITLE 17—COPYRIGHTS

Chapter 1.—SUBJECT MATTER AND SCOPE OF COPYRIGHT

§ 101. Definitions

As used in this title, the following terms and their variant forms mean the following:

An "anonymous work" is a work on the copies or phonorecords of which no natural person is identified as author.

"Audiovisual works" are works that consist of a series of related images which are intrinsically intended to be shown by the use of machines or devices such as projectors, viewers, or electronic equipment, together with accompanying sounds, if any, regardless of the nature of the material objects, such as films or tapes, in which the works are embodied.

The "best edition" of a work is the edition, published in the United States at any time before the date of deposit, that the Library of Congress determines to be most suitable for its purposes.

A person's "children" are that person's immediate offspring, whether legitimate or not, and any children legally adopted by that person.

A "collective work" is a work, such as a periodical issue, anthology, or encyclopedia, in which a number of contributions, constituting separate and independent works in themselves, are assembled into a collective whole.

A "compilation" is a work formed by the collection and assembling of preexisting materials or of data that are selected, coordinated, or arranged in such a way that the resulting work as a whole constitutes an original work of authorship. The term "compilation" includes collective works.

"Copies" are material objects, other than phonorecords, in which a work is fixed by any method now known or later developed, and from which the work can be perceived, reproduced, or otherwise communicated, either directly or with the aid of a machine or device. The term "copies" includes the material object, other than a phonorecord, in which the work is first fixed.

"Copyright owner", with respect to any one of the exclusive rights comprised in a copyright, refers to the owner of that particular right.

A work is "created" when it is fixed in a copy or phonorecord for the first time; where a work is prepared over a period of time, the portion of it that has been fixed at any particular time constitutes the work as of that time, and where the work has been prepared in different versions, each version constitutes a separate work.

A "derivative work" is a work based upon one or more preexisting works, such as a translation, musical arrangement, dramatization, fictionalization, motion picture version, sound recording, art reproduction, abridgment, condensation, or any other form in which a work may be recast, transformed, or adapted. A work consisting of editorial revisions, annotations, elaborations, or other modifications which, as a whole, represent an original work of authorship, is a "derivative work".

A "device", "machine", or "process" is one now known or later developed.

To "display" a work means to show a copy of it, either directly or by means of a film, slide, television image, or any other device or process or, in the case of a motion picture or other audiovisual work, to show individual images nonsequentially.

A work is "fixed" in a tangible medium of expression when its embodiment in a copy or phonorecord, by or under the authority of the author, is sufficiently permanent or stable to permit it to be perceived, reproduced, or otherwise communicated for a period of more than transitory duration. A work consisting of sounds, images, or both, that are being transmitted, is "fixed" for purposes of this title if a fixation of the work is being made simultaneously with its transmission.

The terms "including" and "such as" are illustrative and not limitative.

A "joint work" is a work prepared by two or more authors with the intention that their contributions be merged into inseparable or interdependent parts of a unitary whole.

"Literary works" are works, other than audiovisual works, expressed in words, numbers, or other verbal or numerical symbols or indicia, regardless of the nature of the material objects, such as books, periodicals, manuscripts, phonorecords, film, tapes, disks, or cards, in which they are embodied.

"Motion pictures" are audiovisual works consisting of a series of related images which, when shown in succession, impart an impression of motion, together with accompanying sounds, if any.

To "perform" a work means to recite, render, play, dance, or act it, either directly or by means of any device or process or, in the case of a motion picture or other audiovisual work, to show its images in any sequence or to make the sounds accompanying it audible.

"Phonorecords" are material objects in which sounds, other than those accompanying a motion picture or other audiovisual work, are fixed by any method now known or later developed, and from which the sounds can be perceived, reproduced, or otherwise communicated, either directly or with the aid of a machine or device. The term "phonorecords" includes the material object in which the sounds are first fixed.

"Pictorial, graphic, and sculptural works" include two-dimensional and three-dimensional works of fine, graphic, and applied art, photographs, prints and art reproductions, maps, globes, charts, technical drawings, diagrams, and models. Such works shall include works of artistic craftsmanship insofar as their form but not their mechanical or utilitarian aspects are concerned; the design of a useful article, as defined in this section, shall be considered a pictorial, graphic, or sculptural work only if, and only to the extent that, such design incorporates pictorial, graphic, or sculptural features that can be identified separately from, and are capable of existing independently of, the utilitarian aspects of the article.

A "pseudonymous work" is a work on the copies or phonorecords of which the author is identified under a fictitious name.

"Publication" is the distribution of copies or phonorecords of a work to the public by sale or other transfer of ownership, or by rental, lease, or lending. The offering to distribute copies or phonorecords to a group of persons for purposes of further distribution, public performance, or public display, constitutes publication. A public performance or display of a work does not of itself constitute publication.

To perform or display a work "publicly" means—

(1) to perform or display it at a place open to the public or at any place where a substantial number of persons outside of a normal circle of a family and its social acquaintances is gathered; or

(2) to transmit or otherwise communicate a performance or display of the work to a place specified by clause (1) or to the public, by means of any device or processs, whether the members of the public capable of receiving the performance or display receive it in the same place or in separate places and at the same time or at different times.

"Sound recordings" are works that result from the fixation of a series of musical, spoken, or other sounds, but not including the sounds accompanying a motion picture or other audiovisual work, regardless of the nature of the material objects, such as disks, tapes, or other phonorecords, in which they are embodied.

"State" includes the District of Columbia and the Commonwealth of Puerto Rico, and any territories to which this title is made applicable by an Act of Congress.

A "transfer of copyright ownership" is an assignment, mortgage, exclusive license, or any other conveyance, alienation, or hypothecation of a copyright or of any of the exclusive rights comprised in a copyright, whether or not it is limited in time or place of effect, but not including a nonexclusive license.

A "transmission program" is a body of material that, as an aggregate, has been produced for the sole purpose of transmission to the public in sequence and as a unit.

To "transmit" a performance or display is to communicate it by any device or process whereby images or sounds are received beyond the place from which they are sent.

The "United States", when used in a geographical sense, comprises the several States, the District of Columbia and the Commonwealth of Puerto Rico, and the organized territories under the jurisdiction of the United States Government.

A "useful article" is an article having an intrinsic utilitarian function that is not merely to portray the appearance of the article or to convey information. An article that is normally a part of a useful article is considered a "useful article".

The author's "widow" or "widower" is the author's surviving spouse under the law of the author's domicile at the time of his or her death, whether or not the spouse has later remarried.

A "work of the United States Government" is a work prepared by an officer or employee of the United States Government as part of that person's official duties.

A "work made for hire" is—

(1) a work prepared by an employee within the scope of his or her employment; or

(2) a work specially ordered or commissioned for use as a contribution to a collective work, as a part of a motion picture or other audiovisual work, as a translation, as a supplementary work, as a compilation, as an instructional text, as a test, as answer material for a test, or as an atlas, if the parties expressly agree in a written instrument signed by them that the work shall be considered a work made for hire. For the purpose of the foregoing sentence, a "supplementary work" is a work prepared for publication as a secondary adjunct to a work by another author for the purpose of introducing, concluding, illustrating, explaining, revising, commenting upon, or assisting in the use of the other work, such as forewords, afterwords, pictorial illustrations, maps, charts, tables, editorial notes, musical arrangements, answer material for tests, bibliographies, appendixes, and indexes, and an "instructional text" is a literary, pictorial, or graphic work prepared for publication and with the purpose of use in systematic instructional activities.

§ 102. Subject matter of copyright: In general

(a) Copyright protection subsists, in accordance with this title, in original works of authorship fixed in any tangible medium of expression, now known or later developed, from which they can be perceived, reproduced, or otherwise communicated, either directly or with the aid of a machine or device. Works of authorship include the following categories:

(1) literary works;
(2) musical works, including any accompanying words;
(3) dramatic works, including any accompanying music;
(4) pantomimes and choreographic works;
(5) pictorial, graphic, and sculptural works;
(6) motion pictures and other audiovisual works; and
(7) sound recordings.

(b) In no case does copyright protection for an original work of authorship extend to any idea, procedure, process, system, method of operation, concept, principle, or discovery, regardless of the form in which it is described, explained, illustrated, or embodied in such work.

§ 103. Subject matter of copyright: Compilations and derivative works

(a) The subject matter of copyright as specified by section 102 includes compilations and derivative works, but protection for a work employing preexisting material in which copyright subsists does not extend to any part of the work in which such material has been used unlawfully.

(b) The copyright in a compilation or derivative work extends only to the material contributed by the author of such work, as distinguished from the preexisting material employed in the work, and does not imply any exclusive right in the preexisting material. The copyright in such work is independent of, and does not affect or enlarge the scope, duration, ownership, or subsistence of, any copyright protection in the preexisting material.

§ 104. Subject matter of copyright: National origin

(a) UNPUBLISHED WORKS.—The works specified by sections 102 and 103, while unpublished, are subject to protection under this title without regard to the nationality or domicile of the author.

(b) PUBLISHED WORKS.—The works specified by sections 102 and 103, when published, are subject to protection under this title if—

(1) on the date of first publication, one or more of the authors is a national or domiciliary of the United States, or is a national, domiciliary, or sovereign authority of a foreign nation that is a party to a copyright treaty to which the United States is also a party, or is a stateless person, wherever that person may be domiciled; or

(2) the work is first published in the United States or in a foreign nation that, on the date of first publication, is a party to the Universal Copyright Convention; or

(3) the work is first published by the United Nations or any of its specialized agencies, or by the Organization of American States; or

(4) the work comes within the scope of a Presidential proclamation. Whenever the President finds that a particular foreign nation extends, to works by authors who are nationals or domiciliaries of the United States or to works that are first published in the United States, copyright protection on substantially the same basis as that on which the foreign nation extends protection to works of its own nationals and domiciliaries and works first published in that nation, the President may by proclamation extend protection under this title to works of which one or more

of the authors is, on the date of first publication, a national, domiciliary, or sovereign authority of that nation, or which was first published in that nation. The President may revise, suspend, or revoke any such proclamation or impose any conditions or limitations on protection under a proclamation.

§ 105. Subject matter of copyright: United States Government works

Copyright protection under this title is not available for any work of the United States Government, but the United States Government is not precluded from receiving and holding copyrights transferred to it by assignment, bequest, or otherwise.

§ 106. Exclusive rights in copyrighted works

Subject to sections 107 through 118, the owner of copyright under this title has the exclusive rights to do and to authorize any of the following:

(1) to reproduce the copyrighted work in copies or phonorecords;

(2) to prepare derivative works based upon the copyrighted work;

(3) to distribute copies or phonorecords of the copyrighted work to the public by sale or other transfer of ownership, or by rental, lease, or lending;

(4) in the case of literary, musical, dramatic, and choreographic works, pantomimes, and motion pictures and other audiovisual works, to perform the copyrighted work publicly; and

(5) in the case of literary, musical, dramatic, and choreographic works, pantomimes, and pictorial, graphic, or sculptural works, including the individual images of a motion picture or other audiovisual work, to display the copyrighted work publicly.

§ 107. Limitations on exclusive rights: Fair use

Notwithstanding the provisions of section 106, the fair use of a copyrighted work, including such use by reproduction in copies or phonorecords or by any other means specified by that section, for purposes such as criticism, comment, news reporting, teaching (including multiple copies for classroom use), scholarship, or research, is not an infringement of copyright. In determining whether the use made of a work in any particular case is a fair use the factors to be considered shall include—

(1) the purpose and character of the use, including whether such use is of a commercial nature or is for nonprofit educational purposes;

(2) the nature of the copyrighted work;

(3) the amount and substantiality of the portion used in relation to the copyrighted work as a whole; and

(4) the effect of the use upon the potential market for or value of the copyrighted work.

§ 108. Limitations on exclusive rights: Reproduction by libraries and archives

(a) Notwithstanding the provisions of section 106, it is not an infringement of copyright for a library or archives, or any of its employees acting within the scope of their employment, to reproduce no more than one copy or phonorecord of a work, or to distribute such copy or phonorecord, under the conditions specified by this section, if—

(1) the reproduction or distribution is made without any purpose of direct or indirect commercial advantage;

(2) the collections of the library or archives are (i) open to the public, or (ii) available not only to researchers affiliated with the library or archives or with the institution of which it is a part, but also to other persons doing research in a specialized field; and

(3) the reproduction or distribution of the work includes a notice of copyright.

(b) The rights of reproduction and distribution under this section apply to a copy or phonorecord of an unpublished work duplicated in facsimile form solely for purposes of preservation and security or for deposit for research use in another library or archives of the type described by clause (2) of subsection (a), if the copy or phonorecord reproduced is currently in the collections of the library or archives.

(c) The right of reproduction under this section applies to a copy or phonorecord of a published work duplicated in facsimile form solely for the purpose of replacement of a copy or phonorecord that is damaged, deteriorating, lost, or stolen, if the library or archives has, after a reasonable effort, determined that an unused replacement cannot be obtained at a fair price.

(d) The rights of reproduction and distribution under this section apply to a copy, made from the collection of a library or archives where the user makes his or her request or from that of another library or archives, of no more than one article or other contribution to a copyrighted collection or periodical issue, or to a copy or phonorecord of a small part of any other copyrighted work, if—

(1) the copy or phonorecord becomes the property of the user, and the library or archives has had no notice that the copy or phonorecord would be used for any purpose other than private study, scholarship, or research; and

(2) the library or archives displays prominently, at the place where orders are accepted, and includes on its order form, a warning of copyright in accordance with requirements that the Register of Copyrights shall prescribe by regulation.

(e) The rights of reproduction and distribution under this section apply to the entire work, or to a substantial part of it, made from the collection of a library or archives where the user makes his or her request or from that of another library or archives, if the library or archives has first determined, on the basis of a reasonable investigation, that a copy or phonorecord of the copyrighted work cannot be obtained at a pair price, if—

(1) the copy or phonorecord becomes the property of the user, and the library or archives has had no notice that the copy or phonorecord would be used for any purpose other than private study, scholarship, or research; and

(2) the library or archives displays prominently, at the place where orders are accepted, and includes on its order form, a warning of copyright in accordance with requirements that the Register of Copyrights shall prescribe by regulation.

(f) Nothing in this section—

(1) shall be construed to impose liability for copyright infringement upon a library or archives or its employees for the unsupervised use of reproducing equipment located on its premises: *Provided*, That such equipment displays a notice that the making of a copy may be subject to the copyright law;

(2) excuses a person who uses such reproducing equipment or who requests a copy or phonorecord under subsection (d) from liability for copyright infringement for any such act, or for any later use of such copy or phonorecord, if it exceeds fair use as provided by section 107;

(3) shall be construed to limit the reproduction and distribution by lending of a limited number of copies and excerpts by a library or archives of an audiovisual news program, subject to clauses (1), (2), and (3) of subsection (a) ; or

(4) in any way affects the right of fair use as provided by section 107, or any contractual obligations assumed at any time by the library or archives when it obtained a copy or phonorecord of a work in its collections.

(g) The rights of reproduction and distribution under this section extend to the isolated and unrelated reproduction or distribution of a single copy or phonorecord of the same material on separate occasions, but do not extend to cases where the library or archives, or its employee—

(1) is aware or has substantial reason to believe that it is engaging in the related or concerted reproduction or distribution of multiple copies or phonorecords of the same material, whether made on one occasion or over a period of time, and whether intended for aggregate use by one or more individuals or for separate use by the individual members of a group; or

(2) engages in the systematic reproduction or distribution of single or multiple copies or phonorecords of material described in subsection (d) : *Provided,* That nothing in this clause prevents a library or archives from participating in interlibrary arrangements that do not have, as their purpose or effect, that the library or archives receiving such copies or phonorecords for distribution does so in such aggregate quantities as to substitute for a subscription to or purchase of such work.

(h) The rights of reproduction and distribution under this section do not apply to a musical work, a pictorial, graphic or sculptural work, or a motion picture or other audiovisual work other than an audiovisual work dealing with news, except that no such limitation shall apply with respect to rights granted by subsections (b) and(c), or with respect to pictorial or graphic works published as illustrations, diagrams, or similar adjuncts to works of which copies are reproduced or distributed in accordance with subsections (d) and (e).

(i) Five years from the effective date of this Act, and at five-year intervals thereafter, the Register of Copyrights, after consulting with representatives of authors, book and periodical publishers, and other owners of copyrighted materials, and with representatives of library users and librarians, shall submit to the Congress a report setting forth the extent to which this section has achieved the intended statutory balancing of the rights of creators, and the needs of users. The report should also describe any problems that may have arisen, and present legislative or other recommendations, if warranted.

§ 109. Limitations on exclusive rights: Effect of transfer of particular copy or phonorecord

(a) Notwithstanding the provisions of section 106(3), the owner of a particular copy or phonorecord lawfully made under this title, or any person authorized by such owner, is entitled, without the authority of the copyright owner, to sell or otherwise dispose of the possession of that copy or phonorecord.

(b) Notwithstanding the provisions of section 106(5), the owner of a particular copy lawfully made under this title, or any person authorized by such owner, is entitled, without the authority of the copyright owner, to display that copy publicly, either directly or by the projection of no more than one image at a time, to viewers present at the place where the copy is located.

(c) The privileges prescribed by subsections (a) and (b) do not, unless authorized by the coyright owner, extend to any person who has acquired possession of the copy or phonorecord from the copyright owner, by rental, lease, loan, or otherwise, without acquiring ownership of it.

§ 110. Limitations on exclusive rights: Exemption of certain performances and displays

Notwithstanding the provisions of section 106, the following are not infringements of copyright:

(1) performance or display of a work by instructors or pupils in the course of face-to-face teaching activities of a nonprofit educational institution, in a classroom or similar place devoted to instruction, unless, in the case of a motion picture or other audio-visual work, the performance, or the display of individual images, is given by means of a copy that was not lawfully made under this title, and that the person responsible for the performance knew or had reason to believe was not lawfully made;

(2) performance of a nondramatic literary or musical work or display of a work, by or in the course of a transmission, if—

(A) the performance or display is a regular part of the systematic instructional activities of a governmental body or a nonprofit educational institution; and

(B) the performance or display is directly related and of material assistance to the teaching content of the transmission; and

(C) the transmission is made primarily for—

(i) reception in classrooms or similar places normally devoted to instruction, or

(ii) reception by persons to whom the transmission is directed because their disabilities or other special circumstances prevent their attendance in classrooms or similar places normally devoted to instruction, or

(iii) reception by officers or employees of governmental bodies as a part of their official duties or employment;

(3) performance of a nondramatic literary or musical work or of a dramatico-musical work of a religious nature, or display of a work, in the course of services at a place of worship or other religious assembly;

(4) performance of a nondramatic literary or musical work otherwise than in a transmission to the public, without any purpose of direct or indirect commercial advantage and without payment of any fee or other compensation for the performance to any of its performers, promoters, or organizers, if—

(A) there is no direct or indirect admission charge; or

(B) the proceeds, after deducting the reasonable costs of producing the performance, are used exclusively for educational, religious, or charitable purposes and not for private financial gain, except where the copyright owner has served notice of objection to the performance under the following conditions;

(i) the notice shall be in writing and signed by the copyright owner or such owner's duly authorized agent; and

(ii) the notice shall be served on the person responsible for the performance at least seven days before the date of the performance, and shall state the reasons for the objection; and

(iii) the notice shall comply, in form, content, and manner of service, with requirements that the Register of Copyrights shall prescribe by regulation;

(5) communication of a transmission embodying a performance or display of a work by the public reception of the transmission on a single receiving apparatus of a kind commonly used in private homes, unless—

(A) a direct charge is made to see or hear the transmission; or

(B) the transmission thus received is further transmitted to the public;

(6) performance of a nondramatic musical work by a governmental body or a nonprofit agricultural or horticultural organization, in the course of an annual agricultural or horticultural fair or exhibition conducted by such body or organization; the exemption provided by this clause shall extend to any liability for copyright infringement that would otherwise be imposed on such body or organization, under doctrines of vicarious liability or related infringement, for a performance by a concessionnaire, business establishment, or other person at such fair or exhibition, but shall not excuse any such person from liability for the performance;

(7) performance of a nondramatic musical work by a vending establishment open to the public at large without any direct or indirect admission charge, where the sole purpose of the performance is to promote the retail sale of copies or phonorecords of the work, and the performance is not transmitted beyond the place where the establishment is located and is within the immediate area where the sale is occurring;

(8) performance of a nondramatic literary work, by or in the course of a transmission specifically designed for and primarily directed to blind or other handicapped persons who are unable to read normal printed material as a result of their handicap, or deaf or other handicapped persons who are unable to hear the aural signals accompanying a transmission of visual signals, if the performance is made without any purpose of direct or indirect commercial advantage and its transmission is made through the facilities of: (i) a governmental body; or (ii) a noncommercial educational broadcast station (as defined in section 397 of title 47); or (iii) a radio subcarrier authorization (as defined in 47 CFR 73.293–73.295 and 73.593–73.595); or (iv) a cable system (as defined in section 111(f)).

(9) performance on a single occasion of a dramatic literary work published at least ten years before the date of the performance, by or in the course of a transmission specifically designed for and primarily directed to blind or other handicapped persons who are unable to read normal printed material as a result of their handicap, if the performance is made without any purpose of direct or indirect commercial advantage and its transmission is made through the facilities of a radio subcarrier authorization referred to in clause (8)(iii), *Provided*, That the provisions of this clause shall not be applicable to more than one performance of the same work by the same performers or under the auspices of the same organization.

§ 111. Limitations on exclusive rights: Secondary transmissions

(a) CERTAIN SECONDARY TRANSMISSIONS EXEMPTED.—The secondary transmission of a primary transmission embodying a performance or display of a work is not an infringement of copyright if—

(1) the secondary transmission is not made by a cable system, and consists entirely of the relaying, by the management of a hotel, apartment house, or similar establishment, of signals transmitted by a broadcast station licensed by the Federal Communications Commission, within the local service area of such station, to the private lodgings of guests or residents of such establishment, and no direct charge is made to see or hear the secondary transmission; or

(2) the secondary transmission is made solely for the purpose and under the conditions specified by clause (2) of section 110; or

(3) the secondary transmission is made by any carrier who has no direct or indirect control over the content or selection of the primary transmission or over the particular recipients of the secondary transmission, and whose activities with respect to the secondary transmission consist solely of providing wires, cables, or other communications channels for the use of others: *Provided*, That the provisions of this clause extend only to the activities of said carrier with respect to secondary transmissions and do not exempt from liability the activities of others with respect to their own primary or secondary transmissions; or

(4) the secondary transmission is not made by a cable system but is made by a governmental body, or other nonprofit organization, without any purpose of direct or indirect commercial advantage, and without charge to the recipients of the secondary transmission other than assessments necessary to defray the actual and reasonable costs of maintaining and operating the secondary transmission service.

(b) SECONDARY TRANSMISSION OF PRIMARY TRANSMISSION TO CONTROLLED GROUP.—Notwithstanding the provisions of subsections (a) and (c), the secondary transmission to the public of a primary transmission embodying a performance or display of a work is actionable as an act of infringement under section 501, and is fully subject to the remedies provided by sections 502 through 506 and 509, if the primary transmission is not made for reception by the public at large but is controlled and limited to reception by particular members of the public: *Provided*, however, That such secondary transmission is not actionable as an act of infringement if—

(1) the primary transmission is made by a broadcast station licensed by the Federal Communications Commission; and

(2) the carriage of the signals comprising the secondary transmission is required under the rules, regulations, or authorizations of the Federal Communications Commission; and

(3) the signal of the primary transmitter is not altered or changed in any way by the secondary transmitter.

(c) SECONDARY TRANSMISSIONS BY CABLE SYSTEMS.—

(1) Subject to the provisions of clauses (2), (3), and (4) of this subsection, secondary transmissions to the public by a cable system of a primary transmission made by a broadcast station licensed by the Federal Communications Commission or by an appropriate governmental authority of Canada or Mexico and embodying a performance or display of a work shall be subject to compulsory licensing upon compliance with the requirements of subsection (d) where the carriage of the signals comprising the secondary transmission is permissible under the rules, regulations, or authorizations of the Federal Communications Commission.

(2) Notwithstanding the provisions of clause (1) of this subsection, the willful or repeated secondary transmission to the public by a cable system of a primary transmission made by a

broadcast station licensed by the Federal Communications Commission or by an appropriate governmental authority of Canada or Mexico and embodying a performance or display of a work is actionable as an act of infringement under section 501, and is fully subject to the remedies provided by sections 502 through 506 and 509, in the following cases:

    (A) where the carriage of the signals comprising the secondary transmission is not permissible under the rules, regulations, or authorizations of the Federal Communications Commission; or

    (B) where the cable system has not recorded the notice specified by subsection (d) and deposited the statement of account and royalty fee required by subsection (d).

(3) Notwithstanding the provisions of clause (1) of this subsection and subject to the provisions of subsection (e) of this section, the secondary transmission to the public by a cable system of a primary transmission made by a broadcast station licensed by the Federal Communications Commission or by an appropriate governmental authority of Canada or Mexico and embodying a performance or display of a work is actionable as an act of infringement under section 501, and is fully subject to the remedies provided by sections 502 through 506 and sections 509 and 510, if the content of the particular program in which the performance or display is embodied, or any commercial advertising or station announcements transmitted by the primary transmitter during, or immediately before or after, the transmission of such program, is in any way willfully altered by the cable system through changes, deletions, or additions, except for the alteration, deletion, or substitution of commercial advertisements performed by those engaged in television commercial advertising market research: *Provided*, That the research company has obtained the prior consent of the advertiser who has purchased the original commercial advertisement, the television station broadcasting that commercial advertisement, and the cable system performing the secondary transmission: *And provided further*, That such commercial alteration, deletion, or substitution is not performed for the purpose of deriving income from the sale of that commercial time.

(4) Notwithstanding the provisions of clause (1) of this subsection, the secondary transmission to the public by a cable system of a primary transmission made by a broadcast station licensed by an appropriate governmental authority of Canada or Mexico and embodying a performance or display of a work is actionable as an act of infringement under section 501, and is fully subject to the remedies provided by sections 502 through 506 and section 509, if (A) with respect to Canadian signals, the community of the cable system is located more than 150 miles from the United States-Canadian border and is also located south of the forty-second parallel of latitude, or (B) with respect to Mexican signals, the secondary transmission is made by a cable system which received the primary transmission by means other than direct interception of a free space radio wave emitted by such broadcast television station, unless prior to April 15, 1976, such cable system was actually carrying, or was specifically authorized to carry, the signal of such foreign station on the system pursuant to the rules, regulations, or authorizations of the Federal Communications Commission.

(d) COMPULSORY LICENSE FOR SECONDARY TRANSMISSIONS BY CABLE SYSTEMS.—

(1) For any secondary transmission to be subject to compulsory licensing under subsection (c), the cable system shall, at least one month before the date of the commencement of operations of the cable system or within one hundred and eighty days after the enactment of this Act, whichever is later, and thereafter within thirty days after each occasion on which the ownership or control or the signal carriage complement of the cable system changes, record in the Copyright Office a notice including a statement of the identity and address of the person who owns or operates the secondary transmission service or has power to exercise primary control over it, together with the name and location of the primary transmitter or primary transmitters whose signals are regularly carried by the cable system, and thereafter, from time to time, such further information as the Register of Copyrights, after consultation with the Copyright Royalty Tribunal (if and when the Tribunal has been constituted), shall prescribe by regulation to carry out the purpose of this clause.

(2) A cable system whose secondary transmissions have been subject to compulsory licensing under subsection (c) shall, on a semiannual basis, deposit with the Register of Copyrights, in accordance with requirements that the Register shall, after consultation with the Copyright Royalty Tribunal (if and when the Tribunal has been constituted), prescribe by regulation—

(A) a statement of account, covering the six months next preceding, specifying the number of channels on which the cable system made secondary transmissions to its subscribers, the names and locations of all primary transmitters whose transmissions were further transmitted by the cable system, the total number of subscribers, the gross amounts paid to the cable system for the basic service of providing secondary transmissions of primary broadcast transmitters, and such other data as the Register of Copyrights may, after consultation with the Copyright Royalty Tribunal (if and when the Tribunal has been constituted), from time to time prescribe by regulation. Such statement shall also include a special statement of account covering any nonnetwork television programming that was carried by the cable system in whole or in part beyond the local service area of the primary transmitter, under rules, regulations, or authorizations of the Federal Communications Commission permitting the substitution or addition of signals under certain circumstances, together with logs showing the times, dates, stations, and programs involved in such substituted or added carriage; and

(B) except in the case of a cable system whose royalty is specified in subclause (C) or (D), a total royalty fee for the period covered by the statement, computed on the basis of specified percentages of the gross receipts from subscribers to the cable service during said period for the basic service of providing secondary transmissions of primary broadcast transmitters, as follows:

(i) 0.675 of 1 per centum of such gross receipts for the privilege of further transmitting any nonnetwork programing of a primary transmitter in whole or in part beyond the local service area of such primary transmitter, such amount to be applied against the fee, if any, payable pursuant to paragraphs (ii) through (iv);

(ii) 0.675 of 1 per centum of such gross receipts for the first distant signal equivalent;

(iii) 0.425 of 1 per centum of such gross receipts for each of the second, third, and fourth distant signal equivalents;

(iv) 0.2 of 1 per centum of such gross receipts for the fifth distant signal equivalent and each additional distant signal equivalent thereafter; and

in computing the amounts payable under paragraph (ii) through (iv), above, any fraction of a distant signal equivalent shall be computed at its fractional value and, in the case of any cable system located partly within and partly without the local service area of a primary transmitter, gross receipts shall be limited to those gross receipts derived from subscribers located without the local service area of such primary transmitter; and

(C) if the actual gross receipts paid by subscribers to a cable system for the period covered by the statement for the basic service of providing secondary transmissions of primary broadcast transmitters total $80,000 or less, gross receipts of the cable system for the purpose of this subclause shall be computed by subtracting from such actual gross receipts the amount by which $80,000 exceeds such actual gross receipts, except that in no case shall a cable system's gross receipts be reduced to less than $3,000. The royalty fee payable under this subclause shall be 0.5 of 1 per centum, regardless of the number of distant signal equivalents, if any; and

(D) if the actual gross receipts paid by subscribers to a cable system for the period covered by the statement, for the basic service of providing secondary transmissions of primary broadcast transmitters, are more than $80,000 but less than $160,000, the royalty fee payable under this subclause shall be (i) 0.5 of 1 per centum of any gross receipts up to $80,000; and (ii) 1 per centum of any gross receipts in excess of $80,000 but less than $160,000, regardless of the number of distant signal equivalents, if any.

(3) The Register of Copyrights shall receive all fees deposited under this section and, after deducting the reasonable costs incurred by the Copyright Office under this section, shall deposit the balance in the Treasury of the United States, in such manner as the Secretary of the Treasury directs. All funds held by the Secretary of the Treasury shall be invested in interest-bearing United States securities for later distribution with interest by the Copyright Royalty Tribunal as provided by this title. The Register shall submit to the Copyright Royalty Tribunal, on a semiannual basis, a compilation of all statements of account covering the relevant six-month period provided by clause (2) of this subsection.

(4) The royalty fees thus deposited shall, in accordance with the procedures provided by clause (5), be distributed to those among the following copyright owners who claim that their works were the subject of secondary transmissions by cable systems during the relevant semiannual period:

(A) any such owner whose work was included in a secondary transmission made by a cable system of a nonnetwork television program in whole or in part beyond the local service area of the primary transmitter; and

(B) any such owner whose work was included in a secondary transmission identified in a special statement of account deposited under clause (2)(A); and

(C) any such owner whose work was included in nonnetwork programing consisting exclusively of aural signals carried by a cable system in whole or in part beyond the local service area of the primary transmitter of such programs.

(5) The royalty fees thus deposited shall be distributed in accordance with the following procedures:

(A) During the month of July in each year, every person claiming to be entitled to compulsory license fees for secondary transmissions shall file a claim with the Copyright Royalty Tribunal, in accordance with requirements that the Tribunal shall prescribe by regulation. Notwithstanding any provisions of the antitrust laws, for purposes of this clause any claimants may agree among themselves as to the proportionate division of compulsory licensing fees among them, may lump their claims together and file them jointly or as a single claim, or may designate a common agent to receive payment on their behalf.

(B) After the first day of August of each year, the Copyright Royalty Tribunal shall determine whether there exists a controversy concerning the distribution of royalty fees. If the Tribunal determines that no such controversy exists, it shall, after deducting its reasonable administrative costs under this section, distribute such fees to the copyright owners entitled, or to their designated agents. If the Tribunal finds the existence of a controversy, it shall, pursuant to chapter 8 of this title, conduct a proceeding to determine the distribution of royalty fees.

(C) During the pendency of any proceeding under this subsection, the Copyright Royalty Tribunal shall withhold from distribution an amount sufficient to satisfy all claims with respect to which a controversy exists, but shall have discretion to proceed to distribute any amounts that are not in controversy.

(e) NONSIMULTANEOUS SECONDARY TRANSMISSIONS BY CABLE SYSTEMS.—

(1) Notwithstanding those provisions of the second paragraph of subsection (f) relating to nonsimultaneous secondary transmissions by a cable system, any such transmissions are actionable as an act of infringement under section 501, and are fully subject to the remedies provided by sections 502 through 506 and sections 509 and 510, unless—

(A) the program on the videotape is transmitted no more than one time to the cable system's subscribers; and

(B) the copyrighted program, episode, or motion picture videotape, including the commercials contained within such program, episode, or picture, is transmitted without deletion or editing; and

(C) an owner or officer of the cable system (i) prevents the duplication of the videotape while in the possession of the system, (ii) prevents unauthorized duplication while in the possession of the facility making the videotape for the system if the system owns or controls the facility, or takes reasonable precautions to prevent such duplication if it does not own or control the facility, (iii) takes adequate precautions to prevent duplication while the tape is being transported, and (iv) subject to clause (2), erases or destroys, or causes the erasure or destruction of, the videotape; and

(D) within forty-five days after the end of each calendar quarter, an owner or officer of the cable system executes an affidavit attesting (i) to the steps and precautions taken to prevent duplication of the videotape, and (ii) subject to clause (2), to the erasure or destruction of all videotapes made or used during such quarter; and

(E) such owner or officer places or causes each such affidavit, and affidavits received pursuant to clause (2)(C), to be placed in a file, open to public inspection, at such system's main office in the community where the transmission is made or in the nearest community where such system maintains an office; and

(F) the nonsimultaneous transmission is one that the cable system would be authorized to transmit under the rules, regulations, and authorizations of the Federal Communications Commission in effect at the time of the nonsimultaneous transmission if the transmission had been made simultaneously, except that this subclause shall not apply to inadvertent or accidental transmissions.

(2) If a cable system transfers to any person a videotape of a program nonsimultaneously transmitted by it, such transfer is actionable as an act of infringement under section 501, and is fully subject to the remedies provided by sections 502 through 506 and 509, except that, pursuant to a written, nonprofit contract providing for the equitable sharing of the costs of such videotape and its transfer, a videotape nonsimultaneously transmitted by it, in accordance with clause (1), may be transferred by one cable system in Alaska to another system in Alaska, by one cable system in Hawaii permitted to make such nonsimultaneous transmissions to another such cable system in Hawaii, or by one cable system in Guam, the Northern Mariana Islands, or the Trust Territory of the Pacific Islands, to another cable system in any of those three territories, if—

(A) each such contract is available for public inspection in the offices of the cable systems involved, and a copy of such contract is filed, within thirty days after such contract is entered into, with the Copyright Office (which Office shall make each such contract available for public inspection); and

(B) the cable system to which the videotape is transferred complies with clause (1)(A), (B), (C)(i), (iii), and (iv), and (D) through (F); and

(C) such system provides a copy of the affidavit required to be made in accordance with clause (1)(D) to each cable system making a previous nonsimultaneous transmission of the same videotape.

(3) This subsection shall not be construed to supersede the exclusivity protection provisions of any existing agreement, or any such agreement hereafter entered into, between a cable system and a television broadcast station in the area in which the cable system is located, or a network with which such station is affiliated.

(4) As used in this subsection, the term "videotape", and each of its variant forms, means the reproduction of the images and

sounds of a program or programs broadcast by a television broadcast station licensed by the Federal Communications Commission, regardless of the nature of the material objects, such as tapes or films, in which the reproduction is embodied.

(f) DEFINITIONS.—As used in this section, the following terms and their variant forms mean the following:

A "primary transmission" is a transmission made to the public by the transmitting facility whose signals are being received and further transmitted by the secondary transmission service, regardless of where or when the performance or display was first transmitted.

A "secondary transmission" is the further transmitting of a primary transmission simultaneously with the primary transmission, or nonsimultaneously with the primary transmission if by a "cable system" not located in whole or in part within the boundary of the forty-eight contiguous States, Hawaii, or Puerto Rico: *Provided, however*, That a nonsimultaneous further transmission by a cable system located in Hawaii of a primary transmission shall be deemed to be a secondary transmission if the carriage of the television broadcast signal comprising such further transmission is permissible under the rules, regulations, or authorizations of the Federal Communications Commission.

A "cable system" is a facility, located in any State, Territory, Trust Territory, or Possession, that in whole or in part receives signals transmitted or programs broadcast by one or more television broadcast stations licensed by the Federal Communications Commission, and makes secondary transmissions of such signals or programs by wires, cables, or other communications channels to subscribing members of the public who pay for such service. For purposes of determining the royalty fee under subsection (d)(2), two or more cable systems in contiguous communities under common ownership or control or operating from one head-end shall be considered as one system.

The "local service area of a primary transmitter", in the case of a television broadcast station, comprises the area in which such station is entitled to insist upon its signal being retransmitted by a cable system pursuant to the rules, regulations, and authorizations of the Federal Communications Commission in effect on April 15, 1976, or in the case of a television broadcast station licensed by an appropriate governmental authority of Canada or Mexico, the area in which it would be entitled to insist upon its signal being retransmitted if it were a television broadcast station subject to such rules, regulations, and authorizations. The "local service area of a primary transmitter", in the case of a radio broadcast station, comprises the primary service area of such station, pursuant to the rules and regulations of the Federal Communications Commission.

A "distant signal equivalent" is the value assigned to the secondary transmission of any nonnetwork television programing carried by a cable system in whole or in part beyond the local service area of the primary transmitter of such programing. It is computed by assigning a value of one to each independent station and a value of one-quarter to each network station and noncommercial educational station for the nonnetwork programing so carried pursuant to the rules, regulations, and authorizations of the Federal Communications Commission. The foregoing values for independent, network, and noncommercial educational stations are subject, however, to the following exceptions and limitations. Where the rules and regulations of the Federal Communications Commission require a cable system to omit the further transmission of a particular program and such rules and regulations also permit the substitution of another program embodying a performance or display of a work in place of the omitted transmission, or where such rules and regulations in effect on the date of enactment of this Act permit a cable system, at its election, to effect such deletion and substitution of a nonlive program or to carry additional programs not transmitted by primary transmitters within whose local service area the cable system is located, no value shall be assigned for the substituted or additional program; where the rules, regulations, or authorizations of the Federal Communications Commission in effect on the date of enactment of this Act permit a cable system, at its election, to omit the further transmission of a particular program and such rules, regulations, or authorizations also permit the substitution of another program embodying a performance or display of a work in place of the omitted transmission, the value assigned for the substituted or additional program shall be, in the case of a live program, the value of one full distant signal equivalent multiplied by a fraction that has as its numerator the number of days in the year in which such substitution occurs and as its denominator the number of days in the year. In the case of a station carried pursuant to the late-night or specialty programing rules of the Federal Communications Commission, or a station carried on a part-time basis where full-time carriage is not possible because the cable system lacks the activated channel capacity to retransmit on a full-time basis all signals which it is authorized to carry, the values for independent, network, and noncommercial educational stations set forth above, as the case may be, shall be multiplied by a fraction which is equal to the ratio of the broadcast hours of such station carried by the cable system to the total broadcast hours of the station.

A "network station" is a television broadcast station that is owned or operated by, or affiliated with, one or more of the television networks in the United States providing nationwide transmissons, and that transmits a substantial part of the programing supplied by such networks for a substantial part of that station's typical broadcast day.

An "independent station" is a commercial television broadcast station other than a network station.

A "noncommercial educational station" is a television station that is a noncommercial educational broadcast station as defined in section 397 of title 47.

§ 112. Limitations on exclusive rights: Ephemeral recordings

(a) Notwithstanding the provisions of section 106, and except in the case of a motion picture or other audiovisual work, it is not an infringement of copyright for a transmitting organization entitled to transmit to the public a performance or display of a work, under a license or transfer of the copyright or under the limitations on exclusive rights in sound recordings specified by section 114(a), to make no more than one copy or phonorecord of a particular transmission program embodying the performance or display, if—

(1) the copy or phonorecord is retained and used solely by the transmitting organization that made it, and no further copies or phonorecords are reproduced from it; and

(2) the copy or phonorecord is used solely for the transmitting organization's own transmissions within its local service area, or for purposes of archival preservation or security; and

(3) unless preserved exclusively for archival purposes, the copy or phonorecord is destroyed within six months from the date the transmission program was first transmitted to the public.

(b) Notwithstanding the provisions of section 106, it is not an infringement of copyright for a governmental body or other nonprofit organization entitled to transmit a performance or display of a work, under section 110(2) or under the limitations on exclusive rights in sound recordings specified by section 114(a), to make no more than thirty copies or phonorecords of a particular transmission program embodying the performance or display, if—

(1) no further copies or phonorecords are reproduced from the copies or phonorecords made under this clause; and

(2) except for one copy or phonorecord that may be preserved exclusively for archival purposes, the copies or phonorecords are destroyed within seven years from the date the transmission program was first transmitted to the public.

(c) Notwithstanding the provisions of section 106, it is not an infringement of copyright for a governmental body or other nonprofit organization to make for distribution no more than one copy or phonorecord, for each transmitting organization specified in clause (2) of this subsection, of a particular transmission program embodying a performance of a nondramatic musical work of a religious nature, or of a sound recording of such a musical work, if—

(1) there is no direct or indirect charge for making or distributing any such copies or phonorecords; and

(2) none of such copies or phonorecords is used for any performance other than a single transmission to the public by a transmitting organization entitled to transmit to the public a performance of the work under a license or transfer of the copyright; and

(3) except for one copy or phonorecord that may be preserved exclusively for archival purposes, the copies or phonorecords are all destroyed within one year from the date the transmission program was first transmitted to the public.

(d) Notwithstanding the provisions of section 106, it is not an infringement of copyright for a governmental body or other nonprofit organization entitled to transmit a performance of a work under section 110(8) to make no more than ten copies or phonorecords embodying the performance, or to permit the use of any such copy or phonorecord by any governmental body or nonprofit organization entitled to transmit a performance of a work under section 110(8), if—

(1) any such copy or phonorecord is retained and used solely by the organization that made it, or by a governmental body or nonprofit organization entitled to transmit a performance of a work under section 110(8), and no further copies or phonorecords are reproduced from it; and

(2) any such copy or phonorecord is used solely for transmissions authorized under section 110(8), or for purposes of archival preservation or security; and

(3) the governmental body or nonprofit organization permitting any use of any such copy or phonorecord by any governmental body or nonprofit organization under this subsection does not make any charge for such use.

(e) The transmission program embodied in a copy or phonorecord made under this section is not subject to protection as a derivative work under this title except with the express consent of the owners of copyright in the preexisting works employed in the program.

§ 113. Scope of exclusive rights in pictorial, graphic, and sculptural works

(a) Subject to the provisions of subsections (b) and (c) of this section, the exclusive right to reproduce a copyrighted pictorial, graphic, or sculptural work in copies under section 106 includes the right to reproduce the work in or on any kind of article, whether useful or otherwise.

(b) This title does not afford, to the owner of copyright in a work that portrays a useful article as such, any greater or lesser rights with respect to the making, distribution, or display of the useful article so portrayed than those afforded to such works under the law, whether title 17 or the common law or statutes of a State, in effect on December 31, 1977, as held applicable and construed by a court in an action brought under this title.

(c) In the case of a work lawfully reproduced in useful articles that have been offered for sale or other distribution to the public, copyright does not include any right to prevent the making, distribution, or display of pictures or photographs of such articles in connection with advertisements or commentaries related to the distribution or display of such articles, or in connection with news reports.

§ 114. Scope of exclusive rights in sound recordings

(a) The exclusive rights of the owner of copyright in a sound recording are limited to the rights specified by clauses (1), (2), and (3) of section 106, and do not include any right of performance under section 106(4).

(b) The exclusive right of the owner of copyright in a sound recording under clause (1) of section 106 is limited to the right to duplicate the sound recording in the form of phonorecords, or of copies of motion pictures and other audiovisual works, that directly or indirectly recapture the actual sounds fixed in the recording. The exclusive right of the owner of copyright in a sound recording under clause (2) of section 106 is limited to the right to prepare a derivative work in which the actual sounds fixed in the sound recording are rearranged, remixed, or otherwise altered in sequence or quality. The exclusive rights of the owner of copyright in a sound recording under clauses (1) and (2) of section 106 do not extend to the making or duplication of another sound recording that consists entirely of an independent fixation of other sounds, even though such sounds imitate or simulate those in the copyrighted sound recording. The exclusive rights of the owner of copyright in a sound recording under clauses (1), (2), and (3) of section 106 do not apply to sound recordings included in educational television and radio programs (as defined in section 397 of title 47) distributed or transmitted by or through public broadcasting entities (as defined by section 118(g)) : *Provided*, That copies or phonorecords of said programs are not commercially distributed by or through public broadcasting entities to the general public.

(c) This section does not limit or impair the exclusive right to perform publicly, by means of a phonorecord, any of the works specified by section 106(4).

(d) On January 3, 1978, the Register of Copyrights, after consulting with representatives of owners of copyrighted materials, representatives of the broadcasting, recording, motion picture, entertainment industries, and arts organizations, representatives of organized labor and performers of copyrighted materials, shall submit to the Congress a report setting forth recommendations as to whether this section should be amended to provide for performers and copyright owners of copyrighted material any performance rights in such material. The report should describe the status of such rights in foreign countries, the views of major interested parties, and specific legislative or other recommendations, if any.

§ 115. Scope of exclusive rights in nondramatic musical works: Compulsory license for making and distributing phonorecords

In the case of nondramatic musical works, the exclusive rights provided by clauses (1) and (3) of section 106, to make and to distribute phonorecords of such works, are subject to compulsory licensing under the conditions specified by this section.

(a) AVAILABILITY AND SCOPE OF COMPULSORY LICENSE.—

(1) When phonorecords of a nondramatic musical work have been distributed to the public in the United States under the authority of the copyright owner, any other person may, by complying with the provisions of this section, obtain a compulsory license to make and distribute phonorecords of the work. A person may obtain a compulsory license only if his or her primary purpose in making phonorecords is to distribute them to the public for private use. A person may not obtain a compulsory license for use of the work in the making of phonorecords duplicating a sound recording fixed by another, unless: (i) such sound recording was fixed lawfully; and (ii) the making of the phonorecords was authorized by the owner of copyright in the sound recording or, if the sound recording was fixed before February 15, 1972, by any person who fixed the sound recording pursuant to an express license from the owner of the copyright in the musical work or pursuant to a valid compulsory license for use of such work in a sound recording.

(2) A compulsory license includes the privilege of making a musical arrangement of the work to the extent necessary to conform it to the style or manner of interpretation of the performance involved, but the arrangement shall not change the basic melody or fundamental character of the work, and shall not be subject to protection as a derivative work under this title, except with the express consent of the copyright owner.

(b) NOTICE OF INTENTION TO OBTAIN COMPULSORY LICENSE.—

(1) Any person who wishes to obtain a compulsory license under this section shall, before or within thirty days after making, and before distributing any phonorecords of the work, serve notice of intention to do so on the copyright owner. If the registration or other public records of the Copyright Office do not identify the copyright owner and include an address at which notice can be served, it shall be sufficient to file the notice of intention in the Copyright Office. The notice shall comply, in form, content, and manner of service, with requirements that the Register of Copyrights shall prescribe by regulation.

(2) Failure to serve or file the notice required by clause (1) forecloses the possibility of a compulsory license and, in the absence of a negotiated license, renders the making and distribution of phonorecords actionable as acts of infringement under section 501 and fully subject to the remedies provided by sections 502 through 506 and 509.

(c) ROYALTY PAYABLE UNDER COMPULSORY LICENSE.—

(1) To be entitled to receive royalties under a compulsory license, the copyright owner must be identified in the registration or other public records of the Copyright Office. The owner is entitled to royalties for phonorecords made and distributed after

being so identified, but is not entitled to recover for any phono-records previously made and distributed.

(2) Except as provided by clause (1), the royalty under a compulsory license shall be payable for every phonorecord made and distributed in accordance with the license. For this purpose, a phonorecord is considered "distributed" if the person exercising the compulsory license has voluntarily and permanently parted with its possession. With respect to each work embodied in the phonorecord, the royalty shall be either two and three-fourths cents, or one-half of one cent per minute of playing time or fraction thereof, whichever amount is larger.

(3) Royalty payments shall be made on or before the twentieth day of each month and shall include all royalties for the month next preceding. Each monthly payment shall be made under oath and shall comply with requirements that the Register of Copyrights shall prescribe by regulation. The Register shall also prescribe regulations under which detailed cumulative annual statements of account, certified by a certified public accountant, shall be filed for every compulsory license under this section. The regulations covering both the monthly and the annual statements of account shall prescribe the form, content, and manner of certification with respect to the number of records made and the number of records distributed.

(4) If the copyright owner does not receive the monthly payment and the monthly and annual statements of account when due, the owner may give written notice to the licensee that, unless the default is remedied within thirty days from the date of the notice, the compulsory license will be automatically terminated. Such termination renders either the making or the distribution, or both, of all phonorecords for which the royalty has not been paid, actionable as acts of infringement under section 501 and fully subject to the remedies provided by sections 502 through 506 and 509.

§ 116. Scope of exclusive rights in nondramatic musical works: Public performances by means of coin-operated phonorecord players

(a) LIMITATION ON EXCLUSIVE RIGHT.—In the case of a nondramatic musical work embodied in a phonorecord, the exclusive right under clause (4) of section 106 to perform the work publicly by means of a coin-operated phonorecord player is limited as follows:

(1) The proprietor of the establishment in which the public performance takes place is not liable for infringement with respect to such public performance unless—

(A) such proprietor is the operator of the phonorecord player; or

(B) such proprietor refuses or fails, within one month after receipt by registered or certified mail of a request, at a time during which the certificate required by clause (1)(C) of subsection (b) is not affixed to the phonorecord player, by the copyright owner, to make full disclosure, by registered or certified mail, of the identity of the operator of the phonorecord player.

(2) The operator of the coin-operated phonorecord player may obtain a compulsory license to perform the work publicly on that phonorecord player by filing the application, affixing the certificate, and paying the royalties provided by subsection (b).

(b) RECORDATION OF COIN-OPERATED PHONORECORD PLAYER, AFFIXATION OF CERTIFICATE, AND ROYALTY PAYABLE UNDER COMPULSORY LICENSE.—

(1) Any operator who wishes to obtain a compulsory license for the public performance of works on a coin-operated phonorecord player shall fulfill the following requirements:

(A) Before or within one month after such performances are made available on a particular phonorecord player, and during the month of January in each succeeding year that such performances are made available on that particular phonorecord player, the operator shall file in the Copyright Office, in accordance with requirements that the Register of Copyrights, after consultation with the Copyright Royalty Tribunal (if and when the Tribunal has been constituted), shall prescribe by regulation, an application containing the name and address of the operator of the phonorecord player and the manufacturer and serial number or other explicit identification of the phonorecord player, and deposit with the Register of Copyrights a royalty fee for the current calendar year of $8 for that particular phonorecord player. If such performances are made available on a particular phonorecord player for the first time after July 1 of any year, the royalty fee to be deposited for the remainder of that year shall be $4.

(B) Within twenty days of receipt of an application and a royalty fee pursuant to subclause (A), the Register of Copyrights shall issue to the applicant a certificate for the phonorecord player.

(C) On or before March 1 of the year in which the certificate prescribed by subclause (B) of this clause is issued, or within ten days after the date of issue of the certificate, the operator shall affix to the particular phonorecord player, in a position where it can be readily examined by the public, the certificate, issued by the Register of Copyrights under subclause (B), of the latest application made by such operator under subclause (A) of this clause with respect to that phonorecord player.

(2) Failure to file the application, to affix the certificate, or to pay the royalty required by clause (1) of this subsection renders the public performance actionable as an act of infringement under section 501 and fully subject to the remedies provided by sections 502 through 506 and 509.

(c) DISTRIBUTION OF ROYALTIES.—

(1) The Register of Copyrights shall receive all fees deposited under this section and, after deducting the reasonable costs incurred by the Copyright Office under this section, shall deposit the balance in the Treasury of the United States, in such manner as the Secretary of the Treasury directs. All funds held by the Secretary of the Treasury shall be invested in interest-bearing United States securities for later distribution with interest by the Copyright Royalty Tribunal as provided by this title. The Register shall submit to the Copyright Royalty Tribunal, on an annual basis, a detailed statement of account covering all fees received for the relevant period provided by subsection (b).

(2) During the month of January in each year, every person claiming to be entitled to compulsory license fees under this section for performances during the preceding twelve-month period shall file a claim with the Copyright Royalty Tribunal, in accordance with requirements that the Tribunal shall prescribe by regulation. Such claim shall include an agreement to accept as final,

except as provided in section 810 of this title, the determination of the Copyright Royalty Tribunal in any controversy concerning the distribution of royalty fees deposited under subclause (A) of subsection (b)(1) of this section to which the claimant is a party. Notwithstanding any provisions of the antitrust laws, for purposes of this subsection any claimants may agree among themselves as to the proportionate division of compulsory licensing fees among them, may lump their claims together and file them jointly or as a single claim, or may designate a common agent to receive payment on their behalf.

(3) After the first day of October of each year, the Copyright Royalty Tribunal shall determine whether there exists a controversy concerning the distribution of royalty fees deposited under subclause (A) of subsection (b)(1). If the Tribunal determines that no such controversy exists, it shall, after deducting its reasonable administrative costs under this section, distribute such fees to the copyright owners entitled, or to their designated agents. If it finds that such a controversy exists, it shall, pursuant to chapter 8 of this title, conduct a proceeding to determine the distribution of royalty fees.

(4) The fees to be distributed shall be divided as follows:

(A) to every copyright owner not affiliated with a performing rights society, the pro rata share of the fees to be distributed to which such copyright owner proves entitlement.

(B) to the performing rights societies, the remainder of the fees to be distributed in such pro rata shares as they shall by agreement stipulate among themselves, or, if they fail to agree, the pro rata share to which such performing rights societies prove entitlement.

(C) during the pendency of any proceeding under this section, the Copyright Royalty Tribunal shall withhold from distribution an amount sufficient to satisfy all claims with respect to which a controversy exists, but shall have discretion to proceed to distribute any amounts that are not in controversy.

(5) The Copyright Royalty Tribunal shall promulgate regulations under which persons who can reasonably be expected to have claims may, during the year in which performances take place, without expense to or harassment of operators or proprietors of establishments in which phonorecord players are located, have such access to such establishments and to the phonorecord players located therein and such opportunity to obtain information with respect thereto as may be reasonably necessary to determine, by sampling procedures or otherwise, the proportion of contribution of the musical works of each such person to the earnings of the phonorecord players for which fees shall have been deposited. Any person who alleges that he or she has been denied the access permitted under the regulations prescribed by the Copyright Royalty Tribunal may bring an action in the United States District Court for the District of Columbia for the cancellation of the compulsory license of the phonorecord player to which such access has been denied, and the court shall have the power to declare the compulsory license thereof invalid from the date of issue thereof.

(d) CRIMINAL PENALTIES.—Any person who knowingly makes a false representation of a material fact in an application filed under clause (1)(A) of subsection (b), or who knowingly alters a certificate issued under clause (1)(B) of subsection (b) or knowingly affixes such a certificate to a phonorecord player other than the one it covers, shall be fined not more than $2,500.

(e) DEFINITIONS.—As used in this section, the following terms and their variant forms mean the following:

(1) A "coin-operated phonorecord player" is a machine or device that—

(A) is employed solely for the performance of non-dramatic musical works by means of phonorecords upon being activated by insertion of coins, currency, tokens, or other monetary units or their equivalent;

(B) is located in an establishment making no direct or indirect charge for admission;

(C) is accompanied by a list of the titles of all the musical works available for performance on it, which list is affixed to the phonorecord player or posted in the establishment in a prominent position where it can be readily examined by the public; and

(D) affords a choice of works available for performance and permits the choice to be made by the patrons of the establishment in which it is located.

(2) An "operator" is any person who, alone or jointly with others:

(A) owns a coin-operated phonorecord player; or

(B) has the power to make a coin-operated phonorecord player available for placement in an establishment for purposes of public performance; or

(C) has the power to exercise primary control over the selection of the musical works made available for public performance on a coin-operated phonorecord player.

(3) A "performing rights society" is an association or corporation that licenses the public performance of nondramatic musical works on behalf of the copyright owners, such as the American Society of Composers, Authors and Publishers, Broadcast Music, Inc., and SESAC, Inc.

§ 117. Scope of exclusive rights: Use in conjunction with computers and similar information systems

Notwithstanding the provisions of sections 106 through 116 and 118, this title does not afford to the owner of copyright in a work any greater or lesser rights with respect to the use of the work in conjunction with automatic systems capable of storing, processing, retrieving, or transferring information, or in conjunction with any similar device, machine, or process, than those afforded to works under the law, whether title 17 or the common law or statutes of a State, in effect on December 31, 1977, as held applicable and construed by a court in an action brought under this title.

§ 118. Scope of exclusive rights: Use of certain works in connection with noncommercial broadcasting

(a) The exclusive rights provided by section 106 shall, with respect to the works specified by subsection (b) and the activities specified by subsection (d), be subject to the conditions and limitations prescribed by this section.

(b) Not later than thirty days after the Copyright Royalty Tribunal has been constituted in accordance with section 802, the Chairman of the Tribunal shall cause notice to be published in the Federal Register of the initiation of proceedings for the purpose of determining reasonable terms and rates of royalty payments for the activities specified by subsection (d) with respect to published nondramatic musical works and published pictorial, graphic, and sculptural works during a period beginning as provided in clause (3) of this subsection and ending on December 31, 1982. Copyright owners and public broadcasting entities shall negotiate in good faith and cooperate fully with the Tribunal in an effort to reach reasonable and expeditious results. Notwithstanding any provision of the antitrust laws, any owners of copyright in works specified by this subsection and any public broadcasting entities, respectively, may negotiate and agree upon the terms and rates of royalty payments and the proportionate division of fees paid among various copyright owners, and may designate common agents to negotiate, agree to, pay, or receive payments.

(1) Any owner of copyright in a work specified in this subsection or any public broadcasting entity may, within one hundred and twenty days after publication of the notice specified in this subsection, submit to the Copyright Royalty Tribunal proposed licenses covering such activities with respect to such works. The Copyright Royalty Tribunal shall proceed on the basis of the proposals submitted to it as well as any other relevant information. The Copyright Royalty Tribunal shall permit any interested party to submit information relevant to such proceedings.

(2) License agreements voluntarily negotiated at any time between one or more copyright owners and one or more public broadcasting entities shall be given effect in lieu of any determination by the Tribunal: *Provided,* That copies of such agreements are filed in the Copyright Office within thirty days of execution in accordance with regulations that the Register of Copyrights shall prescribe.

(3) Within six months, but not earlier than one hundred and twenty days, from the date of publication of the notice specified in this subsection the Copyright Royalty Tribunal shall make a determination and publish in the Federal Register a schedule of rates and terms which, subject to clause (2) of this subsection, shall be binding on all owners of copyright in works specified by this subsection and public broadcasting entities, regardless of whether or not such copyright owners and public broadcasting entities have submitted proposals to the Tribunal. In establishing such rates and terms the Copyright Royalty Tribunal may consider the rates for comparable circumstances under voluntary license agreements negotiated as provided in clause (2) of this subsection. The Copyright Royalty Tribunal shall also establish requirements by which copyright owners may receive reasonable notice of the use of their works under this section, and under which records of such use shall be kept by public broadcasting entities.

(4) With respect to the period beginning on the effective date of this title and ending on the date of publication of such rates and terms, this title shall not afford to owners of copyright or public broadcasting entities any greater or lesser rights with respect to the activities specified in subsection (d) as applied to works specified in this subsection than those afforded under the law in effect on December 31, 1977, as held applicable and construed by a court in an action brought under this title.

(c) The initial procedure specified in subsection (b) shall be repeated and concluded between June 30 and December 31, 1982, and at five-year intervals thereafter, in accordance with regulations that the Copyright Royalty Tribunal shall prescribe.

(d) Subject to the transitional provisions of subsection (b) (4), and to the terms of any voluntary license agreements that have been negotiated as provided by subsection (b) (2), a public broadcasting entity may, upon compliance with the provisions of this section, including the rates and terms established by the Copyright Royalty Tribunal under subsection (b) (3), engage in the following activities with respect to published nondramatic musical works and published pictorial, graphic, and sculptural works:

(1) performance or display of a work by or in the course of a transmission made by a noncommercial educational broadcast station referred to in subsection (g); and

(2) production of a transmission program, reproduction of copies or phonorecords of such a transmission program, and distribution of such copies or phonorecords, where such production, reproduction, or distribution is made by a nonprofit institution or organization solely for the purpose of transmissions specified in clause (1); and

(3) the making of reproductions by a governmental body or a nonprofit institution of a transmission program simultaneously with its transmission as specified in clause (1), and the performance or display of the contents of such program under the conditions specified by clause (1) of section 110, but only if the reproductions are used for performances or displays for a period of no more than seven days from the date of the transmission specified in clause (1), and are destroyed before or at the end of such period. No person supplying, in accordance with clause (2), a reproduction of a transmission program to governmental bodies or nonprofit institutions under this clause shall have any liability as a result of failure of such body or institution to destroy such reproduction: *Provided*, That it shall have notified such body or institution of the requirement for such destruction pursuant to this clause: *And provided further*, That if such body or institution itself fails to destroy such reproduction it shall be deemed to have infringed.

(e) Except as expressly provided in this subsection, this section shall have no applicability to works other than those specified in subsection (b).

(1) Owners of copyright in nondramatic literary works and public broadcasting entities may, during the course of voluntary negotiations, agree among themselves, respectively, as to the terms and rates of royalty payments without liability under the antitrust laws. Any such terms and rates of royalty payments shall be effective upon filing in the Copyright Office, in accordance with regulations that the Register of Copyrights shall prescribe.

(2) On January 3, 1980, the Register of Copyrights, after consulting with authors and other owners of copyright in nondramatic literary works and their representatives, and with public broadcasting entities and their representatives, shall submit to the Congress a report setting forth the extent to which voluntary licensing arrangements have been reached with respect to the use of nondramatic literary works by such broadcast stations. The report should also describe any problems that may have arisen, and present legislative or other recommendations, if warranted.

(f) Nothing in this section shall be construed to permit, beyond the limits of fair use as provided by section 107, the unauthorized dramatization of a nondramatic musical work, the production of a transmission program drawn to any substantial extent from a published compilation of pictorial, graphic, or sculptural works, or the unauthorized use of any portion of an audiovisual work.

(g) As used in this section, the term "public broadcasting entity" means a noncommercial educational broadcast station as defined in section 397 of title 47 and any nonprofit institution or organization engaged in the activities described in clause (2) of subsection (d).

Chapter 2.—COPYRIGHT OWNERSHIP AND TRANSFER

Sec.

§ 201. Ownership of copyright

(a) INITIAL OWNERSHIP.—Copyright in a work protected under this title vests initially in the author or authors of the work. The authors of a joint work are coowners of copyright in the work.

(b) WORKS MADE FOR HIRE.—In the case of a work made for hire, the employer or other person for whom the work was prepared is considered the author for purposes of this title, and, unless the parties have expressly agreed otherwise in a written instrument signed by them, owns all of the rights comprised in the copyright.

(c) CONTRIBUTIONS TO COLLECTIVE WORKS.—Copyright in each separate contribution to a collective work is distinct from copyright in the collective work as a whole, and vests initially in the author of the contribution. In the absence of an express transfer of the copyright or of any rights under it, the owner of copyright in the collective work is presumed to have acquired only the privilege of reproducing and distributing the contribution as part of that particular collective work, any revision of that collective work, and any later collective work in the same series.

(d) TRANSFER OF OWNERSHIP.—

(1) The ownership of a copyright may be transferred in whole or in part by any means of conveyance or by operation of law, and may be bequeathed by will or pass as personal property by the applicable laws of intestate succession.

(2) Any of the exclusive rights comprised in a copyright, including any subdivision of any of the rights specified by section 106, may be transferred as provided by clause (1) and owned separately. The owner of any particular exclusive right is entitled, to the extent of that right, to all of the protection and remedies accorded to the copyright owner by this title.

(e) INVOLUNTARY TRANSFER.—When an individual author's ownership of a copyright, or of any of the exclusive rights under a copyright, has not previously been transferred voluntarily by that individual author, no action by any governmental body or other official or organization purporting to seize, expropriate, transfer, or exercise rights of ownership with respect to the copyright, or any of the exclusive rights under a copyright, shall be given effect under this title.

§ 202. Ownership of copyright as distinct from ownership of material object

Ownership of a copyright, or of any of the exclusive rights under a copyright, is distinct from ownership of any material object in which the work is embodied. Transfer of ownership of any material object, including the copy or phonorecord in which the work is first fixed, does not of itself convey any rights in the copyrighted work embodied in the object; nor, in the absence of an agreement, does transfer of ownership of a copyright or of any exclusive rights under a copyright convey property rights in any material object.

§ 203. Termination of transfers and licenses granted by the author

(a) CONDITIONS FOR TERMINATION.—In the case of any work other than a work made for hire, the exclusive or nonexclusive grant of a transfer or license of copyright or of any right under a copyright, executed by the author on or after January 1, 1978, otherwise than by will, is subject to termination under the following conditions:

(1) In the case of a grant executed by one author, termination of the grant may be effected by that author or, if the author is dead, by the person or persons who, under clause (2) of this subsection, own and are entitled to exercise a total of more than one-half of that author's termination interest. In the case of a grant executed by two or more authors of a joint work, termination of the grant may be effected by a majority of the authors who executed it; if any of such authors is dead, the termination interest of any such author may be exercised as a unit by the person or persons who, under clause (2) of this subsection, own and are entitled to exercise a total of more than one-half of that author's interest.

(2) Where an author is dead, his or her termination interest is owned, and may be exercised, by his widow or her widower and his or her children or grandchildren as follows:

(A) the widow or widower owns the author's entire termination interest unless there are any surviving children or grandchildren of the author, in which case the widow or widower owns one-half of the author's interest;

(B) the author's surviving children, and the surviving children of any dead child of the author, own the author's entire termination interest unless there is a widow or widower, in which case the ownership of one-half of the author's interest is divided among them;

(C) the rights of the author's children and grandchildren are in all cases divided among them and exercised on a per stirpes basis according to the number of such author's children represented; the share of the children of a dead child in a termination interest can be exercised only by the action of a majority of them.

(3) Termination of the grant may be effected at any time during a period of five years beginning at the end of thirty-five years from the date of execution of the grant; or, if the grant covers the right of publication of the work, the period begins at the end of thirty-five years from the date of publication of the work under the grant or at the end of forty years from the date of execution of the grant, whichever term ends earlier.

(4) The termination shall be effected by serving an advance notice in writing, signed by the number and proportion of owners of termination interests required under clauses (1) and (2) of this subsection, or by their duly authorized agents, upon the grantee or the grantee's successor in title.

(A) The notice shall state the effective date of the termination, which shall fall within the five-year period specified by clause (3) of this subsection, and the notice shall be served not less than two or more than ten years before that date. A copy of the notice shall be recorded in the Copyright Office before the effective date of termination, as a condition to its taking effect.

(B) The notice shall comply, in form, content, and manner of service, with requirements that the Register of Copyrights shall prescribe by regulation.

(5) Termination of the grant may be effected notwithstanding any agreement to the contrary, including an agreement to make a will or to make any future grant.

(b) EFFECT OF TERMINATION.—Upon the effective date of termination, all rights under this title that were covered by the terminated grants revert to the author, authors, and other persons owning termination interests under clauses (1) and (2) of subsection (a), including those owners who did not join in signing the notice of termination under clause (4) of subsection (a), but with the following limitations:

(1) A derivative work prepared under authority of the grant before its termination may continue to be utilized under the terms of the grant after its termination, but this privilege does not extend to the preparation after the termination of other derivative works based upon the copyrighted work covered by the terminated grant.

(2) The future rights that will revert upon termination of the grant become vested on the date the notice of termination has been served as provided by clause (4) of subsection (a). The rights vest in the author, authors, and other persons named in, and in the proportionate shares provided by, clauses (1) and (2) of subsection (a).

(3) Subject to the provisions of clause (4) of this subsection, a further grant, or agreement to make a further grant, of any right covered by a terminated grant is valid only if it is signed by the same number and proportion of the owners, in whom the right has vested under clause (2) of this subsection, as are required to terminate the grant under clauses (1) and (2) of subsection (a). Such further grant or agreement is effective with respect to all of the persons in whom the right it covers has vested under clause (2) of this subsection, including those who did not join in signing it. If any person dies after rights under a terminated grant have vested in him or her, that person's legal representatives, legatees, or heirs at law represent him or her for purposes of this clause.

(4) A further grant, or agreement to make a further grant, of any right covered by a terminated grant is valid only if it is made after the effective date of the termination. As an exception, however, an agreement for such a further grant may be made between the persons provided by clause (3) of this subsection and the original grantee or such grantee's successor in title, after the notice of termination has been served as provided by clause (4) of subsection (a).

(5) Termination of a grant under this section affects only those rights covered by the grants that arise under this title, and in no way affects rights arising under any other Federal, State, or foreign laws.

(6) Unless and until termination is effected under this section, the grant, if it does not provide otherwise, continues in effect for the term of copyright provided by this title.

§ 204. Execution of transfers of copyright ownership

(a) A transfer of copyright ownership, other than by operation of law, is not valid unless an instrument of conveyance, or a note or memorandum of the transfer, is in writing and signed by the owner of the rights conveyed or such owner's duly authorized agent.

(b) A certificate of acknowledgement is not required for the validity of a transfer, but is prima facie evidence of the execution of the transfer if—

(1) in the case of a transfer executed in the United States, the certificate is issued by a person authorized to administer oaths within the United States; or

(2) in the case of a transfer executed in a foreign country, the certificate is issued by a diplomatic or consular officer of the United States, or by a person authorized to administer oaths whose authority is proved by a certificate of such an officer.

§ 205. Recordation of transfers and other documents

(a) CONDITIONS FOR RECORDATION.—Any transfer of copyright ownership or other document pertaining to a copyright may be recorded in the Copyright Office if the document filed for recordation bears the actual signature of the person who executed it, or if it is accompanied by a sworn or official certification that it is a true copy of the original, signed document.

(b) CERTIFICATE OF RECORDATION.—The Register of Copyrights shall, upon receipt of a document as provided by subsection (a) and of the fee provided by section 708, record the document and return it with a certificate of recordation.

(c) RECORDATION AS CONSTRUCTIVE NOTICE.—Recordation of a document in the Copyright Office gives all persons constructive notice of the facts stated in the recorded document, but only if—

(1) the document, or material attached to it, specifically identifies the work to which it pertains so that, after the document is indexed by the Register of Copyrights, it would be revealed by a reasonable search under the title or registration number of the work; and

(2) registration has been made for the work.

(d) RECORDATION AS PREREQUISITE TO INFRINGEMENT SUIT.—No person claiming by virtue of a transfer to be the owner of copyright or of any exclusive right under a copyright is entitled to institute an infringement action under this title until the instrument of transfer under which such person claims has been recorded in the Copyright Office, but suit may be instituted after such recordation on a cause of action that arose before recordation.

(e) PRIORITY BETWEEN CONFLICTING TRANSFERS.—As between two conflicting transfers, the one executed first prevails if it is recorded, in the manner required to give constructive notice under subsection (c), within one month after its execution in the United States or within two months after its execution outside the United States, or at any time before recordation in such manner of the later transfer. Otherwise the later transfer prevails if recorded first in such manner, and if taken in good faith, for valuable consideration or on the basis of a binding promise to pay royalties, and without notice of the earlier transfer.

(f) PRIORITY BETWEEN CONFLICTING TRANSFER OF OWNERSHIP AND NONEXCLUSIVE LICENSE.—A nonexclusive license, whether recorded or not, prevails over a conflicting transfer of copyright ownership if the license is evidenced by a written instrument signed by the owner of the rights licensed or such owner's duly authorized agent, and if—

(1) the license was taken before execution of the transfer; or

(2) the license was taken in good faith before recordation of the transfer and without notice of it.

Chapter 3.—DURATION OF COPYRIGHT

Sec.
301. Preemption with respect to other laws.
302. Duration of copyright: Works created on or after January 1, 1978.
303. Duration of copyright: Works created but not published or copyrighted before January 1, 1978.
304. Duration of copyright: Subsisting copyrights.
305. Duration of copyright: Terminal date.

§ 301. Preemption with respect to other laws

(a) On and after January 1, 1978, all legal or equitable rights that are equivalent to any of the exclusive rights within the general scope of copyright as specified by section 106 in works of authorship that are fixed in a tangible medium of expression and come within the subject matter of copyright as specified by sections 102 and 103, whether created before or after that date and whether published or unpublished, are governed exclusively by this title. Thereafter, no person is entitled to any such right or equivalent right in any such work under the common law or statutes of any State.

(b) Nothing in this title annuls or limits any rights or remedies under the common law or statutes of any State with respect to—

(1) subject matter that does not come within the subject matter of copyright as specified by sections 102 and 103, including works of authorship not fixed in any tangible medium of expression; or

(2) any cause of action arising from undertakings commenced before January 1, 1978; or

(3) activities violating legal or equitable rights that are not equivalent to any of the exclusive rights within the general scope of copyright as specified by section 106.

(c) With respect to sound recordings fixed before February 15, 1972, any rights or remedies under the common law or statutes of any State shall not be annulled or limited by this title until February 15, 2047. The preemptive provisions of subsection (a) shall apply to any such rights and remedies pertaining to any cause of action arising from undertakings commenced on and after February 15, 2047. Notwithstanding the provisions of section 303, no sound recording fixed before February 15, 1972, shall be subject to copyright under this title before, on, or after February 15, 2047.

(d) Nothing in this title annuls or limits any rights or remedies under any other Federal statute.

§ 302. Duration of copyright: Works created on or after January 1, 1978

(a) IN GENERAL.—Copyright in a work created on or after January 1, 1978, subsists from its creation and, except as provided by the following subsections, endures for a term consisting of the life of the author and fifty years after the author's death.

(b) JOINT WORKS.—In the case of a joint work prepared by two or more authors who did not work for hire, the copyright endures for a term consisting of the life of the last surviving author and fifty years after such last surviving author's death.

(c) ANONYMOUS WORKS, PSEUDONYMOUS WORKS, AND WORKS MADE FOR HIRE.—In the case of an anonymous work, a pseudonymous work, or a work made for hire, the copyright endures for a term of seventy-five years from the year of its first publication, or a term of one hundred years from the year of its creation, whichever expires first. If, before the end of such term, the identity of one or more of the authors of an anonymous or pseudonymous work is revealed in the records of a registration made for that work under subsections (a) or (d) of section 408, or in the records provided by this subsection, the copyright in the work endures for the term specified by subsection (a) or (b), based on the life of the author or authors whose identity has been revealed. Any person having an interest in the copyright in an anonymous or pseudonymous work may at any time record, in records to be maintained by the Copyright Office for that purpose, a statement identifying one or more authors of the work; the statement shall also identify the person filing it, the nature of that person's interest, the source of the information recorded, and the particular work affected, and shall comply in form and content with requirements that the Register of Copyrights shall prescribe by regulation.

(d) RECORDS RELATING TO DEATH OF AUTHORS.—Any person having an interest in a copyright may at any time record in the Copyright Office a statement of the date of death of the author of the copyrighted work, or a statement that the author is still living on a particular date. The statement shall identify the person filing it, the nature of that person's interest, and the source of the information recorded, and shall comply in form and content with requirements that the Register of Copyrights shall prescribe by regulation. The Register shall maintain current records of information relating to the death of authors of copyrighted works, based on such recorded statements and, to the extent the Register considers practicable, on data contained in any of the records of the Copyright Office or in other reference sources.

(e) PRESUMPTION AS TO AUTHOR'S DEATH.—After a period of seventy-five years from the year of first publication of a work, or a period of one hundred years from the year of its creation, whichever expires first, any person who obtains from the Copyright Office a certified report that the records provided by subsection (d) disclose nothing to indicate that the author of the work is living, or died less than fifty years before, is entitled to the benefit of a presumption that the author has been dead for at least fifty years. Reliance in good faith upon this presumption shall be a complete defense to any action for infringement under this title.

§ 303. Duration of copyright: Works created but not published or copyrighted before January 1, 1978

Copyright in a work created before January 1, 1978, but not theretofore in the public domain or copyrighted, subsists from January 1, 1978, and endures for the term provided by section 302. In no case, however, shall the term of copyright in such a work expire before December 31, 2002; and, if the work is published on or before December 31, 2002, the term of copyright shall not expire before December 31, 2027.

§ 304. Duration of copyright: Subsisting copyrights

(a) COPYRIGHTS IN THEIR FIRST TERM ON JANUARY 1, 1978.—Any copyright, the first term of which is subsisting on January 1, 1978, shall endure for twenty-eight years from the date it was originally secured: *Provided*, That in the case of any posthumous work or of any periodical, cyclopedic, or other composite work upon which the copyright was originally secured by the proprietor thereof, or of any work copyrighted by a corporate body (otherwise than as assignee or licensee of the individual author) or by an employer for whom such work is made for hire, the proprietor of such copyright shall be entitled to a renewal and extension of the copyright in such work for the further term of forty-seven years when application for such renewal and extension shall have been made to the Copyright Office and duly registered therein within one year prior to the expiration of the original term of copyright: *And provided further*, That in the case of any other copyrighted work, including a contribution by an individual author to a periodical or to a cyclopedic or other composite work, the author of such work, if still living, or the widow, widower, or children of the author, if the author be not living, or if such author, widow, widower, or children be not living, then the author's executors, or in the absence of a will, his or her next of kin shall be entitled to a renewal and extension of the copyright in such work for a further term of forty-seven years when application for such renewal and extension shall have been made to the Copyright Office and duly registered therein within one year prior to the expiration of the original term of copyright: *And provided further*, That in default of the registration of such application for renewal and extension, the copyright in any work shall terminate at the expiration of twenty-eight years from the date copyright was originally secured.

(b) COPYRIGHTS IN THEIR RENEWAL TERM OR REGISTERED FOR RENEWAL BEFORE JANUARY 1, 1978.—The duration of any copyright, the renewal term of which is subsisting at any time between December 31, 1976, and December 31, 1977, inclusive, or for which renewal registration is made between December 31, 1976, and December 31, 1977, inclusive, is extended to endure for a term of seventy-five years from the date copyright was originally secured.

(c) TERMINATION OF TRANSFERS AND LICENSES COVERING EXTENDED RENEWAL TERM.—In the case of any copyright subsisting in either its first or renewal term on January 1, 1978, other than a copyright in a work made for hire, the exclusive or nonexclusive grant of a transfer or license of the renewal copyright or any right under it, executed before January 1, 1978, by any of the persons designated by the second proviso of subsection (a) of this section, otherwise than by will, is subject to termination under the following conditions:

(1) In the case of a grant executed by a person or persons other than the author, termination of the grant may be effected by the surviving person or persons who executed it. In the case of a grant executed by one or more of the authors of the work, termination of the grant may be effected, to the extent of a particular author's share in the ownership of the renewal copyright, by the author who executed it or, if such author is dead, by the person or persons who, under clause (2) of this subsection, own and are entitled to exercise a total of more than one-half of that author's termination interest.

(2) Where an author is dead, his or her termination interest is owned, and may be exercised, by his widow or her widower and his or her children or grandchildren as follows:

(A) the widow or widower owns the author's entire termination interest unless there are any surviving children or grandchildren of the author, in which case the widow or widower owns one-half of the author's interest;

(B) the author's surviving children, and the surviving children of any dead child of the author, own the author's entire termination interest unless there is a widow or widower, in which case the ownership of one-half of the author's interest is divided among them;

(C) the rights of the author's children and grandchildren are in all cases divided among them and exercised on a per stirpes basis according to the number of such author's children represented; the share of the children of a dead child in a termination interest can be exercised only by the action of a majority of them.

(3) Termination of the grant may be effected at any time during a period of five years beginning at the end of fifty-six years from the date copyright was originally secured, or beginning on January 1, 1978, whichever is later.

(4) The termination shall be effected by serving an advance notice in writing upon the grantee or the grantee's successor in title. In the case of a grant executed by a person or persons other than the author, the notice shall be signed by all of those entitled to terminate the grant under clause (1) of this subsection, or by their duly authorized agents. In the case of a grant executed by one or more of the authors of the work, the notice as to any one author's share shall be signed by that author or his or her duly authorized agent or, if that author is dead, by the number and proportion of the owners of his or her termination interest required under clauses (1) and (2) of this subsection, or by their duly authorized agents.

(A) The notice shall state the effective date of the termination, which shall fall within the five-year period specified by clause (3) of this subsection, and the notice shall be served not less than two or more than ten years before that date. A copy of the notice shall be recorded in the Copyright Office before the effective date of termination, as a condition to its taking effect.

(B) The notice shall comply, in form, content, and manner of service, with requirements that the Register of Copyrights shall prescribe by regulation.

(5) Termination of the grant may be effected notwithstanding any agreement to the contrary, including an agreement to make a will or to make any future grant.

(6) In the case of a grant executed by a person or persons other than the author, all rights under this title that were covered by the terminated grant revert, upon the effective date of termination, to all of those entitled to terminate the grant under clause (1) of this subsection. In the case of a grant executed by one or more of the authors of the work, all of a particular author's rights under this title that were covered by the terminated grant revert, upon the effective date of termination, to that author or, if that author is dead, to the persons owning his or her termination interest under clause (2) of this subsection, including those owners who did not join in signing the notice of termination under clause (4) of this subsection. In all cases the reversion of rights is subject to the following limitations:

(A) A derivative work prepared under authority of the grant before its termination may continue to be utilized under the terms of the grant after its termination, but this privilege does not extend to the preparation after the termination of other derivative works based upon the copyrighted work covered by the terminated grant.

(B) The future rights that will revert upon termination of the grant become vested on the date the notice of termination has been served as provided by clause (4) of this subsection.

(C) Where the author's rights revert to two or more persons under clause (2) of this subsection, they shall vest in those persons in the proportionate shares provided by that clause. In such a case, and subject to the provisions of subclause (D) of this clause, a further grant, or agreement to make a further grant, of a particular author's share with respect to any right covered by a terminated grant is valid only if it is signed by the same number and proportion of the owners, in whom the right has vested under this clause, as are required to terminate the grant under clause (2) of this subsection. Such further grant or agreement is effective with respect to all of the persons in whom the right it covers has vested under this subclause, including those who did not join in signing it. If any person dies after rights under a terminated grant have vested in him or her, that person's legal representatives, legatees, or heirs at law represent him or her for purposes of this subclause.

(D) A further grant, or agreement to make a further grant, of any right covered by a terminated grant is valid only if it is made after the effective date of the termination. As an exception, however, an agreement for such a further grant may be made between the author or any of the persons provided by the first sentence of clause (6) of this subsection, or between the persons provided by subclause (C) of this clause, and the original grantee or such grantee's successor in title, after the notice of termination has been served as provided by clause (4) of this subsection.

(E) Termination of a grant under this subsection affects only those rights covered by the grant that arise under this title, and in no way affects rights arising under any other Federal, State, or foreign laws.

(F) Unless and until termination is effected under this subsection, the grant, if it does not provide otherwise, continues in effect for the remainder of the extended renewal term.

§ 305. Duration of copyright: Terminal date

All terms of copyright provided by sections 302 through 304 run to the end of the calendar year in which they would otherwise expire.

Chapter 4.—COPYRIGHT NOTICE, DEPOSIT, AND REGISTRATION

Sec.
401. Notice of copyright: Visually perceptible copies.
402. Notice of copyright: Phonorecords of sound recordings.
403. Notice of copyright: Publications incorporating United States Government works.
404. Notice of copyright: Contributions to collective works.
405. Notice of copyright: Omission of notice.
406. Notice of copyright: Error in name or date.
407. Deposit of copies or phonorecords for Library of Congress.
408. Copyright registration in general.
409. Application for copyright registration.
410. Registration of claim and issuance of certificate.
411. Registration as prerequisite to infringement suit.
412. Registration as prerequisite to certain remedies for infringement.

§ 401. Notice of copyright: Visually perceptible copies

(a) GENERAL REQUIREMENT.—Whenever a work protected under this title is published in the United States or elsewhere by authority of the copyright owner, a notice of copyright as provided by this section shall be placed on all publicly distributed copies from which the work can be visually perceived, either directly or with the aid of a machine or device.

(b) FORM OF NOTICE.—The notice appearing on the copies, shall consist of the following three elements:

(1) the symbol © (the letter C in a circle), or the word "Copyright", or the abbreviation "Copr."; and

(2) the year of first publication of the work; in the case of compilations or derivative works incorporating previously published material, the year date of first publication of the compilation or derivative work is sufficient. The year date may be omitted where a pictorial, graphic, or sculptural work, with accompanying text matter, if any, is reproduced in or on greeting cards, postcards, stationery, jewelry, dolls, toys, or any useful articles; and

(3) the name of the owner of copyright in the work, or an abbreviation by which the name can be recognized, or a generally known alternative designation of the owner.

(c) POSITION OF NOTICE.—The notice shall be affixed to the copies in such manner and location as to give reasonable notice of the claim of copyright. The Register of Copyrights shall prescribe by regulation, as examples, specific methods of affixation and positions of the notice on various types of works that will satisfy this requirement, but these specifications shall not be considered exhaustive.

§ 402. Notice of copyright: Phonorecords of sound recordings

(a) GENERAL REQUIREMENT.—Whenever a sound recording protected under this title is published in the United States or elsewhere by authority of the copyright owner, a notice of copyright as provided by this section shall be placed on all publicly distributed phonorecords of the sound recording.

(b) FORM OF NOTICE.—The notice appearing on the phonorecords shall consist of the following three elements:

(1) the symbol ℗ (the letter P in a circle) ; and

(2) the year of first publication of the sound recording; and

(3) the name of the owner of copyright in the sound recording, or an abbreviation by which the name can be recognized, or a generally known alternative designation of the owner; if the producer of the sound recording is named on the phonorecord labels or containers, and if no other name appears in conjunction with the notice, the producer's name shall be considered a part of the notice.

(c) POSITION OF NOTICE.—The notice shall be placed on the surface of the phonorecord, or on the phonorecord label or container, in such manner and location as to give reasonable notice of the claim of copyright.

§ 403. Notice of copyright: Publications incorporating United States Government works

Whenever a work is published in copies or phonorecords consisting preponderantly of one or more works of the United States Government, the notice of copyright provided by sections 401 or 402 shall also include a statement identifying, either affirmatively or negatively, those portions of the copies or phonorecords embodying any work or works protected under this title.

§ 404. Notice of copyright: Contributions to collective works

(a) A separate contribution to a collective work may bear its own notice of copyright, as provided by sections 401 through 403. However, a single notice applicable to the collective work as a whole is sufficient to satisfy the requirements of sections 401 through 403 with respect to the separate contributions it contains (not including advertisements inserted on behalf of persons other than the owner of copyright in the collective work), regardless of the ownership of copyright in the contributions and whether or not they have been previously published.

(b) Where the person named in a single notice applicable to a collective work as a whole is not the owner of copyright in a separate contribution that does not bear its own notice, the case is governed by the provisions of section 406(a).

§ 405. Notice of copyright: Omission of notice

(a) EFFECT OF OMISSION ON COPYRIGHT.—The omission of the copyright notice prescribed by sections 401 through 403 from copies or phonorecords publicly distributed by authority of the copyright owner does not invalidate the copyright in a work if—

(1) the notice has been omitted from no more than a relatively small number of copies or phonorecords distributed to the public; or

(2) registration for the work has been made before or is made within five years after the publication without notice, and a reasonable effort is made to add notice to all copies or phonorecords that are distributed to the public in the United States after the omission has been discovered; or

(3) the notice has been omitted in violation of an express requirement in writing that, as a condition of the copyright owner's authorization of the public distribution of copies or phonorecords, they bear the prescribed notice.

(b) EFFECT OF OMISSION ON INNOCENT INFRINGERS.—Any person who innocently infringes a copyright, in reliance upon an authorized copy or phonorecord from which the copyright notice has been omitted, incurs no liability for actual or statutory damages under section 504 for any infringing acts committed before receiving actual notice that registration for the work has been made under section 408, if such person proves that he or she was misled by the omission of notice. In a suit for infringement in such a case the court may allow or disallow recovery of any of the infringer's profits attributable to the infringement, and may enjoin the continuation of the infringing undertaking or may require, as a condition or permitting the continuation of the infringing undertaking, that the infringer pay the copyright owner a reasonable license fee in an amount and on terms fixed by the court.

(c) REMOVAL OF NOTICE.—Protection under this title is not affected by the removal, destruction, or obliteration of the notice, without the authorization of the copyright owner, from any publicly distributed copies or phonorecords.

§ 406. Notice of copyright: Error in name or date

(a) ERROR IN NAME.—Where the person named in the copyright notice on copies or phonorecords publicly distributed by authority of the copyright owner is not the owner of copyright, the validity and ownership of the copyright are not affected. In such a case, however, any person who innocently begins an undertaking that infringes the copyright has a complete defense to any action for such infringement if such person proves that he or she was misled by the notice and began the undertaking in good faith under a purported transfer or license from the person named therein, unless before the undertaking was begun—

(1) registration for the work had been made in the name of the owner of copyright; or

(2) a document executed by the person named in the notice and showing the ownership of the copyright had been recorded. The person named in the notice is liable to account to the copyright owner for all receipts from transfers or licenses purportedly made under the copyright by the person named in the notice.

(b) ERROR IN DATE.—When the year date in the notice on copies or phonorecords distributed by authority of the copyright owner is earlier than the year in which publication first occurred, any period computed from the year of first publication under section 302 is to be computed from the year in the notice. Where the year date is more than one year later than the year in which publication first occurred, the work is considered to have been published without any notice and is governed by the provisions of section 405.

(c) OMISSION OF NAME OR DATE.—Where copies or phonorecords publicly distributed by authority of the copyright owner contain no name or no date that could reasonably be considered a part of the notice, the work is considered to have been published without any notice and is governed by the provisions of section 405.

§ 407. Deposit of copies or phonorecords for Library of Congress

(a) Except as provided by subsection (c), and subject to the provisions of subsection (e), the owner of copyright or of the exclusive right of publication in a work published with notice of copyright in the United States shall deposit, within three months after the date of such publication—

    (1) two complete copies of the best edition; or

    (2) if the work is a sound recording, two complete phonorecords of the best edition, together with any printed or other visually perceptible material published with such phonorecords.

Neither the deposit requirements of this subsection nor the acquisition provisions of subsection (e) are conditions of copyright protection.

(b) The required copies or phonorecords shall be deposited in the Copyright Office for the use or disposition of the Library of Congress. The Register of Copyrights shall, when requested by the depositor and upon payment of the fee prescribed by section 708, issue a receipt for the deposit.

(c) The Register of Copyrights may by regulation exempt any categories of material from the deposit requirements of this section, or require deposit of only one copy or phonorecord with respect to any categories. Such regulations shall provide either for complete exemption from the deposit requirements of this section, or for alternative forms of deposit aimed at providing a satisfactory archival record of a work without imposing practical or financial hardships on the depositor, where the individual author is the owner of copyright in a pictorial, graphic, or sculptural work and (i) less than five copies of the work have been published, or (ii) the work has been published in a limited edition consisting of numbered copies, the monetary value of which would make the mandatory deposit of two copies of the best edition of the work burdensome, unfair, or unreasonable.

(d) At any time after publication of a work as provided by subsection (a), the Register of Copyrights may make written demand for the required deposit on any of the persons obligated to make the deposit under subsection (a). Unless deposit is made within three months after the demand is received, the person or persons on whom the demand was made are liable—

    (1) to a fine of not more than $250 for each work; and

    (2) to pay into a specially designated fund in the Library of Congress the total retail price of the copies or phonorecords demanded, or, if no retail price has been fixed, the reasonable cost of the Library of Congress of acquiring them; and

    (3) to pay a fine of $2,500, in addition to any fine or liability imposed under clauses (1) and (2), if such person willfully or repeatedly fails or refuses to comply with such a demand.

(e) With respect to transmission programs that have been fixed and transmitted to the public in the United States but have not been published, the Register of Copyrights shall, after consulting with the Librarian of Congress and other interested organizations and officials, establish regulations governing the acquisition, through deposit or otherwise, of copies or phonorecords of such programs for the collections of the Library of Congress.

(1) The Librarian of Congress shall be permitted, under the standards and conditions set forth in such regulations, to make a fixation of a transmission program directly from a transmission to the public, and to reproduce one copy or phonorecord from such fixation for archival purposes.

(2) Such regulations shall also provide standards and procedures by which the Register of Copyrights may make written demand, upon the owner of the right of transmission in the United States, for the deposit of a copy or phonorecord of a specific transmission program. Such deposit may, at the option of the owner of the right of transmission in the United States, be accomplished by gift, by loan for purposes of reproduction, or by sale at a price not to exceed the cost of reproducing and supplying the copy or phonorecord. The regulations established under this clause shall provide reasonable periods of not less than three months for compliance with a demand, and shall allow for extensions of such periods and adjustments in the scope of the demand or the methods for fulfilling it, as reasonably warranted by the circumstances. Willful failure or refusal to comply with the conditions prescribed by such regulations shall subject the owner of the right of transmission in the United States to liability for an amount, not to exceed the cost of reproducing and supplying the copy or phonorecord in question, to be paid into a specially designated fund in the Library of Congress.

(3) Nothing in this subsection shall be construed to require the making or retention, for purposes of deposit, of any copy or phonorecord of an unpublished transmission program, the transmission of which occurs before the receipt of a specific written demand as provided by clause (2).

(4) No activity undertaken in compliance with regulations prescribed under clauses (1) or (2) of this subsection shall result in liability if intended solely to assist in the acquisition of copies or phonorecords under this subsection.

§ 408. Copyright registration in general

(a) REGISTRATION PERMISSIVE.—At any time during the subsistence of copyright in any published or unpublished work, the owner of copyright or of any exclusive right in the work may obtain registration of the copyright claim by delivering to the Copyright Office the deposit specified by this section, together with the application and fee specified by sections 409 and 708. Subject to the provisions of section 405(a), such registration is not a condition of copyright protection.

(b) DEPOSIT FOR COPYRIGHT REGISTRATION.—Except as provided by subsection (c), the material deposited for registration shall include—

(1) in the case of an unpublished work, one complete copy or phonorecord;

(2) in the case of a published work, two complete copies or phonorecords of the best edition;

(3) in the case of a work first published outside the United States, one complete copy or phonorecord as so published;

(4) in the case of a contribution to a collective work, one complete copy or phonorecord of the best edition of the collective work.

Copies or phonorecords deposited for the Library of Congress under section 407 may be used to satisfy the deposit provisions of this section, if they are accompanied by the prescribed application and fee, and by any additional identifying material that the Register may, by regulation, require. The Register shall also prescribe regulations establishing requirements under which copies or phonorecords acquired for the Library of Congress under subsection (e) of section 407, otherwise than by deposit, may be used to satisfy the deposit provisions of this section.

(c) ADMINISTRATIVE CLASSIFICATION AND OPTIONAL DEPOSIT.—

(1) The Register of Copyrights is authorized to specify by regulation the administrative classes into which works are to be placed for purposes of deposit and registration, and the nature of the copies or phonorecords to be deposited in the various classes specified. The regulations may require or permit, for particular classes, the deposit of identifying material instead of copies or phonorecords, the deposit of only one copy or phonorecord where two would normally be required, or a single registration for a group of related works. This administrative classification of works has no significance with respect to the subject matter of copyright or the exclusive rights provided by this title.

(2) Without prejudice to the general authority provided under clause (1), the Register of Copyrights shall establish regulations specifically permitting a single registration for a group of works by the same individual author, all first published as contributions to periodicals, including newspapers, within a twelve-month period, on the basis of a single deposit, application, and registration fee, under all of the following conditions—

(A) if each of the works as first published bore a separate copyright notice, and the name of the owner of copyright in the work, or an abbreviation by which the name can be recognized, or a generally known alternative designation of the owner was the same in each notice; and

(B) if the deposit consists of one copy of the entire issue of the periodical, or of the entire section in the case of a newspaper, in which each contribution was first published; and

(C) if the application identifies each work separately, including the periodical containing it and its date of first publication.

(3) As an alternative to separate renewal registrations under subsection (a) of section 304, a single renewal registration may be made for a group of works by the same individual author, all first published as contributions to periodicals, including newspapers, upon the filing of a single application and fee, under all of the following conditions:

(A) the renewal claimant or claimants, and the basis of claim or claims under section 304(a), is the same for each of the works; and

(B) the works were all copyrighted upon their first publication, either through separate copyright notice and registration or by virtue of a general copyright notice in the periodical issue as a whole; and

(C) the renewal application and fee are received not more than twenty-eight or less than twenty-seven years after the thirty-first day of December of the calendar year in which all of the works were first published; and

(D) the renewal application identifies each work separately, including the periodical containing it and its date of first publication.

(d) CORRECTIONS AND AMPLIFICATIONS.—The Register may also establish, by regulation, formal procedures for the filing of an application for supplementary registration, to correct an error in a copyright registration or to amplify the information given in a registration. Such application shall be accompanied by the fee provided by section 708, and shall clearly identify the registration to be corrected or amplified. The information contained in a supplementary registration augments but does not supersede that contained in the earlier registration.

(e) PUBLISHED EDITION OF PREVIOUSLY REGISTERED WORK.—Registration for the first published edition of a work previously registered in unpublished form may be made even though the work as published is substantially the same as the unpublished version.

§ 409. Application for copyright registration

The application for copyright registration shall be made on a form prescribed by the Register of Copyrights and shall include—

(1) the name and address of the copyright claimant;

(2) in the case of a work other than an anonymous or pseudonymous work, the name and nationality or domicile of the author or authors, and, if one or more of the authors is dead, the dates of their deaths;

(3) if the work is anonymous or pseudonymous, the nationality or domicile of the author or authors;

(4) in the case of a work made for hire, a statement to this effect;

(5) if the copyright claimant is not the author, a brief statement of how the claimant obtained ownership of the copyright;

(6) the title of the work, together with any previous or alternative titles under which the work can be identified;

(7) the year in which creation of the work was completed;

(8) if the work has been published, the date and nation of its first publication;

(9) in the case of a compilation or derivative work, an identification of any preexisting work or works that it is based on or incorporates, and a brief, general statement of the additional material covered by the copyright claim being registered;

(10) in the case of a published work containing material of which copies are required by section 601 to be manufactured in the United States, the names of the persons or organizations who performed the processes specified by subsection (c) of section 601 with respect to that material, and the places where those processes were performed; and

(11) any other information regarded by the Register of Copyrights as bearing upon the preparation or identification of the work or the existence, ownership, or duration of the copyright.

§ 410. Registration of claim and issuance of certificate

(a) When, after examination, the Register of Copyrights determines that, in accordance with the provisions of this title, the material deposited constitutes copyrightable subject matter and that the other legal and formal requirements of this title have been met, the Register shall register the claim and issue to the applicant a certificate of registration under the seal of the Copyright Office. The certificate shall contain the information given in the application, together with the number and effective date of the registration.

(b) In any case in which the Register of Copyrights determines that, in accordance with the provisions of this title, the material deposited does not constitute copyrightable subject matter or that the claim is invalid for any other reason, the Register shall refuse registration and shall notify the applicant in writing of the reasons for such refusal.

(c) In any judicial proceedings the certificate of a registration made before or within five years after first publication of the work shall constitute prima facie evidence of the validity of the copyright and of the facts stated in the certificate. The evidentiary weight to be accorded the certificate of a registration made thereafter shall be within the discretion of the court.

(d) The effective date of a copyright registration is the day on which an application, deposit, and fee, which are later determined by the Register of Copyrights or by a court of competent jurisdiction to be acceptable for registration, have all been received in the Copyright Office.

§ 411. Registration as prerequisite to infringement suit

(a) Subject to the provisions of subsection (b), no action for infringement of the copyright in any work shall be instituted until registration of the copyright claim has been made in accordance with this title. In any case, however, where the deposit, application, and fee required for registration have been delivered to the Copyright Office in proper form and registration has been refused, the applicant is entitled to institute an action for infringement if notice thereof, with a copy of the complaint, is served on the Register of Copyrights. The Register may, at his or her option, become a party to the action with respect to the issue of registrability of the copyright claim by entering an appearance within sixty days after such service, but the Register's failure to become a party shall not deprive the court of jurisdiction to determine that issue.

(b) In the case of a work consisting of sounds, images, or both, the first fixation of which is made simultaneously with its transmission, the copyright owner may, either before or after such fixation takes place, institute an action for infringement under section 501, fully subject to the remedies provided by sections 502 through 506 and sections 509 and 510, if, in accordance with requirements that the Register of Copyrights shall prescribe by regulation, the copyright owner—

(1) serves notice upon the infringer, not less than ten or more than thirty days before such fixation, identifying the work and the specific time and source of its first transmission, and declaring an intention to secure copyright in the work; and

(2) makes registration for the work within three months after its first transmission.

§ 412. Registration as prerequisite to certain remedies for infringement

In any action under this title, other than an action instituted under section 411(b), no award of statutory damages or of attorney's fees, as provided by sections 504 and 505, shall be made for—

(1) any infringement of copyright in an unpublished work commenced before the effective date of its registration; or

(2) any infringement of copyright commenced after first publication of the work and before the effective date of its registration, unless such registration is made within three months after the first publication of the work.

Chapter 5.—COPYRIGHT INFRINGEMENT AND REMEDIES

§ 501. Infringement of copyright

(a) Anyone who violates any of the exclusive rights of the copyright owner as provided by sections 106 through 118, or who imports copies or phonorecords into the United States in violation of section 602, is an infringer of the copyright.

(b) The legal or beneficial owner of an exclusive right under a copyright is entitled, subject to the requirements of sections 205 (d) and 411, to institute an action for any infringement of that particular right committed while he or she is the owner of it. The court may require such owner to serve written notice of the action with a copy of the complaint upon any person shown, by the records of the Copyright Office or otherwise, to have or claim an interest in the copyright, and shall require that such notice be served upon any person whose interest is likely to be affected by a decision in the case. The court may require the joinder, and shall permit the intervention, of any person having or claiming an interest in the copyright.

(c) For any secondary transmission by a cable system that embodies a performance or a display of a work which is actionable as an act of infringement under subsection (c) of section 111, a television broadcast station holding a copyright or other license to transmit or perform the same version of that work shall, for purposes of subsection (b) of this section, be treated as a legal or beneficial owner if such secondary transmission occurs within the local service area of that television station.

(d) For any secondary transmission by a cable system that is actionable as an act of infringement pursuant to section 111 (c) (3), the following shall also have standing to sue: (i) the primary transmitter whose transmission has been altered by the cable system; and (ii) any broadcast station within whose local service area the secondary transmission occurs.

§ 502. Remedies for infringement: Injunctions

(a) Any court having jurisdiction of a civil action arising under this title may, subject to the provisions of section 1498 of title 28, grant temporary and final injunctions on such terms as it may deem reasonable to prevent or restrain infringement of a copyright.

(b) Any such injunction may be served anywhere in the United States on the person enjoined; it shall be operative throughout the United States and shall be enforceable, by proceedings in contempt or otherwise, by any United States court having jurisdiction of that person. The clerk of the court granting the injunction shall, when requested by any other court in which enforcement of the injunction is sought, transmit promptly to the other court a certified copy of all the papers in the case on file in such clerk's office.

§ 503. Remedies for infringement: Impounding and disposition of infringing articles

(a) At any time while an action under this title is pending, the court may order the impounding, on such terms as it may deem reasonable, of all copies or phonorecords claimed to have been made or used in violation of the copyright owner's exclusive rights, and of all plates, molds, matrices, masters, tapes, film negatives, or other articles by means of which such copies or phonorecords may be reproduced.

(b) As part of a final judgment or decree, the court may order the destruction or other reasonable disposition of all copies or phonorecords found to have been made or used in violation of the copyright owner's exclusive rights, and of all plates, molds, matrices, masters, tapes, film negatives, or other articles by means of which such copies or phonorecords may be reproduced.

§ 504. Remedies for infringement: Damages and profits

(a) IN GENERAL.—Except as otherwise provided by this title, an infringer of copyright is liable for either—

(1) the copyright owner's actual damages and any additional profits of the infringer, as provided by subsection (b); or

(2) statutory damages, as provided by subsection (c).

(b) ACTUAL DAMAGES AND PROFITS.—The copyright owner is entitled to recover the actual damages suffered by him or her as a result of the infringement, and any profits of the infringer that are attributable to the infringement and are not taken into account in computing the actual damages. In establishing the infringer's profits, the copyright owner is required to present proof only of the infringer's gross revenue, and the infringer is required to prove his or her deductible expenses and the elements of profit attributable to factors other than the copyrighted work.

(c) STATUTORY DAMAGES.—

(1) Except as provided by clause (2) of this subsection, the copyright owner may elect, at any time before final judgment is rendered, to recover, instead of actual damages and profits, an award of statutory damages for all infringements involved in the action, with respect to any one work, for which any one infringer is liable individually, or for which any two or more infringers are liable jointly and severally, in a sum of not less than $250 or more than $10,000 as the court considers just. For the purposes of this subsection, all the parts of a compilation or derivative work constitute one work.

(2) In a case where the copyright owner sustains the burden of proving, and the court finds, that infringement was committed willfully, the court in its discretion may increase the award of statutory damages to a sum of not more than $50,000. In a case where the infringer sustains the burden of proving, and the court finds, that such infringer was not aware and had no reason to believe that his or her acts constituted an infringement of copyright, the court it its discretion may reduce the award of statutory damages to a sum of not less than $100. The court shall remit statutory damages in any case where an infringer believed and had reasonable grounds for believing that his or her use of the copyrighted work was a fair use under section 107, if the infringer was: (i) an employee or agent of a nonprofit educational institution, library, or archives acting within the scope of his or her employment who, or such institution, library, or archives itself, which infringed by reproducing the work in copies or phonorecords; or (ii) a public broadcasting entity which or a person who, as a regular part of the nonprofit activities of a public

broadcasting entity (as defined in subsection (g) of section 118) infringed by performing a published nondramatic literary work or by reproducing a transmission program embodying a performance of such a work.

§ 505. Remedies for infringement: Costs and attorney's fees

In any civil action under this title, the court in its discretion may allow the recovery of full costs by or against any party other than the United States or an officer thereof. Except as otherwise provided by this title, the court may also award a reasonable attorney's fee to the prevailing party as part of the costs.

§ 506. Criminal offenses

(a) CRIMINAL INFRINGEMENT.—Any person who infringes a copyright willfully and for purposes of commercial advantage or private financial gain shall be fined not more than $10,000 or imprisoned for not more than one year, or both: *Provided, however,* That any person who infringes willfully and for purposes of commercial advantage or private financial gain the copyright in a sound recording afforded by subsections (1), (2), or (3) of section 106 or the copyright in a motion picture afforded by subsections (1), (3), or (4) of section 106 shall be fined not more than $25,000 or imprisoned for not more than one year, or both, for the first such offense and shall be fined not more than $50,000 or imprisoned for not more than two years, or both, for any subsequent offense.

(b) FORFEITURE AND DESTRUCTION.—When any person is convicted of any violation of subsection (a), the court in its judgment of conviction shall, in addition to the penalty therein prescribed, order the forfeiture and destruction or other disposition of all infringing copies or phonorecords and all implements, devices, or equipment used in the manufacture of such infringing copies or phonorecords.

(c) FRAUDULENT COPYRIGHT NOTICE.—Any person who, with fraudulent intent, places on any article a notice of copyright or words of the same purport that such person knows to be false, or who, with fraudulent intent, publicly distributes or imports for public distribution any article bearing such notice or words that such person knows to be false, shall be fined not more than $2,500.

(d) FRAUDULENT REMOVAL OF COPYRIGHT NOTICE.—Any person who, with fraudulent intent, removes or alters any notice of copyright appearing on a copy of a copyrighted work shall be fined not more than $2,500.

(e) FALSE REPRESENTATION.—Any person who knowingly makes a false representation of a material fact in the application for copyright registration provided for by section 409, or in any written statement filed in connection with the application, shall be fined not more than $2,500.

§ 507. Limitations on actions

(a) CRIMINAL PROCEEDINGS.—No criminal proceeding shall be maintained under the provisions of this title unless it is commenced within three years after the cause of action arose.

(b) CIVIL ACTIONS.—No civil action shall be maintained under the provisions of this title unless it is commenced within three years after the claim accrued.

§ 508. Notification of filing and determination of actions

(a) Within one month after the filing of any action under this title, the clerks of the courts of the United States shall send written notification to the Register of Copyrights setting forth, as far as is shown by the papers filed in the court, the names and addresses of the parties and the title, author, and registration number of each work involved in the action. If any other copyrighted work is later included in the action by amendment, answer, or other pleading, the clerk shall also send a notification concerning it to the Register within one month after the pleading is filed.

(b) Within one month after any final order or judgment is issued in the case, the clerk of the court shall notify the Register of it, sending with the notification a copy of the order or judgment together with the written opinion, if any, of the court.

(c) Upon receiving the notifications specified in this section, the Register shall make them a part of the public records of the Copyright Office.

§ 509. Seizure and forfeiture

(a) All copies or phonorecords manufactured, reproduced, distributed, sold, or otherwise used, intended for use, or possessed with intent to use in violation of section 506(a), and all plates, molds, matrices, masters, tapes, film negatives, or other articles by means of which such copies or phonorecords may be reproduced, and all electronic, mechanical, or other devices for manufacturing, reproducing, or assembling such copies or phonorecords may be seized and forfeited to the United States.

(b) The applicable procedures relating to (i) the seizure, summary and judicial forfeiture, and condemnation of vessels, vehicles, merchandise, and baggage for violations of the customs laws contained in title 19, (ii) the disposition of such vessels, vehicles, merchandise, and baggage or the proceeds from the sale thereof, (iii) the remission or mitigation of such forfeiture, (iv) the compromise of claims, and (v) the award of compensation to informers in respect of such forfeitures, shall apply to seizures and forfeitures incurred, or alleged to have been incurred, under the provisions of this section, insofar as applicable and not inconsistent with the provisions of this section; except that such duties as are imposed upon any officer or employee of the Treasury Department or any other person with respect to the seizure and forfeiture of vessels, vehicles, merchandise; and baggage under the provisions of the customs laws contained in title 19 shall be performed with respect to seizure and forfeiture of all articles described in subsection (a) by such officers, agents, or other persons as may be authorized or designated for that purpose by the Attorney General.

§ 510. Remedies for alteration of programing by cable systems

(a) In any action filed pursuant to section 111(c)(3), the following remedies shall be available:

(1) Where an action is brought by a party identified in subsections (b) or (c) of section 501, the remedies provided by sections 502 through 505, and the remedy provided by subsection (b) of this section; and

(2) When an action is brought by a party identified in subsection (d) of section 501, the remedies provided by sections 502 and 505, together with any actual damages suffered by such party as a result of the infringement, and the remedy provided by subsection (b) of this section.

(b) In any action filed pursuant to section 111(c)(3), the court may decree that, for a period not to exceed thirty days, the cable system shall be deprived of the benefit of a compulsory license for one or more distant signals carried by such cable system.

Chapter 6.—MANUFACTURING REQUIREMENTS AND IMPORTATION

Sec.
601. Manufacture, importation, and public distribution of certain copies.
602. Infringing importation of copies or phonorecords.
603. Importation prohibitions: Enforcement and disposition of excluded articles.

§ 601. Manufacture, importation, and public distribution of certain copies

(a) Prior to July 1, 1982, and except as provided by subsection (b), the importation into or public distribution in the United States of copies of a work consisting preponderantly of nondramtic literary material that is in the English language and is protected under this title is prohibited unless the portions consisting of such material have been manufactured in the United States or Canada.

(b) The provisions of subsection (a) do not apply—

(1) where, on the date when importation is sought or public distribution in the United States is made, the author of any substantial part of such material is neither a national nor a domiciliary of the United States or, if such author is a national of the United States, he or she has been domiciled outside the United States for a continuous period of at least one year immediately preceding that date; in the case of a work made for hire, the exemption provided by this clause does not apply unless a subsustantial part of the work was prepared for an employer or other person who is not a national or domiciliary of the United States or a domestic corporation or enterprise;

(2) where the United States Customs Service is presented with an import statement issued under the seal of the Copyright Office, in which case a total of no more than two thousand copies of any one such work shall be allowed entry; the import statement shall be issued upon request to the copyright owner or to a person designated by such owner at the time of registration for the work under section 408 or at any time thereafter;

(3) where importation is sought under the authority or for the use, other than in schools, of the Government of the United States or of any State or political subdivision of a State;

(4) where importation, for use and not for sale, is sought—

(A) by any person with respect to no more than one copy of any work at any one time;

(B) by any person arriving from outside the United States, with respect to copies forming part of such person's personal baggage; or

(C) by an organization operated for scholarly, educational, or religious purposes and not for private gain, with respect to copies intended to form a part of its library;

(5) where the copies are reproduced in raised characters for the use of the blind; or

(6) where, in addition to copies imported under clauses (3) and (4) of this subsection, no more than two thousand copies of any one such work, which have not been manufactured in the United States or Canada, are publicly distributed in the United States; or

(7) where, on the date when importation is sought or public distribution in the United States is made—

(A) the author of any substantial part of such material is an individual and receives compensation for the transfer or license of the right to distribute the work in the United States; and

(B) the first publication of the work has previously taken place outside the United States under a transfer or license granted by such author to a transferee or licensee who was not a national or domiciliary of the United States or a domestic corporation or enterprise; and

(C) there has been no publication of an authorized edition of the work of which the copies were manufactured in the United States; and

(D) the copies were reproduced under a transfer or license granted by such author or by the transferee or licensee of the right of first publication as mentioned in subclause (B), and the transferee or the licensee of the right of reproduction was not a national or domiciliary of the United States or a domestic corporation or enterprise.

(c) The requirement of this section that copies be manufactured in the United States or Canada is satisfied if—

(1) in the case where the copies are printed directly from type that has been set, or directly from plates made from such type, the setting of the type and the making of the plates have been performed in the United States or Canada; or

(2) in the case where the making of plates by a lithographic or photoengraving process is a final or intermediate step preceding the printing of the copies, the making of the plates has been performed in the United States or Canada; and

(3) in any case, the printing or other final process of producing multiple copies and any binding of the copies have been performed in the United States or Canada.

(d) Importation or public distribution of copies in violation of this section does not invalidate protection for a work under this title. However, in any civil action or criminal proceeding for infringement of the exclusive rights to reproduce and distribute copies of the work, the infringer has a complete defense with respect to all of the nondramatic literary material comprised in the work and any other parts of the work in which the exclusive rights to reproduce and distribute copies are owned by the same person who owns such exclusive rights in the nondramatic literary material, if the infringer proves—

(1) that copies of the work have been imported into or publicly distributed in the United States in violation of this section by or with the authority of the owner of such exclusive rights; and

(2) that the infringing copies were manufactured in the United States or Canada in accordance with the provisions of subsection (c); and

(3) that the infringement was commenced before the effective date of registration for an authorized edition of the work, the copies of which have been manufactured in the United States or Canada in accordance with the provisions of subsection (c).

(e) In any action for infringement of the exclusive rights to reproduce and distribute copies of a work containing material required by this section to be manufactured in the United States or Canada, the copyright owner shall set forth in the complaint the names of the persons or organizations who performed the processes specified by subsection (c) with respect to that material, and the places where those processes were performed.

§ 602. Infringing importation of copies or phonorecords

(a) Importation into the United States, without the authority of the owner of copyright under this title, of copies or phonorecords of a work that have been acquired outside the United States is an infringement of the exclusive right to distribute copies or phonorecords under section 106, actionable under section 501. This subsection does not apply to—

(1) importation of copies or phonorecords under the authority or for the use of the Government of the United States or of any State or political subdivision of a State, but not including copies or phonorecords for use in schools, or copies of any audiovisual work imported for purposes other than archival use;

(2) importation, for the private use of the importer and not for distribution, by any person with respect to no more than one copy or phonorecord of any one work at any one time, or by any person arriving from outside the United States with respect to copies or phonorecords forming part of such person's personal baggage; or

(3) importation by or for an organization operated for scholarly, educational, or religious purposes and not for private gain, with respect to no more than one copy of an audiovisual work solely for its archival purposes, and no more than five copies or phonorecords of any other work for its library lending or archival purposes, unless the importation of such copies or phonorecords is part of an activity consisting of systematic reproduction or distribution, engaged in by such organization in violation of the provisions of section 108(g)(2).

(b) In a case where the making of the copies or phonorecords would have constituted an infringement of copyright if this title had been applicable, their importation is prohibited. In a case where the copies or phonorecords were lawfully made, the United States Customs Service has no authority to prevent their importation unless the provisions of section 601 are applicable. In either case, the Secretary of the Treasury is authorized to prescribe, by regulation, a procedure under which any person claiming an interest in the copyright in a particular work may, upon payment of a specified fee, be entitled to notification by the Customs Service of the importation of articles that appear to be copies or phonorecords of the work.

§ 603. Importation prohibitions: Enforcement and disposition of excluded articles

(a) The Secretary of the Treasury and the United States Postal Service shall separately or jointly make regulations for the enforcement of the provisions of this title prohibiting importation.

(b) These regulations may require, as a condition for the exclusion of articles under section 602—

(1) that the person seeking exclusion obtain a court order enjoining importation of the articles; or

(2) that the person seeking exclusion furnish proof, of a specified nature and in accordance with prescribed procedures, that the copyright in which such person claims an interest is valid and that the importation would violate the prohibition in section 602; the person seeking exclusion may also be required to post a surety bond for any injury that may result if the detention or exclusion of the articles proves to be unjustified.

(c) Articles imported in violation of the importation prohibitions of this title are subject to seizure and forfeiture in the same manner as property imported in violation of the customs revenue laws. Forfeited articles shall be destroyed as directed by the Secretary of the Treasury or the court, as the case may be; however, the articles may be returned to the country of export whenever it is shown to the satisfaction of the Secretary of the Treasury that the importer had no reasonable grounds for believing that his or her acts constituted a violation of law.

Chapter 7.—COPYRIGHT OFFICE

§ 701. The Copyright Office: General responsibilities and organization

(a) All administrative functions and duties under this title, except as otherwise specified, are the responsibility of the Register of Copyrights as director of the Copyright Office of the Library of Congress. The Register of Copyrights, together with the subordinate officers and employees of the Copyright Office, shall be appointed by the Librarian of Congress, and shall act under the Librarian's general direction and supervision.

(b) The Register of Copyrights shall adopt a seal to be used on and after January 1, 1978, to authenticate all certified documents issued by the Copyright Office.

(c) The Register of Copyrights shall make an annual report to the Librarian of Congress of the work and accomplishments of the Copyright Office during the previous fiscal year. The annual report of the Register of Copyrights shall be published separately and as a part of the annual report of the Librarian of Congress.

(d) Except as provided by section 706(b) and the regulations issued thereunder, all actions taken by the Register of Copyrights under this title are subject to the provisions of the Administrative Procedure Act of June 11, 1946, as amended (c. 324, 60 Stat. 237, title 5, United States Code, Chapter 5, Subchapter II and Chapter 7).

§ 702. Copyright Office regulations

The Register of Copyrights is authorized to establish regulations not inconsistent with law for the administration of the functions and duties made the responsibility of the Register under this title. All regulations established by the Register under this title are subject to the approval of the Librarian of Congress.

§ 703. Effective date of actions in Copyright Office

In any case in which time limits are prescribed under this title for the performance of an action in the Copyright Office, and in which the last day of the prescribed period falls on a Saturday, Sunday, holiday, or other nonbusiness day within the District of Columbia or the Federal Government, the action may be taken on the next succeeding business day, and is effective as of the date when the period expired.

§ 704. Retention and disposition of articles deposited in Copyright Office

(a) Upon their deposit in the Copyright Office under sections 407 and 408, all copies, phonorecords, and identifying material, including those deposited in connection with claims that have been refused registration, are the property of the United States Government.

(b) In the case of published works, all copies, phonorecords, and identifying material deposited are available to the Library of Congress for its collections, or for exchange or transfer to any other library. In the case of unpublished works, the Library is entitled, under regulations that the Register of Copyrights shall prescribe, to select any deposits for its collections or for transfer to the National Archives of the United States or to a Federal records center, as defined in section 2901 of title 44.

(c) The Register of Copyrights is authorized, for specific or general categories of works, to make a facsimile reproduction of all or any part of the material deposited under section 408, and to make such reproduction a part of the Copyright Office records of the registration, before transferring such material to the Library of Congress as provided by subsection (b), or before destroying or otherwise disposing of such material as provided by subsection (d).

(d) Deposits not selected by the Library under subsection (b), or identifying portions or reproductions of them, shall be retained under the control of the Copyright Office, including retention in Government storage facilities, for the longest period considered practicable and desirable by the Register of Copyrights and the Librarian of Congress. After that period it is within the joint discretion of the Register and the Librarian to order their destruction or other disposition; but, in the case of unpublished works, no deposit shall be knowingly or intentionally destroyed or otherwise disposed of during its term of copyright unless a facsimile reproduction of the entire deposit has been made a part of the Copyright Office records as provided by subsection (c).

(e) The depositor of copies, phonorecords, or identifying material under section 408, or the copyright owner of record, may request retention, under the control of the Copyright Office, of one or more of such articles for the full term of copyright in the work. The Register of Copyrights shall prescribe, by regulation, the conditions under which such requests are to be made and granted, and shall fix the fee to be charged under section 708(a)(11) if the request is granted.

§ 705. Copyright Office records: Preparation, maintenance, public inspection, and searching

(a) The Register of Copyrights shall provide and keep in the Copyright Office records of all deposits, registrations, recordations, and other actions taken under this title, and shall prepare indexes of all such records.

(b) Such records and indexes, as well as the articles deposited in connection with completed copyright registrations and retained under the control of the Copyright Office, shall be open to public inspection.

(c) Upon request and payment of the fee specified by section 708, the Copyright Office shall make a search of its public records, indexes, and deposits, and shall furnish a report of the information they disclose with respect to any particular deposits, registrations, or recorded documents.

§ 706. Copies of Copyright Office records

(a) Copies may be made of any public records or indexes of the Copyright Office; additional certificates of copyright registration and copies of any public records or indexes may be furnished upon request and payment of the fees specified by section 708.

(b) Copies or reproductions of deposited articles retained under the control of the Copyright Office shall be authorized or furnished only under the conditions specified by the Copyright Office regulations.

§ 707. Copyright Office forms and publications

(a) CATALOG OF COPYRIGHT ENTRIES.—The Register of Copyrights shall compile and publish at periodic intervals catalogs of all copyright registrations. These catalogs shall be divided into parts in accordance with the various classes of works, and the Register has discretion to determine, on the basis of practicability and usefulness, the form and frequency of publication of each particular part.

(b) OTHER PUBLICATIONS.—The Register shall furnish, free of charge upon request, application forms for copyright registration and general informational material in connection with the functions of the Copyright Office. The Register also has the authority to publish compilations of information, bibliographies, and other material he or she considers to be of value to the public.

(c) DISTRIBUTION OF PUBLICATIONS.—All publications of the Copyright Office shall be furnished to depository libraries as specified under section 1905 of title 44, and, aside from those furnished free of charge, shall be offered for sale to the public at prices based on the cost of reproduction and distribution.

§ 708. Copyright Office fees

(a) The following fees shall be paid to the Register of Copyrights:

(1) for the registration of a copyright claim or a supplementary registration under section 408, including the issuance of a certificate of registration, $10;

(2) for the registration of a claim to renewal of a subsisting copyright in its first term under section 304(a), including the issuance of a certificate of registration, $6;

(3) for the issuance of a receipt for a deposit under section 407, $2;

(4) for the recordation, as provided by section 205, of a transfer of copyright ownership or other document of six pages or less, covering no more than one title, $10; for each page over six and each title over one, 50 cents additional;

(5) for the filing, under section 115(b), of a notice of intention to make phonorecords, $6;

(6) for the recordation, under section 302(c), of a statement revealing the identity of an author of an anonymous or pseudonymous work, or for the recordation, under section 302(d), of a statement relating to the death of an author, $10 for a document of six pages or less, covering no more than one title; for each page over six and for each title over one, $1 additional;

(7) for the issuance, under section 601, of an import statement, $3;

(8) for the issuance, under section 706, of an additional certificate of registration, $4;

(9) for the issuance of any other certification, $4; the Register of Copyrights has discretion, on the basis of their cost, to fix the fees for preparing copies of Copyright Office records, whether they are to be certified or not;

(10) for the making and reporting of a search as provided by section 705, and for any related services, $10 for each hour or fraction of an hour consumed;

(11) for any other special services requiring a substantial amount of time or expense, such fees as the Register of Copyrights may fix on the basis of the cost of providing the service.

(b) The fees prescribed by or under this section are applicable to the United States Government and any of its agencies, employees, or officers, but the Register of Copyrights has discretion to waive the requirement of this subsection in occasional or isolated cases involving relatively small amounts.

(c) The Register of Copyrights shall deposit all fees in the Treasury of the United States in such manner as the Secretary of the Treasury directs. The Register may, in accordance with regulations that he or she shall prescribe, refund any sum paid by mistake or in excess of the fee required by this section; however, before making a refund in any case involving a refusal to register a claim under section 410(b), the Register may deduct all or any part of the prescribed registration fee to cover the reasonable administrative costs of processing the claim.

§ 709. Delay in delivery caused by disruption of postal or other services

In any case in which the Register of Copyrights determines, on the basis of such evidence as the Register may by regulation require, that a deposit, application, fee, or any other material to be delivered to the Copyright Office by a particular date, would have been received in the Copyright Office in due time except for a general disruption or suspension of postal or other transportation or communications services, the actual receipt of such material in the Copyright Office within one month after the date on which the Register determines that the disruption or suspension of such services has terminated, shall be considered timely.

§ 710. Reproduction for use of the blind and physically handicapped: Voluntary licensing forms and procedures

The Register of Copyrights shall, after consultation with the Chief of the Division for the Blind and Physically Handicapped and other appropriate officials of the Library of Congress, establish by regulation standardized forms and procedures by which, at the time applications covering certain specified categories of nondramatic literary works are submitted for registration under section 408 of this title, the copyright owner may voluntarily grant to the Library of Congress a license to reproduce the copyrighted work by means of Braille or similar tactile symbols, or by fixation of a reading of the work in a phonorecord, or both, and to distribute the resulting copies or phonorecords solely for the use of the blind and physically handicapped and under limited conditions to be specified in the standardized forms.

Chapter 8.—COPYRIGHT ROYALTY TRIBUNAL

§ 801. Copyright Royalty Tribunal: Establishment and purpose

(a) There is hereby created an independent Copyright Royalty Tribunal in the legislative branch.

(b) Subject to the provisions of this chapter, the purposes of the Tribunal shall be—

(1) to make determinations concerning the adjustment of reasonable copyright royalty rates as provided in sections 115 and 116, and to make determinations as to reasonable terms and rates of royalty payments as provided in section 118. The rates applicable under sections 115 and 116 shall be calculated to achieve the following objectives:

(A) To maximize the availability of creative works to the public;

(B) To afford the copyright owner a fair return for his creative work and the copyright user a fair income under existing economic conditions;

(C) To reflect the relative roles of the copyright owner and the copyright user in the product made available to the public with respect to relative creative contribution, technological contribution, capital investment, cost, risk, and contribution to the opening of new markets for creative expression and media for their communication;

(D) To minimize any disruptive impact on the structure of the industries involved and on generally prevailing industry practices.

(2) to make determinations concerning the adjustment of the copyright royalty rates in section 111 solely in accordance with the following provisions:

(A) The rates established by section 111(d)(2)(B) may be adjusted to reflect (i) national monetary inflation or deflation or (ii) changes in the average rates charged cable subscribers for the basic service of providing secondary transmissions to maintain the real constant dollar level of the royalty fee per subscriber which existed as of the date of enactment of this Act: *Provided*, That if the average rates charged cable system subscribers for the basic service of providing secondary transmissions are changed so that the average rates exceed national monetary inflation, no change in the rates established by section 111(d)(2)(B) shall be permitted: *And provided further*, That no increase in the royalty fee shall be permitted based on any reduction in the average number of distant signal equivalents per subscriber. The Commission may consider all factors relating to the maintenance of such level of payments including, as an extenuating factor, whether the cable industry has been restrained by subscriber rate regulating authorities from increasing the rates for the basic service of providing secondary transmissions.

(B) In the event that the rules and regulations of the Federal Communications Commission are amended at any time after April 15, 1976, to permit the carriage by cable systems of additional television broadcast signals beyond the local service area of the primary transmitters of such signals, the royalty rates established by section 111(d)(2)(B) may be adjusted to insure that the rates for the additional distant signal equivalents resulting from such carriage are reasonable in the light of the changes effected by the amendment to such rules and regulations. In determining the reasonableness of rates proposed following an amendment of Federal Communications Commission rules and regulations, the Copyright Royalty Tribunal shall consider, among other factors, the economic impact on copyright owners and users: *Provided*, That no adjustment in royalty rates shall be made under this subclause with respect to any distant signal equivalent or fraction thereof represented by (i) carriage of any signal permitted under the rules and regulations of the Federal Communications Commission in effect on April 15, 1976, or the carriage of a signal of the same type (that is, independent, network, or noncommercial educational) substituted for such permitted signal, or (ii) a television broadcast signal first carried after April 15, 1976, pursuant to an individual waiver of the rules and regulations of the Federal Communications Commission, as such rules and regulations were in effect on April 15, 1976.

(C) In the event of any change in the rules and regulations of the Federal Communications Commission with respect to syndicated and sports program exclusivity after April 15, 1976, the rates established by section 111(d)(2)(B) may be adjusted to assure that such rates are reasonable in light of the changes to such rules and regulations, but any such adjustment shall apply only to the affected television broadcast signals carried on those systems affected by the change.

(D) The gross receipts limitations established by section 111(d)(2)(C) and (D) shall be adjusted to reflect national monetary inflation or deflation or changes in the average rates charged cable system subscribers for the basic service of providing secondary transmissions to maintain the real constant dollar value of the exemption provided by such section; and the royalty rate specified therein shall not be subject to adjustment; and

(3) to distribute royalty fees deposited with the Register of Copyrights under sections 111 and 116, and to determine, in cases where controversy exists, the distribution of such fees.

(c) As soon as possible after the date of enactment of this Act, and no later than six months following such date, the President shall publish a notice announcing the initial appointments provided in section 802, and shall designate an order of seniority among the initially-appointed commissioners for purposes of section 802(b).

§ 802. Membership of the Tribunal

(a) The Tribunal shall be composed of five commissioners appointed by the President with the advice and consent of the Senate for a term of seven years each; of the first five members appointed, three shall be designated to serve for seven years from the date of the notice specified in section 801(c), and two shall be designated to serve for five years from such date, respectively. Commissioners shall be compensated at the highest rate now or hereafter prescribe for grade 18 of the General Schedule pay rates (5 U.S.C. 5332).

(b) Upon convening the commissioners shall elect a chairman from among the commissioners appointed for a full seven-year term. Such chairman shall serve for a term of one year. Thereafter, the most senior commissioner who has not previously served as chairman shall serve as chairman for a period of one year, except that, if all commissioners have served a full term as chairman, the most senior commissioner who has served the least number of terms as chairman shall be designated as chairman.

(c) Any vacancy in the Tribunal shall not affect its powers and shall be filled, for the unexpired term of the appointment, in the same manner as the original appointment was made.

§ 803. Procedures of the Tribunal

(a) The Tribunal shall adopt regulations, not inconsistent with law, governing its procedure and methods of operation. Except as otherwise provided in this chapter, the Tribunal shall be subject to the provisions of the Administrative Procedure Act of June 11, 1946, as amended (c. 324, 60 Stat. 237, title 5, United States Code, chapter 5, subchapter II and chapter 7).

(b) Every final determination of the Tribunal shall be published in the Federal Register. It shall state in detail the criteria that the Tribunal determined to be applicable to the particular proceeding, the various facts that it found relevant to its determination in that proceeding, and the specific reasons for its determination.

§ 804. Institution and conclusion of proceedings

(a) With respect to proceedings under section 801(b)(1) concerning the adjustment of royalty rates as provided in sections 115 and 116, and with respect to proceedings under section 801(b)(2)(A) and (D)—

(1) on January 1, 1980, the Chairman of the Tribunal shall cause to be published in the Federal Register notice of commencement of proceedings under this chapter; and

(2) during the calendar years specified in the following schedule, any owner or user of a copyrighted work whose royalty rates are specified by this title, or by a rate established by the Tribunal, may file a petition with the Tribunal declaring that the petitioner requests an adjustment of the rate. The Tribunal shall make a determination as to whether the applicant has a significant interest in the royalty rate in which an adjustment is requested. If the Tribunal determines that the petitioner has a significant interest, the Chairman shall cause notice of this determination, with the reasons therefor, to be published in the Federal Register, together with notice of commencement of proceedings under this chapter.

(A) In proceedings under section 801(b)(2)(A) and (D), such petition may be filed during 1985 and in each subsequent fifth calendar year.

(B) In proceedings under section 801(b)(1) concerning the adjustment of royalty rates as provided in section 115, such petition may be filed in 1987 and in each subsequent tenth calendar year.

(C) In proceedings under section 801(b)(1) concerning the adjustment of royalty rates under section 116, such petition may be filed in 1990 and in each subsequent tenth calendar year.

(b) With respect to proceedings under subclause (B) or (C) of section 801(b)(2), following an event described in either of those subsections, any owner or user of a copyrighted work whose royalty rates are specified by section 111, or by a rate established by the Tribunal, may, within twelve months, file a petition with the Tribunal declaring that the petitioner requests an adjustment of the rate. In this event the Tribunal shall proceed as in subsection (a)(2), above. Any change in royalty rates made by the Tribunal pursuant to this subsection may be reconsidered in 1980, 1985, and each fifth calendar year thereafter, in accordance with the provisions in section 801(b)(2)(B) or (C), as the case may be.

(c) With respect to proceedings under section 801(b)(1), concerning the determination of reasonable terms and rates of royalty payments as provided in section 118, the Tribunal shall proceed when and as provided by that section.

(d) With respect to proceedings under section 801(b)(3), concerning the distribution of royalty fees in certain circumstances under sections 111 or 116, the Chairman of the Tribunal shall, upon determination by the Tribunal that a controversy exists concerning such distribution, cause to be published in the Federal Register notice of commencement of proceedings under this chapter.

(e) All proceedings under this chapter shall be initiated without delay following publication of the notice specified in this section, and the Tribunal shall render its final decision in any such proceeding within one year from the date of such publication.

§ 805. Staff of the Tribunal

(a) The Tribunal is authorized to appoint and fix the compensation of such employees as may be necessary to carry out the provisions of this chapter, and to prescribe their functions and duties.

(b) The Tribunal may procure temporary and intermittent services to the same extent as is authorized by section 3109 of title 5.

§ 806. Administrative support of the Tribunal

(a) The Library of Congress shall provide the Tribunal with necessary administrative services, including those related to budgeting, accounting, financial reporting, travel, personnel, and procurement. The Tribunal shall pay the Library for such services, either in advance or by reimbursement from the funds of the Tribunal, at amounts to be agreed upon between the Librarian and the Tribunal.

(b) The Library of Congress is authorized to disburse funds for the Tribunal, under regulations prescribed jointly by the Librarian of Congress and the Tribunal and approved by the Comptroller General. Such regulations shall establish requirements and procedures under which every voucher certified for payment by the Library of Congress under this chapter shall be supported with a certification by a duly authorized officer or employee of the Tribunal, and shall prescribe the responsibilities and accountability of said officers and employees of the Tribunal with respect to such certifications.

§ 807. Deduction of costs of proceedings

Before any funds are distributed pursuant to a final decision in a proceeding involving distribution of royalty fees, the Tribunal shall assess the reasonable costs of such proceeding.

§ 808. Reports

In addition to its publication of the reports of all final determinations as provided in section 803(b), the Tribunal shall make an annual report to the President and the Congress concerning the Tribunal's work during the preceding fiscal year, including a detailed fiscal statement of account.

§ 809. Effective date of final determinations

Any final determination by the Tribunal under this chapter shall become effective thirty days following its publication in the Federal Register as provided in section 803(b), unless prior to that time an appeal has been filed pursuant to section 810, to vacate, modify, or correct such determination, and notice of such appeal has been served on all parties who appeared before the Tribunal in the proceeding in question. Where the proceeding involves the distribution of royalty fees under sections 111 or 116, the Tribunal shall, upon the expiration of such thirty-day period, distribute any royalty fees not subject to an appeal filed pursuant to section 810.

§ 810. Judicial review

Any final decision of the Tribunal in a proceeding under section 801(b) may be appealed to the United States Court of Appeals, within thirty days after its publication in the Federal Register by an aggrieved party. The judicial review of the decision shall be had, in accordance with chapter 7 of title 5, on the basis of the record before the Tribunal. No court shall have jurisdiction to review a final decision of the Tribunal except as provided in this section.

TRANSITIONAL AND SUPPLEMENTARY PROVISIONS

SEC. 102. This Act becomes effective on January 1, 1978, except as otherwise expressly provided by this Act, including provisions of the first section of this Act. The provisions of sections 118, 304(b), and chapter 8 of title 17, as amended by the first section of this Act, take effect upon enactment of this Act.

SEC. 103. This Act does not provide copyright protection for any work that goes into the public domain before January 1, 1978. The exclusive rights, as provided by section 106 of title 17 as amended by the first section of this Act, to reproduce a work in phonorecords and to distribute phonorecords of the work, do not extend to any nondramatic musical work copyrighted before July 1, 1909.

SEC. 104. All proclamations issued by the President under section 1(e) or 9(b) of title 17 as it existed on December 31, 1977, or under previous copyright statutes of the United States, shall continue in force until terminated, suspended, or revised by the President.

SEC. 105. (a) (1) Section 505 of title 44 is amended to read as follows:

"§ 505. Sale of duplicate plates

"The Public Printer shall sell, under regulations of the Joint Committee on Printing to persons who may apply, additional or duplicate stereotype or electrotype plates from which a Government publication is printed, at a price not to exceed the cost of composition, the metal, and making to the Government, plus 10 per centum, and the full amount of the price shall be paid when the order is filed.".

(2) The item relating to section 505 in the sectional analysis at the beginning of chapter 5 of title 44, is amended to read as follows:

"505. Sale of duplicate plates.".

(b) Section 2113 of title 44 is amended to read as follows:

"§ 2113. Limitation on liability

"When letters and other intellectual productions (exclusive of patented material, published works under copyright protection, and unpublished works for which copyright registration has been made) come into the custody or possession of the Administrator of General Services, the United States or its agents are not liable for infringement of copyright or analogous rights arising out of use of the materials for display, inspection, research, reproduction, or other purposes.".

(c) In section 1498(b) of title 28, the phrase "section 101(b) of title 17" is amended to read "section 504(c) of title 17".

(d) Section 543(a)(4) of the Internal Revenue Code of 1954, as amended, is amended by striking out "(other than by reason of section 2 or 6 thereof)".

(e) Section 3202(a) of title 39 is amended by striking out clause (5). Section 3206 of title 39 is amended by deleting the words "subsections (b) and (c)" and inserting "subsection (b)" in subsection (a), and by deleting subsection (c). Section 3206(d) is renumbered (c).

(f) Subsection (a) of section 290(e) of title 15 is amended by deleting the phrase "section 8" and inserting in lieu thereof the phrase "section 105".

(g) Section 131 of title 2 is amended by deleting the phrase "deposit to secure copyright," and inserting in lieu thereof the phrase "acquisition of material under the copyright law,".

SEC. 106. In any case where, before January 1, 1978, a person has lawfully made parts of instruments serving to reproduce mechanically a copyrighted work under the compulsory license provisions of section 1(e) of title 17 as it existed on December 31, 1977, such person may continue to make and distribute such parts embodying the same mechanical reproduction without obtaining a new compulsory license under the terms of section 115 of title 17 as amended by the first section of this Act. However, such parts made on or after January 1, 1978, constitute phonorecords and are otherwise subject to the provisions of said section 115.

SEC. 107. In the case of any work in which an ad interim copyright is subsisting or is capable of being secured on December 31, 1977, under section 22 of title 17 as it existed on that date, copyright protection is hereby extended to endure for the term or terms provided by section 304 of title 17 as amended by the first section of this Act.

SEC. 108. The notice provisions of sections 401 through 403 of title 17 as amended by the first section of this Act apply to all copies or phonorecords publicly distributed on or after January 1, 1978. However, in the case of a work published before January 1, 1978, compliance with the notice provisions of title 17 either as it existed on December 31, 1977, or as amended by the first section of this Act, is adequate with respect to copies publicly distributed after December 31, 1977.

SEC. 109. The registration of claims to copyright for which the required deposit, application, and fee were received in the Copyright Office before January 1, 1978, and the recordation of assignments of copyright or other instruments received in the Copyright Office before January 1, 1978, shall be made in accordance with title 17 as it existed on December 31, 1977.

SEC. 110. The demand and penalty provisions of section 14 of title 17 as it existed on December 31, 1977, apply to any work in which copyright has been secured by publication with notice of copyright on or before that date, but any deposit and registration made after that date in response to a demand under that section shall be made in accordance with the provisions of title 17 as amended by the first section of this Act.

SEC. 111. Section 2318 of title 18 of the United States Code is amended to read as follows:

"§ 2318. Transportation, sale or receipt of phonograph records bearing forged or counterfeit labels

"(a) Whoever knowingly and with fraudulent intent transports, causes to be transported, receives, sells, or offers for sale in interstate or foreign commerce any phonograph record, disk, wire, tape, film, or other article on which sounds are recorded, to which or upon which is stamped, pasted, or affixed any forged or counterfeited label, knowing the label to have been falsely made, forged, or counterfeited shall be fined not more than $10,000 or imprisoned for not more than one year, or both, for the first such offense and shall be fined not more than $25,000 or imprisoned for not more than two years, or both, for any subsequent offense.

"(b) When any person is convicted of any violation of subsection (a), the court in its judgment of conviction shall, in addition to the penalty therein prescribed, order the forfeiture and destruction or other disposition of all counterfeit labels and all articles to which counterfeit labels have been affixed or which were intended to have had such labels affixed.".

"(c) Except to the extent they are inconsistent with the provisions of this title, all provisions of section 509, title 17, United States Code, are applicable to violations of subsection (a).".

SEC. 112. All causes of action that arose under title 17 before January 1, 1978, shall be governed by title 17 as it existed when the cause of action arose.

SEC. 113. (a) The Librarian of Congress (hereinafter referred to as the "Librarian") shall establish and maintain in the Library of Congress a library to be known as the American Television and Radio Archives (hereinafter referred to as the "Archives"). The purpose of the Archives shall be to preserve a permanent record of the television and radio programs which are the heritage of the people of the United States and to provide access to such programs to historians and scholars without encouraging or causing copyright infringement.

(1) The Librarian, after consultation with interested organizations and individuals, shall determine and place in the Archives such copies and phonorecords of television and radio programs transmitted to the public in the United States and in other countries which are of present or potential public or cultural interest, historical significance, cognitive value, or otherwise worthy of preservation, including copies and phonorecords of published and unpublished transmission programs—

(A) acquired in accordance with sections 407 and 408 of title 17 as amended by the first section of this Act; and

(B) transferred from the existing collections of the Library of Congress; and

(C) given to or exchanged with the Archives by other libraries, archives, organizations, and individuals; and

(D) purchased from the owner thereof.

(2) The Librarian shall maintain and publish appropriate catalogs and indexes of the collections of the Archives, and shall make such collections available for study and research under the conditions prescribed under this section.

(b) Notwithstanding the provisions of section 106 of title 17 as amended by the first section of this Act, the Librarian is authorized with respect to a transmission program which consists of a regularly scheduled newscast or on-the-spot coverage of news events and, under standards and conditions that the Librarian shall prescribe by regulation—

(1) to reproduce a fixation of such a program, in the same or another tangible form, for the purposes of preservation or security or for distribution under the conditions of clause (3) of this subsection; and

(2) to compile, without abridgment or any other editing, portions of such fixations according to subject matter, and to reproduce such compilations for the purpose of clause (1) of this subsection; and

(3) to distribute a reproduction made under clause (1) or (2) of this subsection—

(A) by loan to a person engaged in research; and

(B) for deposit in a library or archives which meets the requirements of section 108(a) of title 17 as amended by the first section of this Act,

in either case for use only in research and not for further reproduction or performance.

(c) The Librarian or any employee of the Library who is acting under the authority of this section shall not be liable in any action for copyright infringement committed by any other person unless the Librarian or such employee knowingly participated in the act of infringement committed by such person. Nothing in this section shall be construed to excuse or limit liability under title 17 as amended by the first section of this Act for any act not authorized by that title or this section, or for any act performed by a person not authorized to act under that title or this section.

(d) This section may be cited as the "American Television and Radio Archives Act".

SEC. 114. There are hereby authorized to be appropriated such funds as may be necessary to carry out the purposes of this Act.

SEC. 115. If any provision of title 17, as amended by the first section of this Act, is declared unconstitutional, the validity of the remainder of this title is not affected.

Approved October 19, 1976.

APPENDIX 2
TEXT OF THE COPYRIGHT ACT OF 1909

Boldface numbers in the margin of the text (e.g., **N1, N2,** etc.) refer to notes at the end of this appendix. These notes represent amendments made to the Copyright Act of 1909 up to the time of the enactment of the 1976 Copyright Law. Ellipses have been inserted to indicate deletions of nonpertinent material from the original document's footnotes.

Title 17—Copyrights

(Revised to January 1, 1973)

Chapter 1—Registration of Copyrights

§ 1. EXCLUSIVE RIGHTS AS TO COPYRIGHTED WORKS.—Any person entitled thereto, upon complying with the provisions of this title, shall have the exclusive right:

(a) To print, reprint, publish, copy, and vend the copyrighted work;

(b) To translate the copyrighted work into other languages or dialects, or make any other version thereof, if it be a literary work; to dramatize it if it be a nondramatic work; to convert it into a novel or other nondramatic work if it be a drama; to arrange or adapt it if it be a musical work; to complete, execute, and finish it if it be a model or design for a work of art;

(c) To deliver, authorize the delivery of, read, or present the copyrighted work in public for profit if it be a lecture, sermon, address or similar production, or other nondramatic literary work; to make or procure the making of any transcription or record thereof by or from which, in whole or in part, it may in any manner or by any method be exhibited, delivered, presented, produced, or reproduced; and to play or perform it in public for profit, and to exhibit, represent, produce, or reproduce it in any manner or by any method whatsoever. The damages for the infringement by broadcast of any work referred to in this subsection shall not exceed the sum of $100 where the infringing broadcaster shows that he was not aware that he was infringing and that such infringement could not have been reasonably foreseen; and

(d) To perform or represent the copyrighted work publicly if it be a drama or, if it be a dramatic work and not reproduced in copies for sale, to vend any manuscript or any record whatsoever thereof; to make or to procure the making of any transcription or record thereof by or from which, in whole or in part, it may in any manner or by any method be exhibited, performed, represented, produced, or reproduced; and to exhibit, perform, represent, produce, or reproduce it in any manner or by any method whatsoever; and

(e) To perform the copyrighted work publicly for profit if it be a musical composition; and for the purpose of public performance for profit, and for the purposes set forth in subsection (a) hereof, to make any arrangement or setting of it or of the melody of it in any system of notation or any form of record in which the thought of an author may be recorded and from which it may be read or reproduced: *Provided,* That the provisions of this title, so far as they secure copyright controlling the parts of instruments serving to reproduce mechanically the musical work, shall include only compositions published and copyrighted after July 1, 1909, and shall not include the works of a foreign author or composer unless the foreign state or nation of which such author or composer is a citizen or subject grants, either by treaty, convention, agreement, or law, to citizens of the United States similar rights. And as a condition of extending the copyright control to such mechanical reproductions, that whenever the owner of a musical copyright has used or permitted or knowingly acquiesced in the use of the copyrighted work upon the parts of instruments serving to reproduce mechanically the musical work, any other person may make similar use of the copyrighted work upon the payment to the copyright proprietor of a royalty of 2 cents on each such part manufactured, to be paid by the manufacturer thereof; and the copyright proprietor may require, and if so the manufacturer shall furnish, a report under oath on the 20th day of each month on the number of parts of instruments manufactured during the previous month serving to reproduce mechanically said musical work, and royalties shall be due on the parts manufactured during any month upon the 20th of the next succeeding month. The payment of the royalty provided for by this section shall free the articles or devices for which such royalty has been paid from further contribution to the copyright except in case of public performance for profit. It shall be the duty of the copyright owner, if he uses the musical composition himself for the manufacture of parts of instruments serving to reproduce mechanically the musical work, or licenses others to do so, to file notice thereof, accompanied by a recording fee, in the copyright office, and any failure to file such notice shall be a complete defense to any suit, action, or proceeding for any infringement of such copyright.

In case of failure of such manufacturer to pay to the copyright proprietor within thirty days after demand in writing the full sum of royalties due at said rate at the date of such demand, the court may award taxable costs to the plaintiff and a reasonable counsel fee, and the court may, in its discretion, enter judgment therein for any sum in addition over the amount found to be due as royalty in accordance with the terms of this title, not exceeding three times such amount.

The reproduction or rendition of a musical composition by or upon coin-operated machines shall not be deemed a public performance for profit unless a fee is charged for admission to the place where such reproduction or rendition occurs.

(f) [1] To reproduce and distribute to the public by sale or other transfer of ownership, or by rental, lease, or lending, reproductions of the copyrighted work if it be a sound recording: *Provided*, That the exclusive right of the owner of a copyright in a sound recording to reproduce it is limited to the right to duplicate the sound recording in a tangible form that directly or indirectly recaptures the actual sounds fixed in the recording: *Provided further*, That this right does not extend to the making or duplication of another sound recording that is an independent fixation of other sounds, even though such sounds imitate or simulate those in the copyrighted sound recording; or to reproductions made by transmitting organizations exclusively for their own use.

§ 2. RIGHTS OF AUTHOR OR PROPRIETOR OF UNPUBLISHED WORK.— Nothing in this title shall be construed to annul or limit the right of the author or proprietor of an unpublished work, at common law or in equity, to prevent the copying, publication, or use of such unpublished work without his consent, and to obtain damages therefor.

§ 3. PROTECTION OF COMPONENT PARTS OF WORK COPYRIGHTED; COMPOSITE WORKS OR PERIODICALS.—The copyright provided by this title shall protect all the copyrightable component parts of the work copyrighted, and all matter therein in which copyright is already subsisting, but without extending the duration or scope of such copyright. The copyright upon composite works or periodicals shall give to the proprietor thereof all the rights in respect thereto which he would have if each part were individually copyrighted under this title.

§ 4. ALL WRITINGS OF AUTHOR INCLUDED.—The works for which copyright may be secured under this title shall include all the writings of an author.

§ 5. CLASSIFICATION OF WORKS FOR REGISTRATION.—The application for registration shall specify to which of the following classes the work in which copyright is claimed belongs:

---

[1] Section 1(f) was added by the Act of October 15, 1971, Pub. L. 92–140, 85 Stat. 391. This act also added section 5(n), added a sentence at the end of section 19, amended the first sentence of section 20, and added three sentences at the end of section 26. The Act specified that the provisions cited in this footnote shall take effect four months after its enactment, that these provisions "shall apply only to sound recordings fixed, published, and copyrighted on and after the effective date of this Act and before January 1, 1975," and that nothing in title 17, United States Code, as amended by these provisions "shall be applied retrospectively or be construed as affecting in any way rights with respect to sound recordings fixed before the effective date of this Act."

N1

(a) Books, including composite and cyclopedic works, directories, gazetteers, and other compilations.

(b) Periodicals, including newspapers.

(c) Lectures, sermons, addresses (prepared for oral delivery).

(d) Dramatic or dramatico-musical compositions.

(e) Musical compositions.

(f) Maps.

(g) Works of art; models or designs for works of art.

(h) Reproductions of a work of art.

(i) Drawings or plastic works of a scientific or technical character.

(j) Photographs.

(k) Prints and pictorial illustrations including prints or labels used for articles of merchandise.

(l) Motion-picture photoplays.

(m) Motion pictures other than photoplays.

(n) [1] Sound recordings.

The above specifications shall not be held to limit the subject matter of copyright as defined in section 4 of this title, nor shall any error in classification invalidate or impair the copyright protection secured under this title.

§ 6. REGISTRATION OF PRINTS AND LABELS.—Commencing July 1, 1940, the Register of Copyrights is charged with the registration of claims to copyright properly presented, in all prints and labels published in connection with the sale or advertisement of articles of merchandise, including all claims to copyright in prints and labels pending in the Patent Office and uncleared at the close of business June 30, 1940. There shall be paid for registering a claim of copyright in any such print or label not a trade-mark $6, which sum shall cover the expense of furnishing a certificate of such registration, under the seal of the Copyright Office, to the claimant of copyright.

§ 7. COPYRIGHT ON COMPILATIONS OF WORKS IN PUBLIC DOMAIN OR OF COPYRIGHTED WORKS; SUBSISTING COPYRIGHTS NOT AFFECTED.— Compilations or abridgments, adaptations, arrangements, dramatizations, translations, or other versions of works in the public domain or of copyrighted works when produced with the consent of the proprietor of the copyright in such works, or works republished with new matter, shall be regarded as new works subject to copyright under the provisions of this title; but the publication of any such new works shall not affect the force or validity of any subsisting copyright upon

---

[1] Section 5(n) was added by the Act of October 15, 1971, Pub. L. 92–140, 85 Stat. 391. [. . .]

the matter employed or any part thereof, or be construed to imply an exclusive right to such use of the original works, or to secure or extend copyright in such original works.

§ 8. COPYRIGHT NOT TO SUBSIST IN WORKS IN PUBLIC DOMAIN, OR PUBLISHED PRIOR TO JULY 1, 1909, AND NOT ALREADY COPYRIGHTED, OR GOVERNMENT PUBLICATIONS; PUBLICATION BY GOVERNMENT OF COPYRIGHTED MATERIAL.—No copyright shall subsist in the original text of any work which is in the public domain, or in any work which was published in this country or any foreign country prior to July 1, 1909, and has not been already copyrighted in the United States, or in any publication of the United States Government, or any reprint, in whole or in part, thereof, except that the Postmaster General may secure copyright on behalf of the United States in the whole or any part of the publications authorized by section 2506 of title 39.[1]

The publication or republication by the Government, either separately or in a public document, of any material in which copyright is subsisting shall not be taken to cause any abridgment or annulment of the copyright or to authorize any use or appropriation of such copyright material without the consent of the copyright proprietor.

§ 9. AUTHORS OR PROPRIETORS, ENTITLED: ALIENS.—The author or proprietor of any work made the subject of copyright by this title, or his executors, administrators, or assigns, shall have copyright for such work under the conditions and for the terms specified in this title: *Provided, however,* That the copyright secured by this title shall extend to the work of an author or proprietor who is a citizen or subject of a foreign state or nation only under the conditions described in subsections (a), (b), or (c) below:

(a) When an alien author or proprietor shall be domiciled within the United States at the time of the first publication of his work; or

(b) When the foreign state or nation of which such author or proprietor is a citizen or subject grants, either by treaty, convention, agreement, or law, to citizens of the United States the benefit of copyright on substantially the same basis as to its own citizens, or copyright protection, substantially equal to the protection secured to such foreign author under this title or by treaty; or when such foreign state or nation is a party to an international agreement which provides for reciprocity in the granting of copyright, by the terms of which agreement the United States may, at its pleasure, become a party thereto.

---

[1] A further exception was provided by a statute enacted in 1968, Pub. L. 90–396, 82 Stat. 339, 340, amending Title 15 of the United States Code (15 U.S.C. 272), authorizing the Secretary of Commerce, at section 290(e), to secure copyright and renewal thereof on behalf of the United States as author or proprietor "in all or any part of any standard reference data which he prepares or makes available under this chapter."

The existence of the reciprocal conditions aforesaid shall be determined by the President of the United States, by proclamation made from time to time, as the purposes of this title may require: *Provided,* That whenever the President shall find that the authors, copyright owners, or proprietors of works first produced or published abroad and subject to copyright or to renewal of copyright under the laws of the United States, including works subject to ad interim copyright, are or may have been temporarily unable to comply with the conditions and formalities prescribed with respect to such works by the copyright laws of the United States, because of the disruption or suspension of facilities essential for such compliance, he may by proclamation grant such extension of time as he may deem appropriate for the fulfillment of such conditions or formalities by authors, copyright owners, or proprietors who are citizens of the United States or who are nationals of countries which accord substantially equal treatment in this respect to authors, copyright owners, or proprietors who are citizens of the United States: *Provided further,* That no liability shall attach under this title for lawful uses made or acts done prior to the effective date of such proclamation in connection with such works, or in respect to the continuance for one year subsequent to such date of any business undertaking or enterprise lawfully undertaken prior to such date involving expenditure or contractual obligation in connection with the exploitation, production, reproduction, circulation, or performance of any such work.

The President may at any time terminate any proclamation authorized herein or any part thereof or suspend or extend its operation for such period or periods of time as in his judgment the interests of the United States may require.

(c) When the Universal Copyright Convention, signed at Geneva on September 6, 1952, shall be in force [1] between the United States of America and the foreign state or nation of which such author is a citizen or subject, or in which the work was first published. Any work to which copyright is extended pursuant to this subsection shall be exempt from the following provisions of this title: (1) The requirement in section 1 (e) that a foreign state or nation must grant to United States citizens mechanical reproduction rights similar to those specified therein; (2) the obligatory deposit requirements of the first sentence of section 13; (3) the provisions of sections 14, 16, 17, and 18; (4) the import prohibitions of section 107, to the extent that they are related to the manufacturing requirements of section 16; and (5) the require-

---

[1] The Universal Copyright Convention came into force with respect to the United States of America on September 16, 1955. [...]

ments of sections 19 and 20 : *Provided, however,* That such exemptions shall apply only if from the time of first publication all the copies of the work published with the authority of the author or other copyright proprietor shall bear the symbol © accompanied by the name of the copyright proprietor and the year of first publication placed in such manner and location as to give reasonable notice of claim of copyright.

Upon the coming into force of the Universal Copyright Convention in a foreign state or nation as hereinbefore provided, every book or periodical of a citizen or subject thereof in which ad interim copyright was subsisting on the effective date of said coming into force shall have copyright for twenty-eight years from the date of first publication abroad without the necessity of complying with the further formalities specified in section 23 of this title.

The provisions of this subsection shall not be extended to works of an author who is a citizen of, or domiciled in the United States of America regardless of place of first publication, or to works first published in the United States.

§ 10. PUBLICATION OF WORK WITH NOTICE.—Any person entitled thereto by this title may secure copyright for his work by publication thereof with the notice of copyright required by this title; and such notice shall be affixed to each copy thereof published or offered for sale in the United States by authority of the copyright proprietor, except in the case of books seeking ad interim protection under section 22 of this title.

§ 11. REGISTRATION OF CLAIM AND ISSUANCE OF CERTIFICATE.—Such person may obtain registration of his claim to copyright by complying with the provisions of this title, including the deposit of copies, and upon such compliance the Register of Copyrights shall issue to him the certificates provided for in section 209 of this title.

§ 12. WORKS NOT REPRODUCED FOR SALE.—Copyright may also be had of the works of an author, of which copies are not reproduced for sale, by the deposit, with claim of copyright, of one complete copy of such work if it be a lecture or similar production or a dramatic, musical, or dramatico-musical composition; of a title and description, with one print taken from each scene or act, if the work be a motion-picture photoplay; of a photographic print if the work be a photograph; of a title and description, with not less than two prints taken from different sections of a complete motion picture, if the work be a motion picture other than a photoplay; or of a photograph or other identifying reproduction thereof, if it be a work of art or a plastic work or drawing. But the privilege of registration of copyright secured hereunder shall not exempt the copyright proprietor from the deposit of copies, under sections 13 and 14 of this title, where the work is later reproduced in copies for sale.

§ 13. DEPOSIT OF COPIES AFTER PUBLICATION; ACTION OR PROCEEDING FOR INFRINGEMENT.—After copyright has been secured by publication of the work with the notice of copyright as provided in section 10 of this title, there shall be promptly deposited in the Copyright Office or in the mail addressed to the Register of Copyrights, Washington, District of Columbia, two complete copies of the best edition thereof then published, or if the work is by an author who is a citizen or subject of a foreign state or nation and has been published in a foreign country, one complete copy of the best edition then published in such foreign country, which copies or copy, if the work be a book or periodical, shall have been produced in accordance with the manufacturing provisions specified in section 16 of this title; or if such work be a contribution to a periodical, for which contribution special registration is requested, one copy of the issue or issues containing such contribution; or if the work belongs to a class specified in subsections (g), (h), (i) or (k) of section 5 of this title, and if the Register of Copyrights determines that it is impracticable to deposit copies because of their size, weight, fragility, or monetary value he may permit the deposit of photographs or other identifying reproductions in lieu of copies of the work as published under such rules and regulations as he may prescribe with the approval of the Librarian of Congress; or if the work is not reproduced in copies for sale there shall be deposited the copy, print, photograph, or other identifying reproduction provided by section 12 of this title, such copies or copy, print, photograph, or other reproduction to be accompanied in each case by a claim of copyright. No action or proceeding shall be maintained for infringement of copyright in any work until the provisions of this title with respect to the deposit of copies and registration of such work shall have been complied with.

§ 14. SAME; FAILURE TO DEPOSIT; DEMAND; PENALTY.—Should the copies called for by section 13 of this title not be promptly deposited as provided in this title, the Register of Copyrights may at any time after the publication of the work, upon actual notice, require the proprietor of the copyright to deposit them, and after the said demand shall have been made, in default of the deposit of copies of the work within three months from any part of the United States, except an outlying territorial possession of the United States, or within six months from any outlying territorial possession of the United States, or from any foreign country, the proprietor of the copyright shall be liable to a fine of $100 and to pay to the Library of Congress twice the amount of the retail price of the best edition of the work, and the copyright shall become void.

§ 15. SAME; POSTMASTER'S RECEIPT; TRANSMISSION BY MAIL WITHOUT COST.—The postmaster to whom are delivered the articles deposited as provided in sections 12 and 13 of this title shall, if requested, give a receipt therefor and shall mail them to their destination without cost to the copyright claimant.

§ 16. MECHANICAL WORK TO BE DONE IN UNITED STATES.—Of the printed book or periodical specified in section 5, subsections (a) and (b), of this title, except the original text of a book or periodical of foreign origin in a language or languages other than English, the text of all copies accorded protection under this title, except as below provided, shall be printed from type set within the limits of the United States, either by hand or by the aid of any kind of typesetting machine, or from plates made within the limits of the United States from type set therein, or, if the text be produced by lithographic process, or photoengraving process, then by a process wholly performed within the limits of the United States, and the printing of the text and binding of the said book shall be performed within the limits of the United States; which requirements shall extend also to the illustrations within a book consisting of printed text and illustrations produced by lithographic process, or photoengraving process, and also to separate lithographs or photoengravings, except where in either case the subjects represented are located in a foreign country and illustrate a scientific work or reproduce a work of art: *Provided, however,* That said requirements shall not apply to works in raised characters for the use of the blind, or to books or periodicals of foreign origin in a language or languages other than English, or to works printed or produced in the United States by any other process than those above specified in this section, or to copies of books or periodicals, first published abroad in the English language, imported into the United States within five years after first publication in a foreign state or nation up to the number of fifteen hundred copies of each such book or periodical if said copies shall contain notice of copyright in accordance with sections 10, 19, and 20 of this title and if ad interim copyright in said work shall have been obtained pursuant to section 22 of this title prior to the importation into the United States of any copy except those permitted by the provisions of section 107 of this title: *Provided further,* That the provisions of this section shall not affect the right of importation under the provisions of section 107 of this title.

§ 17. AFFIDAVIT TO ACCOMPANY COPIES.—In the case of the book the copies so deposited shall be accompanied by an affidavit under the official seal of any officer authorized to administer oaths within the United States, duly made by the person claiming copyright or by his duly authorized agent or representative residing in the United States, or by the printer who has printed the book, setting forth that the copies deposited have been printed from type set within the limits of the

United States or from plates made within the limits of the United States from type set therein; or, if the text be produced by lithographic process, or photoengraving process, that such process was wholly performed within the limits of the United States and that the printing of the text and binding of the said book have also been performed within the limits of the United States. Such affidavit shall state also the place where and the establishment or establishments in which such type was set or plates made or lithographic process, or photoengraving process or printing and binding were performed and the date of the completion of the printing of the book or the date of publication.

§ 18. MAKING FALSE AFFIDAVIT.—Any person who, for the purpose of obtaining registration of a claim to copyright, shall knowingly make a false affidavit as to his having complied with the above conditions shall be deemed guilty of a misdemeanor, and upon conviction thereof shall be punished by a fine of not more than $1,000, and all of his rights and privileges under said copyright shall thereafter be forfeited.

§ 19. NOTICE; FORM.[1]—The notice of copyright required by section 10 of this title shall consist either of the word "Copyright", the abbreviation "Copr.", or the symbol ©, accompanied by the name of the copyright proprietor, and if the work be a printed literary, musical, or dramatic work, the notice shall include also the year in which the copyright was secured by publication. In the case, however, of copies of works specified in subsections (f) to (k), inclusive, of section 5 of this title, the notice may consist of the letter C enclosed within a circle, thus ©, accompanied by the initials, monogram, mark, or symbol of the copyright proprietor: *Provided*, That on some accessible portion of such copies or of the margin, back, permanent base, or pedestal, or of the substance on which such copies shall be mounted, his name shall appear. But in the case of works in which copyright was subsisting on July 1, 1909, the notice of copyright may be either in one of the forms prescribed herein or may consist of the following words: "Entered according to Act of Congress, in the year   , by A. B., in the office of the Librarian of Congress, at Washington, D.C.," or, at his option, the word "Copyright", together with the year the copyright was entered and the name of the party by whom it was taken out; thus, "Copyright, 19—, by A. B." In the case of reproductions of works specified in subsection (n) of section 5 of this title, the notice shall consist of the symbol ℗ (the letter P in a circle), the year of first publication of the sound recording, and the name of the owner of copyright in the sound recording, or an abbreviation by which the name can be recognized, or a generally known alternative designation of the owner:

---

[1] The last sentence of section 19 was added by the Act of October 15, 1971, Pub. L. 92–140, 85 Stat. 391.[...]

Provided, That if the producer of the sound recording is named on the labels or containers of the reproduction, and if no other name appears in conjunction with the notice, his name shall be considered a part of the notice.

§ 20. SAME; PLACE OF APPLICATION OF; ONE NOTICE IN EACH VOLUME OR NUMBER OF NEWSPAPER OR PERIODICAL.[1]—The notice of copyright shall be applied, in the case of a book or other printed publication, upon its title page or the page immediately following, or if a periodical either upon the title page or upon the first page of text of each separate number or under the title heading, or if a musical work either upon its title page or the first page of music, or if a sound recording on the surface of reproductions thereof or on the label or container in such manner and location as to give reasonable notice of the claim of copyright. One notice of copyright in each volume or in each number of a newspaper or periodical published shall suffice.

§ 21. SAME; EFFECT OF ACCIDENTAL OMISSION FROM COPY OR COPIES.—Where the copyright proprietor has sought to comply with the provisions of this title with respect to notice, the omission by accident or mistake of the prescribed notice from a particular copy or copies shall not invalidate the copyright or prevent recovery for infringement against any person who, after actual notice of the copyright, begins an undertaking to infringe it, but shall prevent the recovery of damages against an innocent infringer who has been misled by the omission of the notice; and in a suit for infringement no permanent injunction shall be had unless the copyright proprietor shall reimburse to the innocent infringer his reasonable outlay innocently incurred if the court, in its discretion, shall so direct.

§ 22. AD INTERIM PROTECTION OF BOOK OF PERIODICAL PUBLISHED ABROAD.—In the case of a book or periodical first published abroad in the English language, the deposit in the Copyright Office, not later than six months after its publication abroad, of one complete copy of the foreign edition, with a request for the reservation of the copyright and a statement of the name and nationality of the author and of the copyright proprietor and of the date of publication of the said book or periodical, shall secure to the author or proprietor an ad interim copyright therein, which shall have all the force and effect given to copyright by this title, and shall endure until the expiration of five years after the date of first publication abroad.

§ 23. SAME; EXTENSION TO FULL TERM.—Whenever within the period of such ad interim protection an authorized edition of such

---

[1] The first sentence of section 20 was amended by the Act of October 15, 1971, Pub. L. 92–140, 85 Stat. 391. [. . .]

books or periodicals shall be published within the United States, in accordance with the manufacturing provisions specified in section 16 of this title, and whenever the provisions of this title as to deposit of copies, registration, filing of affidavits, and the printing of the copyright notice shall have been duly complied with, the copyright shall be extended to endure in such book or periodical for the term provided in this title.

§ 24. DURATION; RENEWAL AND EXTENSION.[1]—The copyright secured by this title shall endure for twenty-eight years from the date of first publication, whether the copyrighted work bears the author's true name or is published anonymously or under an assumed name: *Provided*, That in the case of any posthumous work or of any periodical, cyclopedic, or other composite work upon which the copyright was originally secured by the proprietor thereof, or of any work copyrighted by a corporate body (otherwise than as assignee or licensee of the individual author) or by an employer for whom such work is made for hire, the proprietor of such copyright shall be entitled to a renewal and extension of the copyright in such work for the further term of twenty-eight years when application for such renewal and extension shall have been made to the copyright office and duly registered therein within one year prior to the expiration of the original term of copyright: *And provided further*, That in the case of any other copyrighted work, including a contribution by an individual author to a periodical or to a cyclopedic or other composite work, the author of such work, if still living, or the widow, widower, or children of the author, if the author be not living, or if such author, widow, widower, or children be not living, then the author's executors, or in the absence of a will, his next of kin shall be entitled to a renewal and extension of the copyright in such work for a further term of twenty-eight years when application for such renewal and extension shall have been made to the copyright office and duly registered therein within one year prior to the expiration of the original term of copyright:[2] *And provided further*, That in default of the registration of such application for renewal and extension, the copyright in any work shall determine at the expiration of twenty-eight years from first publication.

---

[1] Private Law 92–60, enacted December 15, 1971, provides specially for a term of 75 years from that date, or from the later date of first publication, for the various editions of "Science and Health" by Mary Baker Eddy. [...]
further information is needed on this subject.

[2] A series of eight acts, the most recent being the Act of October 25, 1972, Pub. L. 92–566, 86 Stat. 1170, which cites the seven earlier acts, has extended until December 31, 1974, copyrights previously renewed in which the second term would otherwise have expired between September 19, 1962 and December 31, 1974. [...]

§ 25. Renewal of Copyrights Registered in Patent Office Under Repealed Law.—Subsisting copyrights originally registered in the Patent Office prior to July 1, 1940, under section 3 of the act of June 18, 1874, shall be subject to renewal in behalf of the proprietor upon application made to the Register of Copyrights within one year prior to the expiration of the original term of twenty-eight years.

§ 26. Terms Defined.[1]—In the interpretation and construction of this title "the date of publication" shall in the case of a work of which copies are reproduced for sale or distribution be held to be the earliest date when copies of the first authorized edition were placed on sale, sold, or publicly distributed by the proprietor of the copyright or under his authority, and the word "author" shall include an employer in the case of works made for hire. For the purposes of this section and sections 10, 11, 13, 14, 21, 101, 106, 109, 209, 215, but not for any other purpose, a reproduction of a work described in subsection 5(n) shall be considered to be a copy thereof. "Sound recordings" are works that result from the fixation of a series of musical, spoken, or other sounds, but not including the sounds accompanying a motion picture. "Reproductions of sound recordings" are material objects in which sounds other than those accompanying a motion picture are fixed by any method now known or later developed, and from which the sounds can be perceived, reproduced, or otherwise communicated, either directly or with the aid of a machine or device, and include the "parts of instruments serving to reproduce mechanically the musical work", "mechanical reproductions", and "interchangeable parts, such as discs or tapes for use in mechanical music-producing machines" referred to in sections 1(e) and 101(e) of this title.

§ 27. Copyright Distinct From Property in Object Copyrighted; Effect of Sale of Object, and of Assignment of Copyright.—The copyright is distinct from the property in the material object copyrighted, and the sale or conveyance, by gift or otherwise, of the material object shall not of itself constitute a transfer of the copyright, nor shall the assignment of the copyright constitute a transfer of the title to the material object; but nothing in this title shall be deemed to forbid, prevent, or restrict the transfer of any copy of a copyrighted work the possession of which has been lawfully obtained.

§ 28. Assignments and Bequests.—Copyright secured under this title or previous copyright laws of the United States may be assigned, granted, or mortgaged by an instrument in writing signed by the proprietor of the copyright, or may be bequeathed by will.

---

[1] The last three sentences of section 26 were added by the Act of October 15, 1971, Pub. L. 92–140, 85 Stat. 391. [...]

§ 29. SAME; EXECUTED IN FOREIGN COUNTRY; ACKNOWLEDGMENT AND CERTIFICATE.—Every assignment of copyright executed in a foreign country shall be acknowledged by the assignor before a consular officer or secretary of legation of the United States authorized by law to administer oaths or perform notarial acts. The certificate of such acknowledgment under the hand and official seal of such consular officer or secretary of legation shall be prima facie evidence of the execution of the instrument.

§ 30. SAME; RECORD.—Every assignment of copyright shall be recorded in the copyright office within three calendar months after its execution in the United States or within six calendar months after its execution without the limits of the United States, in default of which it shall be void as against any subsequent purchaser or mortgagee for a valuable consideration, without notice, whose assignment has been duly recorded.

§ 31. SAME; CERTIFICATE OF RECORD.—The Register of Copyrights shall, upon payment of the prescribed fee, record such assignment, and shall return it to the sender with a certificate of record attached under seal of the copyright office, and upon the payment of the fee prescribed by this title he shall furnish to any person requesting the same a certified copy thereof under the said seal.

§ 32. SAME; USE OF NAME OF ASSIGNEE IN NOTICE.—When an assignment of the copyright in a specified book or other work has been recorded the assignee may substitute his name for that of the assignor in the statutory notice of copyright prescribed by this title.

Chapter 2—Infringement Proceedings [1]

§ 101. Infringement:
    (a) Injunction.
    (b) Damages and profits; amounts; other remedies.
    (c) Impounding during action.
    (d) Destruction of infringing copies and plates.
    (e) Interchangeable parts for use in mechanical music-producing machines.
§ 104. Willful infringement for profit.
§ 105. Fraudulent notice of copyright, or removal or alteration of notice.
§ 106. Importation of article bearing false notice or piratical copies of copyrighted work.
§ 107. Importation, during existence of copyright, of piratical copies, or of copies not produced in accordance with section 16 of this title.
§ 108. Forfeiture and destruction of articles prohibited importation.
§ 109. Importation of prohibited articles; regulations; proof of deposit of copies by complainants.

---

[1] Sections 101(f), 102, 103, 110, and 111 were repealed by the Act of June 25, 1948, ch. 646, § 39, 62 Stat. 869, at 931, 936, and 996, effective September 1, 1948. However, see sections 1338, 1400, 1498, and 2072, Title 28, United States Code.

§ 101. INFRINGEMENT.—If any person shall infringe the copyright in any work protected under the copyright laws of the United States such person shall be liable:

(a) INJUNCTION.—To an injunction restraining such infringement;

(b) DAMAGES AND PROFITS; AMOUNT; OTHER REMEDIES.—To pay to the copyright proprietor such damages as the copyright proprietor may have suffered due to the infringement, as well as all the profits which the infringer shall have made from such infringement, and in proving profits the plaintiff shall be required to prove sales only, and the defendant shall be required to prove every element of cost which he claims, or in lieu of actual damages and profits, such damages as to the court shall appear to be just, and in assessing such damages the court may, in its discretion, allow the amounts as hereinafter stated, but in case of a newspaper reproduction of a copyrighted photograph, such damages shall not exceed the sum of $200 nor be less than the sum of $50, and in the case of the infringement of an undramatized or non-dramatic work by means of motion pictures, where the infringer shall show that he was not aware that he was infringing, and that such infringement could not have been reasonably foreseen, such damages shall not exceed the sum of $100; and in the case of an infringement of a copyrighted dramatic or dramatico-musical work by a maker of motion pictures and his agencies for distribution thereof to exhibitors, where such infringer shows that he was not aware that he was infringing a copyrighted work, and that such infringements could not reasonably have been foreseen, the entire sum of such damages recoverable by the copyright proprietor from such infringing maker and his agencies for the distribution to exhibitors of such infringing motion picture shall not exceed the sum of $5,000 nor be less than $250, and such damages shall in no other case exceed the sum of $5,000 nor be less than the sum of $250, and shall not be regarded as a penalty. But the foregoing exceptions shall not deprive the copyright proprietor of any other remedy given him under this law, nor shall the limitation as to the amount of recovery apply to infringements occurring after the actual notice to a defendant, either by service of process in a suit or other written notice served upon him.

First. In the case of a painting, statue, or sculpture, $10 for every infringing copy made or sold by or found in the possession of the infringer or his agents or employees;

Second. In the case of any work enumerated in section 5 of this title, except a painting, statue, or sculpture, $1 for every infringing copy made or sold by or found in the possession of the infringer or his agents or employees;

Third. In the case of a lecture, sermon, or address, $50 for every infringing delivery;

Fourth. In the case of a dramatic or dramatico-musical or a choral or orchestral composition, $100 for the first and $50 for every subsequent infringing performance; in the case of other musical compositions $10 for every infringing performance;

(c) IMPOUNDING DURING ACTION.—To deliver up on oath, to be impounded during the pendency of the action, upon such terms and conditions as the court may prescribe, all articles alleged to infringe a copyright;

(d) DESTRUCTION OF INFRINGING COPIES AND PLATES.—To deliver up on oath for destruction all the infringing copies or devices, as well as all plates, molds, matrices, or other means for making such infringing copies as the court may order.

(e)[1] INTERCHANGEABLE PARTS FOR USE IN MECHANICAL MUSIC-PRODUCING MACHINES.—Interchangeable parts, such as discs or tapes for use in mechanical music-producing machines adapted to reproduce copyrighted musical works, shall be considered copies of the copyrighted musical works which they serve to reproduce mechanically for the purposes of this section 101 and sections 106 and 109 of this title, and the unauthorized manufacture, use, or sale of such interchangeable parts shall constitute an infringement of the copyrighted work rendering the infringer liable in accordance with all provisions of this title dealing with infringements of copyright and, in a case of willful infringement for profit, to criminal prosecution pursuant to section 104 of this title. Whenever any person, in the absence of a license agreement, intends to use a copyrighted musical composition upon the parts of instruments serving to reproduce mechanically the musical work, relying upon the compulsory license provision of this title, he shall serve notice of such intention, by registered mail, upon the copyright proprietor at his last address disclosed by the records of the copyright office, sending to the copyright office a duplicate of such notice.

[(f) See footnote 1, page 205, *supra*.]

[§ 102. See footnote 1, page 205, *supra*.]

[§ 103. See footnote 1, page 205, *supra*.]

---

[1] The former section 101(e) was deleted in its entirety and the present language was substituted by the Act of October 15, 1971, Pub. L. 92–140, 85 Stat. 391, effective immediately upon enactment.

§ 104. WILLFUL INFRINGEMENT FOR PROFIT.—Any person who will-
N3 fully and for profit shall infringe any copyright secured by this title,
or who shall knowingly and willfully aid or abet such infringement,
shall be deemed guilty of a misdemeanor, and upon conviction thereof
shall be punished by imprisonment for not exceeding one year or by
a fine of not less than $100 nor more than $1,000, or both, in the discretion of the court: *Provided, however,* That nothing in this title
shall be so construed as to prevent the performance of religious or
secular works such as oratorios, cantatas, masses, or octavo choruses
by public schools, church choirs, or vocal societies, rented, borrowed,
or obtained from some public library, public school, church choir,
school choir, or vocal society, provided the performance is given for
charitable or educational purposes and not for profit.

§ 105. FRAUDULENT NOTICE OF COPYRIGHT, OR REMOVAL OR ALTERA-
TION OF NOTICE.—Any person who, with fraudulent intent, shall insert
or impress any notice of copyright required by this title, or words of
the same purport, in or upon any uncopyrighted article, or with
fraudulent intent shall remove or alter the copyright notice upon any
article duly copyrighted shall be guilty of a misdemeanor, punishable
by a fine of not less than $100 and not more than $1,000. Any person
who shall knowingly issue or sell any article bearing a notice of United
States copyright which has not been copyrighted in this country, or
who shall knowingly import any article bearing such notice or words
of the same purport, which has not been copyrighted in this country,
shall be liable to a fine of $100.

§ 106. IMPORTATION OF ARTICLE BEARING FALSE NOTICE OR PIRATICAL
COPIES OF COPYRIGHTED WORK.—The importation into the United
States of any article bearing a false notice of copyright when there is
no existing copyright thereon in the United States, or of any piratical
copies of any work copyrighted in the United States, is prohibited.

§ 107. IMPORTATION, DURING EXISTENCE OF COPYRIGHT, OF PIRATICAL
COPIES, OR OF COPIES NOT PRODUCED IN ACCORDANCE WITH SECTION 16
OF THIS TITLE.—During the existence of the American copyright in
any book the importation into the United States of any piratical copies
thereof or of any copies thereof (although authorized by the author
or proprietor) which have not been produced in accordance with the
manufacturing provisions specified in section 16 of this title, or any
plates of the same not made from type set within the limits of the
United States, or any copies thereof produced by lithographic or photoengraving process not performed within the limits of the United
States, in accordance with the provisions of section 16 of this title,
is prohibited: *Provided, however,* That, except as regards piratical
copies, such prohibition shall not apply:

(a) To works in raised characters for the use of the blind.

(b) To a foreign newspaper or magazine, although containing matter copyrighted in the United States printed or reprinted by authority of the copyright proprietor, unless such newspaper or magazine contains also copyright matter printed or reprinted without such authorization.

(c) To the authorized edition of a book in a foreign language or languages of which only a translation into English has been copyrighted in this country.

(d) To any book published abroad with the authorization of the author or copyright proprietor when imported under the circumstances stated in one of the four subdivisions following, that is to say:

First. When imported, not more than one copy at one time, for individual use and not for sale; but such privilege of importation shall not extend to a foreign reprint of a book by an American author copyrighted in the United States.

Second. When imported by the authority or for the use of the United States.

Third. When imported, for use and not for sale, not more than one copy of any such book in any one invoice, in good faith by or for any society or institution incorporated for educational, literary, philosophical, scientific or religious purposes, or for the encouragement of the fine arts, or for any college, academy, school, or seminary of learning, or for any State, school, college, university, or free public library in the United States.

Fourth. When such books form parts of libraries or collections purchased en bloc for the use of societies, institutions, or libraries designated in the foregoing paragraph, or form parts of the libraries or personal baggage belonging to persons or families arriving from foreign countries and are not intended for sale: *Provided*, That copies imported as above may not lawfully be used in any way to violate the rights of the proprietor of the American copyright or annul or limit the copyright protection secured by this title, and such unlawful use shall be deemed an infringement of copyright.

§ 108. FORFEITURE AND DESTRUCTION OF ARTICLES PROHIBITED IMPORTATION.—Any and all articles prohibited importation by this title which are brought into the United States from any foreign country (except in the mails) shall be seized and forfeited by like proceedings as those provided by law for the seizure and condemnation of property imported into the United States in violation of the customs revenue laws. Such articles when forfeited shall be destroyed in such manner as the Secretary of the Treasury or the court, as the case may be, shall direct: *Provided, however*, That all copies of authorized editions of copyright books imported in the mails or otherwise in violation of the provisions of this title may be exported and returned to the country of export whenever it is shown to the satisfaction of the Secretary of the Treasury, in a written application, that such importation does not involve willful negligence or fraud.

§ 109. IMPORTATION OF PROHIBITED ARTICLES; REGULATIONS; PROOF OF DEPOSIT OF COPIES BY COMPLAINANTS.—The Secretary of the Treasury and the Postmaster General are hereby empowered and required to make and enforce individually or jointly such rules and regulations as shall prevent the importation into the United States of articles prohibited importation by this title, and may require, as conditions precedent to exclusion of any work in which copyright is claimed, the copyright proprietor or any person claiming actual or potential injury by reason of actual or contemplated importations of copies of such work to file with the Post Office Department or the Treasury Department a certificate of the Register of Copyrights that the provisions of section 13 of this title have been fully complied with, and to give notice of such compliance to postmasters or to customs officers at the ports of entry in the United States in such form and accompanied by such exhibits as may be deemed necessary for the practical and efficient administration and enforcement of the provisions of sections 106 and 107 of this title.

[§ 110. See footnote 1, page 205, *supra.*]

[§ 111. See footnote 1, page 205, *supra.*]

§ 112. INJUNCTIONS; SERVICE AND ENFORCEMENT.—Any court mentioned in section 1338 of Title 28 or judge thereof shall have power, upon complaint filed by any party aggrieved, to grant injunctions to prevent and restrain the violation of any right secured by this title, according to the course and principles of courts of equity, on such terms as said court or judge may deem reasonable. Any injunction that may be granted restraining and enjoining the doing of anything forbidden by this title may be served on the parties against whom such injunction may be granted anywhere in the United States, and shall be operative throughout the United States and be enforceable by proceedings in contempt or otherwise by any other court or judge possessing jurisdiction of the defendants.

§ 113. TRANSMISSION OF CERTIFIED COPIES OF PAPERS FOR ENFORCEMENT OF INJUNCTION BY OTHER COURT.—The clerk of the court or judge granting the injunction, shall, when required so to do by the court hearing the application to enforce said injunction, transmit without delay to said court a certified copy of all the papers in said cause that are on file in his office.

§ 114. REVIEW OF ORDERS, JUDGMENTS, OR DECREES.—The orders, judgments, or decrees of any court mentioned in section 1338 of Title

28 arising under the copyright laws of the United States may be reviewed on appeal in the manner and to the extent now provided by law for the review of cases determined in said courts, respectively.

§ 115. LIMITATIONS.—(a) CRIMINAL PROCEEDINGS.—No criminal proceedings shall be maintained under the provisions of this title unless the same is commenced within three years after the cause of action arose.

(b) CIVIL ACTIONS.—No civil action shall be maintained under the provisions of this title unless the same is commenced within three years after the claim accrued.

§ 116. COSTS; ATTORNEY'S FEES.—In all actions, suits, or proceedings under this title, except when brought by or against the United States or any officer thereof, full costs shall be allowed, and the court may award to the prevailing party a reasonable attorney's fee as part of the costs.

Chapter 3—Copyright Office

§ 201. Copyright office ; preservation of records.
§ 202. Register, assistant register, and subordinates.
§ 203. Same ; deposit of moneys received ; reports.
§ 204. Same ; bond.
§ 205. Same ; annual report.
§ 206. Seal of copyright office.
§ 207. Rules for registration of claims.
§ 208. Record books in copyright office.
§ 209. Certificates of registration; effect as evidence; receipt for copies deposited.
§ 210. Catalogs of copyright entries ; effect as evidence.
§ 211. Same ; distribution and sale ; disposal of proceeds.
§ 212. Records and works deposited in copyright office open to public inspection ; taking copies of entries.
§ 213. Disposition of articles deposited in office.
§ 214. Destruction of articles deposited in office remaining undisposed of ; removal of by author or proprietor ; manuscripts of unpublished works.
§ 215. Fees.
§ 216. When the day for taking action falls on Saturday, Sunday, or a holiday.

§ 201. COPYRIGHT OFFICE; PRESERVATION OF RECORDS.—All records and other things relating to copyrights required by law to be preserved shall be kept and preserved in the copyright office, Library of Congress, District of Columbia, and shall be under the control of the register of copyrights, who shall, under the direction and supervision of the Librarian of Congress, perform all the duties relating to the registration of copyrights.

§ 202. REGISTER, ASSISTANT REGISTER, AND SUBORDINATES.—There shall be appointed by the Librarian of Congress a Register of Copyrights, and one Assistant Register of Copyrights, who shall have authority during the absence of the Register of Copyrights to attach the copyright office seal to all papers issued from the said office and to sign such certificates and other papers as may be necessary. There shall also be appointed by the Librarian such subordinate assistants to the register as may from time to time be authorized by law.

§ 203. SAME; DEPOSIT OF MONEYS RECEIVED; REPORTS.—The Register of Copyrights shall make daily deposits in some bank in the District of Columbia, designated for this purpose by the Secretary of the Treasury as a national depository, of all moneys received to be applied as copyright fees, and shall make weekly deposits with the Secretary of the Treasury, in such manner as the latter shall direct, of all copyright fees actually applied under the provisions of this title, and annual deposits of sums received which it has not been possible to apply as copyright fees or to return to the remitters, and shall also make monthly reports to the Secretary of the Treasury and to the Librarian of Congress of the applied copyright fees for each calendar month, together with a statement of all remittances received, trust funds on hand, moneys refunded, and unapplied balances.

§ 204. SAME; BOND.—The Register of Copyrights shall give bond to the United States in the sum of $20,000, in form to be approved by the General Counsel for the Department of the Treasury and with sureties satisfactory to the Secretary of the Treasury, for the faithful discharge of his duties.

§ 205. SAME; ANNUAL REPORT.—The Register of Copyrights shall make an annual report to the Librarian of Congress, to be printed in the annual report on the Library of Congress, of all copyright business for the previous fiscal year, including the number and kind of works which have been deposited in the copyright office during the fiscal year, under the provisions of this title.

§ 206. SEAL OF COPYRIGHT OFFICE.—The seal used in the copyright office on July 1, 1909, shall be the seal of the copyright office, and by it all papers issued from the copyright office requiring authentication shall be authenticated.

§ 207. RULES FOR REGISTRATION OF CLAIMS.[1]—Subject to the approval of the Librarian of Congress, the Register of Copyrights shall be authorized to make rules and regulations for the registration of claims to copyright as provided by this title.

§ 208. RECORD BOOKS IN COPYRIGHT OFFICE.—The Register of Copyrights shall provide and keep such record books in the copyright office as are required to carry out the provisions of this title, and when-

---

[1] Published in the *Federal Register* and Title 37 of the *Code of Federal Regulations*.
[. . .]

ever deposit has been made in the copyright office of a copy of any work under the provisions of this title he shall make entry thereof.

§ 209. CERTIFICATE OF REGISTRATION; EFFECT AS EVIDENCE; RECEIPT FOR COPIES DEPOSITED.—In the case of each entry the person recorded as the claimant of the copyright shall be entitled to a certificate of registration under seal of the copyright office, to contain the name and address of said claimant, the name of the country of which the author of the work is a citizen or subject, and when an alien author domiciled in the United States at the time of said registration, then a statement of that fact, including his place of domicile, the name of the author (when the records of the copyright office shall show the same), the title of the work which is registered for which copyright is claimed, the date of the deposit of the copies of such work, the date of publication if the work has been reproduced in copies for sale, or publicly distributed, and such marks as to class designation and entry number as shall fully identify the entry. In the case of a book, the certificate shall also state the receipt of the affidavit, as provided by section 17 of this title, and the date of the completion of the printing, or the date of the publication of the book, as stated in the said affidavit. The Register of Copyrights shall prepare a printed form for the said certificate, to be filled out in each case as above provided for in the case of all registrations made after July 1, 1909, and in the case of all previous registrations so far as the copyright office record books shall show such facts, which certificate, sealed with the seal of the copyright office, shall, upon payment of the prescribed fee, be given to any person making application for the same. Said certificate shall be admitted in any court as prima facie evidence of the facts stated therein. In addition to such certificate the register of copyrights shall furnish, upon request, without additional fee, a receipt for the copies of the work deposited to complete the registration.

§ 210. CATALOG OF COPYRIGHT ENTRIES; EFFECT AS EVIDENCE.—The Register of Copyrights shall fully index all copyright registrations and assignments and shall print at periodic intervals a catalog of the titles of articles deposited and registered for copyright, together with suitable indexes, and at stated intervals shall print complete and indexed catalog for each class of copyright entries, and may thereupon, if expedient, destroy the original manuscript catalog cards containing the titles included in such printed volumes and representing the entries made during such intervals. The current catalog of copyright entries and the index volumes herein provided for shall be admitted in any court as prima facie evidence of the facts stated therein as regards any copyright registration.

§ 211. SAME; DISTRIBUTION AND SALE; DISPOSAL OF PROCEEDS.—The said printed current catalogs as they are issued shall be promptly distributed by the Superintendent of Documents to the collectors of customs of the United States and to the postmasters of all exchange offices of receipt of foreign mails, in accordance with revised list of such collectors of customs and postmasters prepared by the Secretary of the Treasury and the Postmaster General, and they shall also be furnished in whole or in part to all parties desiring them at a price to be determined by the Register of Copyrights for each part of the catalog not exceeding $75 for the complete yearly catalog of copyright entries. The consolidated catalogs and indexes shall also be supplied to all persons ordering them at such prices as may be fixed by the Register of Copyrights, and all subscriptions for the catalogs shall be received by the Superintendent of Documents, who shall forward the said publications; and the moneys thus received shall be paid into the Treasury of the United States and accounted for under such laws and Treasury regulations as shall be in force at the time.

§ 212. RECORDS AND WORKS DEPOSITED IN COPYRIGHT OFFICE OPEN TO PUBLIC INSPECTION; TAKING COPIES OF ENTRIES.—The record books of the copyright office, together with the indexes to such record books, and all works deposited and retained in the copyright office, shall be open to public inspection; and copies may be taken of the copyright entries actually made in such record books, subject to such safeguards and regulations as shall be prescribed by the Register of Copyrights and approved by the Librarian of Congress.

§ 213. DISPOSITION OF ARTICLES DEPOSITED IN OFFICE.—Of the articles deposited in the copyright office under the provisions of the copyright laws of the United States, the Librarian of Congress shall determine what books and other articles shall be transferred to the permanent collections of the Library of Congress, including the law library, and what other books or articles shall be placed in the reserve collections of the Library of Congress for sale or exchange, or be transferred to other governmental libraries in the District of Columbia for use therein.

§ 214. DESTRUCTION OF ARTICLES DEPOSITED IN OFFICE REMAINING UNDISPOSED OF; REMOVAL OF BY AUTHOR OR PROPRIETOR; MANUSCRIPTS OF UNPUBLISHED WORKS.—Of any articles undisposed of as above provided, together with all titles and correspondence relating thereto, the Librarian of Congress and the Register of Copyrights jointly shall, at suitable intervals, determine what of these received during any period of years it is desirable or useful to preserve in the permanent files of the copyright office, and, after due notice as hereinafter provided, may within their discretion cause the remaining articles and other things to be destroyed: *Provided*, That there shall be printed in the Catalog of Copyright Entries from February to November, inclusive, a statement of the years of receipt of such articles and a notice to permit any author, copyright proprietor, or other lawful claimant to claim and remove before the expiration of the month of December of that year anything found which relates to any of his productions deposited or registered for copyright within the period of years stated, not reserved or disposed of as provided for in this title. No manuscript of an unpublished work shall be destroyed during its term of copyright without specific notice to the copyright proprietor of record, permitting him to claim and remove it.

§ 215. FEES.—The Register of Copyrights shall receive, and the persons to whom the services designated are rendered shall pay, the following fees:

For the registration of a claim to copyright in any work, including a print or label used for articles of merchandise, $6; for the registration of a claim to renewal of copyright, $4; which fees shall include a certificate for each registration: *Provided*, That only one registration fee shall be required in the case of several volumes of the same book published and deposited at the same time: *And provided further*, That with respect to works of foreign origin, in lieu of payment of the copyright fee of $6 together with one copy of the work and application, the foreign author or proprietor may at any time within six months from the date of first publication abroad deposit in the Copyright Office an application for registration and two copies of the work which shall be accompanied by a catalog card in form and content satisfactory to the Register of Copyrights.

For every additional certificate of registration, $2.

For certifying a copy of an application for registration of copyright, and for all other certifications, $3.

For recording every assignment, agreement, power of attorney or other paper not exceeding six pages, $5; for each additional page or less, 50 cents; for each title over one in the paper recorded, 50 cents additional.

For recording a notice of use, or notice of intention to use, $3, for each notice of not more than five titles; and 50 cents for each additional title.

For any requested search of Copyright Office records, works deposited, or other available material, or services rendered in connection therewith, $5, for each hour of time consumed.

§ 216. WHEN THE DAY FOR TAKING ACTION FALLS ON SATURDAY, SUNDAY, OR A HOLIDAY.—When the last day for making any deposit or application, or for paying any fee, or for delivering any other material to the Copyright Office falls on Saturday, Sunday, or a holiday within the District of Columbia, such action may be taken on the next succeeding business day.

NOTES

1. By the Act of December 31, 1974, Pub. L. 93-573, 88 Stat. 1873, the phrase "and before January 1, 1975" was stricken.

2. By the Act of December 31, 1974, Pub. L. 93-573, 88 Stat. 1873, the December 31, 1974 date was further extended until December 31, 1976.

3. By the Act of December 31, 1974, Pub. L. 93-573, 88 Stat. 1873, Section 104 was amended to read as follows:

§ 104. Willful infringement for profit

(a) Except as provided in subsection (b), any person who willfully and for profit shall infringe any copyright secured by this title, or who shall knowingly and willfully aid or abet such infringement, shall be deemed guilty of a misdemeanor, and upon conviction thereof shall be punished by imprisonment for not exceeding one year or by a fine of not less than $100 nor more than $1,000, or both, in the discretion of the court: *Provided, however,* That nothing in this title shall be so construed as to prevent the performance of religious or secular works such as oratorios, cantatas, masses, or octavo choruses by public schools, church choirs, or vocal societies, rented, borrowed, or obtained from some public library, public school, church choir, school choir, or vocal society, provided the performance is given for charitable or educational purposes and not for profit.

(b) Any person who willfully and for profit shall infringe any copyright provided by section 1 (f) of this title, or who should knowingly and willfully aid or abet such infringement, shall be fined not more than $25,000 or imprisoned not more than one year, or both, for the first offense and shall be fined not more than $50,000 or imprisoned not more than two years, or both, for any subsequent offense.

APPENDIX 3
FAIR USE GUIDELINES: SECTION 107

Notwithstanding the general exclusive rights that a copyright owner has, they are not infringed upon by the fair use of a copyrighted work [107]. This is not a new concept. "Fair use," as a judicial doctrine, was part of our copyright law even before the Copyright Act of 1909. Nonetheless, the scope of its application to educational uses of copyrighted materials has not been significantly developed in court cases. In 1975, members of the House Judiciary Committee encouraged representatives of educators and publishers to meet together to develop some standards as to permissible educational uses of copyrighted materials. Meetings were held and resulted in the two sets of guidelines included in this appendix. The guidelines do not have the binding effect of a law. However, they are part of the new law's legislative history, and the Senate–House Conference report on the bill states that the conferees accept them "as part of their understanding of fair use."

Guidelines on Educational Copying from Books and Periodicals

The purpose of the following guidelines is to state the minimum and not the maximum standards of educational fair use under Secton 107 of H.R. 2223. The parties agree that the conditions determining the extent of permissible copying for educational purposes may change in the future; that certain types of copying permitted under these guidelines may not be permissible in the future; and conversely that in the future other types of copying not permitted under these guidelines may be permissible under revised guidelines.

Moreover, the following statement of guidelines is not intended to limit the types of copying permitted under the standards of fair use under judicial decision and which are stated in Secton 107 of the Copyright Revision Bill. There may be instances in which copying which does not fall within the guidelines stated below may nonetheless be permitted under the criteria of fair use.

I. SINGLE COPYING FOR TEACHERS

A single copy may be made of any of the following by or for a teacher at his or her individual request for his or her scholarly research or use in teaching or preparation to teach a class:

A. A chapter from a book;

B. An article from a periodical or newspaper;

    C. A short story, short essay or short poem, whether or not from a collective work;

    D. A chart, graph, diagram, drawing, cartoon, or picture from a book, periodical, or newspaper.

II. MULTIPLE COPIES FOR CLASSROOM USE

Multiple copies (not to exceed, in any event, more than one copy per pupil in a course) may be made by or for the teacher giving the course for classroom use or discussion; *provided that*:

    A. The copying meets the tests of brevity and spontaneity as defined below; *and,*

    B. Meets the cumulative effect test as defined below; *and,*

    C. Each copy includes a notice of copyright.

Definitions

Brevity

    i. Poetry: (a) A complete poem if less than 250 words and if printed on not more than two pages, or (b) from a longer poem, an excerpt of not more than 250 words.

    ii. Prose: (a) Either a complete article, story or essay of less than 2,500 words, or (b) an excerpt from any prose work of not more than 1,000 words or 10% of the work, whichever is less, but in any event a minimum of 500 words.

    [Each of the numerical limits stated in "i" and "ii" above may be expanded to permit the completion of an unfinished line of a poem or of an unfinished prose paragraph.]

    iii. Illustration: One chart, graph, diagram, drawing, cartoon or picture per book or per periodical issue.

    iv. "Special" works: Certain works in poetry, prose or in "poetic prose" which often combine language with illustrations and which are intended sometimes for children and at other times for a more general audience fall short of 2,500 words in their entirety. Paragraph "ii" above, notwithstanding such "special works," may not be reproduced in their entirety; however, an excerpt comprising not more than two of the published pages of such special work and containing not more than 10% of the words found in the text thereof, may be reproduced.

Spontaneity

    i. The copying is at the instance and inspiration of the individual teacher, and

    ii. The inspiration and decision to use the work and the moment of its use for maximum teaching effectiveness are so close in time that it would be unreasonable to expect a timely reply to a request for permission.

Cumulative Effect

    i. The copying of the material is for only one course in the school in which the copies are made.

    ii. Not more than one short poem, article, story, essay or two excerpts may be copied from the same author, nor more than three from the same collective work or periodical volume during one class term.

iii. There shall not be more than nine instances of such multiple copying for one course during one class term.

[The limitations stated in "ii" and "iii" above shall not apply to current news periodicals and newspapers and current news sections of other periodicals.]

III. PROHIBITIONS AS TO I AND II ABOVE

Notwithstanding any of the above, the following shall be prohibited:

A. Copying shall not be used to create or to replace or substitute for anthologies, compilations or collective works. Such replacement or substitution may occur whether copies of various works or excerpts therefrom are accumulated or are reproduced and used separately.

B. There shall be no copying of or from works intended to be "consumable" in the course of study or of teaching. These include workbooks, exercises, standardized tests and test booklets and answer sheets and like consumable material.

C. Copying shall not:
   a. substitute for the purchase of books, publisher's reprints or periodicals;
   b. be directed by higher authority;
   c. be repeated with respect to the same item by the same teacher from term to term.

D. No charge shall be made to the student beyond the actual cost of the photocopying.

Guidelines for Educational Uses of Music

The purpose of the following guidelines is to state the minimum and not the maximum standards of educational fair use under Section 107 of H. R. 2223. The parties agree that the conditions determining the extent of permissible copying for educational purposes may change in the future; that certain types of copying permitted under these guidelines may not be permissible in the future; and conversely that in the future other types of copying not permitted under these guidelines may be permissible under revised guidelines.

Moreover, the following statement of guidelines is not intended to limit the types of copying permitted under the standards of fair use under judicial decision and which are stated in Section 107 of the Copyright Revision Bill. There may be instances in which copying which does not fall within the guidelines stated below may nonetheless be permitted under the criteria of fair use.

A. PERMISSIBLE USES

1. Emergency copying to replace purchased copies which for any reason are not available for an imminent performance, provided purchased replacement copies shall be substituted in due course.

2. For academic purposes other than performance, single or multiple copies of excerpts of works may be made, provided that the excerpts do not comprise a part of the whole which would constitute a performable unit such as a

section, movement or area, but in no case more than (10%) of the whole work. The number of copies shall not exceed one copy per pupil.
3. Printed copies which have been purchased may be edited or simplified, provided that the fundamental character of the work is not distorted or the lyrics, if any, altered, or lyrics added if none exist.
4. A single copy of recordings of performances by students may be made for evaluation or rehearsal purposes and may be retained by the educational institution or individual teacher.
5. A single copy of a sound recording (such as a tape, disc or cassette) of copyrighted music may be made from sound recordings owned by an educational institution or an individual teacher for the purpose of constructing aural exercises or examinations and may be retained by the educational institution or individual teacher. (This pertains only to the copyright of the music itself and not to any copyright which may exist in the sound recording.)

B. PROHIBITIONS

1. Copying to create or replace or substitute for anthologies, compilations or collective works.
2. Copying of or from works intended to be "consumable" in the course of study or of teaching, such as workbooks, exercises, standardized tests and answer sheets and like material.
3. Copying for the purpose of performance, except as in A(1) above.
4. Copying for the purpose of substituting for the purchase of music, except as in A(1) and A(2) above.
5. Copying without inclusion of the copyright notice which appears on the printed copy.

APPENDIX 4
LIBRARY REPRODUCTION GUIDELINES:
SECTION 108

This appendix is composed of excerpts from the September 29, 1976, Senate–House Conference report.

Conference Substitute

The conference substitute adopts the provisions of section 108 as amended by the House bill. In doing so, the conferees have noted two letters dated September 22, 1976, sent respectively to John L. McClellan, Chairman of the Senate Judiciary Subcommittee on Patents, Trademarks, and Copyrights, and to Robert W. Kastenmeier, Chairman of the House Judiciary Subcommittee on Courts, Civil Liberties, and the Administration of Justice. The letters, from the Chairman of the National Commission on New Technological Uses of Copyrighted Works (CONTU), Stanley H. Fuld, transmitted a document consisting of "guidelines interpreting the provision in subsection 108(g)(2) of S. 22, as approved by the House Committee on the Judiciary." Chairman Fuld's letters explain that, following lengthy consultations with the parties concerned, the Commission adopted these guidelines as fair and workable and with the hope that the conferees on S. 22 may find that they merit inclusion in the conference report. The letters add that, although time did not permit securing signatures of the representatives of the principal library organizations or of the organizations representing publishers and authors on these guidelines, the Commission had received oral assurances from these representatives that the guidelines are acceptable to their organizations.

The conference committee understands that the guidelines are not intended as, and cannot be considered, explicit rules or directions governing any and all cases, now or in the future. It is recognized that their purpose is to provide guidance in the most commonly encountered interlibrary photocopying situations, that they are not intended to be limiting or determinative in themselves or with respect to other situations, and that they deal with an evolving situation that will undoubtedly require their continuous reevaluation and adjustment. With these qualifications, the conference committee agrees that the guidelines are a reasonable interpretation of the proviso of section 108(g)(2) in the most common situations to which they apply today.

The text of the library reproduction guidelines appears on the following two pages.

Photocopying—Interlibrary Arrangements

INTRODUCTION

Subsection 108(g)(2) of the bill deals, among other things, with limits on interlibrary arrangements for photocopying. It prohibits systematic photocopying of copyrighted materials but permits interlibrary arrangements "that do not have, as their purpose or effect, that the library or archives receiving such copies or phonorecords for distribution does so in such aggregate quantities as to substitute for a subscription to or purchase of such work."

The National Commission on New Technological Uses of Copyrighted Works offered its good offices to the House and Senate subcommittees in bringing the interested parties together to see if agreement could be reached on what a realistic definition would be of "such aggregate quantities." The Commission consulted with the parties and suggested the interpretation which follows, on which there has been substantial agreement by the principal library, publisher, and author organizations. The Commission considers the guidelines which follow to be a workable and fair interpretation of the intent of the proviso portion of subsection 108(g)(2).

These guidelines are intended to provide guidance in the application of section 108 to the most frequently encountered interlibrary case: a library's obtaining from another library, in lieu of interlibrary loan, copies of articles from relatively recent issues of periodicals—those published within five years prior to the date of the request. The guidelines do not specify what aggregate quantity of copies of an article or articles published in a periodical, the issue date of which is more than five years prior to the date when the request for the copy thereof is made, constitutes a substitute for a subscription to such periodical. The meaning of the proviso to subsection 108(g)(2) in such case is left to future interpretation.

The point has been made that the present practice on interlibrary loans and use of photocopies in lieu of loans may be supplemented or even largely replaced by a system in which one or more agencies or institutions, public or private, exist for the specific purpose of providing a central source for photocopies. Of course, these guidelines would not apply to such a situation.

GUIDELINES FOR THE PROVISO OF SUBSECTION 108(g)(2)

1. As used in the proviso of subsection 108(g)(2), the words ". . . such aggregate quantities as to substitute for a subscription to or purchase of such work" shall mean:
   (a) with respect to any given periodical (as opposed to any given issue of a periodical), filled requests of a library or archives (a "requesting entity") within any calendar year for a total of six or more copies of an article or articles published in such periodical within five years prior to the date of the request. These guidelines specifically shall not apply, directly or indirectly, to any request of a requesting entity for a copy or copies of an article or articles published in any issue of a periodical, the publication date of which is more than five years prior to the date when the request is made. These guidelines do not define the meaning, with respect to such a request, of ". . . such aggregate quantities as to substitute for a subscription to [such periodical]."

(b) with respect to any other material described in subsection 108(d) (including fiction and poetry), filled requests of a requesting entity within any calendar year for a total of six or more copies or phonorecords of or from any given work (including a collective work) during the entire period when such material shall be protected by copyright.

2. In the event that a requesting entity—

(a) shall have in force or shall have entered an order for a subscription to a periodical, or

(b) has within its collection, or shall have entered an order for, a copy or phonorecord of any other copyrighted work,

material from either category of which it desires to obtain by copy from another library or archives (the "supplying entity"), because the material to be copied is not reasonably available for use by the requesting entity itself, then the fulfillment of such request shall be treated as though the requesting entity made such copy from its own collection. A library or archives may request a copy or phonorecord from a supplying entity only under those circumstances where the requesting entity would have been able, under the other provisions of section 108, to supply such copy from materials in its own collection.

3. No request for a copy or phonorecord of any material to which these guidelines apply may be fulfilled by the supplying entity unless such request is accompanied by a representation by the requesting entity that the request was made in conformity with these guidelines.

4. The requesting entity shall maintain records of all requests made by it for copies or phonorecords of any materials to which these guidelines apply and shall maintain records of the fulfillment of such requests, which records shall be retained until the end of the third complete calendar year after the end of the calendar year in which the respective request shall have been made.

5. As part of the review provided for in subsection 108(i), these guidelines shall be reviewed not later than five years from the effective date of this bill.

APPENDIX 5
U.S. INTERNATIONAL
COPYRIGHT RELATIONS

The material in this appendix derives from Copyright Office Circular 38 of September 1975, which discusses international copyright protection generally. It is followed by Copyright Office Circular R38a of November 1977, which reports on international copyright relations of the United States. Note: Ellipses denote material deleted from the text.

From Copyright Office Circular 38

GENERAL INFORMATION ABOUT INTERNATIONAL COPYRIGHT PROTECTION

Sources of Protection in Other Countries

There is no such thing as an "international copyright" that will automatically protect an author's writings throughout the entire world. Protection against unauthorized use in a particular country depends basically on the national laws of that country. However, most countries do offer protection to foreign works under certain conditions, and these conditions have been greatly simplified by international copyright treaties and conventions.

An author who wishes to copyright his work in a particular country should first find out the extent of protection for foreign works in that country. If possible he should do this before his work is published anywhere, since protection may often depend on the facts existing at the time of first publication.

If the country in which protection is sought is a party to one of the international copyright conventions discussed below, the work may generally be protected by complying with the conditions of the convention. Even if the work cannot be brought under an international convention, protection under the specific provisions of the country's national laws may still be possible. There are, however, some countries that offer little or no copyright protection for foreign works under any circumstances.

The Universal Copyright Convention

The Universal Copyright Convention (the UCC) is an international treaty to which the United States is a party. The UCC, as drafted at Geneva in 1952, came into force on September 16, 1955. The UCC, as revised at Paris in 1971, came into force on July 10, 1974. As of January 1, 1975, some 65 countries are members of one or both versions. The practical purpose of the UCC is to reduce to a minimum the formalities for securing copyright among participating countries.

As a general rule, the UCC requires a participating country to give the same protection to foreign works that meet the Convention requirements as it gives to its own domestic works. To qualify for protection under the Convention, a work must have been written by a national of a participating country, or must have been published for the first time in a participating country.

The "Berne" Conventions

The Berne Convention of 1886 and its five revisions (Paris, 1896; Berlin, 1908; Rome, 1928; Brussels, 1948; Paris, 1971) have established the International Union for the Protection of Literary and Artistic Works, better known as the Berne Union. As of January 1, 1975, some 65 countries, not including the United States, have adhered to one or more of these conventions and are therefore members of the Berne Union. Protection under these conventions is extended without formalities to works by nationals of any country on the sole condition that first publication take place in a country that belongs to the Berne Union.

The Pan-American Conventions

Western Hemisphere copyright relations are governed to some extent by a series of seven Pan-American Conventions. Among these, the Buenos Aires Convention of 1910 has been ratified by the United States and 17 Latin American nations. It specifies that authors of any contracting country who have secured copyright in their own country will enjoy in each of the other countries the rights it accords its own works, if the work contains "a statement indicating the reservation of the property right."

Although the words "All Rights Reserved," their Spanish-language equivalent "Todos los derechos reservados," or "Copyright Reserved" are often used to denote the reservation of copyright in those countries of the Western Hemisphere (except the United States) that have ratified the Buenos Aires Convention of 1910, such words are not required by the copyright law (Title 17 of the United States Code), have no effect as far as U.S. law is concerned, and should not be considered a substitute for the notice of copyright prescribed by U.S. law.

Bilateral Arrangements and National Laws

In addition to the multilateral copyright conventions discussed above, there are some bilateral treaties or similar arrangements governing the copyright relations of two countries between themselves. Some countries also have laws granting protection to foreign works under certain conditions without regard to any international conventions or treaties. In all of these cases the extent of protection and the requirements for securing copyright vary from country to country.

The Phonogram Convention

The Convention for the Protection of Producers of Phonograms Against Unauthorized Duplication of Their Phonograms was concluded at Geneva in 1971. Under the terms of this convention, adhering countries provide international protection against the making or importation of unauthorized duplicates of phonograms (sound recordings) for distribution to the public. This convention entered into force on April 18, 1973; as of January 1, 1975, some 15 countries were members of the Phonogram Convention. For information on United States copyright for sound recordings, write to the Copyright Office for free circulars on this subject.[. . .]

COPYRIGHT PROTECTION IN OTHER COUNTRIES FOR UNITED STATES WORKS

Protection for U.S. Works Under the Universal Copyright Convention

It is possible for a work by a U.S. author to be published in such a way that it secures copyright protection in the United States and, at the same time, in the other countries that are parties to the Universal Copyright Convention. For this result to be accomplished, all published copies of the work must bear a copyright notice that satisfies both the notice provisions of the UCC, [. . .] and also the notice requirements of the U.S. law.

The copyright notice must consist of the symbol © accompanied by the name of the copyright owner and the year date of publication.[. . .]

Protection Other Than the UCC for U.S. Works

The United States is a party to the Buenos Aires Convention of 1910 and, as explained in Section [. . .] above [General Information about International Copyright Protection], works by U.S. authors may be protected in other member countries if the published copies contain a statement that copyright is reserved. Protection for U.S. works in countries that are members of the Berne Union can be obtained by first or simultaneous publication in a Union country, although difficult legal questions can arise as to what constitutes a genuine "first" or "simultaneous" publication in a particular case. In order to be protected, in some countries it may be necessary for an American author to comply with specific statutory requirements or administrative regulations, which vary from country to country.

From Copyright Office Circular R38a

GENERAL INFORMATION

This sets forth U.S. copyright relations of current interest with the other independent nations of the world. Each entry gives country name (and alternate name) and a statement of copyright relations. The following code is used:

Bilateral	Bilateral copyright relations with the United States by virtue of a proclamation or treaty, as of the date given. Where there is more than one proclamation or treaty, only the date of the first one is given.
BAC	Party to the Buenos Aires Convention of 1910, as of the date given. U.S. ratification deposited with the Government of Argentina, May 1, 1911; proclaimed by the President of the United States, July 13, 1914.
None	No copyright relations with the United States.

Phonogram	Party to the Convention for the Protection of Producers of Phonograms Against Unauthorized Duplication of Their Phonograms, Geneva, 1971, as of the date given. The effective date for the United States was March 10, 1974.

Foreign sound recordings fixed and published on or after February 15, 1972, with the special notice of copyright prescribed by law (e.g., ℗ 1977 Doe Records, Inc.), may be entitled to U.S. copyright protection only if the author is a citizen of one of the countries with which the United States maintains bilateral or phonogram convention relations as indicated below.

UCC Geneva	Party to the Universal Copyright Convention, Geneva, 1952, as of the date given. The effective date for the United States was September 16, 1955.
UCC Paris	Party to the Universal Copyright Convention as revised at Paris, 1971, as of the date given. The effective date for the United States was July 10, 1974.
Unclear	Became independent since 1943. Has not established copyright relations with the United States, but may be honoring obligations incurred under former political status.

RELATIONS AS OF SEPTEMBER 30, 1977

Afghanistan
  None
Albania
  None
Algeria
  UCC Geneva Aug. 28, 1973
  UCC Paris July 10, 1974
Andorra
  UCC Geneva Sept. 16, 1955
Angola
  Unclear
Argentina
  Bilateral Aug. 23, 1934
  BAC April 19, 1950
  UCC Geneva Feb. 13, 1958
  Phonogram June 30, 1973
Australia
  Bilateral March 15, 1918
  UCC Geneva May 1, 1969
  Phonogram June 22, 1974
Austria
  Bilateral Sept. 20, 1907
  UCC Geneva July 2, 1957
Bahamas, The
  UCC Geneva July 10, 1973
  UCC Paris Dec. 27, 1976
Bahrain
  None
Bangladesh
  UCC Geneva Aug. 5, 1975
  UCC Paris Aug. 5, 1975

Barbados
  Unclear
Belgium
  Bilateral July 1, 1891
  UCC Geneva Aug. 31, 1960
Benin (formerly Dahomey)
  Unclear
Bhutan
  None
Bolivia
  BAC May 15, 1914
Botswana
  Unclear
Brazil
  Bilateral April 2, 1957
  BAC Aug. 31, 1915
  UCC Geneva Jan. 13, 1960
  UCC Paris Dec. 11, 1975
  Phonogram Nov. 28, 1975
Bulgaria
  UCC Geneva June 7, 1975
  UCC Paris June 7, 1975
Burma
  Unclear
Burundi
  Unclear
Cambodia (Democratic Kampuchea)
  UCC Geneva Sept. 16, 1955
Cameroon
  UCC Geneva May 1, 1973
  UCC Paris July 10, 1974

Canada
Bilateral Jan. 1, 1924
UCC Geneva Aug. 10, 1962
Cape Verde
Unclear
Central African Republic
Unclear
Chad
Unclear
Chile
Bilateral May 25, 1896
BAC June 14, 1955
UCC Geneva Sept. 16, 1955
Phonogram March 24, 1977
China
Bilateral Jan. 13, 1904
Colombia
BAC Dec. 23, 1936
UCC Geneva June 18, 1976
UCC Paris June 18, 1976
Comoros
Unclear
Congo
Unclear
Costa Rica*
Bilateral Oct. 19, 1899
BAC Nov. 30, 1916
UCC Geneva Sept. 16, 1955
Cuba
Bilateral Nov. 17, 1903
UCC Geneva June 18, 1957
Cyprus
Unclear
Czechoslovakia
Bilateral March 1, 1927
UCC Geneva Jan. 6, 1960
Denmark
Bilateral May 8, 1893
UCC Geneva Feb. 9, 1962
Phonogram March 24, 1977
Djibouti
Unclear
Dominican Republic*
BAC Oct. 31, 1912
Ecuador
BAC Aug. 31, 1914
UCC Geneva June 5, 1957
Phonogram Sept. 14, 1974
Egypt
None

El Salvador
Bilateral June 30, 1908
by virtue of Mexico City
Convention, 1902
Equatorial Guinea
Unclear
Ethiopia
None
Fiji
UCC Geneva Oct. 10, 1970
Phonogram April 18, 1973
Finland
Bilateral Jan. 1, 1929
UCC Geneva April 16, 1963
Phonogram April 18, 1973
France
Bilateral July 1, 1891
UCC Geneva Jan. 14, 1956
UCC Paris July 10, 1974
Phonogram April 18, 1973
Gabon
Unclear
Gambia, The
Unclear
Germany
Bilateral April 15, 1892
UCC Geneva with Federal
Republic of Germany Sept. 16,
1955
UCC Paris with Federal
Republic of Germany July 10, 1974
Phonogram with Federal
Republic of Germany May 18, 1974
UCC Geneva with German
Democratic Republic Oct. 5, 1973
Ghana
UCC Geneva Aug. 22, 1962
Greece
Bilateral March 1, 1932
UCC Geneva Aug. 24, 1963
Grenada
Unclear
Guatemala*
BAC March 28, 1913
UCC Geneva Oct. 28, 1964
Phonogram Feb. 1, 1977
Guinea
Unclear
Guinea-Bissau
Unclear

*This country became a party to the Mexico City Convention, 1902, effective June 30, 1908, to which the United States also became a party, effective on the same date. As regards copyright relations with the United States, this convention is considered to have been superseded by adherence of this country and the United States to the Buenos Aires Convention of 1910.

Guyana
  Unclear
Haiti
  BAC Nov. 27, 1919
  UCC Geneva Sept. 16, 1955
Holy See
  (See entry under Vatican City)
Honduras*
  BAC April 27, 1914
Hungary
  Bilateral Oct. 16, 1912
  UCC Geneva Jan. 23, 1971
  UCC Paris July 10, 1974
  Phonogram May 28, 1975
Iceland
  UCC Geneva Dec. 18, 1956
India
  Bilateral Aug. 15, 1947
  UCC Geneva Jan. 21, 1958
  Phonogram Feb. 12, 1975
Indonesia
  Unclear
Iran
  None
Iraq
  None
Ireland
  Bilateral Oct. 1, 1929
  UCC Geneva Jan. 20, 1959
Israel
  Bilateral May 15, 1948
  UCC Geneva Sept. 16, 1955
Italy
  Bilateral Oct. 31, 1892
  UCC Geneva Jan. 24, 1957
  Phonogram March 24, 1977
Ivory Coast
  Unclear
Jamaica
  None
Japan†
  UCC Geneva April 28, 1956
Jordan
  Unclear
Kenya
  UCC Geneva Sept. 7, 1966

UCC Paris July 10, 1974
  Phonogram April 21, 1976
Korea
  Unclear
Kuwait
  Unclear
Laos
  UCC Geneva Sept. 16, 1955
Lebanon
  UCC Geneva Oct. 17, 1959
Lesotho
  Unclear
Liberia
  UCC Geneva July 27, 1956
Libya
  Unclear
Liechtenstein
  UCC Geneva Jan. 22, 1959
Luxembourg
  Bilateral June 29, 1910
  UCC Geneva Oct. 15, 1955
  Phonogram March 5, 1976
Madagascar (Malagasy Republic)
  Unclear
Malawi
  UCC Geneva Oct. 26, 1965
Malaysia
  Unclear
Maldives
  Unclear
Mali
  Unclear
Malta
  UCC Geneva Nov. 19, 1968
Mauritania
  Unclear
Mauritius
  UCC Geneva March 12, 1968
Mexico
  Bilateral Feb. 27, 1896
  BAC April 24, 1964
  UCC Geneva May 12, 1957
  UCC Paris Oct. 31, 1975
  Phonogram Dec. 21, 1973
Monaco
  Bilateral Oct. 15, 1952

*This country became a party to the Mexico City Convention, 1902, effective June 30, 1908, to which the United States also became a party, effective on the same date. As regards copyright relations with the United States, this convention is considered to have been superseded by adherence of this country and the United States to the Buenos Aires Convention of 1910.

†Bilateral copyright relations between Japan and the United States, which were formulated effective May 10, 1906, are considered to have been abrogated and superseded by the adherence of Japan to the UCC Geneva, effective April 28, 1956.

UCC Geneva Sept. 16, 1955
UCC Paris Dec. 13, 1974
Phonogram Dec. 2, 1974
Mongolia
None
Morocco
UCC Geneva May 8, 1972
UCC Paris Jan. 28, 1976
Mozambique
Unclear
Nauru
Unclear
Nepal
None
Netherlands
Bilateral Nov. 20, 1899
UCC Geneva June 22, 1967
New Zealand
Bilateral Dec. 1, 1916
UCC Geneva Sept. 11, 1964
Phonogram Aug. 13, 1976
Nicaragua*
BAC Dec. 15, 1913
UCC Geneva Aug. 16, 1961
Niger
Unclear
Nigeria
UCC Geneva Feb. 14, 1962
Norway
Bilateral July 1, 1905
UCC Geneva Jan. 23, 1963
UCC Paris Aug. 7, 1974
Oman
None
Pakistan
UCC Geneva Sept. 16, 1955
Panama
BAC Nov. 25, 1913
UCC Geneva Oct. 17, 1962
Phonogram June 29, 1974
Papua New Guinea
Unclear
Paraguay
BAC Sept. 20, 1917
UCC Geneva March 11, 1962
Peru
BAC April 30, 1920
UCC Geneva Oct. 16, 1963

Philippines
Bilateral Oct. 21, 1948
UCC status undetermined by
UNESCO. (Copyright Office
considers that UCC relations do
not exist.)
Poland
Bilateral Feb. 16, 1927
UCC Geneva March 9, 1977
UCC Paris March 9, 1977
Portugal
Bilateral July 20, 1893
UCC Geneva Dec. 25, 1956
Qatar
None
Romania
Bilateral May 14, 1928
Rwanda
Unclear
San Marino
None
Sao Tome and Principe
Unclear
Saudi Arabia
None
Senegal
UCC Geneva July 9, 1974
UCC Paris July 10, 1974
Seychelles
Unclear
Sierra Leone
None
Singapore
Unclear
Somalia
Unclear
South Africa
Bilateral July 1, 1924
Soviet Union
UCC Geneva May 27, 1973
Spain
Bilateral July 10, 1895
UCC Geneva Sept. 16, 1955
UCC Paris July 10, 1974
Phonogram Aug. 24, 1974
Sri Lanka (formerly Ceylon)
Unclear
Sudan
Unclear

*This country became a party to the Mexico City Convention, 1902, effective June 30, 1908, to which the United States also became a party, effective on the same date. As regards copyright relations with the United States, this convention is considered to have been superseded by adherence of this country and the United States to the Buenos Aires Convention of 1910.

Surinam
  Unclear
Swaziland
  Unclear
Sweden
  Bilateral June 1, 1911
  UCC Geneva July 1, 1961
  UCC Paris July 10, 1974
  Phonogram April 18, 1973
Switzerland
  Bilateral July 1, 1891
  UCC Geneva March 30, 1956
Syria
  Unclear
Tanzania
  Unclear
Thailand
  Bilateral Sept. 1, 1921
Togo
  Unclear
Tonga
  None
Trinidad and Tobago
  Unclear
Tunisia
  UCC Geneva June 19, 1969
  UCC Paris June 10, 1975
Turkey
  None
Uganda
  Unclear

United Arab Emirates
  None
United Kingdom
  Bilateral July 1, 1891
  UCC Geneva Sept. 27, 1957
  UCC Paris July 10, 1974
  Phonogram April 18, 1973
Upper Volta
  Unclear
Uraguay
  BAC Dec. 17, 1919
Vatican City (Holy See)
  UCC Geneva Oct. 5, 1955
Venezuela
  UCC Geneva Sept. 30, 1966
Vietnam
  Unclear
Western Samoa
  Unclear
Yemen (Aden)
  Unclear
Yemen (San'a)
  None
Yugoslavia
  UCC Geneva May 11, 1966
  UCC Paris July 10, 1974
Zaire
  Unclear
Zambia
  UCC Geneva June 1, 1965

APPENDIX 6
TABLE OF STATUTORY LIMITS ON THE SCOPE OF COPYRIGHT OWNERS' EXCLUSIVE RIGHTS

The new copyright law's section 106 grants the owner of copyright the exclusive right to do and to authorize any of the following:

1. to reproduce the copyrighted work in copies or phonorecords;
2. to develop derivative works based upon the copyrighted work;
3. to distribute copies or phonorecords of the copyrighted work to the public by sale or other transfer of ownership, or by rental, lease, or lending;
4. in the case of literary, musical, dramatic and choreographic works, pantomimes, and motion pictures and audiovisual works, to perform the copyrighted work publicly; and
5. in the case of literary, musical, dramatic and choreographic works, pantomimes, and pictorial, graphic, or sculptural works, including the individual images of a motion picture or other audiovisual work, to display the copyrighted work publicly.

Those exclusive rights are further clarified by section 101, which defines a number of the terms used, i.e.: (a) audiovisual works; (b) copies; (c) derivative works; (d) display; (e) literary work; (f) motion pictures; (g) perform; (h) perform or display publicly; (i) pictorial, graphic, and sculptural works; and (j) phonorecords. These definitions sometimes have the effect of limiting the scope of an exclusive right, compared to what the right would appear to be from a reading of section 106 alone.

In addition to the limits of section 106, described above, and the definitions referred to, there are a number of other statutory provisions which limit the scope of one or more exclusive rights. Most, but not all, of these other statutory provisions are contained in sections 107–118.

The table that follows lists the various sections of the law—other than section 106 itself and the definitions sections—that can expressly limit the scope of one or more exclusive rights in particular circumstances. Many of the statutory provisions are complex; e.g., they apply only to certain types of works or only under certain circumstances, or both. These complexities necessarily are not reflected in the brief headings given and the statute should be referred to for amplification.

233

The fact that there are a great many limitations does not mean that copyright owners' rights are only of modest scope. Many of the limitations apply only to narrow areas of activity.

Generally, the table does not list those types of copyright law limitations that define what is not subject to U.S. copyright [102–105] or that potentially limit the rights of copyright which a transferee of copyright ownership may have [203; 304(a); 304(c)]. However, some of these provisions have been included in the table because they are often thought of as limitations on the scope of copyright. In the statute itself the word *limitation* is used solely, or at least principally, with respect to sections 107–118.

In the right-hand column of the table are listed the particular exclusive rights potentially affected by the section indicated at the left. The exclusive rights are referred to by the numbers associated with them in section 106; i.e., the number 1 is used to refer to the reproduction right; 2 for the derivative work preparation right; 3 for public distribution right; 4 for public performance right; and 5 for public display right.

Section		Activity or Subject Considered	Exclusive Rights Potentially Affected
1	102(b)	Use of ideas, etc.	1, 2, 3, 4, 5
2	103	Use of preexisting material	1, 2, 3, 4, 5
3	107	Fair use	1, 2, 3, 4, 5
4	108	Library reproductions	1, 3
5	109(a)	Transfer of lawful copy	3
6	109(b)	Display of lawful copy	5
7	110(1)	Teaching activities	4, 5
8	110(2)	Teaching activities	4, 5
9	110(3)	Religious services	4, 5
10	110(4)	Certain noncommercial performances	4
11	110(5)	Use of broadcast receivers in public	4, 5
12	110(6)	Agricultural and horticultural fairs	4
13	110(7)	Record and tape vendors	4
14	110(8)	Aid to the handicapped	4
15	110(9)	Aid to the handicapped	4
16	111(a)(1)	Secondary transmissions, hotels, etc.	4, 5
17	111(a)(2)	Secondary transmissions, teaching activities	4, 5
18	111(a)(3)	Secondary transmissions, passive carriers	4, 5
19	111(a)(4)	Secondary transmissions, certain noncommercial cable transmissions	4, 5
20	111(b)	Secondary transmissions, broadcast signals	4, 5
21	111(c)(d)	Cable systems, broadcast signals	4, 5
22	111(e)(f)	Cable systems, nonsimultaneous broadcast signals	1, 4, 5
23	112(a)	Transmission programs	1
24	112(b)	Transmission programs, teaching activities	1
25	112(c)	Transmission programs, certain noncommercial uses	1

Section		Activity or Subject Considered	Exclusive Rights Potentially Affected
26	112(d)	Transmission programs, aid to the handicapped	1
27	112(e)	Transmission programs under section 112	1, 2, 3, 4, 5
28	113(b)	Useful articles	1, 3, 5
29	113(c)	Useful articles; pictures of	3, 5
30	114	Sound recordings	1, 2, 3, 4
31	115	Recorded nondramatic musical works	1, 2, 3
32	115(a)(2)	Musical works; adaptations of	1, 2, 3, 4, 5
33	116	Jukebox performances	4
34	117	Computer applications	1, 2, 3, 4, 5
35	118(d)(1), (2)	Noncommercial broadcasting	1, 3, 4, 5
36	118(d)(3)	Transmission programs, teaching activities	1, 3
37	201(e)	Copyrights obtained by certain involuntary transfers	1, 2, 3, 4, 5
38	204(a)	"Transfer of ownership" not in writing; effect on transferee	1, 2, 3, 4, 5
39	205(e)	Conflicting transfer of ownership—potential effect on one transferee	1, 2, 3, 4, 5
40	205(f)	Conflict between a transfer of ownership and a nonexclusive license-potential effect on the transferee owner	1, 2, 3, 4, 5
41	301(c)	Sound recordings prior to 2/15/72	1, 2, 3
42	302–305	Copyright duration	1, 2, 3, 4, 5
43	405, 406	Potential effects of errors and omissions of copyright notices	1, 2, 3, 4, 5
44	407(e)	Unpublished transmission programs	1
45	601	Manufacturing clause	3
46	602	Importations	3
47	704(b)	Copies deposited with Copyright Office	1, 3
48	704(c)	Copies deposited with Copyright Office	3
49	103 T&S*	Pre-1910 nondramatic musical works	1, 3
50	106 T&S*	Pre-1978 compulsory licenses in nondramatic musical works	1, 3
51	113 T&S*	Television and radio news programs	1, 2, 3

*T&S refers to the Transitional and Supplementary Provisions of the new law.

APPENDIX 7
CROSS-REFERENCE TABLES: 1976 LAW TO 1909 LAW; 1909 LAW TO 1976 LAW

This appendix consists of two cross-reference tables. Table 1 references the sections of the new law to four significant sets of materials on the new law's legislative history and to the old law, the Copyright Act of 1909, as amended. Table 2 references the sections of the old law to the sections of the new. For the full text of the new and old laws see Appendixes 1 and 2 respectively.

The cross-references between the new and the old law's provisions are based on that portion of the House Judiciary Committee's 1976 report, which set forth, in parallel columns, provisions of the then-proposed new law and related provisions of the old law. The cross-reference tables, while useful research aids, should not be considered to list every possible reference. It should also be kept in mind that some provisions of the new law are derived as much from court decisions as from the text of the 1909 Act. For example, fair use existed as a judicial doctrine; now it is an express part of the new legislation. Finally, many of the new law's provisions relate to detailed limitations on performance rights. There are usually no close parallels in the old law because it dealt with limitations on performance rights through general standards.

The legislative history selected for cross-referencing includes the three principal congressional reports explaining the new law's provisions and selected references to the 1976 *Congressional Record*. The three congressional reports are (1) the November 1975 Report of the Senate Committee on the Judiciary; (2) the September 1976 Report of the House Judiciary Committee; and (3) the September 1976 Senate–House Conference Committee Report of the Conference Committee's resolution of the differences between the bill passed by the House and that passed by the Senate. The cross-references to these three sets of reports are extensive, but do not purport to exhaust the cross-referencing possibilities. The formal citations to these three reports may be found at the beginning of the Notes and References section in this volume.

The cross-references to the 1976 *Congressional Record* are selective ones only. The selections merely reflect a judgment as to important material in the 1976 *Congressional Record* relating to particular sections of the new law.

Those who wish to explore the legislative history beyond the material cited in this appendix will find it useful to read a summary of the history of the new law provided by Barbara Ringer, Register of Copyrights, in her 1975 testimony before the relevant subcommittee of the House of Representatives (*Copyright Law Revision: Hearings on H.R. 2223 Before the Subcommittee on Courts, Civil Liberties, and the Administration of Justice*, 94th Cong., 1st sess., ser. no. 36, pt. 1, pp. 95–99, pt. 3, pp. 1794–1806). Also useful are two articles from the May 1977 issue of the *Law Library Journal* (vol. 70, no. 2), published by the American Association of Law Libraries. One article, by Julius J. Marke, is entitled "United States Copyright Revision and Its Legislative History" (pp. 121–132). Mr. Marke is Law Librarian and Professor of Law at New York University, School of Law. The second article, "How to Research Copyright Law" (pp. 171–183), is by Luciana Chee, Librarian, Hofstra University, School of Law Library.

1. The 1976 Copyright Law Cross-Referenced to Selected Legislative History and to the Copyright Act of 1909

Section	Section Caption	Senate Report	House Report	Conf. Report	Congressional Record, Daily Ed. (Vol. 122)	1909 Act Sections
101	Definitions	50	50			26
102	Subject matter of copyright: In general	50–54	51–57			4, 5
103	Subject matter of copyright: Compilations and derivative works	54–55	57–58, 151, 155			7
104	Subject matter of copyright: National origin	55–56	58			9
105	Subject matter of copyright: United States Government works	56–57, 159	58–60, 180	69–70		8
106	Exclusive rights in copyrighted works	57–61	61–65, 79, 82, 105, 106, 107	76		1
107	Limitations on exclusive rights: Fair use	61–67, 69, 145	65–74	70	H10727, 10875–76, 10880–81	
108	Limitations on exclusive rights: Reproduction by libraries and archives	67–71	74–79, 170, 183	70–74	S1545	
109	Limitations on exclusive rights: Effect of transfer of particular copy or phonorecord	71–73	79–81			27

No.	Description					
110	Limitations on exclusive rights: Exemption of certain performances and displays	65, 73–77, 78, 85	72, 81–88, 92, 103–105	74–75	S1546, H10878	1, 104
111	Limitations on exclusive rights: Secondary transmissions	78–83, 141, 155–156, 161	88–101, 102, 103, 159, 164, 173, 175–179	75–76, 80	H10879	
112	Limitations on exclusive rights: Ephemeral recordings	65, 83–86	72, 101–105	74–75		
113	Scope of exclusive rights in pictorial, graphic, and sculptural works	53, 86–87	105–106			
114	Scope of exclusive rights in sound recordings	53–54, 84, 85, 87–88	102, 103, 106–107	76–77		1
115	Scope of exclusive rights in nondramatic musical works: Compulsory license for making and distributing phonorecords	88–94, 97, 156, 159–160, 161	79, 107–111, 173, 177, 181	77		1, 101
116	Scope of exclusive rights in nondramatic musical works: Public performances by means of coin-operated phonorecord players	95–99, 156	111–115, 173, 177, 179	81		1
117	Scope of exclusive rights: Use in conjunction with computers and similar information systems	99–100	116			
118	Scope of exclusive rights:	100–103, 155	72, 116–120,	77–78	H10728	1

1. The 1976 Copyright Law Cross-Referenced to Selected Legislative History and to the Copyright Act of 1909 (Continued)

Section	Section Caption	Senate Report	House Report	Conf. Report	Congressional Record, Daily Ed. (Vol. 122)	1909 Act Sections
	Use of certain works in connection with noncommercial broadcasting		180			
201	Ownership of copyright	103–107, 141	120–124, 146			3, 9, 26, 28
202	Ownership of copyright as distinct from ownership of material object	107–108	124			27
203	Termination of transfers and licenses granted by the author	108–111, 123–124	124–128, 140–141		H10728	24
204	Execution of transfers of copyright ownership	108, 111–112	128–129			28, 29
205	Recordation of transfers and other documents	111–112, 160	128–129, 181–182			30, 31
301	Preemption with respect to other laws	108, 112–116	129–133	78–79	S2042–44, H10910	2
302	Duration of copyright: Works created on or after Jan. 1, 1978	116–121, 132	133–138, 149			24
303	Duration of copyright: Works created but not published or copyrighted before Jan. 1, 1978	121–122	138–139			2

1. The 1976 Copyright Law Cross-Referenced to Selected Legislative History and to the Copyright Act of 1909 (Continued)

Section	Section Caption	Senate Report	House Report	Conf. Report	Congressional Record, Daily Ed. (Vol. 122)	1909 Act Sections
412	Registration as prerequisite to certain remedies for infringement	140, 160	158, 181			
501	Infringement of copyright	141–142	158–160, 164	75–76		
502	Remedies for infringement: Injunctions	142	160			101, 112, 113
503	Remedies for infringement: Impounding and disposition of infringing articles	142–143	160			1, 101
504	Remedies for infringement: Damages and profits	143–145	161–163	79–80		1, 101
505	Remedies for infringement: Costs and attorney's fees	145	163			116
506	Criminal offenses	145–146	163	79–80		104, 105
507	Limitations on actions	146	164			115
508	Notification of filing and determination of actions	146	164			
509	Seizure and forfeiture		164	79, 80		101, 108
510	Remedies for alteration of programming by cable systems		164			

1. The 1976 Copyright Law Cross-Referenced to Selected Legislative History and to the Copyright Act of 1909 (Continued)

Section	Section Caption	Senate Report	House Report	Conf. Report	Congressional Record, Daily Ed. (Vol. 122)	1909 Act Sections
710	Reproductions for use of the blind and physically handicapped: Voluntary licensing forms and procedures	154	173			
801	Copyright Royalty Tribunal: Establishment and purpose	155–158	175–179	81–82	H10728	
802	Membership of the Tribunal	155–158	173–175	81–82		
803	Procedures of the Tribunal	155–158	173–175	81–82		
804	Institution and conclusion of proceedings	155–158	177–179	81–82		
805	Staff of the Tribunal		174–175			
806	Administrative support of the Tribunal		174–175			
807	Deduction of costs of proceedings	158				
808	Reports					
809	Effective date of final determinations					
810	Judicial review	158	179			
102 (T&S)	Effective date	159	180			

Section*	Section Description Transitional and Supplementary Provisions	Senate Report	House Report	Conf. Report	Congressional Record, Daily Ed. (Vol. 122)	1909 Act Sections
103 (T&S)	Pre-1978 public domain works	159	180			1(e)
104 (T&S)	Presidential proclamations					
105 (T&S)	Amendments to titles 2, 15, 26, 28, 39, & 44 of the U.S. Code	159	180			9
106 (T&S)	Compulsory licenses under section 1(e) of the Copyright Act of 1909	159–160	181			1(e)
107 (T&S)	Ad interim copyrights under section 22 of the Copyright Act of 1909	160	181			22
108 (T&S)	Copyright notices under the Copyright Act of 1909	160	181			19, 20
109 (T&S)	Registration of copyright claims and recordation of documents under the Copyright Act of 1909	160–161	181–182			11, 12, 24, 25, 29, 30, 209
110 (T&S)	Demand and penalty provisions under section 14 of the Copyright Act of 1909			80		14
111 (T&S)	Amendment of Title 18 U.S. Code sec. 2318	161	182			

*T&S refers to the Transitional and Supplementary Provisions of the new law.

1. The 1976 Copyright Law Cross-Referenced to Selected Legislative History and to the Copyright Act of 1909 (Continued)

Section*	Section Description Transitional and Supplementary Provisions	Senate Report	House Report	Conf. Report	Congressional Record, Daily Ed. (Vol. 122)	1909 Act Sections
112 (T&S)	Causes of action that arise before Jan. 1, 1978	161	182			
113 (T&S)	American Television and Radio Archives Act		182–183	77, 79		
114 (T&S)	Appropriations					
115 (T&S)	Savings Clause		183			

*T&S refers to the Transitional and Supplementary Provisions of the new law.

2. The Copyright Act of 1909 Cross-Referenced to the 1976 Copyright Law

1909 Act Section	Section Caption	1976 Act Sections
1	Exclusive rights as to copyrighted works	104, 106, 107–118, 504
2	Rights of author or proprietor of unpublished work	301, 303
3	Protection of component parts of work copyrighted; composite works or periodicals	103, 201
4	All writings of author included	102, 301
5	Classification of works for registration	102, 409
6	Registration of prints and labels	408

7	Copyright on compilations of works in public domain or of copyrighted works; subsisting copyrights not affected	103
8	Copyright not to subsist in works in public domain or published prior to July 1, 1909, and not already copyrighted, or Government publications; publication by Government of copyrighted material	105
9	Authors or proprietors entitled; aliens	104, 201
10	Publication of work with notice	102, 401, 402
11	Registration of claim and issuance of certificate	408, 410
12	Works not reproduced for sale	408
13	Deposit of copies after publication; action or proceeding for infringement	407, 408, 411
14	Same; failure to deposit; demand; penalty	407, 408
15	Same; postmaster's receipt; transmission by mail without cost	
16	Mechanical work to be done in United States	601
17	Affidavit to accompany copies	601
18	Making false affidavit	506, 601
19	Notice; form	401, 402
20	Same; place of application of; one notice in each volume or number of newspaper or periodical	401, 402, 404
21	Same; effect of accidental omission from copy or copies	405
22	Ad interim protection of book or periodical published abroad	601, 107 (T&S)*
23	Same; extension to full term	601, 107 (T&S)*
24	Duration; renewal and extension	203, 302, 304
25	Renewal of copyrights registered in Patent Office under repealed law	304
26	Terms defined	101

*T&S refers to the Transitional and Supplementary Provisions of the new law.

2. The Copyright Act of 1909 Cross-Referenced to the 1976 Copyright Law (Continued)

1909 Act Section	Section Caption	1976 Act Sections
27	Copyright distinct from property in object copyrighted; effect of sale of object, and of assignment of copyright	102, 109, 202
28	Assignments and bequests	201, 204
29	Same; executed in foreign country; acknowledgment and certificate	204
30	Same; record	205
31	Same; certificate of record	205
32	Same; use of name of assignee in notice	405
101	Infringement (a) injunction; (b) damages and profits; amounts; other remedies; (c) impounding during action; (d) destruction of infringing copies and plates; (e) interchangeable parts for use in mechanical music-producing machines	115, 502, 503, 504
104	Willful infringement for profit	110, 506
105	Fraudulent notice of copyright, or removal or alteration of notice	506
106	Importation of article bearing false notice or pirated copies of copyrighted work	602
107	Importation, during existence of copyright, of piratical copies, or of copies not produced in accordance with section 16 of this title	601, 602
108	Forfeiture and destruction of articles prohibited importation	603
109	Importation of prohibited articles; regulations; proof of deposit of copies by complainants	603
112	Injunctions; service and enforcement	502

Section	Description	Reference
113	Transmission of certified copies of papers for enforcement of injunction by other court	502
114	Review of orders, judgments, or decrees	
115	Limitations	507
116	Costs; attorney's fees	505
201	Copyright Office; preservation of records	701
202	Register, assistant register, and subordinates	701
203	Same; deposit of moneys received; reports	701
204	Same; bond	701
205	Same; annual report	701
206	Seal of Copyright Office	701
207	Rules for registration of claims	408, 409, 702
208	Record books in Copyright Office	410, 705
209	Certificates of registration; effect as evidence; receipt for copies deposited	409, 410
210	Catalogs of copyright entries; effect as evidence	707
211	Same; distribution and sale; disposal of proceeds	707
212	Records and works deposited in Copyright Office open to public inspection, taking copies of entries	705
213	Disposition of articles deposited in office	704
214	Destruction of articles deposited in office remaining undisposed of; removal of by author or proprietor; manuscripts of unpublished works	704
215	Fees	708
216	When the day for action falls on Saturday, Sunday, or a holiday	703

APPENDIX 8
COPYRIGHT OFFICE APPLICATION
FORMS FOR REGISTRATION

FORM TX

UNITED STATES COPYRIGHT OFFICE
LIBRARY OF CONGRESS
WASHINGTON, D.C. 20559

APPLICATION
FOR
COPYRIGHT
REGISTRATION
for a
Nondramatic Literary Work

HOW TO APPLY FOR COPYRIGHT REGISTRATION:

- **First:** Read the information on this page to make sure Form TX is the correct application for your work.

- **Second:** Open out the form by lifting on the left. Read through the detailed instructions before starting to complete the form.

- **Third:** Complete spaces 1-4 of the application, then turn the entire form over and, after reading the instructions for spaces 5-11, complete the rest of your application. Use typewriter or print in dark ink. Be sure to sign the form at space 10.

- **Fourth:** Detach your completed application from these instructions and send it with the necessary deposit of the work (see below) to: Register of Copyrights, Library of Congress, Washington, D.C. 20559. Unless you have a Deposit Account in the Copyright Office, your application and deposit must be accompanied by a check or money order for $10, payable to: *Register of Copyrights.*

WHEN TO USE FORM TX: Form TX is the appropriate application to use for copyright registration covering nondramatic literary works, whether published or unpublished.

WHAT IS A "NONDRAMATIC LITERARY WORK"? The category of "nondramatic literary works" (Class TX) is very broad. Except for dramatic works and certain kinds of audiovisual works, Class TX includes all types of works written in words (or other verbal or numerical symbols). A few of the many examples of "nondramatic literary works" include fiction, nonfiction, poetry, periodicals, textbooks, reference works, directories, catalogs, advertising copy, and compilations of information.

DEPOSIT TO ACCOMPANY APPLICATION: An application for copyright registration must be accompanied by a deposit representing the entire work for which registration is to be made. The following are the general deposit requirements as set forth in the statute:

Unpublished work: Deposit one complete copy (or phonorecord).

Published work: Deposit two complete copies (or phonorecords) of the best edition.

Work first published outside the United States: Deposit one complete copy (or phonorecord) of the first foreign edition.

Contribution to a collective work: Deposit one complete copy (or phonorecord) of the best edition of the collective work.

These general deposit requirements may vary in particular situations. For further information about copyright deposit, write for Circular R7.

THE COPYRIGHT NOTICE: For published works, the law provides that a copyright notice in a specified form "shall be placed on all publicly distributed copies from which the work can be visually perceived."Use of the copyright notice is the responsibility of the copyright owner and does not require advance permission from the Copyright Office. The required form of the notice for copies generally consists of three elements: (1) the symbol "©", or the word "Copyright", or the abbreviation "Copr."; (2) the year of first publication; and (3) the name of the owner of copyright. For example: "© 1978 Constance Porter" The notice is to be affixed to the copies "in such manner and location as to give reasonable notice of the claim of copyright." Unlike the law in effect before 1978, the new copyright statute provides procedures for correcting errors in the copyright notice, and even for curing the omission of the notice. However, a failure to comply with the notice requirements may still result in the loss of some copyright protection and, unless corrected within five years, in the complete loss of copyright. For further information about the copyright notice and the procedures for correcting errors or omissions, write for Circular R3.

DURATION OF COPYRIGHT: For works that were created after the effective date of the new statute (January 1, 1978), the basic copyright term will be the life of the author and fifty years after the author's death. For works made for hire, and for certain anonymous and pseudonymous works, the duration of copyright will be 75 years from publication or 100 years from creation, whichever is shorter. These same terms of copyright will generally apply to works that had been created before 1978 but had not been published or copyrighted before that date. For further information about the duration of copyright, including the terms of copyrights already in existence before 1978, write for Circular R15a.

251

FORM TX
UNITED STATES COPYRIGHT OFFICE

REGISTRATION NUMBER

TX   TXU

EFFECTIVE DATE OF REGISTRATION

....
Month   Day   Year

DO NOT WRITE ABOVE THIS LINE. IF YOU NEED MORE SPACE, USE CONTINUATION SHEET

(1) Title

TITLE OF THIS WORK: **PREVIOUS OR ALTERNATIVE TITLES:**

If a periodical or serial give: Vol . . . . . . No . . . . Issue Date . . . .

PUBLICATION AS A CONTRIBUTION: (If this work was published as a contribution to a periodical, serial, or collection, give information about the collective work in which the contribution appeared.)

Title of Collective Work: . . . . Vol . . . . . . No . . . . . . Date . . . . Pages . . . .

(2) Author(s)

IMPORTANT: Under the law, the "author" of a "work made for hire" is generally the employer, not the employee (see instructions). If any part of this work was "made for hire" check "Yes" in the space provided, give the employer (or other person for whom the work was prepared) as "Author" of that part, and leave the space for dates blank.

1

NAME OF AUTHOR: **DATES OF BIRTH AND DEATH:**
Born . . . . Died . . . .
    (Year)   (Year)

Was this author's contribution to the work a "work made for hire"?   Yes . . . . . . No . . . . . .

AUTHOR'S NATIONALITY OR DOMICILE: **WAS THIS AUTHOR'S CONTRIBUTION TO THE WORK:**
Citizen of . . . . } or { Domiciled in . . . .
  (Name of Country)   (Name of Country)
Anonymous?   Yes . . . . . . No . . . . . .
Pseudonymous?   Yes . . . . . . No . . . . . .

AUTHOR OF: (Briefly describe nature of this author's contribution)

If the answer to either of these questions is "Yes, see detailed instructions attached.

2

NAME OF AUTHOR: **DATES OF BIRTH AND DEATH:**
Born . . . . Died . . . .
    (Year)   (Year)

Was this author's contribution to the work a "work made for hire"?   Yes . . . . . . No . . . . . .

AUTHOR'S NATIONALITY OR DOMICILE: **WAS THIS AUTHOR'S CONTRIBUTION TO THE WORK:**
Citizen of . . . . } or { Domiciled in . . . .
  (Name of Country)   (Name of Country)
Anonymous?   Yes . . . . . . No . . . . . .
Pseudonymous?   Yes . . . . . . No . . . . . .

AUTHOR OF: (Briefly describe nature of this author's contribution)

If the answer to either of these questions is "Yes, see detailed instructions attached.

3

NAME OF AUTHOR: **DATES OF BIRTH AND DEATH:**
Born . . . . Died . . . .
    (Year)   (Year)

Was this author's contribution to the work a "work made for hire"?   Yes . . . . . . No . . . . . .

AUTHOR'S NATIONALITY OR DOMICILE: **WAS THIS AUTHOR'S CONTRIBUTION TO THE WORK:**
Citizen of . . . . } or { Domiciled in . . . .
  (Name of Country)   (Name of Country)
Anonymous?   Yes . . . . . . No . . . . . .
Pseudonymous?   Yes . . . . . . No . . . . . .

AUTHOR OF: (Briefly describe nature of this author's contribution)

If the answer to either of these questions is "Yes, see detailed instructions attached.

(3) Creation and Publication

YEAR IN WHICH CREATION OF THIS WORK WAS COMPLETED: **DATE AND NATION OF FIRST PUBLICATION:**

Year . . . .

(This information must be given in all cases.)

Date . . . .
    (Month)   (Day)   (Year)

Nation . . . .
    (Name of Country)

(Complete this block ONLY if this work has been published.)

(4) Claimant(s)

NAME(S) AND ADDRESS(ES) OF COPYRIGHT CLAIMANT(S):

TRANSFER: (If the copyright claimant(s) named here in space 4 are different from the author(s) named in space 2, give a brief statement of how the claimant(s) obtained ownership of the copyright.)

* Complete all applicable spaces (numbers 5-11) on the reverse side of this page
* Follow detailed instructions attached
* Sign the form at line 10

DO NOT WRITE HERE
Page 1 of . . . . pages

HOW TO FILL OUT FORM TX

Specific Instructions for Spaces 1-4

> - The line-by-line instructions on this page are keyed to the spaces on the first page of Form TX, printed opposite.
> - Please read through these instructions before you start filling out your application, and refer to the specific instructions for each space as you go along.

SPACE 1: TITLE

- **Title of this Work:** Every work submitted for copyright registration must be given a title that is capable of identifying that particular work. If the copies or phonorecords of the work bear a title (or an identifying phrase that could serve as a title), transcribe its wording completely and exactly on the application. Remember that indexing of the registration and future identification of the work will depend on the information you give here.

- **Periodical or Serial Issue:** Periodicals and other serials are publications issued at intervals under a general title, such as newspapers, magazines, journals, newsletters, and annuals. If the work being registered is an entire issue of a periodical or serial, give the over-all title of the periodical or serial in the space headed "Title of this Work," and add the specific information about the issue in

the spaces provided. If the work being registered is a contribution to a periodical or serial issue, follow the instructions for "Publication as a Contribution."

- **Previous or Alternative Titles:** Complete this space if there are any additional titles for the work under which someone searching for the registration might be likely to look, or under which a document pertaining to the work might be recorded.

- **Publication as a Contribution:** If the work being registered has been published as a contribution to a periodical, serial, or collection, give the title of the contribution in the space headed "Title of this Work." Then, in the line headed "Publication as a Contribution," give information about the larger work in which the contribution appeared.

SPACE 2: AUTHORS

- **General Instructions:** First decide, after reading these instructions, who are the "authors" of this work for copyright purposes. Then, unless the work is a "collective work" (see below), give the requested information about every "author" who contributed any appreciable amount of copyrightable matter to this version of the work. If you need further space, use the attached Continuation Sheet and, if necessary, request additional Continuation Sheets (Form TX/Con).

- **Who is the "Author"?** Unless the work was "made for hire," the individual who actually created the work is its "author." In the case of a work made for hire, the statute provides that "the employer or other person for whom the work was prepared is considered the author."

- **What is a "Work Made for Hire"?** A "work made for hire" is defined as: (1) "a work prepared by an employee within the scope of his or her employment"; or (2) "a work specially ordered or commissioned" for certain uses specified in the statute, but only if there is a written agreement to consider it a "work made for hire."

- **Collective Work:** In the case of a collective work, such as a periodical issue, anthology, collection of essays, or encyclopedia, it is sufficient to give information about the author of the collective work as a whole.

- **Author's Identity Not Revealed:** If an author's contribution is "anonymous" or "pseudonymous," it is not necessary to give the name and dates for that author. However, the citizenship and domicile of the author **must** be given in all cases, and information about the nature of that author's contribution to the work should be included if possible.

- **Name of Author:** The fullest form of the author's name should be given. If

you have checked "Yes" to indicate that the work was "made for hire," give the full legal name of the employer (or other person for whom the work was prepared). You may also include the name of the employee (for example, "Elster Publishing Co., employer for hire of John Ferguson"). If the work is "anonymous" you may: (1) leave the line blank, or (2) state "Anonymous" in the line, or (3) reveal the author's identity. If the work is "pseudonymous" you may (1) leave the line blank, or (2) give the pseudonym and identify it as such (for example: "Huntley Haverstock, pseudonym"), or (3) reveal both the author's name, making clear which is the real name and which is the pseudonym (for example, "Judith Barton, whose pseudonym is Madeleine Elster").

- **Dates of Birth and Death:** If the author is dead, the statute requires that the year of death be included in the application unless the work is anonymous or pseudonymous. The author's birth date is optional, but is useful as a form of identification. Leave this space blank if the author's contribution was a "work made for hire."

- **"Anonymous" or "Pseudonymous" Work:** An author's contribution to a work is "anonymous" if that author is not identified on the copies or phonorecords of the work. An author's contribution to a work is "pseudonymous" if that author is identified on the copies or phonorecords under a fictitious name.

- **Author's Nationality or Domicile:** Give the country of which the author is a citizen, or the country in which the author is domiciled. The statute requires that either nationality or domicile be given in all cases.

- **Nature of Authorship:** After the words "Author of" give a brief general statement of the nature of this particular author's contribution to the work. Examples: "Entire text"; "Co-author of entire text"; "Chapters 11-14"; "Editorial revisions"; "Compilation and English translation"; "Illustrations."

SPACE 3: CREATION AND PUBLICATION

- **General Instructions:** Do not confuse "creation" with "publication." Every application for copyright registration must state "the year in which creation of the work was completed." Give the date and nation of first publication only if the work has been published.

- **Creation:** Under the statute, a work is "created" when it is fixed in a copy or phonorecord for the first time. Where a work has been prepared over a period of time, the part of the work existing in fixed form on a particular date constitutes the created work on that date. The date you give here should be the year in which the author completed the particular version for which registration

is now being sought, even if other versions exist or if further changes or additions are planned.

- **Publication:** The statute defines "publication" as "the distribution of copies or phonorecords of a work to the public by sale or other transfer of ownership, or by rental, lease, or lending"; a work is also "published" if there has been an "offering to distribute copies or phonorecords to a group of persons for purposes of further distribution, public performance, or public display." Give the full date (month, day, year) when, and the country where, publication first occurred. If first publication took place simultaneously in the United States and other countries, it is sufficient to state "U.S.A."

SPACE 4: CLAIMANT(S)

- **Name(s) and Address(es) of Copyright Claimant(s):** Give the name(s) address(es) of the copyright claimant(s) in this work. The statute provides that copyright in a work belongs initially to the author of the work (including, in the case of a work made for hire, the employer or other person for whom the work was prepared). The copyright claimant is either the author of the work or a person or organization that has obtained ownership of the copyright initially belonging to the author.

- **Transfer:** The statute provides that, if the copyright claimant is not the author, the application for registration must contain "a brief statement of how the claimant obtained ownership of the copyright." If any copyright claimant named in space 4 is not an author named in space 2, give a brief, general statement summarizing the means by which that claimant obtained ownership of the copyright.

EXAMINED BY:	APPLICATION RECEIVED:	
CHECKED BY:		FOR COPYRIGHT OFFICE USE ONLY
CORRESPONDENCE: ☐ Yes	DEPOSIT RECEIVED:	
DEPOSIT ACCOUNT FUNDS USED: ☐	REMITTANCE NUMBER AND DATE	

DO NOT WRITE ABOVE THIS LINE. IF YOU NEED ADDITIONAL SPACE, USE CONTINUATION SHEET (FORM TX/CON)

PREVIOUS REGISTRATION:

- Has registration for this work, or for an earlier version of this work, already been made in the Copyright Office?   Yes .... No ....
- If your answer is "Yes," why is another registration being sought? (Check appropriate box)
  - ☐ This is the first published edition of a work previously registered in unpublished form.
  - ☐ This is the first application submitted by this author as copyright claimant.
  - ☐ This is a changed version of the work, as shown by line 6 of this application.
- If your answer is "Yes," give: Previous Registration Number .... Year of Registration ....

⑤ Previous Registration

COMPILATION OR DERIVATIVE WORK: (See instructions)

PREEXISTING MATERIAL: (Identify any preexisting work or works that this work is based on or incorporates.)

{ ....

MATERIAL ADDED TO THIS WORK: (Give a brief, general statement of the material that has been added to this work and in which copyright is claimed.)

{ ....

⑥ Compilation or Derivative Work

MANUFACTURERS AND LOCATIONS: (If this is a published work consisting preponderantly of nondramatic literary material in English, the law may require that the copies be manufactured in the United States or Canada for full protection. If so, the names of the manufacturers who performed certain processes, and the places where these processes were performed *must* be given. See instructions for details.)

NAMES OF MANUFACTURERS	PLACES OF MANUFACTURE
....	....
....	....
....	....

⑦ Manufacturing

REPRODUCTION FOR USE OF BLIND OR PHYSICALLY-HANDICAPPED PERSONS: (See instructions)

- Signature of this form at space 10, and a check in one of the boxes here in space 8, constitutes a non-exclusive grant of permission to the Library of Congress to reproduce and distribute solely for the blind and physically handicapped and under the conditions and limitations prescribed by the regulations of the Copyright Office: (1) copies of the work identified in space 1 of this application in Braille (or similar tactile symbols); or (2) phonorecords embodying a fixation of a reading of that work; or (3) both.

  a ☐ Copies and phonorecords   b ☐ Copies Only   c ☐ Phonorecords Only

⑧ License For Handicapped

DEPOSIT ACCOUNT: (If the registration fee is to be charged to a Deposit Account established in the Copyright Office, give name and number of Account.)

Name: ....

Account Number: ....

CORRESPONDENCE: (Give name and address to which correspondence about this application should be sent.)

Name: ....

Address: .... (Apt.)

.... (City)   (State)   (ZIP)

⑨ Fee and Correspondence

CERTIFICATION: ✱ I, the undersigned, hereby certify that I am the: (Check one)

☐ author ☐ other copyright claimant ☐ owner of exclusive right(s) ☐ authorized agent of: ....
(Name of author or other copyright claimant, or owner of exclusive right(s))

of the work identified in this application and that the statements made by me in this application are correct to the best of my knowledge.

☞ Handwritten signature: (X) ....

Typed or printed name. .... Date ....

⑩ Certification (Application must be signed)

MAIL CERTIFICATE TO	**⑪ Address For Return of Certificate**

....
(Name)

....
(Number, Street and Apartment Number)

....
(City)   (State)   (ZIP code)

(Certificate will be mailed in window envelope)

✱ 17 U.S.C. § 506(e): Any person who knowingly makes a false representation of a material fact in the application for copyright registration provided for by section 409, or in any written statement filed in connection with the application, shall be fined not more than $2,500.

☼ U. S. GOVERNMENT PRINTING OFFICE : 1977 O - 248-641

PRIVACY ACT ADVISORY STATEMENT
Required by the Privacy Act of 1974 (Public Law 93-579)

AUTHORITY FOR REQUESTING THIS INFORMATION
• Title 17, U.S.C., Secs. 409 and 410

FURNISHING THE REQUESTED INFORMATION IS
• Voluntary

BUT IF THE INFORMATION IS NOT FURNISHED
• It may be necessary to delay or refuse registration
• You may not be entitled to certain relief, remedies, and benefits provided in chapters 4 and 5 of title 17, U.S.C.

PRINCIPAL USES OF REQUESTED INFORMATION
• Establishment and maintenance of a public record
• Examination of the application for compliance with legal requirements

OTHER ROUTINE USES
• Public inspection and copying
• Preparation of public indexes

• Preparation of public catalogs of copyright registrations
• Preparation of search reports upon request

NOTE
• No other advisory statement will be given you in connection with this application
• Please retain this statement and refer to it if we communicate with you regarding this application

INSTRUCTIONS FOR FILLING OUT SPACES 5-11 OF FORM TX

SPACE 5: PREVIOUS REGISTRATION

• **General Instructions:** The questions in space 5 are intended to find out whether an earlier registration has been made for this work and, if so, whether there is any basis for a new registration. As a general rule, only one basic copyright registration can be made for the same version of a particular work.

• **Same Version:** If this version is substantially the same as the work covered by a previous registration, a second registration is not generally possible unless: (1) the work has been registered in unpublished form and a second registration is now being sought to cover the first published edition, or (2) someone other than the author is identified as copyright claimant in the earlier registration, and the author is now seeking registration in his or her own name. If either

of these two exceptions apply, check the appropriate box and give the earlier registration number and date. Otherwise, do not submit Form TX; instead, write the Copyright Office for information about supplementary registration or recordation of transfers of copyright ownership.

• **Changed Version:** If the work has been changed, and you are now seeking registration to cover the additions or revisions, check the third box in space 5, give the earlier registration number and date, and complete both parts of space 6.

• **Previous Registration Number and Date:** If more than one previous registration has been made for the work, give the number and date of the latest registration.

SPACE 6: COMPILATION OR DERIVATIVE WORK

• **General Instructions:** Complete both parts of space 6 if this work is a "compilation," or "derivative work," or both, and if it incorporates one or more earlier works that have already been published or registered for copyright, or that have fallen into the public domain. A "compilation" is defined as "a work formed by the collection and assembling of preexisting materials or of data that are selected, coordinated, or arranged in such a way that the resulting work as a whole constitutes an original work of authorship." A "derivative work" is "a work based on one or more preexisting works." Examples of derivative works include translations, fictionalizations, arrangements, abridgments, condensations, or "any other form in which a work may be recast, transformed, or adapted." Derivative works also include works "consisting of editorial revisions, annotations, elaborations, or other modifications" if these changes, as a whole, represent an original work of authorship.

• **Preexisting Material:** If the work is a compilation, give a brief, general statement describing the nature of the material that has been compiled. Example: "Compilation of all published 1917 speeches of Woodrow Wilson." In the case of a derivative work, identify the preexisting work that has been recast, transformed, or adapted. Example: "Russian version of Goncharov's 'Oblomov'."

• **Material Added to this Work:** The statute requires a "brief, general statement of the additional material covered by the copyright claim being registered." This statement should describe all of the material in this particular version of the work that: (1) represents an original work of authorship; (2) has not fallen into the public domain; and (3) has not been previously published; and (4) has not been previously registered for copyright in unpublished form. Examples: "Foreword, selection, arrangement, editing, critical annotations"; "Revisions throughout; chapters 11-17 entirely new."

SPACE 7: MANUFACTURING PROVISIONS

• **General Instructions:** The copyright statute currently provides, as a general rule, and with a number of exceptions, that the copies of a published work "consisting preponderantly of nondramatic literary material that is in the English language" be manufactured in the United States or Canada in order to be lawfully imported and publicly distributed in the United States. At the present time, applications for copyright registration covering published works that consist mainly of nondramatic matter in English must, in most cases, identify those who performed certain processes in manufacturing the copies, together with the places where those processes were performed. *Please note:* The information must be given even if the copies were manufactured outside the United States or Canada; registration will be made regardless of the places of manufacture identified in space 7. In general, the processes covered

by this provision are: (1) typesetting and plate-making (where a typographic process preceded the actual printing); (2) the making of plates by a lithographic or photoengraving process (where this was a final or intermediate step before printing); and (3) the final printing and binding processes (in all cases). Leave space 7 blank if your work is unpublished or is not in English.

• **Import Statement:** As an exception to the manufacturing provisions, the statute prescribes that, where manufacture has taken place outside the United States or Canada, a maximum of 2000 copies of the foreign edition can be imported into the United States without affecting the copyright owner's rights. For this purpose, the Copyright Office will issue an import statement upon request and payment of a fee of $3 at the time of registration or at any later time. For further information about import statements, ask for circular R62.

SPACE 8: REPRODUCTION FOR USE OF BLIND OR PHYSICALLY-HANDICAPPED PERSONS

• **General Instructions:** One of the major programs of the Library of Congress is to provide Braille editions and special recordings of works for the exclusive use of the blind and physically handicapped. In an effort to simplify and speed up the copyright licensing procedures that are a necessary part of this program, section 710 of the copyright statute provides for the establishment of a voluntary licensing system to be tied in with copyright registration. Under this system, the owner of copyright in a nondramatic literary work has the option, at the time of registration on Form TX, to grant to the Library of Congress a license to reproduce and distribute Braille editions or "talking books" or "talking magazines" of the work being registered. The Copyright Office regulations

provide that, under the license, the reproduction and distribution must be solely for the use of persons who are certified by competent authority as unable to read normal printed material as a result of physical limitations. The license is nonexclusive, and may be terminated upon 90 days notice. For further information, write for Circular R63.

• **How to Grant the License:** The license is entirely voluntary. If you wish to grant it, check one of the three boxes in space 8. Your check in one of these boxes, together with your signature in space 10, will mean that the Library of Congress can proceed to reproduce and distribute under the license without further paperwork.

SPACES 9, 10, 11: FEE, CORRESPONDENCE, CERTIFICATION, RETURN ADDRESS

• **Deposit Account and Mailing Instructions (Space 9):** If you maintain a Deposit Account in the Copyright Office, identify it in space 9. Otherwise you will need to send the registration fee of $10 with your application. The space headed "Correspondence" should contain the name and address of the person to be consulted if correspondence about this application becomes necessary.

• **Certification (Space 10):** The application is not acceptable unless it bears the handwritten signature of the author or other copyright claimant, or of the owner of exclusive right(s), or of the duly authorized agent of such author, claimant, or owner.

• **Address for Return of Certificate (Space 11):** The address box must be completed legibly, since the certificate will be returned in a window envelope.

CONTINUATION SHEET FOR FORM TX

FORM TX/CON
UNITED STATES COPYRIGHT OFFICE

- If at all possible, try to fit the information called for into the spaces provided on Form TX.
- If you do not have space enough for all of the information you need to give on Form TX, use this continuation sheet and submit it with Form TX.
- If you submit this continuation sheet, leave it attached to Form TX. Or, if it becomes detached, clip (do not tape or staple) and fold the two together before submitting them.
- **PART A** of this sheet is intended to identify the basic application. **PART B** is a continuation of Space 2. **PART C** is for the continuation of Spaces 1, 4, 6, or 7. The other spaces on Form TX call for specific items of information, and should not need continuation.

REGISTRATION NUMBER
TX   TXU
EFFECTIVE DATE OF REGISTRATION
....
(Month)   (Day)   (Year)
CONTINUATION SHEET RECEIVED
Page _____ of _____ pages

DO NOT WRITE ABOVE THIS LINE: FOR COPYRIGHT OFFICE USE ONLY

(A)

Identification of Application

IDENTIFICATION OF CONTINUATION SHEET: This sheet is a continuation of the application for copyright registration on Form TX, submitted for the following work:
- TITLE (Give the title as given under the heading "Title of this Work" in Space 1 of Form TX)
....
- NAME(S) AND ADDRESS(ES) OF COPYRIGHT CLAIMANT(S): Give the name and address of at least one copyright claimant as given in Space 4 of Form TX.)
....

(B)

Continuation of Space 2

NAME OF AUTHOR:

Was this author's contribution to the work a "work made for hire"?   Yes...... No......

DATES OF BIRTH AND DEATH:
Born .... Died ....
(Year)   (Year)

AUTHOR'S NATIONALITY OR DOMICILE:
Citizen of .... } or { Domiciled in ....
(Name of Country)   (Name of Country)

WAS THIS AUTHOR'S CONTRIBUTION TO THE WORK:
Anonymous?   Yes...... No......
Pseudonymous? Yes...... No......

AUTHOR OF: (Briefly describe nature of this author's contribution)

If the answer to either of these questions is "Yes, see detailed instructions attached.

NAME OF AUTHOR:

Was this author's contribution to the work a "work made for hire"?   Yes...... No......

DATES OF BIRTH AND DEATH:
Born .... Died ....
(Year)   (Year)

AUTHOR'S NATIONALITY OR DOMICILE:
Citizen of .... } or { Domiciled in ....
(Name of Country)   (Name of Country)

WAS THIS AUTHOR'S CONTRIBUTION TO THE WORK:
Anonymous?   Yes...... No......
Pseudonymous? Yes...... No......

AUTHOR OF: (Briefly describe nature of this author's contribution)

If the answer to either of these questions is "Yes, see detailed instructions attached.

NAME OF AUTHOR:

Was this author's contribution to the work a "work made for hire"?   Yes...... No......

DATES OF BIRTH AND DEATH:
Born .... Died ....
(Year)   (Year)

AUTHOR'S NATIONALITY OR DOMICILE:
Citizen of .... } or { Domiciled in ....
(Name of Country)   (Name of Country)

WAS THIS AUTHOR'S CONTRIBUTION TO THE WORK:
Anonymous?   Yes...... No......
Pseudonymous? Yes...... No......

AUTHOR OF: (Briefly describe nature of this author's contribution)

If the answer to either of these questions is "Yes, see detailed instructions attached.

(C)

Continuation of other Spaces

CONTINUATION OF (Check which):   ☐ Space 1   ☐ Space 4   ☐ Space 6   ☐ Space 7

FORM VA

UNITED STATES COPYRIGHT OFFICE
LIBRARY OF CONGRESS
WASHINGTON, D.C. 20559

APPLICATION FOR COPYRIGHT REGISTRATION
for a
Work of the Visual Arts

HOW TO APPLY FOR COPYRIGHT REGISTRATION:

- **First:** Read the information on this page to make sure Form VA is the correct application for your work.

- **Second:** Open out the form by pulling this page to the left. Read through the detailed instructions before starting to complete the form.

- **Third:** Complete spaces 1-4 of the application, then turn the entire form over and, after reading the instructions for spaces 5-9, complete the rest of your application. Use typewriter or print in dark ink. Be sure to sign the form at space 8.

- **Fourth:** Detach your completed application from these instructions and send it with the necessary deposit of the work (see below) to: Register of Copyrights, Library of Congress, Washington, D.C. 20559. Unless you have a Deposit Account in the Copyright Office, your application and deposit must be accompanied by a check or money order for $10, payable to: *Register of Copyrights.*

WHEN TO USE FORM VA: Form VA is the appropriate form to use for copyright registration covering works of the visual arts. Both published and unpublished works can be registered on Form VA.

WHAT IS A "WORK OF THE VISUAL ARTS"? This category consists of "pictorial, graphic, or sculptural works," including two-dimensional and three-dimensional works of fine, graphic, and applied art, photographs, prints and art reproductions, maps, globes, charts, technical drawings, diagrams, and models.

WHAT DOES COPYRIGHT PROTECT? Copyright in a work of the visual arts protects those pictorial, graphic, or sculptural elements that, either alone or in combination, represent an "original work of authorship." The statute declares: "In no case does copyright protection for an original work of authorship extend to any idea, procedure, process, system, method of operation, concept, principle, or discovery, regardless of the form in which it is described, explained, illustrated, or embodied in such work."

WORKS OF ARTISTIC CRAFTSMANSHIP AND DESIGNS: "Works of artistic craftsmanship" are registrable on Form VA, but the statute makes clear that protection extends to "their form" and not to "their mechanical or utilitarian aspects." The "design of a useful article" is considered copyrightable "only if, and only to the extent that, such design incorporates pictorial, graphic, or sculptural features that can be identified separately from, and are capable of existing independently of, the utilitarian aspects of the article."

LABELS AND ADVERTISEMENTS: Works prepared for use in connection with the sale or advertisement of goods and services are registrable if they contain "original work of authorship." Use Form VA if the copyrightable material in the work you are registering is mainly pictorial or graphic; use Form TX if it consists mainly of text. *NOTE:* Words and short phrases such as names, titles, and slogans cannot be protected by copyright, and the same is true of standard symbols, emblems, and other commonly-used graphic designs that are in the public domain. When used commercially, material of that sort can sometimes be protected under State laws of unfair competition or under the Federal trademark laws. For information about trademark registration, write to the Commissioner of Patents and Trademarks, Washington, D.C. 20231.

DEPOSIT TO ACCOMPANY APPLICATION: An application for copyright registration must be accompanied by a deposit representing the entire work for which registration is to be made. The following are the general deposit requirements for works of the visual arts, as set forth in the statute:

Unpublished work: Deposit one complete copy.

Published work: Deposit two complete copies of the best edition.

Work first published outside the United States: Deposit one complete copy of the first foreign edition.

Contribution to a collective work: Deposit one complete copy of the best edition of the collective work.

These general deposit requirements will vary in particular situations. In most cases, where the copies in which the work has been reproduced are three-dimensional, the Copyright Office Regulations provide for the deposit of identifying material (such as photographs or drawings) meeting certain requirements. For further information about the deposit requirements for works of the visual arts, see the reverse side of this sheet. For general information about copyright deposit, write for Circular R7.

DURATION OF COPYRIGHT: For works that were created after the effective date of the new statute (January 1, 1978), the basic copyright term will be the life of the author and fifty years after the author's death. For works made for hire, and for certain anonymous and pseudonymous works, the duration of copyright will be 75 years from publication or 100 years from creation, whichever is shorter. These same terms of copyright will generally apply to works that had been created before 1978 but had not been published or copyrighted before that date. For further information about the duration of copyright, including the terms of copyrights already in existence before 1978, write for Circular R15a.

FORM VA

UNITED STATES COPYRIGHT OFFICE

REGISTRATION NUMBER

VA   VAU

EFFECTIVE DATE OF REGISTRATION

....
Month   Day   Year

DO NOT WRITE ABOVE THIS LINE. IF YOU NEED ADDITIONAL SPACE, USE CONTINUATION SHEET (FORM VA/CON)

(1) Title

TITLE OF THIS WORK:

NATURE OF THIS WORK: (See instructions)

Previous or Alternative Titles:...

PUBLICATION AS A CONTRIBUTION: (If this work was published as a contribution to a periodical, serial, or collection, give information about the collective work in which the contribution appeared.)

Title of Collective Work:.. Vol...... No...... Date................. Pages...............

(2) Author(s)

IMPORTANT: Under the law, the "author" of a "work made for hire" is generally the employer, not the employee (see instructions). If any part of this work was "made for hire" check "Yes" in the space provided, give the employer (or other person for whom the work was prepared) as "Author" of that part, and leave the space for dates blank.

1

NAME OF AUTHOR:

DATES OF BIRTH AND DEATH:
Born.......... Died..........
(Year)   (Year)

Was this author's contribution to the work a "work made for hire"? Yes...... No......

AUTHOR'S NATIONALITY OR DOMICILE:
Citizen of......................... } or { Domiciled in.........................
(Name of Country)   (Name of Country)

WAS THIS AUTHOR'S CONTRIBUTION TO THE WORK:
Anonymous? Yes...... No......
Pseudonymous? Yes...... No......

AUTHOR OF: (Briefly describe nature of this author's contribution)

If the answer to either of these questions is "Yes," see detailed instructions attached.

2

NAME OF AUTHOR:

DATES OF BIRTH AND DEATH:
Born.......... Died..........
(Year)   (Year)

Was this author's contribution to the work a "work made for hire"? Yes...... No......

AUTHOR'S NATIONALITY OR DOMICILE:
Citizen of......................., } or { Domiciled in.........................
(Name of Country)   (Name of Country)

WAS THIS AUTHOR'S CONTRIBUTION TO THE WORK:
Anonymous? Yes...... No......
Pseudonymous? Yes...... No......

AUTHOR OF: (Briefly describe nature of this author's contribution)

If the answer to either of these questions is "Yes," see detailed instructions attached.

3

NAME OF AUTHOR:

DATES OF BIRTH AND DEATH:
Born.......... Died..........
(Year)   (Year)

Was this author's contribution to the work a "work made for hire"? Yes...... No......

AUTHOR'S NATIONALITY OR DOMICILE:
Citizen of......................... } or { Domiciled in.........................
(Name of Country)   (Name of Country)

WAS THIS AUTHOR'S CONTRIBUTION TO THE WORK:
Anonymous? Yes...... No......
Pseudonymous? Yes...... No......

AUTHOR OF: (Briefly describe nature of this author's contribution)

If the answer to either of these questions is "Yes," see detailed instructions attached.

(3) Creation and Publication

YEAR IN WHICH CREATION OF THIS WORK WAS COMPLETED:

Year..........

(This information must be given in all cases.)

DATE AND NATION OF FIRST PUBLICATION:

Date..
(Month)   (Day)   (Year)

Nation..
(Name of Country)

(Complete this block ONLY if this work has been published.)

(4) Claimant(s)

NAME(S) AND ADDRESS(ES) OF COPYRIGHT CLAIMANT(S):

TRANSFER: (If the copyright claimant(s) named here in space 4 are different from the author(s) named in space 2, give a brief statement of how the claimant(s) obtained ownership of the copyright.)

* Complete all applicable spaces (numbers 5-9) on the reverse side of this page
* Follow detailed instructions attached
* Sign the form at line 8

DO NOT WRITE HERE

Page 1 of........ pages

HOW TO FILL OUT FORM VA
Specific Instructions for Spaces 1-4

> - The line-by-line instructions on this page are keyed to the spaces on the first page of Form VA, printed opposite.
> - Please read through these instructions before you start filling out your application, and refer to the specific instructions for each space as you go along.

SPACE 1: TITLE

- **Title of this Work:** Every work submitted for copyright registration must be given a title that is capable of identifying that particular work. If the copies of the work bear a title (or an identifying phrase that could serve as a title), transcribe its wording completely and exactly on the application; otherwise give the work a short descriptive title, making it as explicit as possible. Remember that indexing of the registration and future identification of the work will depend on the information you give here.

- **Previous or Alternative Titles:** Complete this line if there are any additional titles for this work under which someone searching for the registration might be likely to look, or under which a document pertaining to the work might be recorded.

- **Publication as a Contribution:** If the work being registered has been published as a contribution to a periodical, serial, or collection, give the title of the contribution in the space headed "Title of this Work." Then, in the line headed "Publication as a Contribution," give information about the larger work in which the contribution appeared.

- **Nature of this Work:** Briefly describe the nature or character of the pictorial, graphic, or sculptural work being registered for copyright. Examples: "Oil Painting"; "Charcoal Drawing"; "Etching"; "Sculpture"; "Map"; "Photograph"; "Scale Model"; "Lithographic Print"; "Jewelry Design"; "Fabric Design".

SPACE 2: AUTHORS

- **General Instructions:** First decide, after reading these instructions, who are the "authors" of this work for copyright purposes. Then, unless the work is a "collective work" (see below), give the requested information about every "author" who contributed any appreciable amount of copyrightable matter to this version of the work. If you need further space, use the attached Continuation Sheet and, if necessary, request additional Continuation Sheets (Form VA/Con).

- **Who Is the "Author"?** Unless the work was "made for hire," the individual who actually created the work is its "author." In the case of works of the visual arts, "authors" include artists, cartographers, sculptors, painters, photographers, printmakers, and all others who create pictorial, graphic, or sculptural material. Where a work is made for hire, the statute provides that "the employer or other person for whom the work was prepared is considered the author."

- **What Is a "Work Made for Hire"?** A "work made for hire" is defined as: (1) "a work prepared by an employee within the scope of his or her employment"; or (2) "a work specially ordered or commissioned" for certain uses specified in the statute, but only if there is a written agreement to consider it a "work made for hire."

- **Collective Work:** In the case of a collective work, such as a catalog of paintings or a collection of cartoons by various artists, it is sufficient to give information about the author of the collective work as a whole.

- **Author's Identity Not Revealed:** If an author's contribution is "anonymous" or "pseudonymous," it is not necessary to give the name and dates for that author. However, the citizenship and domicile of the author **must** be given in all cases, and information about the nature of that author's contribution to the work should be included if possible.

- **Name of Author:** The fullest form of the author's name should be given. If you have checked "Yes" to indicate that the work was "made for hire," give the full legal name of the employer (or other person for whom the work was prepared). You may also include the name of the employee (for example: "Fremont Enterprises, Inc., employer for hire of L.B. Jeffries"). If the work is "anonymous" you may: (1) leave the line blank, or (2) state "Anonymous" in the line. or (3) reveal the author's identity. If the work is "pseudonymous" you may (1) leave the line blank, or (2) give the pseudonym and identify it as such (for example: "Richard Heldar, pseudonym"), or (3) reveal the author's name, making clear which is the real name and which is the pseudonym (for example, "Henry Leek, whose pseudonym is Priam Farrel").

- **Dates of Birth and Death:** If the author is dead, the statute requires that the year of death be included in the application unless the work is anonymous or pseudonymous. The author's birth date is optional, but is useful as a form of identification. Leave this space blank if the author's contribution was a "work made for hire."

- **"Anonymous" or "Pseudonymous" Work:** An author's contribution to a work is "anonymous" if that author is not identified on the copies of the work. An author's contribution to a work is "pseudonymous" if that author is identified on the copies under a fictitious name.

- **Author's Nationality or Domicile:** Give the country of which the author is a citizen, or the country in which the author is domiciled. The statute requires that either nationality or domicile be given in all cases.

- **Nature of Authorship:** After the words "Author of" give a brief general statement of the nature of this particular author's contribution to the work. Examples: "Painting"; "Photograph"; "Silk Screen Reproduction"; "Co-author of Cartographic Material"; "Technical Drawing"; "Text and Artwork".

SPACE 3: CREATION AND PUBLICATION

- **General Instructions:** Do not confuse "creation" with "publication." Every application for copyright registration must state "the year in which creation of the work was completed." Give the date and nation of first publication only if the work has been published.

- **Creation:** Under the statute, a work of the visual arts is "created" when it is fixed in a copy for the first time. A work is "fixed" in a copy when its embodiment "is sufficiently permanent or stable to permit it to be perceived, reproduced, or otherwise communicated for a period of more than transitory duration." Where a work has been prepared over a period of time, the part of the work existing in fixed form on a particular date constitutes the created work on that date. The date you give here should be the year in which the author completed the particular version for which registration is now being sought, even if other versions exist or if further changes or additions are planned.

- **Publication:** "Publication" is defined as "the distribution of copies or phonorecords of a work to the public by sale or other transfer of ownership, or by rental, lease, or lending"; a work is also "published" if there has been an "offering to distribute copies or phonorecords to a group of persons for purposes of further distribution, public performance, or public display." The statute makes clear that public display of a work "does not of itself constitute publication." Give the full date (month, day, year) when, and the country where, publication first occurred. If first publication took place simultaneously in the United States and other countries, it is sufficient to state "U.S.A."

SPACE 4: CLAIMANT(S)

- **Name(s) and Address(es) of Copyright Claimant(s):** Give the name(s) and address(es) of the copyright claimant(s) in this work. The statute provides that copyright in a work belongs initially to the author of the work (including, in the case of a work made for hire, the employer or other person for whom the work was prepared). The copyright claimant is either the author of the work or a person or organization that has obtained ownership of the copyright initially belonging to the author.

- **Transfer:** The statute provides that, if the copyright claimant is not the author, the application for registration must contain "a brief statement of how the claimant obtained ownership of the copyright." If any copyright claimant named in space 4 is not an author named in space 2, give a brief, general statement summarizing the means by which that claimant obtained ownership of the copyright.

EXAMINED BY:	APPLICATION RECEIVED:	
CHECKED BY:		FOR COPYRIGHT OFFICE USE ONLY
CORRESPONDENCE: ☐ Yes	DEPOSIT RECEIVED:	
DEPOSIT ACCOUNT FUNDS USED: ☐	REMITTANCE NUMBER AND DATE:	

DO NOT WRITE ABOVE THIS LINE. IF YOU NEED ADDITIONAL SPACE, USE CONTINUATION SHEET (FORM VA/CON)

PREVIOUS REGISTRATION:

- Has registration for this work, or for an earlier version of this work, already been made in the Copyright Office? Yes. . . . . No. . . . .

- If your answer is "Yes," why is another registration being sought? (Check appropriate box)
  - ☐ This is the first published edition of a work previously registered in unpublished form.
  - ☐ This is the first application submitted by this author as copyright claimant.
  - ☐ This is a changed version of the work, as shown by line 6 of the application.

- If your answer is "Yes," give: Previous Registration Number. . . . . Year of Registration. . . . .

(5) Previous Registration

COMPILATION OR DERIVATIVE WORK: (See instructions)

PREEXISTING MATERIAL: (Identify any preexisting work or works that this work is based on or incorporates.)

. . . .
. . . .
. . . .

MATERIAL ADDED TO THIS WORK: (Give a brief. general statement of the material that has been added to this work and in which copy right is claimed.)

. . . .
. . . .
. . . .
. . . .

(6) Compilation or Derivative Work

DEPOSIT ACCOUNT: (If the registration fee is to be charged to a Deposit Account established in the Copyright Office, give name and number of Account.)

Name: . . . .

Account Number: . . . .

CORRESPONDENCE: (Give name and address to which correspondence about this application should be sent.)

Name: . . . .

Address: . . . . (Apt.)

. . . .
(City) (State) (ZIP)

(7) Fee and Correspondence

CERTIFICATION: ✱ I, the undersigned, hereby certify that I am the: (Check one)

☐ author ☐ other copyright claimant ☐ owner of exclusive right(s) ☐ authorized agent of: . . . .
(Name of author or other copyright claimant, or owner of exclusive right(s))
of the work identified in this application and that the statements made by me in this application are correct to the best of my knowledge.

Handwritten signature: (X) . . . .

Typed or printed name: . . . . Date: . . . .

(8) Certification (Application must be signed)

MAIL CERTIFICATE TO

. . . .
(Name)
. . . .
(Number. Street and Apartment Number)
. . . .
(City) (State) (ZIP code)

(Certificate will be mailed in window envelope)

(9) Address For Return of Certificate

✱ 17 U.S.C. § 506(e): FALSE REPRESENTATION – Any person who knowingly makes a false representation of a material fact in the application for copyright registration provided for by section 409. or in any written statement filed in connection with the application. shall be fined not more than $2.500.

☆ U.S. GOVERNMENT PRINTING OFFICE : 1977 O—248-638

Nov. 1977 –300,000

INSTRUCTIONS FOR SPACES 5-9

SPACE 5: PREVIOUS REGISTRATION

• **General Instructions:** The questions in space 5 are intended to find out whether an earlier registration has been made for this work and, if so, whether there is any basis for a new registration. As a general rule, only one basic copyright registration can be made for the same version of a particular work.

• **Same Version:** If this version is substantially the same as the work covered by a previous registration, a second registration is not generally possible unless: (1) the work has been registered in unpublished form and a second registration is now being sought to cover the first published edition, or (2) someone other than the author is identified as copyright claimant in the earlier registration, and the author is now seeking registration in his or her own name. If either of these two exceptions apply, check the appropriate box and give the earlier registration number and date. Otherwise, do not submit Form VA; instead, write the Copyright Office for information about supplementary registration or recordation of transfer of copyright ownership.

• **Changed Version:** If the work has been changed, and you are now seeking registration to cover the additions or revisions, check the third box in space 5, give the earlier registration number and date, and complete both parts of space 6.

• **Previous Registration Number and Date:** If more than one previous registration has been made for the work, give the number and date of the latest registration.

SPACE 6: COMPILATION OR DERIVATIVE WORK

• **General Instructions:** Complete both parts of space 6 if this work is a "compilation," or "derivative work," or both, and if it is based on or incorporates one or more "preexisting works" that are not eligible for registration for one reason or another: works that have already been published or registered, or works that have fallen into the public domain. A "compilation" is defined as "a work formed by the collection and assembling of preexisting materials or of data that are selected, coordinated, or arranged in such a way that the resulting work as a whole constitutes an original work of authorship." A "derivative work" is "a work based on one or more preexisting works." In addition to various forms in which works may be "recast, transformed, or adapted," derivative works include works "consisting of editorial revisions, annotations, elaborations, or other modifications" if these changes, as a whole, represent an original work of authorship.

• **Preexisting Material:** If the work is a compilation, give a brief, general statement describing the nature of the material that has been compiled. Example: "Compilation of 19th Century political cartoons". In the case of a derivative work, identify the preexisting work that has been recast, transformed, or adapted. Examples: "Grünewald Altarpiece"; "19th Century quilt design."

• **Material Added to this Work:** The statute requires a "brief, general statement of the additional material covered by the copyright claim being registered." This statement should describe all of the material in this particular version of the work that: (1) represents an original work of authorship; (2) has not fallen into the public domain; (3) has not been previously published; and (4) has not been previously registered for copyright in unpublished form. Examples: "Adaptation of design and additional artistic work"; "Reproduction of painting by photolithography"; "Additional cartographic material"; "Compilation of photographs."

SPACES 7, 8, 9: FEE, CORRESPONDENCE, CERTIFICATION, RETURN ADDRESS

• **Deposit Account and Mailing Instructions (Space 7):** If you maintain a Deposit Account in the Copyright Office, identify it in space 7. Otherwise you will need to send the registration fee of $10 with your application. The space headed "Correspondence" should contain the name and address of the person to be consulted if correspondence about this application becomes necessary.

• **Certification (Space 8):** The application is not acceptable unless it bears the handwritten signature of the author or other copyright claimant, or of the owner of exclusive right(s), or of the duly authorized agent of such author, claimant, or owner.

• **Address for Return of Certificate (Space 9):** The address box must be completed legibly, since the certificate will be returned in a window envelope.

MORE INFORMATION

THE COPYRIGHT NOTICE: For published works, the law provides that a copyright notice in a specified form "shall be placed on all publicly distributed copies from which the work can be visually perceived." Use of the copyright notice is the responsibility of the copyright owner, and does not require advance permission from the Copyright Office.

• **Form of the Notice:** The required form of the notice for copies generally consists of three elements: (1) the symbol "©", or the word "Copyright", or the abbreviation "Copr."; (2) the year of first publication; and (3) the name of the owner of copyright in the work, or an abbreviation by which the name can be recognized, or a generally known alternative designation of the owner. Example: "© 1978 Samuel Marlove." Under the statute, the year date may be omitted from the notice in cases "where a pictorial, graphic, or sculptural work, with accompanying text matter, if any, is reproduced in or on greeting cards, postcards, stationery, jewelry, dolls, toys, or any useful articles."

• **Position of the Notice:** The notice is to be affixed to the copies "in such manner and location as to give reasonable notice of the claim of copyright."

• **Errors or Omissions:** Unlike the law in effect before 1978, the new copyright statute provides procedures for correcting errors in the copyright notice, and even for curing the omission of the notice. However, a failure to comply with the notice requirements may still result in the loss of some copyright protection and, unless corrected within five years, in the complete loss of copyright. For further information about the copyright notice and the procedures for correcting errors or omissions, write for Circular R3.

FORM OF DEPOSIT FOR WORKS OF THE VISUAL ARTS

Exceptions to General Deposit Requirements. As explained on the reverse side of this page, the statutory deposit requirements (generally one copy for unpublished works and two copies for published works) will vary for particular kinds of works of the visual arts. The copyright law authorizes the Register of Copyrights to issue regulations specifying "the administrative classes into which works are to be placed for purposes of deposit and registration, and the nature of the copies or phonorecords to be deposited in the various classes specified." For particular classes, the regulations may require or permit "the deposit of identifying material instead of copies or phonorecords," or "the deposit of only one copy or phonorecord where two would normally be required."

What Should You Deposit? The detailed requirements with respect to the kind of deposit to accompany an application on Form VA are contained in the Copyright Office Regulations, and are summarized in our Circular R7. The following does not cover all of the deposit requirements, but is intended to give you some general guidance.

• For an unpublished work, the material deposited should represent the entire copyrightable content of the work for which registration is being sought;

• For a published work, the material deposited should generally consist of two complete copies of the best edition. Exceptions:

—For certain types of works, one complete copy may be deposited instead of two. These include greeting cards, postcards, stationery, labels, advertisements, scientific drawings, and globes.

—For most three-dimensional sculptural works, and for certain two-dimensional works, the Copyright Office Regulations require the deposit of identifying material (photographs or drawings in a specified form) rather than copies.

—Under certain circumstances, for works published in five copies or less or in limited, numbered editions, the deposit may consist of one copy or of identifying reproductions.

CONTINUATION SHEET FOR FORM VA

FORM VA/CON

UNITED STATES COPYRIGHT OFFICE

- If at all possible, try to fit the information called for into the spaces provided on Form VA.
- If you do not have space enough for all of the information you need to give on Form VA, use this continuation sheet and submit it with Form VA.
- If you submit this continuation sheet, leave it attached to Form VA. Or, if it becomes detached, clip (do not tape or staple) and fold the two together before submitting them.
- **PART A** of this sheet is intended to identify the basic application. **PART B** is a continuation of Space 2. **PART C** is for the continuation of Spaces 1, 4, or 6. The other spaces on Form VA call for specific items of information, and should not need continuation.

REGISTRATION NUMBER
VA   VAU
EFFECTIVE DATE OF REGISTRATION
(Month)   (Day)   (Year)
CONTINUATION SHEET RECEIVED
Page _____ of _____ pages

DO NOT WRITE ABOVE THIS LINE. FOR COPYRIGHT OFFICE USE ONLY

(A)

Identification of Application

IDENTIFICATION OF CONTINUATION SHEET: This sheet is a continuation of the application for copyright registration on Form VA, submitted for the following work:
- TITLE: (Give the title as given under the heading "Title of this Work" in Space 1 of Form VA.)
....
- NAME(S) AND ADDRESS(ES) OF COPYRIGHT CLAIMANT(S): (Give the name and address of at least one copyright claimant as given in Space 4 of Form VA.)
....

(B)

Continuation of Space 2

☐

NAME OF AUTHOR:

Was this author's contribution to the work a "work made for hire"?   Yes......   No......

DATES OF BIRTH AND DEATH:
Born .... Died ....
(Year)   (Year)

AUTHOR'S NATIONALITY OR DOMICILE:
Citizen of .... } or { Domiciled in ....
(Name of Country)   (Name of Country)

WAS THIS AUTHOR'S CONTRIBUTION TO THE WORK:
Anonymous?   Yes...... No......
Pseudonymous? Yes...... No......
If the answer to either of these questions is "Yes." see detailed instructions attached.

AUTHOR OF: (Briefly describe nature of this author's contribution)

☐

NAME OF AUTHOR:

Was this author's contribution to the work a "work made for hire"?   Yes......   No......

DATES OF BIRTH AND DEATH:
Born .... Died ....
(Year)   (Year)

AUTHOR'S NATIONALITY OR DOMICILE:
Citizen of .... } or { Domiciled in ....
(Name of Country)   (Name of Country)

WAS THIS AUTHOR'S CONTRIBUTION TO THE WORK:
Anonymous?   Yes...... No......
Pseudonymous? Yes...... No......
If the answer to either of these questions is "Yes." see detailed instructions attached.

AUTHOR OF: (Briefly describe nature of this author's contribution)

☐

NAME OF AUTHOR:

Was this author's contribution to the work a "work made for hire"?   Yes......   No......

DATES OF BIRTH AND DEATH:
Born .... Died ....
(Year)   (Year)

AUTHOR'S NATIONALITY OR DOMICILE:
Citizen of .... } or { Domiciled in ....
(Name of Country)   (Name of Country)

WAS THIS AUTHOR'S CONTRIBUTION TO THE WORK:
Anonymous?   Yes...... No......
Pseudonymous? Yes...... No......
If the answer to either of these questions is "Yes." see detailed instructions attached.

AUTHOR OF: (Briefly describe nature of this author's contribution)

(C)

Continuation of Other Spaces

CONTINUATION OF (Check which):   ☐ Space 1   ☐ Space 4   ☐ Space 6

APPLICATION FOR COPYRIGHT REGISTRATION

for a
Work of the Performing Arts

FORM PA

UNITED STATES COPYRIGHT OFFICE
LIBRARY OF CONGRESS
WASHINGTON, D.C. 20559

HOW TO APPLY FOR COPYRIGHT REGISTRATION:

- *First:* Read the information on this page to make sure Form PA is the correct application for your work.

- *Second:* Open out the form by pulling this page to the left. Read through the detailed instructions before starting to complete the form.

- *Third:* Complete spaces 1-4 of the application, then turn the entire form over and, after reading the instructions for spaces 5-9, complete the rest of your application. Use typewriter or print in dark ink. Be sure to sign the form at space 8.

- *Fourth:* Detach your completed application from these instructions and send it with the necessary deposit of the work (see below) to: Register of Copyrights, Library of Congress, Washington, D.C. 20559. Unless you have a Deposit Account in the Copyright Office, your application and deposit must be accompanied by a check or money order for $10, payable to: *Register of Copyrights.*

WHEN TO USE FORM PA: Form PA is the appropriate application to use for copyright registration covering works of the performing arts. Both published and unpublished works can be registered on Form PA.

WHAT IS A "WORK OF THE PERFORMING ARTS"? This category includes works prepared for the purpose of being "performed" directly before an audience or indirectly "by means of any device or process." Examples of works of the performing arts are: (1) musical works, including any accompanying words; (2) dramatic works, including any accompanying music; (3) pantomimes and choreographic works; and (4) motion pictures and other audiovisual works. **Note:** This category does not include sound recordings, which should be registered on Form SR. For more information about copyright in sound recordings, see the reverse side of this sheet.

DEPOSIT TO ACCOMPANY APPLICATION: An application for copyright registration must be accompanied by a deposit representing the entire work for which registration is to be made. The following are the general deposit requirements as set forth in the statute:

Unpublished work: Deposit one complete copy or phonorecord.

Published work: Deposit two complete copies or phonorecords of the best edition.

Work first published outside the United States: Deposit one complete copy or phonorecord of the first foreign edition.

Contribution to a collective work: Deposit one complete copy or phonorecord of the best edition of the collective work.

These general deposit requirements may vary in particular situations. For further information about the specific deposit requirements for particular types of works of the performing arts, see the reverse side of this sheet. For general information about copyright deposit, write for Circular R7.

THE COPYRIGHT NOTICE: For published works, the law provides that a copyright notice in a specified form "shall be placed on all publicly distributed copies from which the work can be visually perceived." Use of the copyright notice is the responsibility of the copyright owner and does not require advance permission from the Copyright Office. The required form of the notice for copies generally consists of three elements: (1) the symbol "©", or the word "Copyright", or the abbreviation "Copr."; (2) the year of first publication; and (3) the name of the owner of copyright. For example: "© 1978 Alexander Hollenius" The notice is to be affixed to the copies "in such manner and location as to give reasonable notice of the claim of copyright." Unlike the law in effect before 1978, the new copyright statute provides procedures for correcting errors in the copyright notice, and even for curing the omission of the notice. However, a failure to comply with the notice requirements may still result in the loss of some copyright protection and, unless corrected within five years, in the complete loss of copyright. For further information about the copyright notice, see the reverse side of this sheet. For additional information concerning the copyright notice and the procedures for correcting errors or omissions, write for Circular R3.

DURATION OF COPYRIGHT: For works that were created after the effective date of the new statute (January 1, 1978), the basic copyright term will be the life of the author and fifty years after the author's death. For works made for hire, and for certain anonymous and pseudonymous works, the duration of copyright will be 75 years from publication or 100 years from creation, whichever is shorter. These same terms of copyright will generally apply to works that had been created before 1978 but had not been published or copyrighted before that date. For further information about the duration of copyright, including the terms of copyrights already in existence before 1978, write for Circular R15a.

FORM PA
UNITED STATES COPYRIGHT OFFICE

REGISTRATION NUMBER

PA   PAU

EFFECTIVE DATE OF REGISTRATION

. . . .
Month   Day   Year

DO NOT WRITE ABOVE THIS LINE. IF YOU NEED MORE SPACE, USE CONTINUATION SHEET (FORM PA/CON)

(1)
Title

TITLE OF THIS WORK:

NATURE OF THIS WORK:
(See instructions)

PREVIOUS OR ALTERNATIVE TITLES:

(2)
Author(s)

IMPORTANT: Under the law, the "author" of a "work made for hire" is generally the employer, not the employee (see instructions). If any part of this work was "made for hire" check "Yes" in the space provided, give the employer (or other person for whom the work was prepared) as "Author" of that part, and leave the space for dates blank.

1

NAME OF AUTHOR:

DATES OF BIRTH AND DEATH:
Born . . . . Died . . . .
(Year)   (Year)

Was this author's contribution to the work a "work made for hire"?   Yes . . . . . .   No . . . . . .

AUTHOR'S NATIONALITY OR DOMICILE:
Citizen of . . . . } or { Domiciled in . . . .
(Name of Country)   (Name of Country)

AUTHOR OF: (Briefly describe nature of this author's contribution)

WAS THIS AUTHOR'S CONTRIBUTION TO THE WORK:
Anonymous?   Yes . . . . . .   No . . . . . .
Pseudonymous? Yes . . . . . .   No . . . . . .
If the answer to either of these questions is "Yes." see detailed instructions attached.

2

NAME OF AUTHOR:

DATES OF BIRTH AND DEATH:
Born . . . . Died . . . .
(Year)   (Year)

Was this author's contribution to the work a "work made for hire"?   Yes . . . . . .   No . . . . . .

AUTHOR'S NATIONALITY OR DOMICILE:
Citizen of . . . . } or { Domiciled in . . . .
(Name of Country)   (Name of Country)

AUTHOR OF: (Briefly describe nature of this author's contribution)

WAS THIS AUTHOR'S CONTRIBUTION TO THE WORK:
Anonymous?   Yes . . . . . .   No . . . . . .
Pseudonymous? Yes . . . . . .   No . . . . . .
If the answer to either of these questions is "Yes." see detailed instructions attached.

3

NAME OF AUTHOR:

DATES OF BIRTH AND DEATH:
Born . . . . Died . . . .
(Year)   (Year)

Was this author's contribution to the work a "work made for hire"?   Yes . . . . . .   No . . . . . .

AUTHOR'S NATIONALITY OR DOMICILE:
Citizen of . . . . } or { Domiciled in . . . .
(Name of Country)   (Name of Country)

AUTHOR OF: (Briefly describe nature of this author's contribution)

WAS THIS AUTHOR'S CONTRIBUTION TO THE WORK:
Anonymous?   Yes . . . . . .   No . . . . . .
Pseudonymous? Yes . . . . . .   No . . . . . .
If the answer to either of these questions is "Yes." see detailed instructions attached.

(3)
Creation and Publication

YEAR IN WHICH CREATION OF THIS WORK WAS COMPLETED:

Year. . . . .
(This information must be given in all cases.)

DATE AND NATION OF FIRST PUBLICATION:
Date. . . . .
(Month)   (Day)   (Year)
Nation . . . .
(Name of Country)
(Complete this block ONLY if this work has been published.)

(4)
Claimant(s)

NAME(S) AND ADDRESS(ES) OF COPYRIGHT CLAIMANT(S):

TRANSFER: (If the copyright claimant(s) named here in space 4 are different from the author(s) named in space 2, give a brief statement of how the claimant(s) obtained ownership of the copyright.)

* Complete all applicable spaces (numbers 5-9) on the reverse side of this page.
* Follow detailed instructions attached.
* Sign the form at line 8.

DO NOT WRITE HERE

Page 1 of . . . . pages

HOW TO FILL OUT FORM PA

Specific Instructions for Spaces 1-4

- The line-by-line instructions on this page are keyed to the spaces on the first page of Form PA, printed opposite.
- Please read through these instructions before you start filling out your application, and refer to the specific instructions for each space as you go along.

SPACE 1: TITLE

- **Title of this Work:** Every work submitted for copyright registration must be given a title that is capable of identifying that particular work. If the copies or phonorecords of the work bear a title (or an identifying phrase that could serve as a title), transcribe its wording completely and exactly on the application. Remember that indexing of the registration and future identification of the work will depend on the information you give here.

  If the work you are registering is an entire "collective work" (such as a collection of plays or songs), give the over-all title of the collection. If you are registering one or more individual contributions to a collective work, give the title of each contribution, followed by the title of the collection. Example: " 'A Song for Elinda' in Old and New Ballads for Old and New People."

- **Nature of this Work:** Briefly describe the general nature or character of the work being registered for copyright. Examples: "Music"; "Song Lyrics"; "Words and Music"; "Drama[2]"; "Musical Play"; "Choreography"; "Pantomime"; "Motion Picture"; "Audiovisual Work".

- **Previous or Alternative Titles:** Complete this space if there are any additional titles for the work under which someone searching for the registration might be likely to look, or under which a document pertaining to the work might be recorded.

SPACE 2: AUTHORS

- **General Instructions:** First decide, after reading these instructions, who are the "authors" of this work for copyright purposes. Then, unless the work is a "collective work" (see below), give the requested information about every "author" who contributed any appreciable amount of copyrightable matter to this version of the work. If you need further space, use the attached Continuation Sheet and, if necessary, request additional Continuation Sheets (Form PA/Con).

- **Who Is the "Author"?** Unless the work was "made for hire," the individual who actually created the work is its "author." In the case of a work made for hire, the statute provides that "the employer or other person for whom the work was prepared is considered the author."

- **What is a "Work Made for Hire"?** A "work made for hire" is defined as: (1) "a work prepared by an employee within the scope of his or her employment"; or (2) "a work specially ordered or commissioned" for certain uses specified in the statute, but only if there is a written agreement to consider it a "work made for hire."

- **Collective Work:** In the case of a collective work, such as a song book or a collection of plays, it is sufficient to give information about the author of the collective work as a whole.

- **Author's Identity Not Revealed:** If an author's contribution is "anonymous" or "pseudonymous," it is not necessary to give the name and dates for that author. However, the citizenship and domicile of the author **must** be given in all cases, and information about the nature of that author's contribution to the work should be included if possible.

- **Name of Author:** The fullest form of the author's name should be given. If you have checked "Yes" to indicate that the work was "made for hire," give the full legal name of the employer (or other person for whom the work was prepared). You may also include the name of the employee (for example: "Music Makers Publishing Co., employer for hire of Lila Crane"). If the work is "anonymous" you may: (1) leave the line blank, or (2) state "Anonymous" in the line, or (3) reveal the author's identity. If the work is "pseudonymous" you may (1) leave the line blank, or (2) give the pseudonym and identify it as such (for example: "Huntley Haverstock, pseudonym"), or (3) reveal the author's name, making clear which is the real name and which is the pseudonym (for example, "Judith Barton, whose pseudonym is Madeleine Elster").

- **Dates of Birth and Death:** If the author is dead, the statute requires that the year of death be included in the application unless the work is anonymous or pseudonymous. The author's birth date is optional, but is useful as a form of identification. Leave this space blank if the author's contribution was a "work made for hire."

- **"Anonymous" or "Pseudonymous" Work:** An author's contribution to a work is "anonymous" if that author is not identified on the copies or phonorecords of the work. An author's contribution to a work is "pseudonymous" if that author is identified on the copies or phonorecords under a fictitious name.

- **Author's Nationality or Domicile:** Give the country of which the author is a citizen, or the country in which the author is domiciled. The statute requires that either nationality or domicile be given in all cases.

- **Nature of Authorship:** After the words "Author of" give a brief general statement of the nature of this particular author's contribution to the work. Examples: "Words"; "Co-Author of Music"; "Words and Music"; "Arrangement"; "Co-Author of Book and Lyrics"; "Dramatization"; "Entire Work"; "Compilation and English Translation"; "Editorial Revisions".

SPACE 3: CREATION AND PUBLICATION

- **General Instructions:** Do not confuse "creation" with "publication." Every application for copyright registration must state "the year in which creation of the work was completed." Give the date and nation of first publication only if the work has been published.

- **Creation:** Under the statute, a work is "created" when it is fixed in a copy or phonorecord for the first time. Where a work has been prepared over a period of time, the part of the work existing in fixed form on a particular date constitutes the created work on that date. The date you give here should be the year in which the author completed the particular version for which registration is now being sought, even if other versions exist or if further changes or additions are planned.

- **Publication:** The statute defines "publication" as "the distribution of copies or phonorecords of a work to the public by sale or other transfer of ownership, or by rental, lease, or lending"; a work is also "published" if there has been an "offering to distribute copies or phonorecords to a group of persons for purposes of further distribution, public performance, or public display." Give the full date (month, day, year) when, and the country where, publication first occurred. If first publication took place simultaneously in the United States and other countries, it is sufficient to state "U.S.A."

SPACE 4: CLAIMANT(S)

- **Name(s) and Address(es) of Copyright Claimant(s):** Give the name(s) and address(es) of the copyright claimant(s) in this work. The statute provides that copyright in a work belongs initially to the author of the work (including, in the case of a work made for hire, the employer or other person for whom the work was prepared). The copyright claimant is either the author of the work or a person or organization that has obtained ownership of the copyright initially belonging to the author.

- **Transfer:** The statute provides that, if the copyright claimant is not the author, the application for registration must contain "a brief statement of how the claimant obtained ownership of the copyright." If any copyright claimant named in space 4 is not an author named in space 2, give a brief general statement summarizing the means by which that claimant obtained ownership of the copyright.

EXAMINED BY:	APPLICATION RECEIVED:	FOR COPYRIGHT OFFICE USE ONLY
CHECKED BY:		
CORRESPONDENCE: ☐ Yes	DEPOSIT RECEIVED:	
DEPOSIT ACCOUNT FUNDS USED: ☐	REMITTANCE NUMBER AND DATE:	

DO NOT WRITE ABOVE THIS LINE. IF YOU NEED ADDITIONAL SPACE, USE CONTINUATION SHEET (FORM PA/CON)

PREVIOUS REGISTRATION:

⑤ Previous Registration

- Has registration for this work, or for an earlier version of this work, already been made in the Copyright Office? Yes .... No ....

- If your answer is "Yes," why is another registration being sought? (Check appropriate box)

  ☐ This is the first published edition of a work previously registered in unpublished form.
  ☐ This is the first application submitted by this author as copyright claimant.
  ☐ This is a changed version of the work, as shown by line 6 of the application.

- If your answer is "Yes," give: Previous Registration Number .... Year of Registration ....

COMPILATION OR DERIVATIVE WORK: (See instructions)

⑥ Compilation or Derivative Work

PREEXISTING MATERIAL: (Identify any preexisting work or works that the work is based on or incorporates.)
....
....
....
....

MATERIAL ADDED TO THIS WORK: (Give a brief, general statement of the material that has been added to this work and in which copyright is claimed.)
....
....
....
....

DEPOSIT ACCOUNT: (If the registration fee is to be charged to a Deposit Account established in the Copyright Office, give name and number of Account.)

Name: ....

Account Number: ....

CORRESPONDENCE: (Give name and address to which correspondence about this application should be sent.)

Name: ....

Address: ....
                                          (Apt.)

....
(City)   (State)   (ZIP)

⑦ Fee and Correspondence

CERTIFICATION: ✻ I, the undersigned, hereby certify that I am the: (Check one)

☐ author ☐ other copyright claimant ☐ owner of exclusive right(s) ☐ authorized agent of: ....
                                                                (Name of author or other copyright claimant, or owner of exclusive right(s))
of the work identified in this application and that the statements made by me in this application are correct to the best of my knowledge.

☞ Handwritten signature: (X) ....

Typed or printed name. .... Date ....

⑧ Certification (Application must be signed)

MAIL CERTIFICATE TO

....
(Name)

....
(Number, Street and Apartment Number)

....
(City)   (State)   (ZIP code)

(Certificate will be mailed in window envelope)

⑨ Address For Return of Certificate

✻ 17 U.S.C. §506(e) FALSE REPRESENTATION—Any person who knowingly makes a false representation of a material fact in the application for copyright registration provided for by section 409, or in any written statement filed in connection with the application, shall be fined not more than $2,500.

✿ U. S. GOVERNMENT PRINTING OFFICE: 1977 O - 248-636

Nov. 1977 - 1, 000, 000

INSTRUCTIONS FOR SPACES 5-9

SPACE 5: PREVIOUS REGISTRATION

• **General Instructions:** The questions in space 5 are intended to find out whether an earlier registration has been made for this work and, if so, whether there is any basis for a new registration. As a general rule, only one basic copyright registration can be made for the same version of a particular work.

• **Same Version:** If this version is substantially the same as the work covered by a previous registration, a second registration is not generally possible unless: (1) the work has been registered in unpublished form and a second registration is now being sought to cover the first published edition, or (2) someone other than the author is identified as copyright claimant in the earlier registration, and the author is now seeking registration in his or her own name. If either of these two exceptions apply, check the appropriate box and give the earlier registration number and date. Otherwise, do not submit Form PA; instead, write the Copyright Office for information about supplementary registration or recordation of transfers of copyright ownership.

• **Changed Version:** If the work has been changed, and you are now seeking registration to cover the additions or revisions, check the third box in space 5, give the earlier registration number and date, and complete both parts of space 6.

• **Previous Registration Number and Date:** If more than one previous registration has been made for the work, give the number and date of the latest registration.

SPACE 6: COMPILATION OR DERIVATIVE WORK

• **General Instructions:** Complete both parts of space 6 if this work is a "compilation," or "derivative work," or both, and if it incorporates one or more earlier works that have already been published or registered for copyright, or that have fallen into the public domain. A "compilation" is defined as "a work formed by the collection and assembling of preexisting materials or of data that are selected, coordinated, or arranged in such a way that the resulting work as a whole constitutes an original work of authorship." A "derivative work" is "a work based on one or more preexisting works." Examples of derivative works include musical arrangements, dramatizations, translations, abridgments, condensations, motion picture versions, or "any other form in which a work may be recast, transformed, or adapted." Derivative works also include works "consisting of editorial revisions, annotations, elaborations, or other modifications" if these changes, as a whole, represent an original work of authorship.

• **Preexisting Material:** If the work is a compilation, give a brief, general statement describing the nature of the material that has been compiled. Example: "Compilation of 19th Century military songs." In the case of a derivative work, identify the preexisting work that has been recast, transformed, or adapted. Example: "French version of Hugo's 'Le Roi s'amuse'."

• **Material Added to this Work:** The statute requires a "brief, general statement of the additional material covered by the copyright claim being registered." This statement should describe all of the material in this particular version of the work that: (1) represents an original work of authorship; and (2) has not fallen into the public domain; and (3) has not been previously published; and (4) has not been previously registered for copyright in unpublished form. Examples: "Arrangement for piano and orchestra"; "Dramatization for television"; "New film version"; "Revisions throughout; Act III completely new".

SPACES 7, 8, 9: FEE, CORRESPONDENCE, CERTIFICATION, RETURN ADDRESS

• **Deposit Account and Mailing Instructions (Space 7):** If you maintain a Deposit Account in the Copyright Office, identify it in space 7. Otherwise you will need to send the registration fee of $10 with your application. The space headed "Correspondence" should contain the name and address of the person to be consulted if correspondence about this application becomes necessary.

• **Certification (Space 8):** The application is not acceptable unless it bears the handwritten signature of the author or other copyright claimant, or of the owner of exclusive right(s), or of the duly authorized agent of such author, claimant, or owner.

• **Address for Return of Certificate (Space 9):** The address box must be completed legibly, since the certificate will be returned in a window envelope.

MORE INFORMATION

A NOTE ON TERMINOLOGY: The following are the meanings given to some of the terms used in the copyright statute:

• **"Works":** "Works" are the basic subject matter of copyright; they are what authors create and copyright protects. The statute draws a sharp distinction between the "work" and "any material object in which the work is embodied."

• **"Copies" and "Phonorecords":** These are the two types of material objects in which "works" are embodied. In general, **"copies"** are objects from which a work can be read or visually perceived, directly or with the aid of a machine or device, such as manuscripts, books, sheet music, film, and videotape. **"Phonorecords"** are objects embodying fixations of sounds, such as audio tapes and phonograph disks. For example, a song (the "work") can be reproduced in sheet music ("copies") or phonograph disks ("phonorecords"), or both.

• **"Sound Recordings":** These are "works," not "copies" or "phonorecords." With one exception, "sound recordings" are "works that result from the fixation of a series of musical, spoken, or other sounds." (The exception is for the audio portions of audiovisual works, including motion picture soundtracks; these are considered an integral part of the audiovisual work as a whole.) "Sound recordings" are registered on Form SR.

Example: When a record company issues a new release, the release will typically involve two distinct "works": the "musical work" that has been recorded, and the "sound recording" as a separate work in itself. The material objects that the record company sends out are "phonorecords": physical reproductions of both the "musical work" and the "sound recording."

FOR A MUSICAL OR DRAMATIC WORK, SHOULD YOU DEPOSIT COPIES OR PHONORECORDS WITH YOUR FORM PA?

• **For registration in unpublished form:**
(1) If the work exists only in one form or the other (copies or phonorecords, but not both), deposit the work in its existing form;
(2) If the work exists in both copies and phonorecords, deposit the form that best represents the musical or dramatic work in which copyright is being claimed.

• **For registration in published form:**
(1) If the work has been published in the form of copies but not phonorecords, deposit two copies of the best edition. If the work has been published in the form of phonorecords only, deposit two phonorecords of the best edition.
(2) If the work has been published in both forms, deposit two copies (**not phonorecords**) of the best edition.
(3) If the work has been first published outside the United States, deposit one copy or phonorecord as first published.

SHOULD YOU FILE FORM PA OR FORM SR? If the musical or dramatic work has been recorded, and both that "work," and the sound recording as a separate "work," are eligible for registration, the application form you should file depends on the following:

• **File only Form PA if:** You are seeking to register only the musical or dramatic work, not the sound recording.

• **File only Form SR if:** The copyright claimant for both the musical or dramatic work and the sound recording is the same, and you are seeking a single registration to cover both of these "works."

• **Separate applications on Forms PA and SR should be filed if:**
(1) The copyright claimant for the musical or dramatic work is different from the copyright claimant for the sound recording; or
(2) You prefer to have separate registrations for the musical or dramatic work **and** the sound recording.

FORM OF COPYRIGHT NOTICE ON PHONORECORDS:

For musical or dramatic works: The copyright notice for musical and dramatic works (for example: "© 1978 George Harvey Bone") is required to appear on "all publicly distributed copies from which the work can be visually perceived." There is no requirement that the notice for musical or dramatic works be placed on phonorecords reproducing them.

For sound recordings: The copyright statute provides that, whenever a sound recording is published, a special notice of copyright (for example: "℗1978 Miriam Haines") "shall be placed on all publicly distributed phonorecords of the sound recording." For further information about the requirements for copyright in sound recordings, write for Form SR and Circular R56.

CONTINUATION SHEET FOR FORM PA

FORM PA/CON

UNITED STATES COPYRIGHT OFFICE

- If at all possible, try to fit the information called for into the spaces provided on Form PA.
- If you do not have space enough for all of the information you need to give on Form PA, use this continuation sheet and submit it with Form PA.
- If you submit this continuation sheet, leave it attached to Form PA. Or, if it becomes detached, clip (do not tape or staple) and fold the two together before submitting them.
- **PART A** of this sheet is intended to identify the basic application. **PART B** is a continuation of Space 2. **PART C** is for the continuation of Spaces 1, 4, or 6. The other spaces on Form PA call for specific items of information, and should not need continuation.

REGISTRATION NUMBER
PA   PAU
EFFECTIVE DATE OF REGISTRATION
.... (Month)   (Day)   (Year)
CONTINUATION SHEET RECEIVED
Page _____ of _____ pages

DO NOT WRITE ABOVE THIS LINE. FOR COPYRIGHT OFFICE USE ONLY

(A)
Identification of Application

IDENTIFICATION OF CONTINUATION SHEET: This sheet is a continuation of the application for copyright registration on Form PA, submitted for the following work:
- TITLE: (Give the title as given under the heading "Title of this Work" in Space 1 of Form PA.)
....
- NAME(S) AND ADDRESS(ES) OF COPYRIGHT CLAIMANT(S): (Give the name and address of at least one copyright claimant as given in Space 4 of Form PA.)
....

(B)
Continuation of Space 2

NAME OF AUTHOR: **DATES OF BIRTH AND DEATH:**
Born .... Died ....
(Year)   (Year)
Was this author's contribution to the work a "work made for hire"?   Yes...... No......

AUTHOR'S NATIONALITY OR DOMICILE: **WAS THIS AUTHOR'S CONTRIBUTION TO THE WORK:**
Citizen of .... } or { Domiciled in ....
(Name of Country)   (Name of Country)
Anonymous?   Yes...... No......
Pseudonymous? Yes...... No......

AUTHOR OF: (Briefly describe nature of this author's contribution)   If the answer to either of these questions is "Yes," see detailed instructions attached.

NAME OF AUTHOR: **DATES OF BIRTH AND DEATH:**
Born .... Died ....
(Year)   (Year)
Was this author's contribution to the work a "work made for hire"?   Yes...... No......

AUTHOR'S NATIONALITY OR DOMICILE: **WAS THIS AUTHOR'S CONTRIBUTION TO THE WORK:**
Citizen of .... } or { Domiciled in ....
(Name of Country)   (Name of Country)
Anonymous?   Yes...... No......
Pseudonymous? Yes...... No......

AUTHOR OF: (Briefly describe nature of this author's contribution)   If the answer to either of these questions is "Yes," see detailed instructions attached.

NAME OF AUTHOR: **DATES OF BIRTH AND DEATH:**
Born .... Died ....
(Year)   (Year)
Was this author's contribution to the work a "work made for hire"?   Yes...... No......

AUTHOR'S NATIONALITY OR DOMICILE: **WAS THIS AUTHOR'S CONTRIBUTION TO THE WORK:**
Citizen of .... } or { Domiciled in ....
(Name of Country)   (Name of Country)
Anonymous?   Yes...... No......
Pseudonymous? Yes...... No......

AUTHOR OF: (Briefly describe nature of this author's contribution)   If the answer to either of these questions is "Yes," see detailed instructions attached.

(C)
Continuation of other Spaces

CONTINUATION OF (Check which):   ☐ Space 1   ☐ Space 4   ☐ Space 6

APPLICATION FOR COPYRIGHT REGISTRATION
for a
Sound Recording

FORM SR

UNITED STATES COPYRIGHT OFFICE
LIBRARY OF CONGRESS
· WASHINGTON, D.C. 20559

HOW TO APPLY FOR COPYRIGHT REGISTRATION:

- *First:* Read the information on this page to make sure Form SR is the correct application for your work.

- *Second:* Open out the form by pulling this page to the left. Read through the detailed instructions before starting to complete the form.

- *Third:* Complete spaces 1-4 of the application, then turn the entire form over and, after reading the instructions for spaces 5-9, complete the rest of your application. Use typewriter or print in dark ink. Be sure to sign the form at space 8.

- *Fourth:* Detach your completed application from these instructions and send it with the necessary deposit of the work (see below) to: Register of Copyrights, Library of Congress, Washington, D.C. 20559. Unless you have a Deposit Account in the Copyright Office, your application and deposit must be accompanied by a check or money order for $10, payable to: *Register of Copyrights.*

WHEN TO USE FORM SR: Form SR is the appropriate application to use for copyright registration covering a sound recording. It should be used where the copyright claim is limited to the sound recording itself, and it should also be used where the same copyright claimant is seeking to register not only the sound recording but also the musical, dramatic, or literary work embodied in the sound recording. Both published and unpublished works can be registered on Form SR.

WHAT IS A "SOUND RECORDING"? With one exception, "sound recordings" are works that result from the fixation of a series of musical, spoken, or other sounds. The exception is for the audio portions of audiovisual works, such as a motion picture soundtrack or an audio cassette accompanying a filmstrip; these are considered an integral part of the audiovisual work as a whole. For further information about "sound recordings" and the distinction between "sound recordings" and "phonorecords," see the reverse side of this sheet. For additional information about copyright in sound recordings, write for Circular R56.

DEPOSIT TO ACCOMPANY APPLICATION: An application for copyright registration must be accompanied by a deposit representing the entire work for which registration is to be made. For registration on Form SR, the following are the general deposit requirements:

Unpublished work: Deposit one complete phonorecord.

Published work: Deposit two complete phonorecords of the best edition, together with "any printed or other visually perceptible material" published with the phonorecords.

Work first published outside the United States: Deposit one complete phonorecord of the work as first published.

Contribution to a collective work: Deposit one complete phonorecord of the best edition of the collective work.

These general deposit requirements may vary in particular situations. For further information about the deposit requirements for sound recordings, see the reverse side of this sheet. For general information about copyright deposit, write for Circular R7.

THE COPYRIGHT NOTICE: For published sound recordings, the law provides that a copyright notice in a specified form "shall be placed on all publicly distributed phonorecords of the sound recording." Use of the copyright notice is the responsibility of the copyright owner and does not require advance permission from the Copyright Office. The required form of the notice for phonorecords generally consists of three elements: (1) the symbol "℗" (the letter P in a circle); (2) the year of first publication of the sound recording; and (3) the name of the owner of copyright. For example: " ℗ 1978 Rittenhouse Record Co." The notice is to be "placed on the surface of the phonorecord, or on the label or container, in such manner and location as to give reasonable notice of the claim of copyright." Unlike the law in effect before 1978, the new copyright statute provides procedures for correcting errors in the copyright notice, and even for curing the omission of the notice. However, a failure to comply with the notice requirements may still result in the loss of some copyright protection and, unless corrected within five years, in the complete loss of copyright. For further information about the copyright notice, see the reverse side of this sheet. For additional information concerning the copyright notice and the procedures for correcting errors or omissions, write for Circular R3.

DURATION OF COPYRIGHT: For works that were created after the effective date of the new statute (January 1, 1978), the basic copyright term will be the life of the author and fifty years after the author's death. For works made for hire, and for certain anonymous and pseudonymous works, the duration of copyright will be 75 years from publication or 100 years from creation, whichever is shorter. These same terms of copyright will generally apply to works that had been created before 1978 but had not been published or copyrighted before that date. Sound recordings fixed before February 15, 1972 are not eligible for registration, but may be protected by state law. For further information about the duration of copyright, including the terms of copyrights already in existence before 1978, write for Circular R15a.

FORM SR

UNITED STATES COPYRIGHT OFFICE

REGISTRATION NUMBER		
SR		SRU

EFFECTIVE DATE OF REGISTRATION

. . . .
Month   Day   Year

DO NOT WRITE ABOVE THIS LINE. IF YOU NEED MORE SPACE, USE CONTINUATION SHEET (FORM SR/CON)

(1) Title

TITLE OF THIS WORK:

Catalog number of sound recording, if any:. . . . .

PREVIOUS OR ALTERNATIVE TITLES:

NATURE OF MATERIAL RECORDED: (Check Which)

☐ Musical   ☐ Musical-Dramatic
☐ Dramatic   ☐ Literary
☐ Other: . . . .
. . . .

(2) Author(s)

IMPORTANT: Under the law, the "author" of a "work made for hire" is generally the employer, not the employee (see instructions). If any part of this work was "made for hire" check "Yes" in the space provided, give the employer (or other person for whom the work was prepared) as "Author" of that part, and leave the space for dates blank.

1

NAME OF AUTHOR:

Was this author's contribution to the work a "work made for hire"? Yes...... No......

DATES OF BIRTH AND DEATH:
Born . . . . Died . . . .
(Year)   (Year)

AUTHOR'S NATIONALITY OR DOMICILE:
Citizen of . . . . } or { Domiciled in . . . .
(Name of Country)   (Name of Country)

AUTHOR OF: (Briefly describe nature of this author's contribution)

WAS THIS AUTHOR'S CONTRIBUTION TO THE WORK:
Anonymous? Yes...... No......
Pseudonymous? Yes...... No......
If the answer to either of these questions is "Yes," see detailed instructions attached.

2

NAME OF AUTHOR:

Was this author's contribution to the work a "work made for hire"? Yes...... No......

DATES OF BIRTH AND DEATH:
Born . . . . Died . . . .
(Year)   (Year)

AUTHOR'S NATIONALITY OR DOMICILE:
Citizen of . . . . } or { Domiciled in . . . .
(Name of Country)   (Name of Country)

AUTHOR OF: (Briefly describe nature of this author's contribution)

WAS THIS AUTHOR'S CONTRIBUTION TO THE WORK:
Anonymous? Yes...... No......
Pseudonymous? Yes...... No......
If the answer to either of these questions is "Yes," see detailed instructions attached.

3

NAME OF AUTHOR:

Was this author's contribution to the work a "work made for hire"? Yes...... No......

DATES OF BIRTH AND DEATH:
Born . . . . Died . . . .
(Year)   (Year)

AUTHOR'S NATIONALITY OR DOMICILE:
Citizen of . . . . } or { Domiciled in . . . .
(Name of Country)   (Name of Country)

AUTHOR OF: (Briefly describe nature of this author's contribution)

WAS THIS AUTHOR'S CONTRIBUTION TO THE WORK:
Anonymous? Yes...... No......
Pseudonymous? Yes...... No......
If the answer to either of these questions is "Yes," see detailed instructions attached.

(3) Creation and Publication

YEAR IN WHICH CREATION OF THIS WORK WAS COMPLETED:

Year. . . . .

(This information must be given in all cases.)

DATE AND NATION OF FIRST PUBLICATION:

Date. . . . .
(Month)   (Day)   (Year)

Nation . . . .
(Name of Country)

(Complete this block ONLY if this work has been published.)

(4) Claimant(s)

NAME(S) AND ADDRESS(ES) OF COPYRIGHT CLAIMANT(S):

TRANSFER: (If the copyright claimant(s) named here in space 4 are different from the author(s) named in space 2, give a brief statement of how the claimant(s) obtained ownership of the copyright.)

• *Complete all applicable spaces (numbers 5-9) on the reverse side of this page*
• *Follow detailed instructions attached*
• *Sign the form at line 8*

DO NOT WRITE HERE
Page 1 of . . . . pages

HOW TO FILL OUT FORM SR

Specific Instructions for Spaces 1-4

- The line-by-line instructions on this page are keyed to the spaces on the first page of Form SR, printed opposite.
- Please read through these instructions before you start filling out your application, and refer to the specific instructions for each space as you go along.

SPACE 1: TITLE

- **Title of this Work:** Every work submitted for copyright registration must be given a title that is capable of identifying that particular work. If the phonorecords of the work bear a title (or an identifying phrase that could serve as a title), transcribe its wording completely and exactly on the application.

  If the work you are registering is an entire "collective work" (such as a compilation of previously-issued recordings), give the over-all title of the collection. If you are registering one or more individual contributions to a collective work, give the title of each contribution, followed by the title of the collection. Example: " 'Perpetual Motion' in *Croatian Folk Songs and Dances*."

- **Nature of Material Recorded:** Indicate the general type or character of the works or other material embodied in the recording. The box marked "Literary" should be checked for nondramatic spoken material of all sorts, including narration, interviews, panel discussions, and training material. If the material recorded is not musical, dramatic, or literary in nature, check "Other" and briefly describe the type of sounds fixed in the recording. For example: "Sound Effects"; "Bird Calls"; "Crowd Noises".

- **Previous or Alternative Titles:** Complete this space if there are any additional titles for the work under which someone searching for the registration might be likely to look, or under which a document pertaining to the work might be recorded.

SPACE 2: AUTHORS

- **General Instructions:** First decide, after reading these instructions, who are the "authors" of this work for copyright purposes. Then, unless the work is a "collective work" (see below), give the requested information about every "author" who contributed any appreciable amount of copyrightable matter to this version of the work.

- **Note:** As explained in more detail elsewhere on this application form, Form SR may be used to apply for a single registration to cover not only a sound recording but also the musical, dramatic, or literary work embodied in that recording, as long as the copyright claimant is the same for both. If you are submitting this Form SR to cover the recorded musical, dramatic, or literary work as well as the sound recording itself, it is important for space 2 to include full information about the various authors of all of the material covered by the copyright claim, making clear the nature of each author's contribution.

- **Who is the "Author"?** Unless the work was "made for hire," the individual who actually created the work is its "author." In the case of a work made for hire, the statute provides that "the employer or other person for whom the work was prepared is considered the author." Authorship of a sound recording may include the performance fixed in the recording, or the creative elements of the recording as such, or both.

- **What is a "Work Made for Hire"?** A "work made for hire" is defined as: (1) "a work prepared by an employee within the scope of his or her employment"; or (2) "a work specially ordered or commissioned" for certain uses specified in the statute, but only if there is a written agreement to consider it a "work made for hire."

- **Collective Work:** In the case of a collective work, such as a compilation of separately-made recordings, it is sufficient to give information about the author of the collective work as a whole.

- **Author's Identity Not Revealed:** If an author's contribution is "anonymous" or "pseudonymous," it is not necessary to give the name and dates for that author. However, the citizenship and domicile of the author **must** be given in all cases, and information about the nature of that author's contribution to the work should be included if possible.

- **Name of Author:** The fullest form of the author's name should be given. If you have checked "Yes" to indicate that the work was "made for hire," give the full legal name of the employer (or other person for whom the work was prepared). You may also include the name of the employee (for example: "Music Makers Record Co., employer for hire of Lila Crane." If the work is "anonymous" you may: (1) leave the line blank, or (2) state "Anonymous" in the line, or (3) reveal the author's identity. If the work is "pseudonymous" you may (1) leave the line blank, or (2) give the pseudonym and identify it as such (for example: "Huntley Haverstock, pseudonym"), or (3) reveal the author's name, making clear which is the real name and which is the pseudonym (for example: "Judith Barton, whose pseudonym is Madeleine Elster").

- **Dates of Birth and Death:** If the author is dead, the statute requires that the year of death be included in the application unless the work is anonymous or pseudonymous. The author's birth date is optional, but is useful as a form of identification. Leave this space blank if the author's contribution was a "work made for hire."

- **"Anonymous" or "Pseudonymous" Work:** An author's contribution to a work is "anonymous" if that author is not identified on the copies or phonorecords of the work. An author's contribution to a work is "pseudonymous" if that author is identified on the copies or phonorecords under a fictitious name.

- **Author's Nationality or Domicile:** Give the country of which the author is a citizen, or the country in which the author is domiciled. The statute requires that either nationality or domicile be given in all cases.

- **Nature of Authorship:** After the words "Author of" give a brief general statement of the nature of this particular author's contribution to the work. If you are submitting this Form SR to cover both the sound recording and the underlying musical, dramatic, or literary work, make sure that the precise nature of each author's contribution is reflected here. Examples where the authorship pertains to the recording: "Sound Recording"; "Performance and Recording"; "Recorded Reading"; "Compilation and Remixing of Sounds". Examples where the authorship relates to the underlying work: "Words and Music"; "Book and Lyrics"; "Co-author of Dialogue and Narration"; "Script of Speech". Examples where the authorship pertains to both: "Words, Music, Performance, Recording"; "Arrangement of Music and Recording"; "Compilation of Poems and Reading"

SPACE 3: CREATION AND PUBLICATION

- **General Instructions:** Do not confuse "creation" with "publication." Every application for copyright registration must state "the year in which creation of the work was completed." Give the date and nation of first publication only if the work has been published.

- **Creation:** Under the statute, a sound recording is "created" when it is fixed in a phonorecord for the first time. A work is "fixed" in a phonorecord when its embodiment "is sufficiently permanent or stable to permit it to be perceived, reproduced, or otherwise communicated for a period of more than transitory duration." Where a work has been prepared over a period of time, the part of the work existing in fixed form on a particular date constitutes the created work on that date. The date you give here should be the year in which the author completed the particular version for which registration is now being sought, even if other versions exist or if further changes or additions are planned.

- **Publication:** The statute defines "publication" as "the distribution of copies or phonorecords of a work to the public by sale or other transfer of ownership, or by rental, lease, or lending"; a work is also "published" if there has been an "offering to distribute copies or phonorecords to a group of persons for purposes of further distribution, public performance, or public display." Give the full date (month, day, year) when, and the country where, publication first occurred. If first publication took place simultaneously in the United States and other countries, it is sufficient to state "U.S.A."

SPACE 4: CLAIMANT(S)

- **Name(s) and Address(es) of Copyright Claimant(s):** Give the name(s) and address(es) of the copyright claimant(s) in this work. The statute provides that copyright in a work belongs initially to the author of the work (including, in the case of a work made for hire, the employer or other person for whom the work was prepared). The copyright claimant is either the author of the work or a person or organization that has obtained ownership of the copyright initially belonging to the author.

- **Transfer:** The statute provides that, if the copyright claimant is not the author, the application for registration must contain "a brief statement of how the claimant obtained ownership of the copyright." If any copyright claimant named in space 4 is not an author named in space 2, give a brief, general statement summarizing the means by which that claimant obtained ownership of the copyright.

EXAMINED BY:	APPLICATION RECEIVED:	
CHECKED BY:		
CORRESPONDENCE: ☐ Yes	DEPOSIT RECEIVED:	FOR COPYRIGHT OFFICE USE ONLY
DEPOSIT ACCOUNT FUNDS USED: ☐	REMITTANCE NUMBER AND DATE:	

DO NOT WRITE ABOVE THIS LINE. IF YOU NEED ADDITIONAL SPACE, USE CONTINUATION SHEET (FORM SR/CON)

PREVIOUS REGISTRATION:

5
Previous Registration

• Has registration for this work, or for an earlier version of this work, already been made in the Copyright Office? Yes. . . . . . . No. . . . . . .

• If your answer is "Yes," why is another registration being sought? (Check appropriate box)
  ☐ This is the first published edition of a work previously registered in unpublished form.
  ☐ This is the first application submitted by this author as copyright claimant.
  ☐ This is a changed version of the work, as shown by line 6 of the application.

• If your answer is "Yes," give: Previous Registration Number. . . . . Year of Registration. . . . .

COMPILATION OR DERIVATIVE WORK: (See instructions)

6
Compilation or Derivative Work

PREEXISTING MATERIAL: (Identify any preexisting work or works that the work is based on or incorporates.)
. . . .
. . . .
. . . .
. . . .

MATERIAL ADDED TO THIS WORK: (Give a brief, general statement of the material that has been added to this work and in which copyright is claimed.)
. . . .
. . . .
. . . .
. . . .

DEPOSIT ACCOUNT: (If the registration fee is to be charged to a Deposit Account established in the Copyright Office, give name and number of Account.)

Name: . . . .

Account Number: . . . .

CORRESPONDENCE: (Give name and address to which correspondence about this application should be sent.)

Name: . . . .

Address: . . . .
                                                                        (Apt.)

. . . .
        (City)   (State)   (ZIP)

7
Fee and Correspondence

CERTIFICATION: ✱ I, the undersigned, hereby certify that I am the: (Check one)

☐ author ☐ other copyright claimant ☐ owner of exclusive right(s) ☐ authorized agent of: . . . .
                                                                        (Name of author or other copyright claimant, or owner of exclusive right(s))
of the work identified in this application and that the statements made by me in this application are correct to the best of my knowledge.

☞ Handwritten signature: (X) . . . .

Typed or printed name: . . . . Date: . . . .

8
Certification
(Application must be signed)

MAIL CERTIFICATE TO

. . . .
                                (Name)
. . . .
                    (Number, Street and Apartment Number)
. . . .
        (City)   (State)   (ZIP code)

(Certificate will be mailed in window envelope)

9
Address For Return of Certificate

✱ 17 U.S.C. § 506(e): FALSE REPRESENTATION—Any person who knowingly makes a false representation of a material fact in the application for copyright registration provided for by section 409, or in any written statement filed in connection with the application, shall be fined not more than $2,500

☆ U.S. GOVERNMENT PRINTING OFFICE : 1977 O—248-637

Nov. 1977—200,000

INSTRUCTIONS FOR SPACES 5-9

SPACE 5: PREVIOUS REGISTRATION

• **General Instructions:** The questions in space 5 are intended to find out whether an earlier registration has been made for this work and, if so, whether there is any basis for a new registration. As a general rule, only one basic copyright registration can be made for the same version of a particular work.

• **Same Version:** If this version is substantially the same as the work covered by a previous registration, a second registration is not generally possible unless: (1) the work has been registered in unpublished form and a second registration is now being sought to cover the first published edition, or (2) someone other than the author is identified as copyright claimant in the earlier registration, and the author is now seeking registration in his or her own name. If either of these two exceptions apply, check the appropriate box and give the earlier registration number and date. Otherwise, do not submit Form SR; instead, write the Copyright Office for information about supplementary registration or recordation of transfer of copyright ownership.

• **Changed Version:** If the work has been changed, and you are now seeking registration to cover the additions or revisions, check the third box in space 5, give the earlier registration number and date, and complete both parts of space 6.

• **Previous Registration Number and Date:** If more than one previous registration has been made for the work, give the number and date of the latest registration.

SPACE 6: COMPILATION OR DERIVATIVE WORK

• **General Instructions:** Complete both parts of space 6 if this work is a "compilation," or "derivative work," or both, and if it is based on or incorporates one or more "preexisting works" that are not eligible for registration for one reason or another: works that have already been published or registered, or works that have fallen into the public domain, or sound recordings that were fixed before February 15, 1972. A "compilation" is defined as "a work formed by the collection and assembling of preexisting materials or of data that are selected, coordinated, or arranged in such a way that the resulting work as a whole constitutes an original work of authorship." A "derivative work" is "a work based on one or more preexisting works." In addition to various forms in which works may be "recast, transformed, or adapted," derivative works include works "consisting of editorial revisions, annotations, elaborations, or other modifications" if these changes, as a whole, represent an original work of authorship.

• **Preexisting Material:** If the work is a compilation, give a brief, general statement describing the nature of the material that has been compiled. Example: "Compilation of 1930 recordings by various Chicago jazz bands." In the case of a derivative work, identify the preexisting work that has been recast, transformed, or adapted. Example: "1945 recording by Sperryville Symphony of Bach Double Concerto."

• **Material Added to this Work:** The statute requires a "brief, general statement of the additional material covered by the copyright claim being registered." This statement should describe all of the material in this particular version of the work that: (1) represents an original work of authorship; (2) has not fallen into the public domain; (3) has not been previously published; (4) has not been previously registered for copyright in unpublished form; and (5) is not a sound recording fixed before February 15, 1972. Examples: "Recorded performances on bands 1 and 3"; "Remixed sounds from original multitrack sound sources"; "New words, arrangement, and additional sounds"

SPACES 7, 8, 9: FEE, CORRESPONDENCE, CERTIFICATION, RETURN ADDRESS

• **Deposit Account and Mailing Instructions (Space 7):** If you maintain a Deposit Account in the Copyright Office, identify it in space 7. Otherwise you will need to send the registration fee of $10 with your application. The space headed "Correspondence" should contain the name and address of the person to be consulted if correspondence about this application becomes necessary.

• **Certification (Space 8):** The application is not acceptable unless it bears the handwritten signature of the author or other copyright claimant, or of the owner of exclusive right(s), or of the duly authorized agent of such author, claimant, or owner.

• **Address for Return of Certificate (Space 9):** The address box must be completed legibly, since the certificate will be returned in a window envelope.

MORE INFORMATION

A NOTE ON TERMINOLOGY: The following are the meanings given to some of the terms used in the copyright statute:

• **"Works":** "Works" are the basic subject matter of copyright; they are what authors create and copyright protects. The statute draws a sharp distinction between the "work" and "any material object in which the work is embodied."

• **"Copies" and "Phonorecords":** These are the two types of material objects in which "works" are embodied. In general, **"copies"** are objects from which a work can be read or visually perceived, directly or with the aid of a machine or device, such as manuscripts, books, sheet music, film, and videotape. **"Phonorecords"** are objects embodying fixations of sounds, such as audio tapes and phonograph disks. For example, a song (the "work") can be reproduced in sheet music ("copies") or phonograph disks ("phonorecords"), or both.

• **"Sound Recordings":** These are "works," not "copies" or "phonorecords." "Sound recordings" are "works that result from the fixation of a series of musical, spoken, or other sounds, but not including the sounds accompanying a motion picture or other audiovisual work."

Example: When a record company issues a new release, the release will typically involve two distinct "works": the "musical work" that has been recorded, and the "sound recording" as a separate work in itself. The material objects that the record company sends out are "phonorecords": physical reproductions of both the "musical work" and the "sound recording."

SHOULD YOU FILE MORE THAN ONE APPLICATION? If your work consists of a recorded musical, dramatic, or literary work, and both that "work," and the sound recording as a separate "work," are eligible for registration, the application form you should file depends on the following:

• **File only Form SR if:** The copyright claimant is the same for both the musical, dramatic, or literary work and for the sound recording, and you are seeking a single registration to cover both of these "works."

• **File only Form PA (or Form TX) if:** You are seeking to register only the musical, dramatic, or literary work, not the sound recording. Form PA is appropriate for works of the performing arts; Form TX is for nondramatic literary works.

• **Separate applications should be filed on Form PA (or Form TX) and on Form SR if:**

(1) The copyright claimant for the musical, dramatic, or literary work is different from the copyright claimant for the sound recording, or

(2) You prefer to have separate registrations for the musical, dramatic, or literary work and for the sound recording.

FORM OF COPYRIGHT NOTICE ON PHONORECORDS:

For sound recordings: The copyright statute provides that, whenever a sound recording is published, a special notice of copyright (for example: "℗ 1978 Miriam Haines") "shall be placed on all publicly distributed phonorecords of the sound recording."

For musical, dramatic, or literary works: The copyright notice for musical, dramatic, and literary works (for example: "© 1978 George Harvey Bone") is required to appear on "all publicly distributed copies from which the work can be visually perceived." There is no requirement that the notice for musical, dramatic, or literary works be placed on phonorecords reproducing them.

CONTINUATION SHEET FOR FORM SR

FORM SR/CON
UNITED STATES COPYRIGHT OFFICE

- If at all possible, try to fit the information called for into the spaces provided on Form SR.
- If you do not have space enough for all of the information you need to give on Form SR, use this continuation sheet and submit it with Form SR.
- If you submit this continuation sheet, leave it attached to Form SR. Or, if it becomes detached, clip (do not tape or staple) and fold the two together before submitting them.
- **PART A** of this sheet is intended to identify the basic application. **PART B** is a continuation of Space 2. **PART C** is for the continuation of Spaces 1, 4, or 6. The other spaces on Form SR call for specific items of information and should not need continuation.

REGISTRATION NUMBER
SR   SRU
EFFECTIVE DATE OF REGISTRATION
....
(Month)   (Day)   (Year)
CONTINUATION SHEET RECEIVED
Page _____ of _____ pages

DO NOT WRITE ABOVE THIS LINE. FOR COPYRIGHT OFFICE USE ONLY

(A)

Identification of Application

IDENTIFICATION OF CONTINUATION SHEET: This sheet is a continuation of the application for copyright registration on Form SR, submitted for the following work:

- TITLE: (Give the title as given under the heading "Title of this Work" in Space 1 of Form SR.)

....

- NAME(S) AND ADDRESS(ES) OF COPYRIGHT CLAIMANT(S): (Give the name and address of at least one copyright claimant as given in Space 4 of Form SR.)

....

(B)

Continuation of Space 2

☐ **NAME OF AUTHOR:**

Was this author's contribution to the work a "work made for hire"? Yes...... No......

AUTHOR'S NATIONALITY OR DOMICILE:

Citizen of .... } or { Domiciled in ....
(Name of Country)   (Name of Country)

AUTHOR OF: (Briefly describe nature of this author's contribution)

DATES OF BIRTH AND DEATH:
Born .... Died ....
(Year)   (Year)

WAS THIS AUTHOR'S CONTRIBUTION TO THE WORK:
Anonymous? Yes...... No......
Pseudonymous? Yes...... No......
If the answer to either of these questions is "Yes," see detailed instructions attached.

☐ **NAME OF AUTHOR:**

Was this author's contribution to the work a "work made for hire"? Yes...... No......

AUTHOR'S NATIONALITY OR DOMICILE:

Citizen of .... } or { Domiciled in ....
(Name of Country)   (Name of Country)

AUTHOR OF: (Briefly describe nature of this author's contribution)

DATES OF BIRTH AND DEATH:
Born .... Died ....
(Year)   (Year)

WAS THIS AUTHOR'S CONTRIBUTION TO THE WORK:
Anonymous? Yes...... No......
Pseudonymous? Yes...... No......
If the answer to either of these questions is "Yes," see detailed instructions attached.

☐ **NAME OF AUTHOR:**

Was this author's contribution to the work a "work made for hire"? Yes...... No......

AUTHOR'S NATIONALITY OR DOMICILE:

Citizen of .... } or { Domiciled in ....
(Name of Country)   (Name of Country)

AUTHOR OF: (Briefly describe nature of this author's contribution)

DATES OF BIRTH AND DEATH:
Born .... Died ....
(Year)   (Year)

WAS THIS AUTHOR'S CONTRIBUTION TO THE WORK:
Anonymous? Yes...... No......
Pseudonymous? Yes...... No......
If the answer to either of these questions is "Yes," see detailed instructions attached.

(C)

Continuation of other Spaces

CONTINUATION OF (Check which):   ☐ Space 1   ☐ Space 4   ☐ Space 6

FORM GR/CP

UNITED STATES COPYRIGHT OFFICE
LIBRARY OF CONGRESS
WASHINGTON, D.C. 20559

THIS FORM:

- Can be used solely as an adjunct to a basic application for copyright registration.
- Is not acceptable unless submitted together with Form TX, Form PA, or Form VA.
- Is acceptable only if the group of works listed on it all qualify for a single copyright registration under 17 U.S.C. § 408 (c)(2).

ADJUNCT APPLICATION
for Copyright Registration for a
Group of Contributions to Periodicals

WHEN TO USE FORM GR/CP: Form GR/CP is the appropriate adjunct application form to use when you are submitting a basic application on Form TX, Form PA, or Form VA, for a group of works that qualify for a single registration under section 408(c)(2) of the copyright statute.

WHEN DOES A GROUP OF WORKS QUALIFY FOR A SINGLE REGISTRATION UNDER 17 U.S.C. §408 (c)(2)?
The statute provides that a single copyright registration for a group of works can be made if **all** of the following conditions are met:

(1) All of the works are by the same author, who is an individual (not an employer for hire); and

(2) All of the works were first published as contributions to periodicals (including newspapers) within a twelve-month period; and

(3) Each of the contributions as first published bore a separate copyright notice, and the name of the owner of copyright in the work (or an abbreviation or alternative designation of the owner) was the same in each notice; and

(4) One copy of the entire periodical issue or newspaper section in which each contribution was first published must be deposited with the application; and

(5) The application must identify each contribution separately, including the periodical containing it and the date of its first publication.

How to Apply for Group Registration:

First: Study the information on this page to make sure that all of the works you want to register together as a group qualify for a single registration.

Second: Turn this page over and read through the detailed instructions for group registration. Decide which form you should use for the basic registration (Form TX for nondramatic literary works; or Form PA for musical, dramatic, and other works of the performing arts; or Form VA for pictorial and graphic works). Be sure that you have all of the information you need before you start filling out both the basic and the adjunct application forms.

Third: Complete the basic application form, following the detailed instructions accompanying it **and the special instructions on the reverse of this page**.

Fourth: Complete the adjunct application on Form GR/CP and mail it, together with the basic application form and the required copy of each contribution, to: Register of Copyrights, Library of Congress, Washington, D.C. 20559. Unless you have a Deposit Account in the Copyright Office, your application and copies must be accompanied by a check or money order for $10, payable to: *Register of Copyrights.*

PROCEDURE FOR GROUP REGISTRATION

TWO APPLICATION FORMS MUST BE FILED

When you apply for a single registration to cover a group of contributions to periodicals, you must submit two application forms:

(1) A basic application on either Form TX, or Form PA, or Form VA. It must contain all of the information required for copyright registration except the titles and information concerning publication of the contributions.

(2) An adjunct application on Form GR/CP. The purpose of this form is to provide separate identification for each of the contributions and to give information about their first publication, as required by the statute.

WHICH BASIC APPLICATION FORM TO USE

The basic application form you choose to submit should be determined by the nature of the contributions you are registering. As long as they meet the statutory qualifications for group registration (outlined on the reverse of this page), the contributions can be registered together even if they are entirely different in nature, type, or content. However, you must choose which of three forms is generally the most appropriate on which to submit your basic application:

Form TX: for nondramatic literary works consisting primarily of text. Examples are fiction, verse, articles, news stories, features, essays, reviews, editorials, columns, quizzes, puzzles, and advertising copy.

Form PA: for works of the performing arts. Examples are music, drama, choreography, and pantomimes.

Form VA: for works of the visual arts. Examples are photographs, drawings, paintings, prints, art reproductions, cartoons, comic strips, charts, diagrams, maps, pictorial ornamentation, and pictorial or graphic material published as advertising.

If your contributions differ in nature, choose the form most suitable for the majority of them. However, if any of the contributions consists preponderantly of nondramatic text matter in English, you should file Form TX for the entire group. This is because Form TX is the only form containing spaces for information about the manufacture of copies, which the statute requires to be given for certain works.

REGISTRATION FEE FOR GROUP REGISTRATION

The fee for registration of a group of contributions to periodicals is $10, no matter how many contributions are listed on Form GR/CP. Unless you maintain a Deposit Account in the Copyright Office, the registration fee must accompany your application forms and copies. Make your remittance payable to: *Register of Copyrights.*

WHAT COPIES SHOULD BE DEPOSITED FOR GROUP REGISTRATION?

The application forms you file for group registration must be accompanied by one complete copy of each contribution listed in Form GR/CP, exactly as the contribution was first published in a periodical. The deposit must consist of the entire issue of the periodical containing the contribution; or, if the contribution was first published in a newspaper, the deposit should consist of the entire section in which the contribution appeared. Tear sheets or proof copies are not acceptable for deposit.

COPYRIGHT NOTICE REQUIREMENTS

For published works, the law provides that a copyright notice in a specified form "shall be placed on all publicly distributed copies from which the work can be visually perceived." The required form of the notice generally consists of three elements: (1) the symbol "©", or the word "Copyright", or the abbreviation "Copr."; (2) the year of first publication of the work; and (3) the name of the owner of copyright in the work, or an abbreviation or alternative form of the name. For example: "© 1978 Samuel Craig"

Among the conditions for group registration of contributions to periodicals, the statute establishes two requirements involving the copyright notice:

(1) Each of the contributions as first published must have borne a separate copyright notice; and

(2) "The name of the owner of copyright in the work, or an abbreviation by which the name can be recognized, or a generally known alternative designation of the owner" must have been the same in each notice.

HOW TO FILL OUT THE BASIC APPLICATION FORM WHEN APPLYING FOR GROUP REGISTRATION

In general, the instructions for filling out the basic application (Form TX, Form PA, or Form VA) apply to group registrations. In addition, please observe the following specific instructions:

Space 1 (Title): Do not give information concerning any of the contributions in space 1 of the basic application. Instead, in the block headed "Title of this Work", state: "See Form GR/CP, attached". Leave the other blocks in space 1 blank.

Space 2 (Author): Give the name and other information concerning the author of all of the contributions listed in Form GR/CP. For group registration, all of the contributions must have been written by the same individual author.

Space 3 (Creation and Publication): In the block calling for the year of creation, give the year of creation of the last of the contributions to be completed. Leave the block calling for the date and nation of first publication blank.

Space 4 (Claimant): Give all of the requested information, which must be the same for all of the contributions listed on Form GR/CP.

Other spaces: Complete all of the applicable spaces, and be sure that the form is signed in the certification space.

HOW TO FILL OUT FORM GR/CP

PART A: IDENTIFICATION OF APPLICATION

• **Identification of Basic Application:** Indicate, by checking one of the boxes, which of the basic application forms (Form TX, or Form PA, or Form VA) you are filing for registration.

• **Identification of Author and Claimant:** Give the name of the individual author exactly as it appears in line 2 of the basic application, and give the name of the copyright claimant exactly as it appears in line 4. These must be the same for all of the contributions listed in Part B of Form GR/CP.

PART B: REGISTRATION FOR GROUP OF CONTRIBUTIONS

• **General Instructions:** Under the statute, a group of contributions to periodicals will qualify for a single registration only if the application "identifies each work separately, including the periodical containing it and its date of first publication." Part B of the Form GR/CP provides lines enough to list 19 separate contributions; if you need more space, use additional Forms GR/CP. If possible, list the contributions in the order of their publication, giving the earliest first. Number each line consecutively.

• **Important:** All of the contributions listed on Form GR/CP must have been published within a single twelve-month period. This does not mean that all of the contributions must have been published during the same calendar year, but it does mean that, to be grouped in a single application, the earliest and latest contributions must not have been published more than twelve months apart. Example: Contributions published on April 1, 1978, July 1, 1978, and March 1, 1979, could be grouped together, but a contribution published on April 15, 1979, could not be registered with them as part of the group.

• **Title of Contribution:** Each contribution must be given a title that is capable of identifying that particular work and of distinguishing it from others. If the contribution as published in the periodical bears a title (or an identifying phrase that could serve as a title), transcribe its wording completely and exactly.

• **Identification of Periodical:** Give the over-all title of the periodical in which the contribution was first published, together with the volume and issue number (if any) and the issue date.

• **Pages:** Give the number of the page of the periodical issue on which the contribution appeared. If the contribution covered more than one page, give the inclusive pages, if possible.

• **First Publication:** The statute defines "publication" as "the distribution of copies or phonorecords of a work to the public by sale or other transfer of ownership, or by rental, lease, or lending"; a work is also "published" if there has been an "offering to distribute copies or phonorecords to a group of persons for purposes of further distribution, public performance, or public display." Give the full date (month, day, and year) when, and the country where, publication of the periodical issue containing the contribution first occurred. If first publication took place simultaneously in the United States and other countries, it is sufficient to state "U.S.A."

NOTE: The advantage of group registration is that it allows any number of works published within a twelve-month period to be registered "on the basis of a single deposit, application, and registration fee." On the other hand, group registration may also have disadvantages under certain circumstances. If infringement of a published work begins before the work has been registered, the copyright owner can still obtain the ordinary remedies for copyright infringement (including injunctions, actual damages and profits, and impounding and disposition of infringing articles). However, in that situation—where the copyright in a published work is infringed before registration is made—the owner cannot obtain special remedies (statutory damages and attorney's fees) unless registration was made within three months after first publication of the work.

ADJUNCT APPLICATION
for
Copyright Registration for a
Group of Contributions to Periodicals

- Use this adjunct form only if your are making a single registration for a group of contributions to periodicals, and you are also filing a basic application on Form TX, Form PA, or Form VA. Follow the instructions, attached.
- Number each line in Part B consecutively. Use additional Forms GR/CP if you need more space.
- Submit this adjunct form with the basic application form. Clip (do not tape or staple) and fold all sheets together before submitting them.

FORM GR/CP

UNITED STATES COPYRIGHT OFFICE

REGISTRATION NUMBER
TX   PA   VA

EFFECTIVE DATE OF REGISTRATION

. . . .
(Month)   (Day)   (Year)

FORM GR/CP RECEIVED

Page _____ of _____ pages

DO NOT WRITE ABOVE THIS LINE. FOR COPYRIGHT OFFICE USE ONLY

(A)
Identification of Application

IDENTIFICATION OF BASIC APPLICATION:
- This application for copyright registration for a group of contributions to periodicals is submitted as an adjunct to an application filed on: (Check which)

☐ Form TX   ☐ Form PA   ☐ Form VA

IDENTIFICATION OF AUTHOR AND CLAIMANT: (Give the name of the author and the name of the copyright claimant in all of the contributions listed in Part B of this form. The names should be the same as the names given in spaces 2 and 4 of the basic application.)

Name of Author: . . . .
Name of Copyright Claimant: . . . .

(B)
Registration For Group of Contributions

COPYRIGHT REGISTRATION FOR A GROUP OF CONTRIBUTIONS TO PERIODICALS: (To make a single registration for a group of works by the same individual author, all first published as contributions to periodicals within a 12-month period (see instructions), give full information about each contribution. If more space is needed, use additional Forms GR/CP.)

☐ Title of Contribution: . . . .
Title of Periodical: . . . . Vol. . . . . . No. . . . . . Issue Date . . . . Pages. . . . .
Date of First Publication:. . . . . Nation of First Publication . . . .
(Month)   (Day)   (Year)   (Country)

☐ Title of Contribution: . . . .
Title of Periodical: . . . . Vol. . . . . . No. . . . . . Issue Date . . . . Pages. . . . .
Date of First Publication:. . . . . Nation of First Publication . . . .
(Month)   (Day)   (Year)   (Country)

☐ Title of Contribution: . . . .↓. . . . .
Title of Periodical: . . . . Vol. . . . . . No. . . . . . Issue Date . . . . Pages. . . . .
Date of First Publication:. . . . . Nation of First Publication . . . .
(Month)   (Day)   (Year)   (Country)

☐ Title of Contribution: . . . .
Title of Periodical: . . . . Vol. . . . . . No. . . . . . Issue Date . . . . Pages. . . . .
Date of First Publication:. . . . . Nation of First Publication . . . .
(Month)   (Day)   (Year)   (Country)

☐ Title of Contribution: . . . .
Title of Periodical: . . . . Vol. . . . . . No. . . . . . Issue Date . . . . Pages. . . . .
Date of First Publication:. . . . . Nation of First Publication . . . .
(Month)   (Day)   (Year)   (Country)

☐ Title of Contribution: . . . .
Title of Periodical: . . . . Vol. . . . . . No. . . . . . Issue Date . . . . Pages. . . . .
Date of First Publication:. . . . . Nation of First Publication . . . .
(Month)   (Day)   (Year)   (Country)

☐ Title of Contribution: . . . .
Title of Periodical: . . . . Vol. . . . . . No. . . . . . Issue Date . . . . Pages. . . . .
Date of First Publication:. . . . . Nation of First Publication . . . .
(Month)   (Day)   (Year)   (Country)

<table>
<tr><td></td><td style="text-align:right">FOR
COPYRIGHT
OFFICE
USE
ONLY</td></tr>
</table>

DO NOT WRITE ABOVE THIS LINE. FOR COPYRIGHT OFFICE USE ONLY

☐ Title of Contribution: ....

Title of Periodical: .... Vol. . . . . . No. . . . . . Issue Date . . . . Pages. . . . .

Date of First Publication:. . . . . Nation of First Publication. . . . .
        (Month)   (Day)   (Year)   (Country)

Ⓑ
Continued

☐ Title of Contribution: ....

Title of Periodical: .... Vol. . . . . . No. . . . . . Issue Date . . . . Pages. . . . .

Date of First Publication:. . . . . Nation of First Publication. . . . .
        (Month)   (Day)   (Year)   (Country)

☐ Title of Contribution: ....

Title of Periodical: .... Vol. . . . . . No. . . . . . Issue Date . . . . Pages. . . . .

Date of First Publication:. . . . . Nation of First Publication. . . . .
        (Month)   (Day)   (Year)   (Country)

☐ Title of Contribution: ....

Title of Periodical: .... Vol. . . . . . No. . . . . . Issue Date . . . . Pages. . . . .

Date of First Publication:. . . . . Nation of First Publication. . . . .
        (Month)   (Day)   (Year)   (Country)

☐ Title of Contribution: ....

Title of Periodical: .... Vol. . . . . . No. . . . . . Issue Date . . . . Pages. . . . .

Date of First Publication:. . . . . Nation of First Publication. . . . .
        (Month)   (Day)   (Year)   (Country)

☐ Title of Contribution: ....

Title of Periodical: .... Vol. . . . . . No. . . . . . Issue Date . . . . Pages. . . . .

Date of First Publication:. . . . . Nation of First Publication. . . . .
        (Month)   (Day)   (Year)   (Country)

☐ Title of Contribution: ....

Title of Periodical: .... Vol. . . . . . No. . . . . . Issue Date . . . . Pages. . . . .

Date of First Publication:. . . . . Nation of First Publication. . . . .
        (Month)   (Day)   (Year)   (Country)

☐ Title of Contribution: ....

Title of Periodical: .... Vol. . . . . . No. . . . . . Issue Date . . . . Pages. . . . .

Date of First Publication:. . . . . Nation of First Publication. . . . .
        (Month)   (Day)   (Year)   (Country)

☐ Title of Contribution: ....

Title of Periodical: .... Vol. . . . . . No. . . . . . Issue Date . . . . Pages. . . . .

Date of First Publication:. . . . . Nation of First Publication. . . . .
        (Month)   (Day)   (Year)   (Country)

☐ Title of Contribution: ....

Title of Periodical: .... Vol. . . . . . No. . . . . . Issue Date . . . . Pages. . . . .

Date of First Publication:. . . . . Nation of First Publication. . . . .
        (Month)   (Day)   (Year)   (Country)

☐ Title of Contribution: ....

Title of Periodical: .... Vol. . . . . . No. . . . . . Issue Date . . . . Pages. . . . .

Date of First Publication:. . . . . Nation of First Publication. . . . .
        (Month)   (Day)   (Year)   (Country)

☐ Title of Contribution: ....

Title of Periodical: .... Vol. . . . . . No. . . . . . Issue Date . . . . Pages. . . . .

Date of First Publication:. . . . . Nation of First Publication. . . . .
        (Month)   (Day)   (Year)   (Country)

☐ Title of Contribution: ....

Title of Periodical: .... Vol. . . . . . No. . . . . . Issue Date . . . . Pages. . . . .

Date of First Publication:. . . . . Nation of First Publication. . . . .
        (Month)   (Day)   (Year)   (Country)

USE THIS FORM WHEN:

- An earlier registration has been made in the Copyright Office; and

- Some of the facts given in that registration are incorrect or incomplete; and

- You want to place the correct or complete facts on record.

FORM CA

UNITED STATES COPYRIGHT OFFICE
LIBRARY OF CONGRESS
WASHINGTON, D.C. 20559

Application for Supplementary Copyright Registration

To Correct or Amplify Information Given in the Copyright Office Record of an Earlier Registration

What is "Supplementary Copyright Registration"? Supplementary registration is a special type of copyright registration provided for in section 408(d) of the copyright law.

Purpose of Supplementary Registration. As a rule, only one basic copyright registration can be made for the same work. To take care of cases where information in the basic registration turns out to be incorrect or incomplete, the law provides for "the filing of an application for supplementary registration, to correct an error in a copyright registration or to amplify the information given in a registration."

Earlier Registration Necessary. Supplementary registration can be made only if a basic copyright registration for the same work has already been completed.

Who May File. Once basic registration has been made for a work, any author or other copyright claimant, or owner of any exclusive right in the work, who wishes to correct or amplify the information given in the basic registration, may submit Form CA.

Please Note:

- Do not use Form CA to correct errors in statements on the copies or phonorecords of the work in question, or to reflect changes in the content of the work. If the work has been changed substantially, you should consider making an entirely new registration for the revised version to cover the additions or revisions.

- Do not use Form CA as a substitute for renewal registration. For works originally copyrighted between January 1, 1950 and December 31, 1977, registration of a renewal claim within strict time limits is necessary to extend the first 28-year copyright term to the full term of 75 years. This cannot be done by filing Form CA.

- Do not use Form CA as a substitute for recording a transfer of copyright or other document pertaining to rights under a copyright. Recording a document under section 205 of the statute gives all persons constructive notice of the facts stated in the document and may have other important consequences in cases of infringement or conflicting transfers. Supplementary registration does not have that legal effect.

How to Apply for Supplementary Registration:

First: Study the information on this page to make sure that filing an application on Form CA is the best procedure to follow in your case.

Second: Turn this page over and read through the specific instructions for filling out Form CA. Make sure, before starting to complete the form, that you have all of the detailed information about the basic registration you will need.

Third: Complete all applicable spaces on this form, following the line-by-line instructions on the back of this page. Use typewriter, or print the information in dark ink.

Fourth: Detach this sheet and send your completed Form CA to: Register of Copyrights, Library of Congress, Washington, D.C. 20559. Unless you have a Deposit Account in the Copyright Office, your application must be accompanied by a check or money order for $10 payable to: *Register of Copyrights.* Do not send copies, phonorecords, or supporting documents with your application, since they cannot be made part of the record of a supplementary registration.

What Happens When a Supplementary Registration is Made? When a supplementary registration is completed, the Copyright Office will assign it a new registration number in the appropriate registration category, and issue a certificate of supplementary registration under that number. The basic registration will not be expunged or cancelled, and the two registrations will both stand in the Copyright Office records. The supplementary registration will have the effect of calling the public's attention to a possible error or omission in the basic registration, and of placing the correct facts or the additional information on official record. Moreover, if the person on whose behalf Form CA is submitted is the same as the person identified as copyright claimant in the basic registration, the Copyright Office will place a note referring to the supplementary registration in its records of the basic registration.

PLEASE READ DETAILED INSTRUCTIONS ON REVERSE

Please read the following line-by-line instructions carefully and refer to them while completing Form CA.

INSTRUCTIONS
For Completing FORM CA (Supplementary Registration)

PART A: BASIC INSTRUCTIONS

• **General Instructions:** The information in this part identifies the basic registration to be corrected or amplified. Each item must agree exactly with the information as it already appears in the basic registration (even if the purpose of filing Form CA is to change one of these items).

• **Title of Work:** Give the title as it appears in the basic registration, including previous or alternative titles if they appear.

• **Registration Number:** This is a series of numerical digits, preceded by one or more letters. The registration number appears in the upper right hand corner of the certificate of registration.

• **Registration Date:** Give the year when the basic registration was completed.

• **Name(s) of Author(s) and Name(s) of Copyright Claimant(s):** Give all of the names as they appear in the basic registration.

PART B: CORRECTION

• **General Instructions:** Complete this part **only** if information in the basic registration was incorrect at the time that basic registration was made. Leave this part blank and complete Part C, instead, if your purpose is to add, update, or clarify information rather than to rectify an actual error.

• **Location and Nature of Incorrect Information:** Give the line number and the heading or description of the the space in the basic registration where the error occurs (for example: "Line number 3 . . . Citizenship of author").

• **Incorrect Information as it Appears in Basic Registration:** Transcribe the erroneous statement exactly as it appears in the basic registration.

• **Corrected Information:** Give the statement as it should have appeared.

• **Explanation of Correction (Optional):** If you wish, you may add an explanation of the error or its correction.

PART C: AMPLIFICATION

• **General Instructions:** Complete this part if you want to provide any of the following: (1) additional information that could have been given but was omitted at the time of basic registration; (2) changes in facts, such as changes of title or address of claimant, that have occurred since the basic registration; or (3) explanations clarifying information in the basic registration.

• **Location and Nature of Information to be Amplified:** Give the line number and the heading or description of the space in the basic registration where the information to be amplified appears.

• **Amplified Information:** Give a statement of the added, updated, or explanatory information as clearly and succinctly as possible.

• **Explanation of Amplification (Optional):** If you wish, you may add an explanation of the amplification.

PARTS D, E, F, G: CONTINUATION, FEE, MAILING INSTRUCTIONS AND CERTIFICATION

• **Continuation (Part D):** Use this space if you do not have enough room in Parts B or C

• **Deposit Account and Mailing Instructions (Part E):** If you maintain a Deposit Account in the Copyright Office, identify it in Part E. Otherwise, you will need to send the registration fee of $10 with your form. The space headed "Correspondence" should contain the name and address of the person to be consulted if correspondence about the form becomes necessary.

• **Certification (Part F):** The application is not acceptable unless it bears the handwritten signature of the author, or other copyright claimant, or of the owner of exclusive right(s), or of the duly authorized agent of such author, claimant, or owner.

• **Address for Return of Certificate (Part G):** The address box must be completed legibly, since the certificate will be returned in a window envelope.

FORM CA
UNITED STATES COPYRIGHT OFFICE

REGISTRATION NUMBER

TX	TXU	PA	PAU	VA	VAU	SR	SRU	RE

Effective Date of Supplementary Registration

. . . .
MONTH   DAY   YEAR

DO NOT WRITE ABOVE THIS LINE—FOR COPYRIGHT OFFICE USE

(A)
Basic Instructions

TITLE OF WORK:

REGISTRATION NUMBER OF BASIC REGISTRATION: | YEAR OF BASIC REGISTRATION:

NAME(S) OF AUTHOR(S): | NAME(S) OF COPYRIGHT CLAIMANT(S):

(B)
Correction

LOCATION AND NATURE OF INCORRECT INFORMATION IN BASIC REGISTRATION:

Line Number . . . . Line Heading or Description . . . .

INCORRECT INFORMATION AS IT APPEARS IN BASIC REGISTRATION:

CORRECTED INFORMATION:

EXPLANATION OF CORRECTION: (Optional)

(C)
Amplification

LOCATION AND NATURE OF INFORMATION IN BASIC REGISTRATION TO BE AMPLIFIED:

Line Number . . . . Line Heading or Description . . . .

AMPLIFIED INFORMATION:

EXPLANATION OF AMPLIFIED INFORMATION: (Optional)

	EXAMINED BY:	FORM CA RECEIVED	FOR COPYRIGHT OFFICE USE ONLY
	CHECKED BY:		
	CORRESPONDENCE ☐ YES	REMITTANCE NUMBER AND DATE	
	REFERENCE TO THIS REGISTRATION ADDED TO BASIC REGISTRATION ☐ YES ☐ NO	DEPOSIT ACCOUNT FUNDS USED ☐	

DO NOT WRITE ABOVE THIS LINE: FOR COPYRIGHT OFFICE USE ONLY

CONTINUATION OF: (Check which): ☐ PART B OR ☐ PART C

D
Continuation

DEPOSIT ACCOUNT: If the registration fee is to be charged to a Deposit Account established in the Copyright Office, give name and number of Account:

Name . . . . Account Number . . . .

CORRESPONDENCE: Give name and address to which correspondence should be sent:

Name . . . . Apt. No. . . . .

Address . . . .
        (Number and Street)   (City)   (State)   (ZIP Code)

E
Deposit
Account and
Mailing
Instructions

CERTIFICATION ✱ I, the undersigned, hereby certify that I am the: (Check one)

☐ author ☐ other copyright claimant ☐ owner of exclusive right(s) ☐ authorized agent of: . . . .
                                                        (Name of author or other copyright claimant, or owner of exclusive right(s))
of the work identified in this application and that the statements made by me in this application are correct to the best of my knowledge.

Handwritten signature: (X) . . . .

Typed or printed name . . . .

Date: . . . .

✱ 17 USC §506(e): FALSE REPRESENTATION—Any person who knowingly makes a false representation of a material fact in the application for copyright registration provided for by section 409, or in any written statement filed in connection with the application, shall be fined not more than $2,500.

F
Certification
(Application
must be
signed)

. . . .
        (Name)

. . . .
        (Number, Street and Apartment Number)

. . . .
        (City)   (State)   (ZIP code)

MAIL CERTIFICATE TO

(Certificate will
be mailed in
window envelope)

G
Address for
Return of
Certificate

Nov. 1977—25,000

FORM RE

UNITED STATES COPYRIGHT OFFICE
LIBRARY OF CONGRESS
WASHINGTON, D.C. 20559

APPLICATION FOR
Renewal Registration

HOW TO REGISTER A RENEWAL CLAIM:

- **First:** Study the information on this page and make sure you know the answers to two questions:

  (1) What are the renewal time limits in your case?

  (2) Who can claim the renewal?

- **Second:** Turn this page over and read through the specific instructions for filling out Form RE. Make sure, before starting to complete the form, that the copyright is now eligible for renewal, that you are authorized to file a renewal claim, and that you have all of the information about the copyright you will need.

- **Third:** Complete all applicable spaces on Form RE, following the line-by-line instructions on the back of this page. Use typewriter, or print the information in dark ink.

- **Fourth:** Detach this sheet and send your completed Form RE to: Register of Copyrights, Library of Congress, Washington, D.C. 20559. Unless you have a Deposit Account in the Copyright Office, your application must be accompanied by a check or money order for $6, payable to: *Register of Copyrights*. Do not send copies, phonorecords, or supporting documents with your renewal application.

WHAT IS RENEWAL OF COPYRIGHT? For works originally copyrighted between January 1, 1950 and December 31, 1977, the statute now in effect provides for a first term of copyright protection lasting for 28 years, with the possibility of renewal for a second term of 47 years. If a valid renewal registration is made for a work, its total copyright term is 75 years (a first term of 28 years, plus a renewal term of 47 years). Example: For a work copyrighted in 1960, the first term will expire in 1988, but if renewed at the proper time the copyright will last through the end of 2035.

SOME BASIC POINTS ABOUT RENEWAL:

(1) There are strict time limits and deadlines for renewing a copyright.

(2) Only certain persons who fall into specific categories named in the law can claim renewal.

(3) The new copyright law does away with renewal requirements for works first copyrighted after 1977. However, copyrights that were already in their first copyright term on January 1, 1978 (that is, works originally copyrighted between January 1, 1950 and December 31, 1977) **still have to be renewed** in order to be protected for a second term.

TIME LIMITS FOR RENEWAL REGISTRATION: The new copyright statute provides that, in order to renew a copyright, the renewal application and fee must be received in the Copyright Office "within one year prior to the expiration of the copyright." It also provides that all terms of copyright will run through the end of the year in which they would otherwise expire. Since all copyright terms will expire on December 31st of their last year, all periods for renewal registration will run from December 31th of the 27th year of the copyright, and will end on December 31st of the following year.

To determine the time limits for renewal in your case:

(1) First, find out the date of original copyright for the work. (In the case of works originally registered in unpublished form, the date of copyright is the date of registration; for published works, copyright begins on the date of first publication.)

(2) Then add 28 years to the year the work was originally copyrighted.

Your answer will be the calendar year during which the copyright will be eligible for renewal, and December 31st of that year will be the renewal deadline. Example: a work originally copyrighted on April 19, 1957, will be eligible for renewal between December 31, 1984, and December 31, 1985.

WHO MAY CLAIM RENEWAL: Renewal copyright may be claimed only by those persons specified in the law. Except in the case of four specific types of works, the law gives the right to claim renewal to the individual author of the work, regardless of who owned the copyright during the original term. If the author is dead, the statute gives the right to claim renewal to certain of the author's beneficiaries (widow and children, executors, or next of kin, depending on the circumstances). The present owner (proprietor) of the copyright is entitled to claim renewal only in four specified cases, as explained in more detail on the reverse of this page.

CAUTION: Renewal registration is possible only if an acceptable application and fee are **received** in the Copyright Office during the renewal period and before the renewal deadline. If an acceptable application and fee are not received before the renewal deadline, the work falls into the public domain and the copyright cannot be renewed. The Copyright Office has no discretion to extend the renewal time limits.

INSTRUCTIONS FOR COMPLETING FORM RE

SPACE 1: RENEWAL CLAIM(S)

• **General Instructions:** In order for this application to result in a valid renewal, space 1 must identify one or more of the persons who are entitled to renew the copyright under the statute. Give the full name and address of each claimant, with a statement of the basis of each claim, using the wording given in these instructions.

• **Persons Entitled to Renew:**

A. The following persons may claim renewal in all types of works except those enumerated in Paragraph B, below:

1. The author, if living. State the claim as: *the author.*

2. The widow, widower, and/or children of the author, if the author is not living. State the claim as: *the widow (widower) of the author* .... (Name of author) and/or *the child (children) of the deceased author* .... (Name of author)

3. The author's executor(s), if the author left a will and if there is no surviving widow, widower, or child. State the claim as: *the executor(s) of the author* .... (Name of author)

4. The next of kin of the author, if the author left no will and if there is no surviving widow, widower, or child. State the claim as: *the next of kin of the deceased author* .... *there being no will.* (Name of author)

B. In the case of the following four types of works, the proprietor (owner of the copyright at the time of renewal registration) may claim renewal:

1. Posthumous work (a work as to which no copyright assignment or other contract for exploitation has occurred during the author's lifetime). State the claim as: *proprietor of copyright in a posthumous work.*

2. Periodical, cyclopedic, or other composite work. State the claim as: *proprietor of copyright in a composite work.*

3. "Work copyrighted by a corporate body otherwise than as assignee or licensee of the individual author." State the claim as: *proprietor of copyright in a work copyrighted by a corporate body otherwise than as assignee or licensee of the individual author.* (This type of claim is considered appropriate in relatively few cases.)

4. Work copyrighted by an employer for whom such work was made for hire. State the claim as: *proprietor of copyright in a work made for hire.*

SPACE 2: WORK RENEWED

• **General Instructions:** This space is to identify the particular work being renewed. The information given here should agree with that appearing in the certificate of original registration.

• **Title:** Give the full title of the work, together with any subtitles or descriptive wording included with the title in the original registration. In the case of a musical composition, give the specific instrumentation of the work.

• **Renewable Matter:** Copyright in a new version of a previous work (such as an arrangement, translation, dramatization, compilation, or work republished with new matter) covers only the additions, changes, or other new material appearing for the first time in that version. If this work was a new version, state in general the new matter upon which copyright was claimed.

• **Contribution to Periodical, Serial, or other Composite Work:** Separate renewal registration is possible for a work published as a contribution to a periodical, serial, or other composite work, whether the contribution was copyrighted independently or as part of the larger work in which it appeared. Each contribution published in a separate issue ordinarily requires a separate renewal registration. However, the new law provides an alternative, permitting groups of periodical contributions by the same individual author to be combined under a single renewal application and fee in certain cases.

If this renewal application covers a single contribution, give all of the requested information in space 2. If you are seeking to renew a group of contributions, include a reference such as "See space 5" in space 2 and give the requested information about all of the contributions in space 5.

SPACE 3: AUTHOR(S)

• **General Instructions:** The copyright secured in a new version of a work is independent of any copyright protection in material published earlier. The only "authors" of a new version are those who contributed copyrightable matter to it. Thus, for renewal purposes, the person who wrote the original version on which the new work is based cannot be regarded as an "author" of the new version, unless that person also contributed to the new matter.

• **Authors of Renewable Matter:** Give the full names of all authors who contributed copyrightable matter to this particular version of the work.

SPACE 4: FACTS OF ORIGINAL REGISTRATION

• **General Instructions:** Each item in space 4 should agree with the information appearing in the original registration for the work. If the work being renewed is a single contribution to a periodical or composite work that was not separately registered, give information about the particular issue in which the contribution appeared. You may leave this space blank if you are completing space 5.

• **Original Registration Number:** Give the full registration number, which is a series of numerical digits, preceded by one or more letters. The registration number appears in the upper right hand corner of the certificate of registration.

• **Original Copyright Claimant:** Give the name in which ownership of the copyright was claimed in the original registration.

• **Date of Publication or Registration:** Give only one date. If the original registration gave a publication date, it should be transcribed here; otherwise the registration was for an unpublished work, and the date of registration should be given.

SPACE 5: GROUP RENEWALS

• **General Instructions:** A single renewal registration can be made for a group of works if all of the following statutory conditions are met: (1) all of the works were written by the same author, who is named in space 3 and who is or was an individual (not an employer for hire); (2) all of the works were first published as contributions to periodicals (including newspapers) and were copyrighted on their first publication; (3) the renewal claimant or claimants, and the basis of claim or claims, is the same for all of the works; (4) the renewal application and fee are "received not more than 28 or less than 27 years after the 31st day of December of the calendar year in which all of the works were first published"; and (5) the renewal application identifies each work separately, including the periodical containing it and the date of first publication.

Time Limits for Group Renewals: To be renewed as a group, all of the contributions must have been first published during the same calendar year. For example, suppose six contributions by the same author were published on April 1, 1960, July 1, 1960, November 1, 1960, February 1, 1961, July 1, 1961, and March 1, 1962. The three 1960 copyrights can be combined and renewed at any time during 1988, and the two 1961 copyrights can be renewed as a group during 1989, but the 1962 copyright must be renewed by itself, in 1990.

Identification of Each Work: Give all of the requested information for each contribution. The registration number should be that for the contribution itself if it was separately registered, and the registration number for the periodical issue if it was not.

SPACES 6, 7 AND 8: FEE, MAILING INSTRUCTIONS, AND CERTIFICATION

• **Deposit Account and Mailing Instructions (Space 6):** If you maintain a Deposit Account in the Copyright Office, identify it in Space 6. Otherwise, you will need to send the renewal registration fee of $6 with your form. The space headed "Correspondence" should contain the name and address of the person to be consulted if correspondence about the form becomes necessary.

• **Certification (Space 7):** The renewal application is not acceptable unless it bears the handwritten signature of the renewal claimant or the duly authorized agent of the renewal claimant.

• **Address for Return of Certificate (Space 8):** The address box must be completed legibly, since the certificate will be returned in a window envelope.

FORM RE
UNITED STATES COPYRIGHT OFFICE

REGISTRATION NUMBER

EFFECTIVE DATE OF RENEWAL REGISTRATION

....
(Month)　(Day)　(Year)

DO NOT WRITE ABOVE THIS LINE.　FOR COPYRIGHT OFFICE USE ONLY

① Renewal Claimant(s)

RENEWAL CLAIMANT(S), ADDRESS(ES), AND STATEMENT OF CLAIM: (See Instructions)

1 Name ....
Address ....
Claiming as ....
(Use appropriate statement from instructions)

2 Name ....
Address ....
Claiming as ....
(Use appropriate statement from instructions)

3 Name ....
Address ....
Claiming as ....
(Use appropriate statement from instructions)

② Work Renewed

TITLE OF WORK IN WHICH RENEWAL IS CLAIMED:

RENEWABLE MATTER:

CONTRIBUTION TO PERIODICAL OR COMPOSITE WORK:

Title of periodical or composite work: ....
If a periodical or other serial, give: Vol. .... No. .... Issue Date ....

③ Author(s)

AUTHOR(S) OF RENEWABLE MATTER:

④ Facts of Original Registration

ORIGINAL REGISTRATION NUMBER: .... **ORIGINAL COPYRIGHT CLAIMANT:**

ORIGINAL DATE OF COPYRIGHT:
- If the original registration for this work was made in published form, give:
  DATE OF PUBLICATION: .... (Month) (Day) (Year)

OR

- If the original registration for this work was made in unpublished form, give:
  DATE OF REGISTRATION: .... (Month) (Day) (Year)

	RENEWAL APPLICATION RECEIVED:	
EXAMINED BY: .... CHECKED BY:		FOR COPYRIGHT OFFICE USE ONLY
DEPOSIT ACCOUNT FUNDS USED: ☐	REMITTANCE NUMBER AND DATE:	

DO NOT WRITE ABOVE THIS LINE

RENEWAL FOR GROUP OF WORKS BY SAME AUTHOR: To make a single registration for a group of works by the same individual author published as contributions to periodicals (see instructions), give full information about each contribution. If more space is needed, request continuation sheet (Form RE/CON).

⑤

Renewal for Group of Works

1
Title of Contribution: ....
Title of Periodical: .... Vol. .... No. .... Issue Date ....
Date of Publication: .... Registration Number. ....
(Month)   (Day)   (Year)

2
Title of Contribution: ....
Title of Periodical: .... Vol. .... No. .... Issue Date ....
Date of Publication: .... Registration Number. ....
(Month)   (Day)   (Year)

3
Title of Contribution: ....
Title of Periodical: .... Vol. .... No. .... Issue Date ....
Date of Publication: .... Registration Number. ....
(Month)   (Day)   (Year)

4
Title of Contribution: ....
Title of Periodical: .... Vol. .... No. .... Issue Date ....
Date of Publication: .... Registration Number. ....
(Month)   (Day)   (Year)

5
Title of Contribution: ....
Title of Periodical: .... Vol. .... No. .... Issue Date ....
Date of Publication: .... Registration Number. ....
(Month)   (Day)   (Year)

6
Title of Contribution: ....
Title of Periodical: .... Vol. .... No. .... Issue Date ....
Date of Publication: .... Registration Number. ....
(Month)   (Day)   (Year)

7
Title of Contribution: ....
Title of Periodical: .... Vol. .... No. .... Issue Date ....
Date of Publication: .... Registration Number. ....
(Month)   (Day)   (Year)

DEPOSIT ACCOUNT: (If the registration fee is to be charged to a Deposit Account established in the Copyright Office, give name and number of Account.)

Name: ....
Account Number: ....

CORRESPONDENCE: (Give name and address to which correspondence about this application should be sent.)

Name: ....
Address: ....
                                    (Apt.)
....
        (City)   (State)   (ZIP)

⑥

Fee and Correspondence

CERTIFICATION: I, the undersigned, hereby certify that I am the: (Check one)
☐ renewal claimant   ☐ duly authorized agent of: ....
                                                        (Name of renewal claimant)
of the work identified in this application, and that the statements made by me in this application are correct to the best of my knowledge.

☞ Handwritten signature: (X) ....

Typed or printed name. ....

Date ....

⑦

Certification (Application must be signed)

....
(Name)
....
(Number, Street and Apartment Number)
....
(City)   (State)   (ZIP code)

MAIL CERTIFICATE TO

(Certificate will be mailed in window envelope)

⑧

Address for Return of Certificate

APPENDIX 9
SELECTED COPYRIGHT OFFICE
REGULATIONS

Warning of Copyright

§201.14 Warnings of copyright for use by certain libraries and archives.

(a) *Definitions.* (1) A "Display Warning of Copyright" is a notice under paragraphs (d) (2) and (e) (2) of section 108 of Title 17 of the United States Code as amended by Pub. L. 94-553. As required by those sections the "Display Warning of Copyright" is to be displayed at the place where orders for copies or phonorecords are accepted by certain libraries and archives.

(2) An "Order Warning of Copyright" is a notice under paragraphs (d) (2) and (e) (2) of section 108 of Title 17 of the United States Code as amended by Pub. L. 94-553. As required by those sections the "Order Warning of Copyright" is to be included on printed forms supplied by certain libraries and archives and used by their patrons for ordering copies or phonorecords.

(b) *Contents.* A Display Warning of Copyright and an Order Warning of Copyright shall consist of a verbatim reproduction of the following notice, printed in such size and form and displayed in such manner as to comply with paragraph (c) of this section:

NOTICE

WARNING CONCERNING COPYRIGHT RESTRICTIONS

The copyright law of the United States (Title 17, United States Code) governs the making of photocopies or other reproductions of copyrighted material.

Under certain conditions specified in the law, libraries and archives are authorized to furnish a photocopy or other reproduction. One of these specified conditions is that the photocopy or reproduction is not to be "used for any purpose other than private study, scholarship, or research." If a user makes a request for, or later uses, a photocopy or reproduction for purposes in excess of "fair use," that user may be liable for copyright infringement.

This institution reserves the right to refuse to accept a copying order if, in its judgment, fulfillment of the order would involve violation of copyright law.

(c) *Form and Manner of Use.* (1) A Display Warning of Copyright shall be printed on heavy paper or other durable material in type at least 18 points in size, and shall be displayed prominently, in such manner and location as to be clearly visible, legible, and comprehensible to a casual observer within the immediate vicinity of the place where orders are accepted.

(2) An Order Warning of Copyright shall be printed within a box located prominently on the order form itself, either on the front side of the form or immediately adjacent to the space calling for the name or signature of the person using the form. The notice shall be printed in type size no smaller than that used predominantly throughout the form, and in no case shall the type size be smaller than 8 points. The notice shall be printed in such manner as to be clearly legible, comprehensible, and readily apparent to a casual reader of the form.

Deposit Requirements

§202.19 Deposit of published copies or phonorecords for the Library of Congress.

(a) *General.* This section prescribes rules pertaining to the deposit of copies and phonorecords of published works for the Library of Congress under section 407 of title 17 of the United States Code, as amended by Pub. L. 94-553. The provisions of this section are not applicable to the deposit of copies and phonorecords for purposes of copyright registration under section 408 of title 17, except as expressly adopted in §202.20 of these regulations.

(b) *Definitions.* For the purposes of this section:

(1) (i) The "best edition" of a work is the edition, published in the United States at any time before the date of deposit, that the Library of Congress determines to be most suitable for its purposes.

(ii) Criteria for selection of the "best edition" from among two or more published editions of the same version of the same work are set forth in the statement entitled "Best Edition of Published Copyrighted Works for the Collections of the Library of Congress" (hereafter referred to as the "Best Edition Statement") in effect at the time of deposit. Copies of the Best Edition Statement are available upon request made to the Acquisitions and Processing Division of the Copyright Office. [The "Best Edition statement" is set forth at the end of this appendix.]

(iii) Where no specific criteria for the selection of the "best edition" are established in the Best Edition Statement, that edition which, in the judgment of the Library of Congress, represents the highest quality for its purposes shall be considered the "best edition." In such cases: (A) When the Copyright Office is aware that two or more editions of a work have been published it will consult with other appropriate officials of the Library of Congress to obtain instructions as to the "best edition" and (except in cases for which special relief is granted) will require deposit of that edition; and (B) when a potential depositor is uncertain which of two or more published editions comprises the "best edition," inquiry should be made to the Acquisitions and Processing Division of the Copyright Office.

(iv) Where differences between two or more "editions" of a work represent variations in copyrightable content, each edition is considered a separate version, and hence a different work, for the purpose of this section, and criteria of "best edition" based on such differences do not apply.

(2) A "complete" copy includes all elements comprising the unit of publication of the best edition of the work, including elements that, if considered separately, would not be copyrightable subject matter or would otherwise be exempt from mandatory deposit requirements under paragraph (c) of this section. In the case of sound recordings, a "complete" phonorecord includes the phonorecord, together with any printed or other visually perceptible material published with such phonorecord (such as textual or pictorial matter appearing on record sleeves or album covers, or embodied in leaflets or booklets included in a sleeve, album, or other container). In the case of a musical composition published only by the rental, lease, or lending of copies consisting of a full score and parts, a full score is a "complete" copy; in the case of a musical composition published only by the rental, lease, or lending of copies consisting of a conductor's score and parts, a conductor's score is a "complete" copy.

(3) The terms "copies," "collective work," "device," "fixed," "literary work," "machine," "motion picture," "phonorecord," "publication," "sound recording," and "useful article," and their variant forms, have the meanings given to them in section 101 of title 17.

(4) "Title 17" means title 17 of the United States Code, as amended by Pub. L. 94-553.

(c) *Exemptions from deposit requirements.* The following categories of material are exempt from the deposit requirements of section 407(a) of title 17:

(1) Diagrams and models illustrating scientific or technical works or formulating scientific or technical information in linear or three-dimensional form, such as an architectural or engineering blueprint, plan, or design, a mechanical drawing, or an anatomical model.

(2) Greeting cards, picture postcards, and stationery.

(3) Lectures, sermons, speeches, and addresses when published individually and not as a collection of the works of one or more authors.

(4) Literary, dramatic, and musical works published only as embodied in phonorecords. This category does not exempt the owner of copyright, or of the exclusive right of publication, in a sound recording resulting from the fixation of such works in a phonorecord from the applicable deposit requirements for the sound recording.

(5) Literary works, including computer programs and automated data bases, published in the United States only in the form of machine-readable copies (such as magnetic tape or disks, punched cards, or the like) from which the work cannot ordinarily be visually perceived except with the aid of a machine or device. Works published in a form requiring the use of a machine or device for purposes of optical enlargement (such as film, filmstrips, slide films and works published in any variety of microform), and works published in visually perceivable form but used in connection with optical scanning devices, are not within this category and are subject to the applicable deposit requirements.

(6) Three-dimensional sculptural works, and any works published only as reproduced in or on jewelry, dolls, toys, games, plaques, floor coverings, wallpaper and similar commercial wall coverings, textile and other fabrics, packaging material, or any useful article. Globes, relief models, and similar cartographic representations of area are not within this category and are subject to the applicable deposit requirements.

(7) Prints, labels, and other advertising matter published in connection with

the rental, lease, lending, licensing, or sale of articles of merchandise, works of authorship, or services.

(8) Tests, and answer material for tests, when published separately from other literary works.

(9) Works first published as individual contributions to collective works. This category does not exempt the owner of copyright, or of the exclusive right of publication, in the collective work as a whole from the applicable deposit requirements for the collective work.

(10) Works first published outside the United States and later published in the United States without change in copyrightable content, if: (i) registration for the work was made under §17 U.S.C. 408 before the work was published in the United States; or (ii) registration for the work was made under 17 U.S.C. 408 after the work was published in the United States but before a demand for deposit is made under 17 U.S.C. 407(d).

(11) Works published only as embodied in a soundtrack that is an integral part of a motion picture. This category does not exempt the owner of copyright, or of the exclusive right of publication, in the motion picture from the applicable deposit requirements for the motion picture.

(12) Motion pictures that consist of television transmission programs and that have been published, if at all, only by reason of a license or other grant to a nonprofit institution of the right to make a fixation of such programs directly from a transmission to the public, with or without the right to make further uses of such fixations.

(d) *Nature of required deposit.* (1) Subject to the provisions of paragraph (d) (2) of this section, the deposit required to satisfy the provisions of section 407(a) of title 17 shall consist of (i) in the case of published works other than sound recordings, two complete copies of the best edition; and (ii) in the case of published sound recordings, two complete phonorecords of the best edition.

(2) In the case of certain published works not exempt from deposit requirements under paragraph (c) of this section, the following special provisions shall apply:

(i) In the case of published three-dimensional cartographic representations of area, such as globes and relief models, the deposit of one complete copy of the best edition of the work will suffice in lieu of the two copies required by paragraph (d) (1) of this section.

(ii) In the case of published motion pictures, the deposit of one complete copy of the best edition of the work will suffice in lieu of the two copies required by paragraph (d) (1) of this section. Any deposit for a published motion picture must be accompanied by a separate description of its contents, such as a continuity, pressbook, or synopsis. Unless selected by the Library of Congress for addition to its collections within thirty days from the date the deposit is received in the Copyright Office, all copies of motion pictures deposited under this section will be returned to the depositor by the Copyright Office, without right of recall.

(iii) In the case of any published work deposited in the form of a hologram, the deposit shall be accompanied by: (A) Two sets of precise instructions for displaying the image fixed in the hologram; and (B) two sets of identifying material in compliance with §202.21 of these regulations and clearly showing the displayed image.

(iv) In any case where an individual author is the owner of copyright in a published pictorial or graphic work and (A) less than five copies of the work have been published, or (B) the work has been published and sold or offered for sale in a limited edition consisting of no more than three hundred numbered copies, the deposit of one complete copy of the best edition of the work or, alternatively, the deposit of photographs or other identifying material in compliance with §202.21 of these regulations, will suffice in lieu of the two copies required by paragraph (d) (1) of this section.

(v) In the case of a musical composition published only by the rental, lease, or lending of copies, the deposit of one complete copy of the best edition will suffice in lieu of the two copies required by paragraph (d) (1) of this section.

(vi) In the case of published multimedia kits that are prepared for use in systematic instructional activities and that include literary works, audiovisual works, sound recordings, or any combination of such works, the deposit of one complete copy of the best edition will suffice in lieu of the two copies required by paragraph (d) (1) of this section.

(e) *Special relief.* (1) In the case of any published work not exempt from deposit under paragraph (c) of this section, the Register of Copyrights may, after consultation with other appropriate officials of the Library of Congress and upon such conditions as the Register may determine after such consultation: (i) Grant an exemption from the deposit requirements of section 407(a) of title 17 on an individual basis for single works or series or groups of works; or (ii) permit the deposit of one copy or phonorecord, or alternative identifying material, in lieu of the two copies or phonorecords required by paragraph (d) (1) of this section; or (iii) permit the deposit of incomplete copies or phonorecords, or copies or phonorecords other than those normally comprising the best edition.

(2) Any decision as to whether to grant such special relief, and the conditions under which special relief is to be granted, shall be made by the Register of Copyrights after consultation with other appropriate officials of the Library of Congress, and shall be based upon the acquisition policies of the Library of Congress then in force.

(3) Requests for special relief under this paragraph shall be made in writing to the Chief, Acquisitions and Processing Division of the Copyright Office, shall be signed by or on behalf of the owner of copyright or of the exclusive right of publication in the work, and shall set forth specific reasons why the request should be granted.

(f) *Submission and receipt of copies and phonorecords.* (1) All copies and phonorecords deposited in the Copyright Office will be considered to be deposited only in compliance with section 407 of title 17 unless they are accompanied by: (i) An application for registration of claim to copyright, or (ii) a clear written request that they be held for connection with a separately forwarded application. Copies or phonorecords deposited without such an accompanying application or written request will not be connected with or held for receipt of separate applications, and will not satisfy the deposit provisions of section 408 of title 17 or §202.20 of these regulations. Any written request that copies or phonorecords be held for connection with a separately forwarded application must appear in a letter or similar document accompanying the deposit; a request or instruction appearing on the packaging, wrapping, or container for the deposit will not be effective for this purpose.

(2) All copies and phonorecords deposited in the Copyright Office under section 407 of title 17, unless accompanied by written instructions to the contrary, will be considered to be deposited by the person or persons named in the copyright notice on the work.

(3) Upon request by the depositor made at the time of the deposit, the Copyright Office will issue a Certificate of Receipt for the deposit of copies or phonorecords of a work under this section. Certificates of Receipt will be issued in response to requests made after the date of deposit only if the requesting party is identified in the records of the Copyright Office as having made the deposit. In either case, requests for a Certificate of Receipt must be in writing and accompanied by a fee of $2. A Certificate of Receipt will include identification of the depositor, the work deposited, and the nature and format of the copy or phonorecord deposited, together with the date of receipt.

§202.20 Deposit of copies and phonorecords for copyright registration.

(a) *General.* This section prescribes rules pertaining to the deposit of copies and phonorecords of published and unpublished works for the purpose of copyright registration under section 408 of title 17 of the United States Code, as amended by Pub. L. 94-553. The provisions of this section are not applicable to the deposit of copies and phonorecords for the Library of Congress under section 407 of title 17, except as expressly adopted in §202.19 of these regulations.

(b) *Definitions.* For the purposes of this section:

(1) The "best edition" of a work has the meaning set forth in §202.19 (b) (1) of these regulations.

(2) A "complete" copy or phonorecord of an unpublished work is a copy or phonorecord representing the entire copyrightable content of the work for which registration is sought. A "complete" copy or phonorecord of a published work includes all elements comprising the applicable unit of publication of the work. In the case of a contribution to a collective work, a "complete" copy or phonorecord is the entire collective work including the contribution or, in the case of a newspaper, the entire section including the contribution. In the case of published sound recordings, a "complete" phonorecord has the meaning set forth in §202.19(b) (2) of these regulations. In the case of a musical composition published only by the rental, lease, or lending of copies consisting of a full score and parts, a full score is a "complete" copy; in the case of a musical composition published only by the rental, lease, or lending of copies consisting of a conductor's score and parts, a conductor's score is a "complete" copy.

(3) The terms "copy," "collective work," "device," "fixed," "literary work," "machine," "motion picture," "phonorecord," "publication," "sound recording," "transmission program," and "useful article," and their variant forms, have the meanings given to them in section 101 of title 17.

(4) A "secure test" is a non-marketed test administered under supervision at specified centers on specific dates, all copies of which are accounted for and either destroyed or returned to restricted locked storage following each administration. For these purposes a test is not marketed if copies are not sold but it is distributed and used in such a manner that ownership and control of copies remain with the test sponsor or publisher.

(5) "Title 17" means title 17 of the United States Code, as amended by Pub. L. 94-553.

(6) For the purposes of determining the applicable deposit requirements under this §202.20 only, the following shall be considered as unpublished motion pictures: motion pictures that consist of television transmission programs and that have been published, if at all, only by reason of a license or other grant to a nonprofit institution of the right to make a fixation of such programs directly from a transmission to the public, with or without the right to make further uses of such fixations.

(c) *Nature of required deposit.* (1) Subject to the Provisions of paragraph (c) (2) of this section, the deposit required to accompany an application for registration of claim to copyright under section 408 of title 17 shall consist of:

(i) In the case of unpublished works, one complete copy or phonorecord.

(ii) In the case of works first published in the United States before January 1, 1978, two complete copies or phonorecords of the work as first published.

(iii) In the case of works first published in the United States on or after January 1, 1978, two complete copies or phonorecords of the best edition.

(iv) In the case of works first published outside of the United States, whenever published, one complete copy or phonorecord of the work as first published. For the purposes of this section, any works simultaneously first published within and outside of the United States shall be considered to be first published in the United States.

(2) In the case of certain works, the special provisions set forth in this clause shall apply. In any case where this clause specifies that one copy or phonorecord may be submitted, that copy or phonorecord shall represent the best edition, or the work as first published, as set forth in paragraph (c) (1) of this section.

(i) *General.* In the following cases the deposit of one complete copy or phonorecord will suffice in lieu of two copies or phonorecords: (A) Published three-dimensional cartographic representations of area, such as globes and relief models; (B) published diagrams illustrating scientific or technical works or formulating scientific or technical information in linear or other two-dimensional form, such as an architectural or engineering blueprint, or a mechanical drawing; (C) published greeting cards, picture postcards and stationery; (D) lectures, sermons, speeches, and addresses published individually and not as a collection of the works of one or more authors; (E) published contributions to a collective work; (F) musical compositions published only by the rental, lease, or lending of copies; and (G) published multimedia kits that are prepared for use in systematic instructional activities and that include literary works, audiovisual works, sound recordings, or any combination of such works.

(ii) *Motion pictures.* In the case of published motion pictures, the deposit of one complete copy will suffice in lieu of two copies. The deposit of a copy or copies for any published or unpublished motion picture must be accompanied by a separate description of its contents, such as a continuity, pressbook, or synopsis. Unless selected by the Library of Congress for addition to its collections within thirty days from the effective date of registration, all copies of motion pictures deposited under this section will be returned to the applicant by the Copyright Office, without right of recall. In the case of unpublished motion pictures (including television transmission programs that have been fixed and transmitted to the public, but have not been published), the deposit of identifying material in compliance with §202.21 of these regulations may be made and will suffice in lieu of an actual copy.

(iii) *Holograms.* In the case of any work deposited in the form of a hologram, the copy or copies shall be accompanied by: (A) Precise instructions for displaying the image fixed in the hologram; and (B) photographs or other identifying material complying with §202.21 of these regulations and clearly showing the displayed image. The number of sets of instructions and identifying material shall be the same as the number of copies required.

(iv) *Certain pictorial and graphic works.* In any case where an individual author is the owner of copyright in a pictorial or graphic work and (A) the work is unpublished, or (B) less than five copies of the work have been published, or (C) the work has been published and sold or offered for sale in a limited edition consisting of no more than three hundred numbered copies, the deposit of identifying material in compliance with §202.21 of these regulations may be made and will suffice in lieu of actual copies. As an alternative to the deposit of such identifying material, in any such case the deposit of one complete copy will suffice in lieu of two copies.

(v) *Commercial prints and labels.* In the case of prints, labels, and other advertising matter published in connection with the rental, lease, lending, licensing, or sale of articles of merchandise, works of authorship, or services, the deposit of one complete copy will suffice in lieu of two copies. Where the print or label is published in a larger work, such as a newspaper or other periodical, one copy of the entire page or pages upon which it appears may be submitted in lieu of the entire larger work. In the case of prints or labels physically inseparable from a three-dimensional object, identifying material complying with §202.21 of these regulations must be submitted rather than an actual copy or copies.

(vi) *Tests.* In the case of tests, and answer material for tests, published separately from other literary works, the deposit of one complete copy will suffice in lieu of two copies. In the case of any secure test the Copyright Office will return the deposit to the applicant promptly after examination: *Provided,* That sufficient portions, description, or the like are retained so as to constitute a sufficient archival record of the deposit.

(vii) *Machine-readable works.* In cases where an unpublished literary work is fixed, or a published literary work is published in the United States, only in the form of machine-readable copies (such as magnetic tape or disks, punched cards, or the like) from which the work cannot ordinarily be perceived except with the aid of a machine or device,[1] the deposit shall consist of:

(A) For published or unpublished computer programs, one copy of identifying portions of the program, reproduced in a form visually perceptible without the aid of a machine or device, either on paper or in microform. For these purposes, "identifying portions" shall mean either the first and last twenty-five pages or equivalent units of the program if reproduced on paper, or at least the first and last twenty-five pages or equivalent units of the program if reproduced

---

[1]Works published in a form requiring the use of a machine or device for purposes of optical enlargement (such as film, filmstrips, slide films, and works published in any variety of microform), and works published in visually perceptible form but used in connection with optical scanning devices, are not within this category.

in microform, together with the page or equivalent unit containing the copyright notice, if any.

(B) For published and unpublished automated data bases, compilations, statistical compendia, and other literary works so fixed or published, one copy of identifying portions of the work, reproduced in a form visually perceptible without the aid of a machine or device, either on paper or in microform. For these purposes: (1) "identifying portions" shall mean either the first and last twenty-five pages or equivalent units of the work if reproduced on paper, or at least the first and last twenty-five pages or equivalent units of work if reproduced on microform, or, in the case of automated data bases comprising separate and distinct data files, representative portions of each separate data file consisting of either 50 complete data records from each file or the entire file, whichever is less; and (2) "data file" and "file" mean a group of data records pertaining to a common subject matter, regardless of the physical size of the records or the number of data items included in them. (In the case of revised versions of such data bases, the portions deposited must contain representative data records which have been added or modified.) In any case where the deposit comprises representative portions of each separate file of an automated data base as indicated above, it shall be accompanied by a typed or printed descriptive statement containing: The title of the data base; the name and address of the copyright claimant; the name and content of each separate file within the data base, including the subject matter involved, the origin(s) of the data, and the approximate number of individual records within the file; and a description of the exact contents of any machine-readable copyright notice employed in or with the work and the manner and frequency with which it is displayed (e.g., at user's terminal only at sign-on, or continuously on terminal display, or on printouts, etc.). If a visually-perceptible copyright notice is placed on any copies of the work (such as magnetic tape reels) or their container, a sample of such notice must also accompany the statement.

(viii) *Works reproduced in or on sheetlike materials.* In the case of any unpublished work that is fixed, or any published work that is published, only in the form of a two-dimensional reproduction on sheet-like materials such as textile and other fabrics, wallpaper and similar commercial wall coverings, carpeting, floor tile, and similar commercial floor coverings, and wrapping paper and similar packaging material, the deposit shall consist of one copy in the form of an actual swatch or piece of such material sufficient to show all elements of the work in which copyright is claimed and the copyright notice appearing on the work, if any. If the work consists of a repeated pictorial or graphic design, the complete design and at least one repetition must be shown. If the sheet-like material in or on which a published work has been reproduced has been embodied in or attached to a three-dimensional object, such as wearing apparel, furniture, or any other three-dimensional manufactured article, and the work has been published only in that form, the deposit must consist of identifying material complying with §202.21 of these regulations instead of a copy.

(ix) *Works reproduced in or on three-dimensional objects.* In the following cases where the deposit of an actual copy of the work would not lend itself to shelving or flat storage, the deposit must consist of identifying material complying with §202.21 of these regulations instead of a copy or copies: (A) Any three-dimensional sculptural work, including any illustration or formulation of artistic expression or information in three-dimensional form, including statues, carvings, ceramics, moldings, constructions, models, and maquettes (but not including works reproduced by intaglio or relief printing methods on two-dimensional materials such as paper or fabrics); and (B) any two-dimensional or three-dimensional work that, if unpublished, has been fixed or, if published, has been published only in or on jewelry, dolls, toys, games, or any three-dimensional useful article. However, where the work has been fixed or published in or on a useful article that comprises one of the elements of the unit of publication of an educational or instructional kit which also includes a literary or audiovisual work, a sound recording, or any combination of such works, the requirement of this paragraph for the deposit of identifying material shall not apply.

(x) *Soundtracks.* For separate registration of an unpublished work that is fixed, or a published work that is published, only as embodied in a soundtrack that is an integral part of a motion picture, the deposit of identifying material in compliance with §202.21 of these regulations will suffice in lieu of an actual copy or copies of the motion picture.

(xi) *Oversize deposits.* In any case where the deposit otherwise required by this section exceeds ninety-six inches in any dimension, identifying material complying with §202.21 of these regulations must be submitted instead of an actual copy or copies.

(d) *Special relief.* (1) In any case the Register of Copyrights may, after consultation with other appropriate officials of the Library of Congress and upon such conditions as the Register may determine after such consultation: (i) Permit the deposit of one copy or phonorecord, or alternative identifying material, in lieu of the one or two copies or phonorecords otherwise required by paragraph (c) (1) of this section; or (ii) permit the deposit of incomplete copies or phonorecords, or copies or phonorecords other than those normally comprising the best edition.

(2) Any decision as to whether to grant such special relief, and the conditions under which special relief is to be granted, shall be made by the Register of Copyrights after consultation with other appropriate officials of the Library of Congress, and shall be based upon the acquisition policies of the Library of Congress then in force and the archival and examining requirements of the Copyright Office.

(3) Requests for special relief under this paragraph may be combined with requests for special relief under §202.19 (e) of these regulations. Whether so combined or made solely under this paragraph, such requests shall be made in writing to the Chief, Examining Division of the Copyright Office, shall be signed by or on behalf of the person signing the application for registration, and shall set forth specific reasons why the request should be granted.

(e) *Use of copies and phonorecords deposited for the Library of Congress.* Copies and phonorecords deposited for the Library of Congress under section 407 of title 17 and §202.19 of these regulations may be used to satisfy the deposit provisions of this section if they are accompanied by an application for registration of claim to copyright in the work represented by the deposit, or connected with such an application under the conditions set forth in §202.19(f) (1) of these regulations.

§202.21 Deposit of identifying material instead of copies.

(a) *General.* Subject to the specific provisions of paragraphs (f) and (g) of this section, in any case where the deposit of identifying material is permitted or required under §202.19 or §202.20 of these regulations, the material shall consist of photographic prints, transparencies, photostats, drawings, or similar two-dimensional reproductions or renderings of the work, in a form visually perceivable without the aid of a machine or device. In the case of pictorial or graphic works, such material shall reproduce the actual colors employed in the work. In all other cases, such material may be in black and white or may consist of a reproduction of the actual colors.

(b) *Completeness; number of sets.* As many pieces of identifying material as are necessary to show clearly the entire copyrightable content of the work for which deposit is being made, or for which registration is being sought, shall be submitted. Except in cases falling under the provisions of §202.19 (d) (2) (iii) or §202.20 (c) (2) (iii) with respect to holograms, only one set of such complete identifying material is required.

(c) *Size.* All pieces of identifying material must be of uniform size. Photographic transparencies must be 35 mm. in size, and must be fixed in cardboard, plastic, or similar mounts to facilitate identification, handling, and storage. All other types of identifying material must be not less than 5 × 7 inches and not more than 9 × 12 inches, but preferably 8 × 10 inches. Except in the case of transparencies, the image of the work must be either lifesize or larger, or if less than lifesize must be at least four inches in its greatest dimension.

(d) *Title and dimensions.* At least one piece of identifying material must, on its front, back, or mount, indicate the title of the work and an exact measurement of one or more dimensions of the work.

(e) *Copyright notice.* In the case of works published with notice of copyright, the notice and its position on the work must be clearly shown on at least one piece of identifying material. Where necessary because of the size or position of the notice, a separate drawing or the like showing the exact appearance and content of the notice, its dimensions, and its specific position on the work shall be submitted.

(f) For separate registration of an unpublished work that is fixed, or a published work that is published, only as embodied in a soundtrack that is an integral part of a motion picture, identifying material deposited in lieu of an actual copy or copies of the motion picture shall consist of: (1) a transcription of the entire work, or a reproduction of the entire work on a phonorecord; and (2) photographs or other reproductions from the motion picture showing the title of the motion picture, the soundtrack credits, and the copyright notice for the soundtrack, if any. The provisions of paragraphs (b), (c), (d), and (e) of this §202.21 do not apply to identifying material deposited under this paragraph (f).

(g) In the case of unpublished motion pictures (including transmission programs that have been fixed and transmitted to the public, but have not been published), identifying material deposited in lieu of an actual copy shall consist of either: (1) an audio cassette or other phonorecord reproducing the entire soundtrack or other sound portion of the motion picture, and a description of the motion picture; or (2) a set consisting of one frame enlargement or similar visual reproduction from each ten minute segment of the motion picture, and a description of the motion picture. In either case the "description" may be a continuity, a pressbook, or a synopsis, but in all cases it must include: (i) the title or continuing title of the work, and the episode title, if any: (ii) the nature and general content of the program; (iii) the date when the work was first fixed and whether or not fixation was simultaneous with first transmission; (iv) the date of first transmission, if any; (v) the running time; and (vi) the credits appearing on the work, if any. The provisions of paragraphs (b), (c), (d), and (e) of this §202.21 do not apply to identifying material submitted under this paragraph (g).

"BEST EDITION" OF PUBLISHED COPYRIGHTED WORKS FOR THE COLLECTIONS OF THE LIBRARY OF CONGRESS

The Copyright Law (Title 17, United States Code) requires that copies or phonorecords deposited in the Copyright Office be of the "best edition" of the work. The law states that "The 'best edition' of work is the edition, published in the United States at any time before the date of deposit, that the Library of Congress determines to be most suitable for its purposes."

When two or more editions of the same version of a work have been published, the one of the highest quality is generally considered to be the best edition. In judging quality, the Library of Congress will adhere to the criteria set forth below in all but exceptional circumstances.

Where differences between editions represent variations in copyrightable content, each edition is a separate version and "best edition" standards based on such differences do not apply. Each such version is a separate work for the purposes of the Copyright Law.

Appearing below are lists of criteria to be applied in determining the best edition of each of several types of material. The criteria are listed in descending order of importance. In deciding between two editions, a criterion-by-criterion comparison should be made. The edition which first fails to satisfy a criterion is to be considered of inferior quality and will not be an acceptable deposit. For example, if a comparison is made between two hardbound editions of a book, one a trade edition printed on acid-free paper and the other a specially bound edition printed on average paper, the former will be the best edition because the type of paper is a more important criterion than the binding.

Under regulations of the Copyright Office, potential depositors may request authorization to deposit copies or phonorecords of other than the best edition of a specific work (e.g., a microform rather than a printed edition of a serial).

I. PRINTED TEXTUAL MATTER

A. *Paper, Binding, and Packaging:*
   1. Archival-quality rather than less-permanent paper.
   2. Hard cover rather than soft cover.
   3. Library binding rather than commercial binding.
   4. Trade edition rather than book club edition.
   5. Sewn rather than glue-only binding.
   6. Sewn or glued rather than stapled or spiral-bound.
   7. Stapled rather than spiral-bound or plastic-bound.

8. Bound rather than looseleaf, except when future looseleaf insertions are to be issued.
9. Slipcased rather than nonslipcased.
10. With protective folders rather than without (for broadsides).
11. Rolled rather than folded (for broadsides).
12. With protective coatings rather than without (except broadsides, which should not be coated).

B. *Rarity:*
1. Special limited edition having the greatest number of special features.
2. Other limited edition rather than trade edition.
3. Special binding rather than trade binding.

C. *Illustrations:*
1. Illustrated rather than unillustrated.
2. Illustrations in color rather than black and white.

D. *Special Features:*
1. With thumb notches or index tabs rather than without.
2. With aids to use such as overlays and magnifiers rather than without.

E. *Size:*
1. Larger rather than smaller sizes. (Except that large-type editions for the partially-sighted are not required in place of editions employing type of more conventional size.)

II. PHOTOGRAPHS

A. Size and finish, in descending order of preference:
1. The most widely distributed edition.
2. 8 × 10-inch glossy print.
3. Other size or finish.

B. Unmounted rather than mounted.

C. Archival-quality rather than less permanent paper stock or printing process.

III. MOTION PICTURES

A. Film rather than another medium. Film editions are listed below in descending order of preference.
1. Preprint material, by special arrangement.
2. Film gauge in which most widely distributed.
3. 35 mm rather than 16 mm.
4. 16 mm rather than 8 mm.
5. Special formats (e.g., 65 mm) only in exceptional cases.
6. Open reel rather than cartridge or cassette.

B. Videotape rather than videodisc. Videotape editions are listed below in descending order of preference.
1. Tape gauge in which most widely distributed.
2. Two-inch tape.
3. One-inch tape.
4. Three-quarter-inch tape cassette.
5. One-half-inch tape cassette.

IV. OTHER GRAPHIC MATTER

A. *Paper and Printing:*
   1. Archival quality rather than less-permanent paper.
   2. Color rather than black and white.
B. *Size and Content:*
   1. Larger rather than smaller size.
   2. In the case of cartographic works, editions with the greatest amount of information rather than those with less detail.
C. *Rarity:*
   1. The most widely distributed edition rather than one of limited distribution.
   2. In the case of a work published only in a limited, numbered edition, one copy outside the numbered series but otherwise identical.
   3. A photographic reproduction of the original, by special arrangement only.
D. *Text and Other Materials:* 1. Works with annotations, accompanying tabular or textual matter, or other interpretative aids rather than those without them.
E. *Binding and Packaging:*
   1. Bound rather than unbound.
   2. If editions have different binding, apply the criteria in I.A.2–I.A.7, above.
   3. Rolled rather than folded.
   4. With protective coatings rather than without.

V. PHONORECORDS

A. Disc rather than tape.
B. With special enclosures rather than without.
C. Open-reel rather than cartridge.
D. Cartridge rather than cassette.
E. Quadraphonic rather than stereophonic.
F. True stereophonic rather than monaural.
G. Monaural rather than electronically rechanneled stereo.

VI. MUSICAL COMPOSITIONS

A. *Fullness of Score:* 1. *Vocal music:* a. With orchestral accompaniment—
   i. Full score and parts, if any, rather than conductor's score and parts, if any. (In cases of compositions published only by rental, lease, or lending, this requirement is reduced to full score only.)
   ii. Conductor's score and parts, if any, rather than condensed score and parts, if any. (In cases of compositions published only by rental, lease, or lending, this requirement is reduced to conductor's score only.)
   b. Unaccompanied: Open score (each part on separate staff) rather than closed score (all parts condensed to two staves).
   2. *Instrumental music:*
   a. Full score and parts, if any, rather than conductor's score and parts, if any. (In cases of compositions published only by rental, lease, or lending, this requirement is reduced to full score only.)
   b. Conductor's score and parts, if any, rather than condensed score and

parts, if any. (In cases of compositions published only by rental, lease, or lending, this requirement is reduced to conductor's score only.)
B. *Printing and Paper:* 1. Archival-quality rather than less-permanent paper.
C. *Binding and Packaging:*
    1. Special limited editions rather than trade editions.
    2. Bound rather than unbound.
    3. If editions have different binding, apply the criteria in I.A.2–I.A.12, above.
    4. With protective folders rather than without.

VII. MICROFORMS

A. *Related Materials.* 1. With indexes, study guides, or other printed matter rather than without.
B. *Permanence and Appearance:*
    1. Silver halide rather than any other emulsion.
    2. Positive rather than negative.
    3. Color rather than black and white.
C. *Format (newspapers and newspaper-formatted serials):* 1. Reel microfilm rather than any other microform.
D. *Format (all other materials):*
    1. Microfiche rather than reel microfilm.
    2. Reel microfilm rather than microform cassettes.
    3. Microfilm cassettes rather than micro-opaque prints.
E. *Sizes:* 1. 35 mm rather than 16 mm.

VIII. WORKS EXISTING IN MORE THAN ONE MEDIUM

Editions are listed below in descending order of preference.

A. Newspapers, dissertations and theses, newspaper-formatted serials:
    1. Microform.
    2. Printed matter.
B. All other materials:
    1. Printed matter.
    2. Microform.
    3. Phonorecord.

(Effective: January 1, 1978.)

INDEX